Sacred Possessions

Sacred Possessions

Vodou, Santería, Obeah, and the Caribbean

EDITED BY
MARGARITE FERNÁNDEZ OLMOS
AND
LIZABETH PARAVISINI-GEBERT

R RUTGERS UNIVERSITY PRESS
New Brunswick, New Jersey

Library of Congress Cataloging-in-Publication Data

Sacred possessions : Vodou, Santería, Obeah, and the Caribbean /
    edited by Margarite Fernández Olmos and Lizabeth Paravisini-Gebert.
        p. cm.
    Includes bibliographical references and index.
    ISBN 0-8135-2360-5 (cloth : alk. paper). — ISBN 0-8135-2361-3
    (pbk. : alk. paper)
        1. Blacks—Caribbean Area—Religion.   2. Caribbean Area—Religion.
    I. Fernández Olmos, Margarite. II. Paravisini-Gebert, Lizabeth.
    BL2565.S23 1997
    299'.6'09729—dc20   96-18145
                                                                         CIP

British Cataloging-in-Publication information available

Manufactured in the United States of America

Contents

The Shaman Woman, Resistance, and the Powers of
Transformation: A Tribute to Ma Cia in Simone Schwarz-Bart's

Sorcerers, She-Devils, and Shipwrecked Women: Writing

Trans-Caribbean Identity and the Fictional World

Acknowledgments

M y grateful thanks to the Professional Staff Congress of the City University of New York for a research grant and the Wolfe Institute for the Humanities of Brooklyn College for a faculty fellowship, both of which greatly facilitated the successful completion of this project; and to my family, Enrique and Gabriela, for their constant patience and encouragement.
—M.F.O.

I am indebted to the American Association of University Women for a generous fellowship in 1994–1995 for my ongoing study on "Race, Gender, and the Plantation in Caribbean Women's Fiction"; the fellowship was also instrumental in allowing me to complete this project. I am also indebted to Vassar College for a timely sabbatical. I am very grateful to Rick Pantale of Piermont Pictures Video in Piermont, New York, who kindly guided me through his extensive collection of "zombie" films in preparation for the essay included in this collection. My family—Gordon, Carrie, D'Arcy, and little Gordon—were patient and supportive to a fault. They have, as always, all my love.
—L.P.-G.

We are both extremely grateful to our editor at Rutgers University Press, Leslie Mitchner, for her faith in the project and constant support, and to Pamela Fischer, our copyeditor, for her painstaking work and infinite patience.

Excilia Saldaña's "Por el mar del Caribe" is translated here into English with the permission of the poet. Joan Dayan's "Vodoun, or the Voice of the Gods" appeared in *Raritan* 10, no. 3 (winter 1991): 32–57. José Piedra's "From Monkey Tales to Cuban Songs: On Signification" appeared in *Modern Language*

Notes 100, no. 2 (March 1985): 361–390. Alan Richardson's "Romantic Voodoo: Obeah and British Culture, 1797–1807" appeared in *Studies in Romanticism* 32 (spring 1993): 3–28. It is reprinted courtesy of the Trustees of Boston University.

Sacred Possessions

on the sea of the Antilles . . .

—NICOLÁS GUILLÉN

*Sailing on the Caribbean, the ships arrived. They bore blacks, they
    bore whites. The ships arrived.*
*The ships arrived, sailing on the Caribbean: Europe laughing,
    Africa in tears. Africa arrived in tears.*
*Sailing on the Caribbean, Africa arrived in tears; she came with her
    orichas, myths and legends, magic rituals. And awaiting was
    the harquebus, the pillory, the encampments, and abuse; the
    voice of the master awaited: the blacks always below; the
    whip always above. The voice of the master awaited.*
*The voice of the master awaited on the Caribbean Sea, but the
    waves also spoke; and the African drum spoke on the rock's
    hide. The African drum spoke.*
*Sailing on the Caribbean Sea the African drum spoke, the islands were
    peopled; sweat and toil and rebellion and valor; love, dance,
    and song. The islands were peopled.*
*The islands were peopled on the Caribbean Sea, children sprouted:
    white and black, black and white; white, black, mulatto, on
    the Caribbean Sea on which the ships sailed, where the
    drum was heard, where the voice of the master was felt; by
    way of the hides, by way of the whip, hands were clasped:
    yours and mine.*
On the Caribbean Sea, hands were clasped.

—EXCILIA SALDAÑA, *Kele Kele* (1988)
TRANSLATED BY MARGARITE FERNÁNDEZ OLMOS

Introduction

Religious Syncretism and Caribbean Culture

THE CARIBBEAN was the site of the world's first multicultural experiment, the locus of diversity, the cradle of ethnic and cultural syncretism. It is not surprising, then, that as the West seeks to address its increasing eclecticism—the result of the "Thirdworldization" it has undergone as waves of migrants from its former colonies descend on its cities and towns—its scholars turn to the Caribbean for clues to an understanding of this newly encountered "difference." They soon discover, however, that the Caribbean does not readily open itself to scrutiny, that it does not willingly yield its secrets to newcomers, that its kernel is wrapped in layers of ambiguity, that it hides behind languages and cultures adept at "signification." Even scholars born and bred in the region confront the task of shedding light on the slippery perplexity of their islands as a challenge.

In *The Repeating Island*, Cuban novelist and scholar Antonio Benítez-Rojo recalls an anecdote from his youth that strikes chords of recognition in those seeking to decipher for the uninitiated the idiosyncrasies of their home islands. During the 1962 missile crisis, as Cuba awaited nuclear catastrophe and neighborhoods were evacuated, two old black women passed under his window "in a certain kind of way":

> I cannot describe this "certain kind of way": I will say that there was a
> kind of ancient and golden powder between their gnarled legs, a scent
> of basil and mint in their dress, a symbolic, ritual wisdom in their
> gesture and their gay chatter. I knew at once that there would be no
> apocalypse. The swords and the archangels and the beasts and the

trumpets and the breaking of the last seal were not going to come, for
the simple reason that the Caribbean is not an apocalyptic world; it is
not a phallic world in pursuit of the vertical desires of ejaculation and
castration.[1]

He could simply have said that the Caribbean is not a white Judeo-Christian
world to which a Biblical apocalypse *could* come, but this idea is inherent in
his description: this revelation came to him at the sight of two old *black* women
enveloped in their own aura of ancient (that is, African) scents and rhythms,
possessors of a "ritual wisdom" that owed little to, and thought less of, worlds
of archangels and trumpets and last seals; they belonged to the fluidity and
oscillation of Afro-Cuba and swayed to the beat of a *batá* drummer.

Benítez-Rojo's talismanic old black women, conquerors of the Apocalypse,
are flesh-and-blood emblems of a process Edward Brathwaite has described as
"psychic maroonage," the elaboration of "a syncretic vision of African patterns, symbols and communicative cannons (modes of walking, eating, working, inter-relating; musical, artistic, and other practices) which the subordinate
maintains in everyday life even in the course of submitting to large scale socio-
economic pressures of dominance."[2] This process of cultural maroonage, of
Creolization as the creative and innovative means of fending off oppressive
and dehumanizing values, is the key to understanding the multilayeredness
and polyphony of Caribbean cultures.[3] "Compromise," José Piedra maintains
in "From Monkey Tales to Cuban Songs: On Signification," "consisted of a
subtle balance between mimicking and mocking an oppressive code which had
miscalculated the effects of reducing all the participant cultures into a Hispanic symbiosis." In the crucible of the plantation—amid relationships based
on European power and African powerlessness—the slaves' very survival depended on their ability to manipulate and resist their complete absorption into
the core values of the plantation masters.

The coercion and resistance, acculturation and appropriation that typify
the Caribbean experience are most evident in the Creolization of African-
based religious beliefs and practices in the slave societies of the New World.
African religions merged in a dynamic process with European Christian and
Amerindian beliefs to shape syncretic theologies that provide alternative ways
of looking at the world "in a certain kind of way." Powerful repositories of
inner strength and cultural affirmation, the Caribbean's African-derived syncretic religions and healing practices—most notable among them Vodou,
Santería, Obeah, Quimbois, Gagá—have penetrated to the core of cultural
development in the Caribbean, leaving deep imprints on every significant cultural manifestation of the various islands. The Ifá system of divination in
Santería—dependent on "a wealth of narrative materials for the literary manifestations of poetic divination: motifs, themes, pharmacopeia, therapeutic ut-

terances, and practical wisdom in the form of fables and proverbs"—as analyzed by Eugenio Matibag in "Ifá and Interpretation: An Afro-Caribbean Literary Practice," "exemplifies the practices by which a community can preserve, order, and transmit narratives capable of providing coherence and structure to experience."

THESE "DIASPORAN RELIGIONS"—the term was coined by Joseph Murphy—share a Western African or Central African heritage (or both);[4] their various gods, rituals, theologies can easily be traced to common roots. But their most characteristic trait is their dynamism. Not only do they differ from each other in significant ways, but even within a system such as Haitian Vodou the vitality and heterogeneity of beliefs belie the notion of a single tradition. If all these religions can be said to coincide perfectly in one area, it is in their promotion of a ritualized union of the people with the spirit world, in the reciprocity of the link between the spirits and the community. Diasporan liturgies, Murphy contends, are distinctive in the way they work out the relationship between human beings and spirit in community ceremony. The centerpiece of that communal ritual is the phenomenon of possession. As Joan Dayan reminds us in "Vodoun, or the Voice of the Gods," "The language of possession, or the *crise de loa*—that moment when the god inhabits the head of his or her servitor—articulates the reciprocal abiding of human and god." The reciprocity between community and spirit, Murphy underscores, "is expressed in physical work as the community works through word, music, and movement" to summon the spirit, who in turn works through the congregation, "filling human actions with its power."

> Diasporan ceremonies are thus services *for* the spirit, actions of sacrifice and praise to please the spirit. And they are services *of* the spirit, actions undertaken by the spirits to inspire the congregation. Thus the reciprocity of diasporan spirituality is affirmed: service to the spirit is service to the community; and service to the community is service to the spirit. Service is revealed to be the central value of communal life. Service shows the spirit, in ceremony, but also whenever one member serves another. It is "service," in all its elegant multiple meanings, that shows the active quality of the spirituality of the African diaspora.[5]

The term *Vodou* (also *Voodoo, Vodoun,* and *Vaudon*)* evolved from the

---

* The spelling of this and many other terms of African origin used to describe various practices and beliefs is a constant source of debate among scholars and believers. Rather than arbitrarily impose our preferred spelling on all contributors to this book—particularly given the validity of the arguments presented in favor of one or another spelling—we have respected individual preferences throughout.

Dahomedan word *vodu* or *vodun*, meaning spirit or deity, and denotes a religion practiced by some six million Haitians who "serve the *loa*," or spirits. The term encompasses a variety of cultural elements—individual practices and creeds, a complex system of folk medicine, a structure for community justice, a fertile oral tradition, a rich iconography that has nourished Haitian art, a wealth of metaphors of political affirmation. Anna Wexler, in "'I Am Going to See Where My Oungan Is': The Artistry of a Haitian Vodou Flagmaker," for example, discusses these richly sequinned and beaded flags used in Vodou ceremonies to summon the loas as examples of meticulously crafted "ethnic art" whose function is nonetheless profoundly religious; their artistry is intended to enhance their purpose, that of "attract[ing] the spirits into the human gathering, mediating between worlds." Vodou, Leslie Desmangles rightfully contends, is "the folk religion of Haiti that pervades the framework of Haitian culture."[6]

The oldest, least understood, and perhaps most maligned of all Afro-Caribbean belief systems, Vodou has a rich tradition. It was born in the Dahomedan, Congolese, and Nigerian regions of West Africa and was filtered through Roman Catholic symbolism and liturgical traditions. Its deities, the loas (or *mystères*), are multiple and varied. Although generally divided into two main rites or "nations"—the *Rada* pantheon (of Dahomean or Yoruban origin) and the *Petro* (Creole loas originating principally in Haiti)—they elude these superficial categorizations because of their ever-changing manifestations. The gods' "astonishing proliferation," Dayan asserts, is evidence of their "ever being born or reconstructed, dying or being forgotten." Vodou practice centers around a complex system of myths and rituals linking the devotees to the divine entities and the entire spiritual community, with possession of believers by the loa being the system's cornerstone. The hierarchy of involvement may be summarized briefly as the *konesans*, a basic stage of participation; the *hounsi*, or "spouses," of the loa, who represent a more advanced level of commitment; and the male (*houngan*) and female (*mambo*) leaders, who initiate new hounsi and facilitate the community's contact with the deities and ancestral spirits.

In *African Civilizations in the New World*, Roger Bastide differentiates various categories of religious syncretism in the Caribbean. Morphological syncretism ("mosaic syncretism") is based on the juxtaposition and coexistence of African-derived elements and Catholic symbols—the Vodou *pé*, or altars, with stones, wax candles, crosses, statues of saints, and pots containing souls of the dead, for example. Institutional syncretism combines prescribed religious observances by reconciling Christian and African liturgical calendars.[7] Most common, however, is syncretism by correspondence, or what Desmangles calls a "symbiosis by identity," through which an African deity and a Catholic saint became one on the basis of mythical or symbolic similarities. Thus Erzulie, the beautiful water goddess of love who traces her ancestry to Whydah in Dahomey (or Benin) and Oshun in Nigeria, becomes the Virgin Mary. Benin's python god Damballah becomes Saint Patrick, the conqueror of the Irish snakes in Catholic hagiology. Legba, the guardian of destiny who holds the keys to the gates of the underworld, becomes Saint Peter. This symbiosis by identification, Desmangles argues, dates back to the Haitian colonial period; when Catholic missionaries displayed lithographs showing the various symbols associated with the lives of the Christian saints, the slaves associated these symbols with those related to their own gods. French colonial authorities in Haiti, in collusion with the Catholic hierarchy, strove to forbid Vodou practices, leading the slave population to the subterfuge of honoring the African gods through the worship of their Catholic representatives, using them as "a veil behind which they could practice their African religions."[8] Margarite Fernández Olmos, in "Trans-Caribbean Identity and the Fictional World of Mayra Montero," argues for yet another category of religious syncretism, exemplified by the Gagá cult in the Dominican Republic. Gagá, a Vodou-derived practice brought by emigrating Haitian sugarcane workers to the Dominican Republic, where it was transformed and reinterpreted by local folk practices and beliefs, is "an interesting example of nontraditional Caribbean syncretism: instead of a hybridity between the European and the colonized, Gagá exemplifies a secondary type of syncretism, one between (ex)colonized peoples."

Cuban Santería is the outcome of a similar process of accommodation, preservation, and resistance. Derived from Yoruba beliefs and rituals, Santería, also known as "la Regla de Ocha," or the belief system of the *orichas*, honors the deities, or orichas, with strictly prescribed rituals and offerings. As does Haitian Vodou, Cuban Santería reflects the convergence of African beliefs with the Roman Catholic saints (*santos*), whom the slaves were obliged to worship. Like their Haitian counterparts, Cuban slaves "developed multiple levels of discourse to organize their heterogeneous religious experience, referring, in more public and secular contexts, to the Yoruba orishas by the Spanish word santos. Alerted to the energetic devotions to these santos practiced by Afro-Cubans, outsiders labeled their religion santería, 'the way of the saints.'"[9]

In "La Regla de Ocha: The Religious System of Santería," Miguel Barnet notes the importance of the notion of family in Santería practice. A spiritual kinship binds the members of the group, who—within Cuba as well as in Cuban exile communities around the world—are of all races and come from all sectors of Cuban society. Entrance into this spiritual family is obtained through an initiation presided over by a godmother (*madrina*) or godfather (*padrino*) as head of the *ilé*, or religious community. Becoming a true *santera* or *santero* involves unconditional dedication, rigorous discipline, and a lifelong commitment to a particular oricha. Members are believed to have been spiritually chosen by an oricha for initiation. Initiation opens the paths toward spiritual growth, of which there are two: the *camino de Orula*, the way of knowledge and enlightenment, and the *camino de santo*, the way of the spirit. A priest (*babalocha*) or priestess (*iyalocha*) guides the initiate's development. The highest and most intense degree of involvement is attained by the *babalawo*, the master of a method of divination called *Ifá*, who must spend years of difficult training in the traditions, memorize thousands of verses of Ifá poetry in the Yoruba language, familiarize himself with herbalism and ritual theology with a tutor and godfather, and undergo an elaborate initiation ceremony.

Vodou and Santería are group phenomena; the loas and orichas live through and for the community. Obeah, by contrast, is a more individualized system, defined by George Simpson in *Black Religions in the New World* as a Jamaican conjuring practice closely linked to witchcraft.[10] Obeah, as Karla Frye proposes in "'An Article of Faith': Obeah and Hybrid Identities in Elizabeth Nunez-Harrell's *When Rocks Dance*," "is not a religion as such but a system of beliefs grounded in spirituality and an acknowledgment of the supernatural and involving aspects of witchcraft, sorcery, magic, spells, and healing." The term can be traced to the Ashanti and kindred tribes from the Gold Coast of Africa, which were heavily represented in the slave populations of the British colonies. (The Ashanti word *obayifo*, witch or wizard, corrupted into *Obeah*, *Obiah*, or *Obia*.) The practice of Obeah involves the "putting on" and "taking off" of "duppies" or "jumbees" (ghosts or spirits of the dead) for either good or evil purposes. It differs from Vodou and Santería in that its beliefs and rituals are not centered on the participation of the community but involve secret individualized consultations aimed at fostering specific ends.[11] In "'Another Poor Devil of a Human Being . . .': Jean Rhys and the Novel as Obeah," however, Elaine Savory argues her case for a reconsideration of Obeah as central to the notion of community. "Both Catholicism and Obeah function best as communal moral constructs, informing people's relations with one another," she contends in her discussion of Rhys's *Smile Please*, "even when it seems as if the individual Catholic or person who asks the Obeah practitioner for help is alone. The belief system itself is sustained and critiqued by a community." Obeah is analogous to Vodou and Santería, moreover, in the vital cultural role it has played throughout the English-speaking Caribbean. The Obeah-man and Obeah-woman played a prominent role in Caribbean slave societies from the earliest days of the sugar plantations in the West Indies; they functioned as community leaders and repositories of the African folk's cultural heritage.[12] Like its Haitian and Cuban counterparts,

Obeah has permeated the popular imagination and West Indian literature and culture, despite constant efforts by colonial authorities to repress its manifestations and persecute its practitioners.

The vilification and condemnation to which Obeah and other African-derived religions have been subjected throughout the centuries are partly the result of their practitioners' reputed skill in the preparation of natural poisons as spells for retaliatory purposes; Obeah practice, for example, involves the use of animal and natural substances for cures and spells, as does Quimbois in Guadeloupe and Martinique. (In contemporary usage the terms *Obeah-man* and *quimboiseur* are interchangeable with *folk doctor.*) Ivette Romero-Cesareo, in "Sorcerers, She-Devils, and Shipwrecked Women: Writing Religion in French-Caribbean Literature," argues for a focus on the beneficial aspects of these practices, as seen from within the communities in question. In her discussion of Simone Schwarz-Bart's *Pluie et vent sur Télumée Miracle*, she quotes Schwarz-Bart to stress "the healing properties—for both body and soul—of the special baths prepared [for Télumée] by [the shaman woman] Ma Cia, which help her recuperate from the string of tragic events in her life." She would steep in "a big earthen pan waiting for [her] outside her cabin, in the sun, full of water dark with all kinds of magic leaves—paoca, calaba balsam, bride's rose, and the power of Satan"—and ladle the contents ritualistically over her head to "leave behind all the fatigues of the week." Likewise, as Brinda Mehta argues in "The Shaman Woman, Resistance, and the Powers of Transformation: A Tribute to Ma Cia in Simone Schwarz-Bart's *The Bridge of Beyond*," the female shaman figure in African-based Caribbean religions functions as the mediator who paves the way for "the survival and wholeness of entire peoples" through "her universal messages of interconnectedness, unified resistance to oppression, sisterhood, and respect for the environment." But the more common approach has been the sensationalistic exploitation of ritual practices—as uncivilized, unbridled, erotic—for the titillation of the West. Typical of this misrepresentation are denigrating accounts like those that abound in William Seabrook's *The Magic Island*, where he writes of a Vodou ceremony—"not devoid of a certain beauty"—that he claims to have witnessed while in Haiti: "In the red light of torches which made the moon turn pale, leaping, screaming, writhing black bodies, blood-maddened, sex-maddened, god-maddened, drunken, whirled and danced their dark saturnalia, heads thrown weirdly back as if their necks were broken, white teeth and eyeballs gleaming, while couples seizing one another from time to time fled from the circle, as if pursued by furies, into the forest to share and slake their ecstasy."[13]

The censure to which they have been subjected also owes much to the role played by Obeah, Vodou, and other African-based religions in inspiring revolts against European colonial powers. As did Vodou, Alan Richardson explains in "Romantic Voodoo: Obeah and British Culture, 1797–1807," Obeah "provided an 'ideological rallying point' in sanctioning rebellion, afforded meeting places and leaders, and formed a repository for the 'collective memory of the slaves' by preserving African traditions which could be opposed to the dominant colonial culture. Even the illusory promise of invulnerability could provide much needed morale for struggles in which the whites were almost always better armed than the black rebels." The 1760 rebellion of Ashanti slaves in Jamaica under the leadership of Tacky is a case in point. Tacky, who sought to legitimize his leadership position by claiming to have been an African chief, secured the services of an Obeah-man as a magicoreligious co-leader charged with supplying the rebellious slaves with a potion that would make them invulnerable in battle. The defiant slaves came to believe that Tacky could catch any bullet aimed at him and fire it back at the enemy. Although the rebels were subdued after a prolonged and fierce resistance, the colonial authorities, fearful of the role Obeah had played in fostering and sustaining the rebellion, sought immediately (and ultimately unsuccessfully) to prohibit the continuation of the practice.

The parallels with Haitian Vodou are evident; the seeds of Haiti's successful war for independence are said to have been planted by a belief in slave leader Mackandal's legendary powers to predict the future and transform himself into various animals, attributes he used to defy the French authorities. Sabotage by poison was Mackandal's chief strategy, and so powerful was the legend that sprung from the rapidly spreading tales of the fear this sagacious houngan had instilled in the French planters of Haiti that despite his capture and execution by the colonial authorities, the myth of his immortality lived on. A more direct connection between Vodou and popular insurrection can be traced to the oft-told tale of the evening of August 21, 1791, when a wild boar was sacrificed to the loas and the powerful houngan Boukman made a solemn oath to struggle to defeat the French slaveholders, a connection between religion and political resistance that continues in the present day.

In the postcolonial period, Desmangles has argued, Haitian loas like Ogoun were integrated into the framework of Haitian history, becoming identified with the heroes of the revolution, "the symbolic embodiers of Vodouisant's national ideal, the bringers of a higher order which was to be a perfected Haiti." The symbolic link was vigorously stressed during the American occupation of Haiti (1915–1934), the antisuperstition campaigns (1940–1942), and more recently "during weeks of *dechoukaj* (reprisals) in which the masses took to the streets throughout the country to avenge the murders, the theft, and the civil rights abuses of the tontons macoutes during the twenty-nine years of the Duvalier oligarchy."[14] But each affirmation of the rebellious power of the people and their loas has been met by a campaign of defamation against Vodou and its practitioners. "Pro-Western ideologues of 'progress' and 'civilization,'" Lizabeth Paravisini-Gebert writes in "Women Possessed: Eroticism and Exoticism in the Representation of Woman as Zombie," "have derided ritualistic practices of African origin as proof of the Caribbean folk's inability to embrace 'modernity,' of their incapacity for emancipation and sovereignty. Given a glimpse of Caribbean people's resolution to assert their autonomy, they are quick to invoke the titillating figure of the zombie as representative of the Afro-Caribbean folk as bogeyman."

DISCUSSIONS of the correlations among the various Caribbean literatures and cultures have always been fraught with difficulty: conceptual approaches based on colonial patterns have sought to preserve the traditional separations of Caribbean nations, and thus, they preclude a broader pan-Caribbean perspective. Linguistic barriers gain exaggerated importance in debates regarding national and cultural identities, obscuring other manifestations, such as religious syncretism, that tend to unify Caribbean cultural and literary expression.

Edward Brathwaite acknowledged this problem in his seminal 1974 essay, "The African Presence in the Caribbean," where he calls for a heterogeneous, aesthetic approach to, and a broader view of, culture. Anthropologists have long maintained that religion was a pivotal factor in the survival of African culture in the Caribbean. Brathwaite alerts us to the consequences of the role of religion.

> Whenever "religion" is mentioned . . . a *whole cultural complex* is also present. . . . Until, therefore, our definition of "culture" is re-examined in terms of its totality, not simply its Europeanity, we will fail to discover a literature of negritude and, with it, a literature of local authenticity. Likewise, the African presence in Caribbean literature cannot be fully or easily perceived until we redefine the term "literature" to include the nonscribal material of the folk/oral tradition, which, on examination, turns out to have a much longer history than our scribal tradition, to have been more relevant to the majority of our people, and to have had an unquestionably wider provenance.[15]

The goals of revealing thematic connections and textual practices and of penetrating the codes of representation of the syncretic cultures in the Caribbean should in no way be interpreted as a negation of difference or a homogenization of significant sociohistorical variations. Likewise, many of the insights yielded by this type of approach can in some measure be applied to areas outside the Caribbean basin (the focus of this book): Brazil and other Latin American countries, and even certain U.S. cities such as New York and

Miami, reveal the type of cultural amalgamation that characterizes the Caribbean. Nevertheless, an important dimension of Caribbean consciousness has been forged by African-based culture, and it has generated a degree of unity not found in other regional constellations. This dimension distinguishes the region as a whole, offering the possibility of a pan-Caribbean cultural synthesis that stresses unity while maintaining diversity. This dimension of consciousness must receive the recognition it deserves in grounding Caribbean literary and cultural identity.

Paradoxically, another unifying factor of Caribbean cultures is the displacement, the forced or voluntary migration of peoples, which is the foundation of Caribbean societies. This dynamic process of cultural fusion is not exclusively African, European, Chinese, Amerindian, or East Indian, but is composed of one, some, or all of these ethnicities. The contemporary global phenomenon of mass human migration, and the often violent encounters and interactions of peoples and cultures that such migrations have given rise to, have historically been the very basis of colonial and postcolonial Caribbean societies. Consequently, as Abiola Irele has noted, the dynamics of literary and cultural identity in the region have implications that go beyond the area itself. Caribbean literature today, he writes, "can be considered to be positioned at the point of intersection between the reflexes of postmodernism and the emerging field of postcolonial theory. It has become apparent that, in its very thrust, the discursive project of colonized intellectuals has been the rejection of overarching 'master narratives' formulated in the West, in favor of local forms of knowledge and the structures of feeling they enable." He cites as an example the elaboration of the notion of hybridity and cultural ambiguity "as a constitutive principle of modern experience" by various Caribbean writers and intellectuals.

> [This principle provides] a perspective that helps to clarify the
> context in which much of contemporary literature is developing, in
> response to the objective conditions of modern existence. To evoke
> these interconnections, therefore, is to indicate a common field of
> imaginative and intellectual production and of critical discourse in
> both the Third World and the West, one that offers a rich field for
> scholarly exploration. Because of the special intensity of its engage-
> ment with these issues, Caribbean literature has assumed a strategic
> importance in this field.[16]

The persistence and insistence of syncretic African-based belief systems in the literatures and cultures of the Caribbean is the focus of this book which encompasses diverse multi- and interdisciplinary approaches. These approaches are all variations on a common theme: the creative and powerful process of religious syncretism and its social relevance and widespread transcendence within Caribbean cultures. The collaboration and interchange of disciplines as well as the combination of different national and linguistic approaches contribute to the avoidance of a narrow and static perspective and to the expansion of discourse within the field.

Just as a familiarity with Santería can enrich the visual and intellectual impact of a Wilfredo Lam painting or an awareness of sacred drumming can heighten the sensual experience of a performance of Afro-Caribbean music, so too can a consciousness of Caribbean belief systems help us appreciate the beauty and complexity of peoples who have so much to teach about sharing, retaining, incorporating, and tolerating other cultures. Although Benítez-Rojo has ruefully stated of the Caribbean that its "ardent way of conceiving culture . . . owes a lot to each Caribbean person's knowing more or less intuitively that finally the only thing that history's undertow has left to him is his paradoxical culture, and nothing more,"[17] clearly, as his own works and those of many others have demonstrated, the historical legacy of the Caribbean is much more than that. It is to be found in the region's gift for constantly re-creating and redefining itself.

Notes

1. Antonio Benítez-Rojo, *The Repeating Island: The Caribbean and the Postmodern Perspective*, trans. James Maraniss (Durham, N.C.: Duke University Press, 1992), 10.
2. Marc Zimmerman, "The Unity of the Caribbean and Its Literatures," in *Process of Unity in Caribbean Society: Ideologies and Literatures* (Minneapolis: Institute for the Study of Ideologies and Literature, 1983), 43. The concept of "psychic maroonage" is taken from Edward Kamau Brathwaite's *Contradictory Omens* (Mona, Jamaica: Savacou, 1974).
3. Zimmerman, "The Unity of the Caribbean," 43.
4. Joseph M. Murphy, *Working the Spirit: Ceremonies of the African Diaspora* (Boston: Beacon Press, 1994), 6–7.
5. Ibid.
6. Leslie G. Desmangles, *The Faces of the Gods: Vodou and Roman Catholicism in Haiti* (Chapel Hill: University of North Carolina Press, 1992), 1–3.
7. Roger Bastide, *African Civilizations in the New World* (London: C. Hurst, 1971), 154–156.
8. Desmangles, *The Faces of the Gods*, 10–11.
9. Murphy, *Working the Spirit*, 81.
10. George Eaton Simpson, *Black Religions in the New World* (New York: Columbia University Press, 1978), 14. Jay D. Dobbin, *The Jombee Dance of Montserrat: A Study of Trance Ritual in the West Indies* (Columbus: Ohio State University Press, 1986), asserts that certain group activities centered around Obeah beliefs continue to survive as a form of folk religion.
11. In Jamaica and the British West Indies a parallel to Vodou and Santería might be the less generalized Jamaican Shangoism, listed by Simpson alongside Vodou and Santería as a "Neo-African cult."

12. Ivor Morrish, *Obeah, Christ and Rastaman: Jamaica and Its Religion* (Cambridge: James Clarke, 1982), 40.

13. William B. Seabrook, *The Magic Island* (New York: Harcourt, Brace, 1929), 42.

14. Desmangles, *The Faces of the Gods*, 172.

15. Edward Kamau Brathwaite, "The African Presence in the Caribbean," *Daedalus* 103, no. 2 (spring 1974): 74, 78 (emphasis added).

16. Abiola Irele, "Editorial," *Research in African Literatures* 25, no. 2 (summer 1994): 3.

17. Benítez-Rojo, *The Repeating Island*, 166.

Vodoun, or the Voice of the Gods

JOAN DAYAN

Better a jungle in the head than rootless concrete.
                    —DEREK WALCOTT, "Pentecost"

AFTER THE DEPARTURE of "Baby Doc" Duvalier from Haiti in February 1986, amid shouts of "Haiti liberée" and photos of charred "malfaiteurs," a Haitian friend remarked, "You can always invent a new image of Haiti." Perhaps no other Caribbean island has inspired such extreme invention, such impressive paraphrase. Writing in 1887, the Englishman James Anthony Froude called Haiti "the most ridiculous caricature of civilization in the world."[1] But Froude reminded his readers that beneath the tinsel cover of elegance, fashion, and good French, lay the dark and heady substratum of Africa, which for him meant a legacy of cannibalism, blood drinking, and lust.

Vodoun, a word used by the Fon tribe of southern Dahomey to mean "spirit," "god," or "image," is most often used by outsiders to signal the backwardness, indolence, and greed that they feel needs correcting. Photos of mud baths, native eyes opened wide in abandon, and bleeding chickens punctuate articles on Haiti in publications as disparate as *Newsweek*, *Vanity Fair*, and the *New York Review of Books*. For some outsiders, Vodoun promises a refreshing dose of exoticism. William B. Seabrook, writing his *Magic Island* in 1929, during the American occupation of Haiti, told his blasé readers back in New York to get some passion into their lives by putting blood in their Fifth Avenue cocktails: "Perhaps if we mixed a little true sacrificial blood in our synthetic cocktails and flavored them prayerfully with holy fire, our night clubs would be more orgiastically successful and become sacred as temples were in the days of Priapus and Aphrodite."[2]

Tales of zombis, *loup-garous* (sometimes identified as werewolves and some-times as female vampires), snakes, and red-eyed *bakalou baka*, or *pinga maza* (an evil spirit, translated literally as "prenez garde," or beware), though pe-ripheral to the more basic beliefs and practices that articulate the multiple and ambiguous versions of Haitian socioreligious life, have always appealed to foreigners. It should not surprise us that during the American occupation, from 1915 to 1934, tales of cannibalism, torture, and zombis were published in this country. What better way to justify the "civilizing" presence of Ma-rines in Haiti than to project the phantasm of barbarism? What might be dis-missed as harmless but titillating tales of gore and spirits flapping in the night always have serious consequences. And representations of Vodoun have usu-ally served a political purpose, whether President Elie Lescot's support of the Catholic church and its "antisuperstition" campaign in 1941 to clear peasant land for United States rubber production or "Papa Doc" Duvalier's cynical de-formation of what he called a *uniquely* Haitian tradition.

Whenever the repression of the peasantry became more violent than usual, due to the necessities of export or appropriation of lands, Vodoun practices were described—in both the Haitian and the foreign press—as superstition and black magic. In the gritty, not-so-inspiring world of politics and power, a mythologized Haiti of zombis, sorcery, and witchdoctors helps to derail our attention from the real causes of poverty and suffering: economic exploita-tion, color prejudice, and political guile. Indeed, a month after Henry Namphy found himself replaced by a new general, Prosper Avril (later replaced by Ertha Pascal-Trouillot, one more in a series of figures for what has become known as Duvalierism without Duvalier), the *Wall Street Journal* featured an article by Charles McCoy, "Black Magic Casts a Deepening Spell over Troubled Haiti." With such leads as "Werewolves and Cannibals," "The Ship Has Sunk," and "Children of the Drum," McCoy reveals the perennial attachment to an occult Haiti, while giving his readers good reason to lose hope for any form of democracy in such a macabre land. His conclusions have less to do with what Alexander Cockburn once described as the "robust paradigm of inter-vention and exploitation" than with "headless corpses," werewolves "chopped to bits by machete," a Vodoun priest who lost his nose to the devil, and magic potions. As McCoy tells us, "Western notions of progress and development fade in the smoke of a voodoo priest's flaming magic stones." Yet in spite of corruption, illiteracy, disease, and death, McCoy suggests that Haiti still of-fers something to the aspiring tourist. He concludes the article in idyllic tones that elevate Haiti out of the ordinary and ease readers into another spectacle that demands neither thought, responsibility, nor concern: "Haiti is one of the last places on earth where a traveler can still share a glass of rum with a god."

To TALK ABOUT the gods, to write about Vodoun, is no easy matter. Ceremonies and services for the gods, and the gods themselves, vary from region to region. My own knowledge is based on experiences and research in Port-au-Prince and those areas near the capital, Léogane, Croix-des-Missions, and Croix-des-Bouquets. What I say then will be neither exclusive nor binding for other localities. I will also admit that since I believe in much of what I describe, I run risks, both literary and ethical. Finally, to write about Vodoun at a time when the Centre Pompidou in Paris, caught up in the celebration of the hybrid (a more sophisticated version of the current "global studies" phenomenon), produces an exhibition called "Magiciens de la Terre" in which expressive artifacts—from all kinds of places—jostle in fetishistic display, is to be aware of how much out there in the radically "other" can be the occasion for fanciful adventure, grist for the academic mill. Differences are neutralized. We get a slick, homogenized history. Where such sensuous certainty flourishes, as Hegel reminds us, no distinction can find its way. And Emmanuel Levinas confronts the coercions of indeterminacy when he writes: "The despotism of the senses constitutes the source of tyranny."

"Natural communities are finished. Look at Haiti, it's all pastiche and fraud"—a warning from a smart analyst of culture that alerts me to the need for caution when writing about a place turned to as either locus of liberation or proof of regression. For some Haitians Vodoun tyrannizes the land and the people: the gods are always hungry, and even dogs are driven to suicide, jumping out of windows or throwing themselves in front of cars. For others, this religion of resistance and revolution gives collective strength and identity to the disenfranchised. What then are the constraints of this theodicy? How has Vodoun changed in the past fifty years? Is there a logic to its dissolution and retentions: do we see a vital push toward integration or a static cult of the remnant?

Answering these questions is made more difficult when Vodoun practitioners themselves cannot resist the temptation to share stories of the excessive anger of the gods, the revenge of the ancestors, and the blood lust of sorcerers. It is possible that in Haiti, where many invent the unspeakable for the sake of their own fiction—or for the money proffered by eager foreigners—most outsiders will not be able to get at the everyday, the lived reality of a particular locale. As one Haitian intellectual explained to me, "Vodoun is an all-powerful trope. It appeals to everyone's imagination. It has been manipulated throughout history, used by all kinds of people. Everyone gets a piece of it." It is easy enough to see how Vodoun inspires ample associations or impressive speculations. What is less easy to understand is how this religion resists manipulation, how its practices set limits to any universal trope or symbol, and finally, how its rituals confront, absorb, and reconstitute the extremes of idealization or denigration. In thinking about Vodoun we must inhabit—even if risking that fashionable postmodern device—an indeterminate place, not vague so much as very particularized in its many conversions. We must move to a middle ground where laws of identity and contradiction no longer work, where local and sometimes erratic gods summon and urge an insistent ideology or world of reference.

> It is a long way from Guinea
> but the gods still have their places.
>   —EDWARD KAMAU BRATHWAITE, "Homecoming"

WHO ARE the gods of Vodoun? How do they come into your life, and how are they to be served? There are thousands of gods in Haiti; yet the enormous range of divinity is in no way arbitrary. Any one god or loa (also called mystères, anges, saints, or les invisibles) can have multiple emanations, depending on locale, on a particular ritual, on the composition of the hounfort (in the west of Haiti understood both as the temple surroundings and the ceremonial altar), or on their association with particular individuals or family groups. And any Vodoun initiate can, once dead, be turned into a god by a Vodoun priest. The African origin of the gods is complex. Although Legba, the "master of the crossroads," invoked first in every ceremony, comes from Dahomey, some loa are recognized as Congo, Ibo, or Nago spirits while others bear traces of their pasts in other regions of Africa. The loa can be classified according to the numerous groups, nations, or tribes to which they belong. But such a division does not help us to understand the link formed between these tribes in the New World, the loa's wandering from one tribe to another, or the endless transformations of loa as they relate to their servitors. A local god of the mountains and peasant farms, Cousin Zaka, reconstitutes for the Haitian the agrarian rites of a submerged Amerindian past, as Papa Dessalines adapts Ogoun, the West African warrior god (who "walks" in Haiti in his various aspects), to the exigencies of the Haitian war of independence.

The institution of slavery, in wrenching individuals from their native land and from their names and their origins, produced communities of belief that would ever be distinguished from the mood or character of Western religion. The gods came to the New World. In their travels something unique would happen to the possibility of nostos. When the gods left Africa, they taught their people how to live the epic of displacement. No longer simply identifiable in terms of parentage or place, they would come into the heads of their people and there urge a return to a thought of origin, a place as urgent as it was irretrievable. "The gods do not die. They go under the sea." So Sabine, Derek Walcott's new Ulysses, leaves Trinidad, takes the schooner Flight, and descends into the shades: "I taking a sea-bath, I gone down the road."

The loa live *en bas de l'eau,* under the waters, in an unlocatable place called "Guinée." Though clearly distinguished from *les morts,* the spirits of the dead, they share their home with the ancestors. When loa come to visit their "children," whether in a formal, public ceremony or in private times of dream or individual communion, they come by way of the *chemin de l'eau,* or water road. Thus Jacques Roumain in *Guinée,* as translated by Langston Hughes,

> It is the long road to Guinea
> Where your fathers await you
>   without impatience.
> Along the way, they talk,
> They wait.
> This is the hour when the streams rattle
>   like beads of bone.

Since no one really knows what goes on down under the waters or how the loa relate to each other and to the dead, talk about the gods usually ends up being about the ways in which men and women serve or resist their "mysteries," or how the gods themselves respond to the vicissitudes of life in the corporeal world.

If the kingdom of the gods remains indescribable or obscure, their presence on earth is precisely apprehended. The experience of Vodoun, at least in traditional practice, takes place in a community that articulates itself around the hounfort. The hounfort includes a central dwelling of one or more rooms, circumscribed by a large area called the *peristyle* (or *tonnelle,* usually covered like a shed) in the middle of which is the *poteau-mitan,* or center post, that images the traffic between heaven and earth. Some writers have interpreted the post as the means of descent for the loa to earth. It would be more accurate to see the post as the place where the way up and the way down are no longer contradictory, for as we have seen, the loa ascend *or* descend: coming up out of the waters and into the heads of their people.

Since the loa have left their watery dwelling to visit earth, they must be made comfortable, which means receiving some material compensation such as food, drink, music, and dance for their journey. In some hounfort there are rooms or houses for the loa. These sanctuaries are referred to as the *caye-mystère,* the *bagi* or *sobagi,* and contain one or more altars to the gods. Each god has his or her own altar, which contains a mélange of objects, flowers, plates of food and drink, *cruches* or *govis*—the earthen jars or bottles belonging to the spirits of the dead—and the *pots-de-tête,* which contain the hairs or nail parings of the initiates there kept safe from harm.

In his *Voodoo in Haiti,* Alfred Métraux describes the *bagi* as "a veritable junk shop"; and if we forget the negative connotations expressed here, the

description would be quite accurate.[3] For the loa's room is an elaborately com-
piled habitation, where the loa can find on display their special things. These
pieces of property are not only tokens of devotion, preserved by the *houngan*,
or priest, for the gods, but they make up the lineaments and capture the idio-
syncracies of the loa. On the walls hang the Catholic chromolithographs or
color prints of the saints adopted, or redefined as counterparts of the loa.
(Damballah-Wèdo, the fertile snake god of the waters, is figured as St. Patrick
with serpents under his feet. Here, identification is made with the snakes as
Damballah and not with the Christian symbolism of spirits crushed under-
foot.) And those who are possessed, who become the temporary vessel for the
gods, come to the room to get the clothes and objects they need in order to
represent the god they have momentarily become. The loa do not all have
rooms of their own, for they are far too numerous. And even though they sometimes make exorbitant, though not usually gratuitous demands on their devotees, they don't mind sharing their rooms with other gods, as long as the altars
are kept separate.

These spatial arrangements—the organization of the hounfort and the
objects contained in the altar room or bagi—confirm and elaborate the civil
organization of Vodoun. When there is no ceremony going on, all kinds of
daily activities take place throughout the court and peristyle. And although
every hounfort varies, depending on region, wealth, or local custom, the space
always allows the cooperative participation of all members. Chairs usually form
a circle around the ceremonial ground, and no one—not even the uninitiated—is excluded from access to religious ritual.

Here I should add that not every hounfort is so elaborated. As Haitians
migrate to New York, Miami, Canada, or France, the gods move indoors, to
be served in basements or corners of apartments. I will return to what we might
think of as the gods *à la dérive*, but for now I should emphasize that the details of ritual and the necessities of service—especially food and drink—are
maintained, even in exile. A table for Damballah set up for his ceremony in
a Brooklyn basement—obviously no poteau-mitan here—displayed fried bananas in sugar, a cup of water, a plate of biscuits, a plate of cookies, a cup of
coffee, an egg on a saucer, a saucer containing rice in milk with cinnamon,
three cakes, a bouquet of flowers in a vase, bottles of rum and orange liqueur.

The accumulated waste, what Edward Kamau Brathwaite has called the
"claypots, shards, ruins" of the contemporary Caribbean, is not revised out of
the sacred. Never elusive, abstract, or idealized, the gods themselves demand
habitations that serve them the treasures as well as the detritus of Haiti. What
appears as randomness is actually a tough commitment to the facts of *this* world.
The gods relate to and are activated by things that do not conform to cravings
for purity or longings for transcendence.

It is not easy to grasp the close, reciprocal, even palpable relation of the Haitian to his gods. And yet the vital connection between human and divinity—between thoughts of the beyond and the claims of the present—uneasily and endlessly reformed or redressed, remains the ground for the collective exercise of Vodoun. As a young practitioner of Vodoun, now in New York, explained, "The loa are in the people not in the place. They follow their *cheval* (horse) anywhere, across the ocean and into their homes." Or as René Depestre, the Haitian novelist and poet, now living in Lézignan-Corbières, told me: "The gods never die, for they gain sustenance from the most intimate moments of their people; and they suffer, for they are implicated in the general zombification of Haitians."

> *They manifest themselves. They become incarnate in*
> *the bodies of their servitors. They eat, drink, talk,*
> *dance in the person of their medium. Some gods make*
> *themselves men all day long. . . . And the person*
> *possessed . . . becomes god, he is the god in flesh and*
> *bones.*
>
> —DR. LOUIS MARS

THE LANGUAGE of possession, or the *crise de loa*—that moment when the god inhabits the head of his or her servitor—articulates the reciprocal abiding of human and god. The "horse" is said to be mounted and ridden by the god. The event is not a matter of domination, but a kind of double movement of attenuation and expansion. For make no mistake about it, the loa cannot appear in epiphany, cannot be made manifest on earth without the person who becomes the temporary receptacle or mount. And the possessed gives herself up to become an instrument in a social and collective drama. This experience of election, its shock of communion, is not evidence of psychic disruption, or proof of pathology, but rather a result of the most intense discipline and study. Not everyone can be possessed, for not everyone can know how to respond to the demands and expectations of her god (see Figure 1).

The Vodoun servitors, most often women, are called *hounsi*, or spirit-wives. Those who have been initiated into the mysteries and have passed the trial by fire (the ceremony *brûler zin*) are born anew as *hounsi kanzo*, as opposed to the *hounsi bossale* (from the Spanish *bozal*, meaning wild or untamed, and originally applied to the slaves newly arrived from Africa, as opposed to the Creole slaves born in the New World). When loa possess the hounsi bossale, the experience is dangerous and unpredictable, for the loa can be as undisciplined as their "horses." In order to become hounsi kanzo, you must have a mastery of your self, be prepared to receive the loa and, most of all, to localize and control what for the uninitiated remains vague or unreal.

Figure 1. Mambo La Merci Benjamin goes into trance, supported by *hounsi*. *Photo: Joan Dayan (Bel Air, Haiti, 1970)*.

The loa do not correlate with objects in the natural world nor with specific human activities. Instead their identities are formed by their relation with each other and by their interaction with those they claim as their servitors. Any individual god—unless "bought" or "stolen"—conforms to some extent with the character and inclinations of its nation or human family. Looked at from the vantage of Western religions, the Vodoun gods might seem to lack a necessary grandeur, offering themselves to the spectacle of ceremony with a kind of rough immediacy.

Since the gods cannot be classified according to rank—an old African god as Legba might well find himself in the company of the colonial, Creole god Ti-Jean-Pied-Fin—their appearance might seem anarchic. And one god can have many emanations, whether regarded as members of the same family or as different manifestations of the same deity. To take Erzulie, the most contradictory of loa, known most generally as "Maîtresse Erzulie," both virgin and lady of love, served by spinsters and prostitutes: not only does she "walk" as Erzulie-Fréda in the "douce" Rada rites of Dahomey, but she walks in the Petro rites as well, as Erzulie-gé-rouge (with red eyes) or Erzulie Mapian. She also shares with the other Petro loa, all born in Haiti—and for many, closely associated with the war of independence—a tough, brute, or "dure" temperament. And yet the astonishing multiplicity of gods resists this simple division of loa into the two major groups, Rada or Petro. When Milo Rigaud attempted to classify and list the loa, he admitted, "Scarcely one hundred pages would suffice to mention all the loas." His list in *Secrets of Voodoo* demonstrates the astonishing proliferation of gods and names.[4] Erzulie appears as: Grande Erzulie, Erzulie Toro (the Bull), Erzulie Fréda, Erzulie-gé-rouge, Erzulie Mapian (Louse), Erzulie-dos-bas (Low Back), Erzulie Zandor, Erzulie Boum'ba, Erzulie-séverine-belle-femme, Erzulie Dantor (see Figure 2).

One of the reasons it is so difficult to codify the gods of Haiti is that they are ever being born or reconstructed, dying or being forgotten. The established tutelary gods like Damballah, Legba, Ogoun, Erzulie-Fréda, or Chango remain. But there are other kinds of gods, sometimes called *les dieux de circonstance* or *de politique*. Ever testifying to the labor of resistance and change, Vodoun comprehends multiple stories in its realizations. Milo Rigaud tells the story of a loa he "knew" called "Captain Daybas," not Haitian, not African, but a United States Marine:

> This mystery of the African pantheon was, formerly, an officer of the American marines; doubtless attracted by vodoun, he became an initiate; the magic priesthood of the hounfort to which he belonged made a "vodoun" [spirit] of his soul after his death. . . . Ever since, Captain Daybas, a vodoun loa, descends to possess his adepts like the other loa—and, when his adepts are "mounted" by him, they forget

Figure 2. Wall painting of Ezili Dantò (Erzulie Dantor). *Photo: Joan Dayan (Bainet, Haiti, 1986).*

their Creole in order to speak only English throughout their possession.

It has been said that the rigor, authority, and cruelty of the American Marines so struck the Haitian imagination that many of the foreigners' qualities showed up in the contours or expressions of other loa. Imagine the Irish Catholic church making a saint of Oliver Cromwell. The American occupation of Haiti is remembered by many as the most degrading, and ultimately the most destructive, experience since slavery. But in Vodoun things are never simple. Whenever Captain Daybas appears, history is in some sense reconceived and made part of the present political and economic scene. God and servitor speak the memory of a particular colonial relation in all its caprices of power: we are pressed to think again about any ideology of domination, about the peculiar relation *between* those who called themselves "masters" and those who found themselves "servants."

Nowhere does the divide between an oral and written history become so apparent as when we consider the making of a hero. While no writer, as far as I know, has ever poeticized the story of Dessalines, Dessalines remains the only Black Jacobin who became a loa. "Dessalines, Dessalines, démanbré [the ravaged], / Viv la libèté." Legend has it that the blood oath of Bois-Caïman began the slave revolt in 1791. In Bois-Caïman a Vodoun service was convened by the houngan Boukman and a *mambo* (priestess) who, as far as I know, remains unnamed (the fate of most women who fought in Haiti's many revolts against slavery and foreign intrusion). Today, the ceremony of Bois-Caïman is one of the most fierce deeds of recollection: it relives the ferocity of the struggle for independence, with the militant Petro deities, whose identities were forged in the New World struggles, at the center of the service. Some Vodoun practitioners say that the loa do not let them forget the tribulations of slavery, and the defeats of the Spanish, English, and French, all those *blancs* during the thirteen years of revolt. (In Haiti you can't translate *blancs* literally. Most often it does not mean white but foreigner. A black from the United States would be called blanc.) In 1804 Dessalines declared the independence of Saint-Domingue, recalling the original Amerindian inhabitants when he chose the name "Haiti," which means mountainous lands. For Aimé Césaire, when the slaves revolted, a literature was born: "the first epic of the New World was written by Haitians, by Toussaint, Christophe, and Dessalines."[5] Yet another epic continues to be told in Vodoun: a story passed on through generations of Haitians who remember the gods and ancestors left out of books, who bear witness to what the standard histories would never tell.

Although all practitioners of Vodoun will tell you they believe in the supreme God, *le bon dieu*, that singular power is surely absent from the pressing concerns of the Haitian rural communities. It is the loa who understand, experience, and manifest the poverty of a land whose history they bear—quite literally—in their bones. Although no relations of power or classification by status are structurally specified in Vodoun practice, a strong collectivity is implied. And what first seemed to be random or interchangeable—haphazard visitations by indiscriminate gods—might well suggest another kind of relatedness, something more akin to an extended family, with ties both inherited and communal.

In Jacques-Stephen Alexis's extraordinary 1957 novel *Les Arbres musiciens*, based on the 1941 antisuperstition campaign and the simultaneous United States rubber production program, SHADA, the Vodoun priest or houngan Bois d'Orme, knowing that his community's lands are to be appropriated by the government, that his peasants will be dispossessed and the loa scattered, recollects the attributes of "these gods in the image of men." His words remain a moving, if somewhat sentimental literary document of the close, familial relation between gods and humans, linked through time by their land.

> Sometimes he rebelled against the loa, he had blasphemed their
> name . . . but deep down he loved them. . . . He had been faithful to
> them like a dog. He was their chosen one and his heart had to beat
> with joy. . . . He had kept pure of all stain an old tradition, the knot of
> fidelity that bound a people to their most ancient values.[6]

Perhaps the very idea of reciprocity is being endlessly redefined (or reimagined) by these gods. The relations between human and gods are not necessarily harmonious: spirit and matter do not dwell together unperturbed. Gods sometimes accept rather undignified treatment by their devotees. One adept I know recounted long arguments and cursing bouts with her loa. "The gods do not like to lose face. It's not like Jesus Christ. They become you and you become them." While the servitor has to submit to the demands of the gods, the loa can only express themselves by materializing in the bodies of sometimes recalcitrant individuals. In terms of the often ambiguous processes by which Vodoun practice constitutes itself, the charge of randomness is no longer surprising. Nor is interchangeability—the erosion of such powerful dualisms as body and soul, exaltation and mortification—shocking in the logic of a religion that works through and questions what it means to be equal: in equilibrium or correspondence.

When pronounced in Creole, *loa* (written in standard Haitian orthography as *lwa*) sounds like *loi* in French—a phonic resemblance that no doubt made things rather difficult for the colonialist. It would be interesting to know what those possessed by the *loi d'état* thought the slaves were doing when they prayed to and called for their loa. In Creole, after all, the term for law is *lwa* or *lalwa*. So, some Frenchman at some time made sure to distinguish the difficult but abiding connection between the spirit and the law.

The appearance of the gods, and even the cult of the ancestors, are operative only in a social world: the spirits are always, for better or for worse, functions of rather exigent—though sometimes temporary—sociopolitical situations. In this cosmology, the laws of creation are never abstract. No Mallarméan *traduction verbale de l'univers*, perceived as the spider's threads one hoards tight within the self. No spiritual release from an unseen, inward force. But rather some kind of appreciated balance, an envisioned harmony within and without, voices inside and out competing with and reshaping each other. The correspondence is efficacious only because it builds on the fragmentary and contingent. Even possession by a loa is built up out of a disjunction that is never healed. As Walcott knows in "Laventville," when he laments "a life we never found, / customs and gods that are not born again," only to make a place for the voice of the gods.[7]

At the beginning of every ceremony Atibon Legba, also called Alegba, the guardian of the roads, of all paths or openings, must be invoked, "Atibon Legba, l'ouvri bayè pou moin!" (Atibon Legba, open the gate for me!) No longer the energetic trickster of Dahomey, identified with sun and sex, he manifests himself in Haiti as "Papa Legba of the Old Bones." Very old, he lives out the loss suffered by his people. The carved phallus that used to represent him on the soil of Dahomey has become a gnarled crutch-crane, fitted into his crotch. And yet Legba's very presence is cause for that pleasure that can only come from recognition. To invoke Legba is to bear the weight of his legacy. "Alegba, maché, non! / N'ap pôté Atibon Legba!" (Walk on, then, Alegba! / We are carrying Atibon Legba!) (See Figure 3.)

Never metamorphosed out of history or embellished into dream, Legba opens the way to memory, not fantasy. Indeed, perhaps the best way to get at the difference between Vodoun and Christianity is to put the passages of Legba next to the ascension of Christ. I recall the suffering Christs of Mathias Grünewald. In the central panel of his Isenheim altarpiece of 1515, Christ bears the wear and tear of mortality and the wounds of crucifixion, and although the harrowing image remains with us, we know that he ascended to eternity, shedding the marred husk. But Legba is called upon again and again, whenever a ceremony takes place, and ceremonies take place for all kinds of reasons. And every time he comes, he can be identified by this body marked by a shattered history. "Atibon Legba rivé lan bayé-a / Nou vié, oh!" (Atibon Legba has arrived at the gate / We are old, oh!) Or as the exiled René Depestre retells Legba's story in the militant "Epiphanies of the Voodoo Gods" in *A Rainbow for the Christian West*:

Figure 3. Wall painting of the three Trinities. *Photo: Joan Dayan (Port-au-Prince, Haiti, 1970).*

I arrive covered with dust
I am the great black Ancestor
. . . .
I arrive exhausted from my travels
And I thrust my great age
Over the tracks where
Your white betrayals crawl![8]

The loa are the Mafia.

—A HAITIAN IN NEW YORK

THE DEVOTEE refers to his loa not only as *anges*, *mystères*, or *saints*, or *les invisibles*, but also as *diables*. Here we see the crossing of languages and terms that is so much a part of the transformative processes of Vodoun. For the practitioner has internalized the language of Christian demonization, taught him by the priest or pastor in order to wean him from belief, but usually ending up reinforcing the presence of the gods in his or her life. As Drexel Woodson tells it, thinking of his field work in Dondon in northern Haiti, "If you ask someone what is your religion, they answer, 'I'm Catholic, and I serve the gods.'"

How do the facts of a social world—mores, economics, and histories—penetrate our very comprehension of a religious theology? In *The Predicament of Culture*, James Clifford insists that we stop seeing "local narratives" as clues to either a lost paradise or present corruption. Instead, he urges us to see how rituals, language, and cultures are "invented and revived in complex, oppositional contexts."[9] By incorporating and consuming (or as one rather well-read houngan told me, "by cannibalizing") the trappings, prayers, and representations of Catholicism, Vodoun has been able to survive attempts to threaten, weaken, or destroy it. Never static, but adapting itself to the quirks of history and the moods of the "civilizer," Vodoun combines African belief, Catholic practices, and even the newest fads of consumption into its heady amalgam: Papa Legba appears in epiphany with a Coca-Cola bottle in his hand (though the foreign receptacle contains the alcoholic drink *clairin*), and Guédé smokes his favorite cigarettes. Vodoun thus bears the hybrid history of the Caribbean, including in its practices not only the succession of local beliefs but the fragmented devices of those who came to colonize. The increasing number of Protestant sects in Haiti, however—with their emphasis on personal gain and prohibition of rum, dance, and drums—seems to have demonstrated what Edmund Wilson in *Red, Black, Blond and Olive* predicted forty years ago: you can't be Protestant and serve the gods.[10]

Since the perpetual colonization of Haiti was apparently made easier by the missionaries, both Catholic and Protestant, who promised to rid those converted of the curse of savagery, Vodoun as trope could work wonders in many directions. Whether constructing Haiti alternately as "Black France" or as what Césaire called the "African Antilles," historians would find in Vodoun a uniqueness essential to varying constructions of civilization and savagery. Most striking is the way Vodoun became synonymous with the Haitian nation, especially when François Duvalier contrived his myth of authenticity, his peculiar brand of *noirisme* or "black essence."

Since Duvalier's cynical exploitation of Vodoun for political ends, perhaps it is more difficult to see Vodoun as a practice of collective liberation and renewed consciousness. Duvalier mimed the chief Haitian death god, the master of the cemeteries, "Baron Samedi," not only by wearing his emblematic dark glasses and black bowler hat, but by sending thousands to the grave, the Baron's express habitation. Once connected to accounts of blood-drinking in the palace and the eating of enemies on the roads, Vodoun became less a place of survival (or "marronage") and more a signal for sorcery, terror, and the gratuitous exploits of the dread *Tontons Macoutes*, Duvalier's secret police. Duvalier's impersonation of Baron Samedi was effective. Recently a friend told me her story of Duvalier's funeral. "His coffin was carried through Port-au-Prince. And as it passed through the crowds, suddenly the winds came taking everything away with him. It was a clear day of blue skies, but the spirit of Duvalier roared and blew, leaving us in darkness."

It is difficult to tell where religion ends and magic begins. Even the best of gods, those of the Rada (Arada) rite from Alladah or Dahomey, can some-times do evil, while a tough deity like Marinette-Bois-Chèche (Marinette-Dry-Bones) of the Petro rite, known for her bloody behavior and preference for pimento, gunpowder, and gasoline, can be calmed if served properly. The gods have multiple attributes: they can be tyrannical, greedy, protective, or faith-ful. It all depends on how they are served. Though quick to anger and some-times insatiable, the proper performance of ritual, the careful modifications in service by the houngan, and consistent devotions by the believer can re-strain and to some extent monitor the gods' perturbations.

You cannot always know where the powers of evil reside. As Laënnec Hurbon writes in *Le Barbare imaginaire*, "the spirits which one serves in all innocence can, from one day to the next, declare themselves murderers, greedy for blood and for 'human flesh!'"[11] You must move carefully through a land-scape filled with spirits, angry ancestors, and *wanga* (charms or spells). Paul Moral, writing some twenty years ago in *Le Paysan haïtien*, described how many of the old customs and services had lost their force as the large familial com-munities had crumbled.[12] Superstitions replaced the collective and ancestral rituals, attesting to "the defensive character of the popular religion." The best guide through this uncertainty and fear is the houngan or *gangan*, the priest, doctor, and counsel of his community. In some regions the mambo has pow-ers equal to the houngan. And as Vodoun has made its way to New York, she most often leads the service for the gods, who find themselves in what might be called, taking Bob Shacochi's lead, "The Next New World."

According to most accounts, the houngan distinguishes himself from the *boco*, who can use his supernatural powers for evil: "il sert des deux mains" means that he serves both good and evil. Like most progressive Haitian intel-lectuals, Alexis cautiously separates the Rada nation of loa, "the pure vodoun arada," practiced by the houngan Bois-d'Orme, from the satanic sorcery of the boco Danger Dossou, *le gangan macoute* (the bogey gangan). In practice, how-ever, the distinction between religion and sorcery made by aligning the gods according to Rada and Petro, and the division between houngan and boco, is not always so absolute. In the north of Haiti boco means houngan. And the houngan must be familiar with magic in order to fight against the machina-tions of sorcerers.

Although the threat of sorcery is always present for the believer—haunted by fears of evil spirits, hexes, and revenants—magic remains on the periphery of Vodoun. The focus or kernel of the religion remains the cult of the dead, comprising all the filial obligations toward the ancestors, the placating of the various household gods (the *loa héritage* or *loa racine*, either connected to the family land or received directly from either parents or ancestors). In the continuing labor of self-definition realized as a collective drive, even in the process of emigration and modernization, these rituals remain: those of *initiation*, or *brûler zin*, the ceremony of the "boiling pots," during which the initiate who knows how to "tie fire" has been elevated to the status of *kanzo*; *mystic marriage*, or marriage with a loa; the major death ceremony *déssounin* (called *dégradation* in the north of Haiti); and the *possession*, or mounting of humans by gods. Whether inherited loa that come with the land or those loa "in your blood" or the loa *maît-tête* (master of the head) received in initiation, they are always distinguished from the bad gods who cannot be trusted, those known as *loa volé* or *loa acheté*, paid or enticed into service by contract with a boco or ritual specialist who might well have more money or other tempting "goods" than the houngan (see Figure 4).

WHAT HAS happened to the loa of Haiti? Why has there been an increase in tales of secret sects, *baka* (red-eyed evil spirits, often in the shape of animals), and zombis, as the traditional religion tied to land, memory, and family disintegrates? The Haitian peasant has always been poor, but in the past few years, with the continued move to the cities (forced by programs to get peasants into assembly industries and by repeated massacres of peasant organizations), the loa have lost their ancestral places. They have also lost their favorite offerings. The loa need to be fed, and one of the most important ceremonies is the *manger-loa*. Every loa has a preferred food, and any variation in the expected offering can result in the loa's desertion or revenge. Now, the poorer the Haitian the less he or she can offer his or her god; and as the gods become more inaccessible, their presence can sometimes be forced by unscrupulous methods. "If the gods are not with you, then you have to go to a boco and buy them."

How can the gods be lured away from the heads of their servitors? How are they coaxed out of the blood of their human family member? These questions are not easy to answer. The very notion of *what constitutes a person* or *identity* is indelibly tied to the loa, whose lineaments are in turn dependent on the contingent and human.

In Haiti the relation between human and god is reciprocal. It is said that when the people are happy, the loa are happy and show their pleasure by appearing more often. The *petit bon ange*, the *gros bon ange*, and the *corps cadavre* (*kadav-kó* in Creole) constitute the three parts of individual identity in Haitian thought. The petit bon ange, the source of consciousness and affect, depends upon the loa for protection, for keeping it steady and bound to the person. The gros bon ange, also called *ombre-cadavre*, is the double of the

Figure 4. Wall painting of a *baka*, or evil spirit (on left), "walking" with a *machann*, or market woman. *Photo: Joan Dayan (Bainet, Haiti, 1986).*

material body—something like our idea of *spiritus*—but understood as the shadow cast by the body on the mind. According to François Duvalier's colleague in ethnographic investigation, Lorimer Denis, in his 1956 essay "Le Cimetière," the gros bon ange can easily detach itself from the body. Denis describes it taking trips during sleep in a manner reminiscent of Locke's "wandering soul." Its adventures during this time of wandering become the substance of dream. When Denis's "big good angel" wanders, it might be seized by a sorcerer, never to return to its fleshly abode.[13]

The three-part structure of Haitian identity is difficult to comprehend, and accounts are often contradictory. What matters here is that the petit bon ange remains inseparable from all that constitutes our personality—or thinking matter—and the loa, penetrating the petit bon ange during possession, depends on its force for support. Without the loa, the petit bon ange in turn loses its necessary anchor: the petit bon ange will be free-floating, attaching itself to anything, or in its dislocation be stolen by a sorcerer and turned into a zombi. For the Haitian there is no more powerful emblem of apathy, anonymity, and loss. For what is a zombi but a husk without substance, a human emptied of affect or will? As Haitians starve and lose their loa, zombis roam the countryside with increasing frequency. A vicious cycle: once the loa is not supported by the petit bon ange, and no longer possesses (or manifests itself to) its chosen identity—dancing in the head of its horse—the loa is lost, and, dispossessed, it roams the countryside, bereft and rapacious.

The economics of Haiti provoke the anger of the gods, and the vicissitudes of Vodoun. Marie Chauvet, surely the most demystifying of Haitian novelists—sent into exile in 1968 after the publication of her stunning *Amour, Colère, et Folie* (Love, anger, and madness)—knew how to articulate the vengeance of the gods. In her 1961 *Fonds des nègres*, the houngan Beauville warns:

> Do you know what the drums are used for now? To make the rich in the city dance. They are taken around the parlors, they are taken down the streets to be sold. . . . Ah! misery could make you sell your teeth and your skin. . . . But negroes displease the loa: they are selling their beliefs and even their ceremonies. But not a cent will remain in the hollow of their hands. It is the curse of the loa.[14]

As the family and root loa (loa héritage and loa racine) disappear, the loa acheté increase. Traditional relationships deteriorate. Money makes possible unspeakable bargains. The acquisitive function of sorcerers—those who answer the call of greed and not healing or preservation—becomes indispensable to survival. As one houngan in Port-au-Prince told me, faith in the beneficent loa has been so undermined by recent events in Haiti that the terrified Vodoun adept turns to the dealer in bad magic—"fighting the devil with the devil"—known as the *djab* (called *djablesse* if a woman). As Jamaica Kincaid warns in *At the Bottom of the River*, "Take good care when you see a beautiful woman. A jablesse always tries to look like a beautiful woman."[15]

More than thirty years ago, Maya Deren, filmmaker and Vodoun initiate, emphasized how religious practice interacts with social or collective needs. In her 1953 book, *Divine Horsemen*, she wrote: "The best condition for magical action is not the primitive community with its collective emphasis, but the modern community, with its individualistic emphasis, and it is here that one may experience the pre-eminent spectacle of the magician at work."[16] For Deren, as for many other observers, those who worked for profit were not to be confused with those who worked for good, variously defined as cosmic, mystical, and collective, those who possessed, as spiritual leaders, what Haitians call *connaissance*, or understanding.

Collective fantasies are volatile. As things get wilder in Haiti—toxic trash from Philadelphia dumped at Gonaives and sold to peasants as fertilizer, contraband rice, and cocaine—the rumors get more gruesome. But the most horrible projections of the victimized are no worse than the macabre facts of their daily life. If more Haitians talk about the gratuitous violence of the secret sects (*rouges*) in the countryside, who merge indiscriminately with criminal loa, the army, and *drogués*, these reports of random terror were no doubt effected by the plight of a population confronted with the terrorism of Papa Doc Duvalier. Imagine what must have happened to Haitians who live in the countryside, separated from the political center of Port-au-Prince, unable to read the constitution or know its laws, when they saw their worst fears enacted by the Tontons Macoutes. And what was Papa Doc, as we have seen, but the perfect realization of an angry, retributive Baron Samedi?

Night was always a terrible time for those who believed in devils, baka, and the *zobops* or *cochon gris* who like to *manger moune* (eat persons). Now, not even the nonbelievers leave their homes after dark. What is significant here is the severe disarticulation of the Haitian imagination. Political realities—a chaos of instrumentalization and greed—merge with a destructive syncretism. Groups with machine guns out to steal from the rich in Petionville, disappointed gods, and zombis who serve the memory of Papa Doc form a reservoir of curious, recycled, and incomprehensible facts. What voice, and of which gods, is the question that continues to haunt me.

I am Cap'tain Zombi
I drink through my ears
I listen with ten fingers
                    —RENÉ DEPESTRE, "Cap'tain Zombi"

MORE MONEY, most often acquired by the wrong people in the wrong way, not only buys loa but produces more zombis. If we look at Wade Davis's celebrated discovery of the secret zombi powder, we must keep the economics of the situation in mind. The ethnobotanist arrives in the poorest country in the Western hemisphere loaded with money. When he says he is looking for the zombi drug, the boco will certainly oblige: he not only gives Davis the recipe, but makes sure the requisite skulls, bones, and blood are ready for viewing. Davis's sensational 1985 report from Haiti, *The Serpent and the Rainbow* (turned into a Hollywood horror film directed by Wes Craven—publicized by the runner "Don't bury me, I'm not dead!"—and recycled three years later in a highbrow version, *Passage of Darkness*), remains the best recent example of what it means to confuse Vodoun with the practice of sorcerers and secret societies (*Bizango, Vin'BaingDing*—Blood, Pain, Excrement—or *San poel*). And although Davis claims that he wants to rescue the Haitian people and their religion from misunderstanding and prejudice, the images that conclude this book tell another story: "I turned to a man pressed close beside me and saw his arm, riddled with needles and small blades, and the blood running copiously over the scars of past years. . . . He too was possessed, like the youth straddling the dying bull, or the dancers and the women wallowing in the mud."[17]

In Jean Rhys's *Wide Sargasso Sea*, the white Englishman Rochester, obsessed by his Creole wife Antoinette (the Bertha in the attic of Brontë's *Jane Eyre*), comes across a definition of the zombi: "A zombi is a dead person who seems to be alive or a living person who is dead. A zombi can also be the spirit of a place."[18] Born out of the experience of slavery and the sea passage from Africa to the New World, the zombi tells the story of colonization: the reduction of human into thing for the ends of capital. For the Haitian no fate is to be more feared. In a contemporary Caribbean of development American style, the zombi phenomenon obviously goes beyond the machinations of the local boco. As Depestre puts it, "This fantastic process of reification and assimilation means the total loss of my identity, the psychological annihilation of my being, my zombification."[19] And Laënnec Hurbon explains how the zombi stories produce and capitalize on an internalization of slavery and passivity, making the victims of an oppressive economic and social system the cause: "The phantasm of the zombi . . . does nothing but attest to the fulfillment of a system that moves the victim to internalize his condition."[20]

In Haiti there are many forms of death and perpetual rites for the dead.

As Roger Bastide has written, "The dead remain hidden in us." But the zombis, those soulless husks deprived of freedom and forced to work as slaves, remain the ultimate sign of loss and dispossession. Indeed, the ritual of possession, when the human surrenders his or her identity momentarily to the loa—making the self the receptacle of a god—should be understood as the opposite of zombification. As other rites deteriorate, those connected to the dead and dying remain vital and obligatory. The most critical ritual in Vodoun is déssounin, the separation of the dead from his or her loa. The loa *maît-tête* must be freed from the cadaver, so that the individual's petit bon ange can move beyond death, joining the ancestors beneath the waters, or becoming a new protective spirit. At the moment of the spirit's passage, however, a sorcerer's magic can take the petit bon ange, leaving the *zombi cadavre*. Besides what is known as the zombi "in flesh and bones," forced to work as a domestic or in the fields, the zombi is also a spirit that can be "put" or "sent on" someone to turn them into the living dead.

> *Her body she always usta say might be in Tatem, but*
> *her mind was long gone with the Ibos.*
> —PAULE MARSHALL, *Praisesong for the Widow*

For my friend who grew up in Port-au-Prince but now lives in New York, Vodoun is a thing of evil, of gods asking for what you cannot give, or looking to the right and to the left, fearing that someone somewhere might have put the meat on you. As she put it, "If you have one foot in this world and one foot in the next, then everything is simultaneously out of control and in control of alternately the right and the wrong people." And yet, she added, her very reaction against Vodoun always brings her closer to her mother's gods. They still visit her in her dreams. And when she goes to church, the loa tell her about the Haiti she has left behind. Sometimes she feels bad, as if she betrayed those who still fight to be "tall in her head." "They have fought for a long time. When my grandmother in Haiti became a Seventh-Day Adventist and threw her loa's wine, food, playing cards, and candles into the latrine, the loa went underground. But when my mother turned five, she became very ill. Her mind shook, and she lost it, until she let the family loa come back."

Alexis's houngan Bois-d'Orme, before his death and the wrenching of his people from their lands and their loa, reflected: "I know that the loa live in the earth, in the rivers, under the sea, in the waters of the lake, in the sun when it rises or sets, in the seasons, in the harvests, in the smile of the stars. . . . How could they not live eternally in the heart of men?"[21] Though a bit more romanticized, the message is the same for most Haitians practicing Vodoun today. The gods do not die. Even when you pray to the Good God alone and his martyred son, your gods will remind you of Bois-Caïman, when gods and slaves answered the sound of the conch shell, the *lambi* that began the Haitian Revolution.

Gods born out of blood. Phantoms stored in the minds of a people, making visible whenever they visit their faithful those times that might be forgotten. I recall the story Aunt Cuney tells Avey Johnson in Paule Marshall's *Praisesong for the Widow.* The Africans who arrived in Tatem, South Carolina, took one look at their chains, one look back over the waters, and one more look ahead of them to the new country. Then they just turned around and walked across the waters back to Africa never to be seen again.

> They had seen what they had seen and those Ibos was
> stepping! And they didn't bother getting back into the
> small boats drawed up here—boats take too much
> time. They just kept walking right out over the
> river. . . . Left the white folks standin' back here with
> they mouth hung open and they taken off down the
> river on foot. Stepping. . . . They feets was gonna take
> 'em wherever they was going that day.[22]

AVEY JOHNSON'S quest leads her away from North White Plains, New York, to Ti Morne, Carriacou, where she remembers her "Old Parents," "The Long-Time People." Amid the fragments of song, a muddle of names and dances, the "bare bones" and "burn-out ends," Avey makes it across the waters. And her home, her "native land," is no exotic Africa precious to those who would make an icon of loss. Her return depends upon a labor of mind, a difficult process of experience and recall: "Thoughts—new thoughts—vague and half-formed slowly beginning to fill the emptiness."[23]

Notes

Throughout I use the term *Vodoun* to describe the belief system of the Haitian majority. The orthography of the term "vodou" is still somewhat vexed and variable. French authors fluctuate between *Vadoux, voudoo, vôdou,* and *vodou,* while many English writers use *Vodoun* to distinguish it from the Voodoo so evocative of black magic. I have most often used a French translation of Vodoun words, since writers still struggle over the varying orthography of Haitian Creole, and for most readers the French spelling is still more familiar, since it has been used by ethnographers as well as Haitian novelists.

1. James Anthony Froude, *The English in the West Indies or The Bow of Ulysses* (New York: Scribner's, 1888), 343.
2. William B. Seabrook, *The Magic Island* (New York: Harcourt, Brace, 1929), 43.
3. Alfred Métraux, *Voodoo in Haiti,* trans. Hugo Charteris (New York: Schocken, 1972), 80.
4. Milo Rigaud, *Secrets of Voodoo* (New York: Arco, 1969).
5. Aimé Césaire, interviewed by René Depestre in *Pour la révolution, pour la poésie*

(Montreal: Editions Leméac, 1974), 166. The interview also appeared in the English edition of Césaire's *Discours sur le colonialisme* (Discourse on colonialism), trans. Joan Pinkham (New York and London: Monthly Review Press, 1972), 74.

6. Jacques-Stephen Alexis, *Les Arbres musiciens* (Paris: Editions Gallimard, 1957), 140.

7. Derek Walcott, "Laventville," in *Collected Poems, 1948–1984* (New York: Farrar, Straus & Giroux, 1986).

8. Translated by Joan Dayan. For an earlier version see René Depestre, "Epiphanies of the Vodoun Gods," in *A Rainbow for the Christian West*, trans. Joan Dayan (Amherst: University of Massachusetts Press, 1977), 123.

9. James Clifford, *The Predicament of Culture: Twentieth-Century Ethnography, Literature, and Art* (Cambridge: Harvard University Press, 1988), 16.

10. Edmund Wilson, *Red, Black, Blond and Olive: Studies in Four Civilizations (Zuni, Haiti, Soviet Russia, Israel)* (London: W. H. Allen, 1956), 130–134.

11. Laënnec Hurbon, *Le Barbare imaginaire* (Paris: Les Editions du Cerf, 1988).

12. Paul Moral, *Le Paysan haïtien: Etude sur la vie rurale en Haiti* (Port-au-Prince: Editions Fardin, 1978).

13. Lorimer Denis, "Le Cimetière," *Bulletin du Bureau d'Ethnologie* (Port-au-Prince) 13 (1956): 1–16.

14. Marie Chauvet, *Fonds des nègres* (Port-au-Prince: Editions Henri Deschamps, 1961), 131.

15. Jamaica Kincaid, "In the Night," in *At the Bottom of the River* (New York: Random House, Vintage Books, 1985), 9.

16. Maya Deren, *Divine Horsemen: The Living Gods of Haiti* (1953; reprint, Kingston, N.Y.: McPherson, 1970), 200.

17. Wade Davis, *The Serpent and the Rainbow* (New York: Warner Books, 1985), 329.

18. Jean Rhys, *Wide Sargasso Sea* (New York: Norton, 1982), 107.

19. René Depestre, *Bonjour et adieu à la négritude* (Paris: Editions Robert Laffont, 1980), 97–98.

20. Hurbon, *Le Barbare imaginaire*.

21. Alexis, *Les Arbres musiciens*, 346.

22. Paule Marshall, *Praisesong for the Widow* (New York: Dutton, 1984), 38–39.

23. Ibid., 240.

Women Possessed

LIZABETH PARAVISINI-GEBERT

Eroticism and Exoticism in the Representation of Woman as Zombie

They are dead bodies—zombies, the living dead, corpses taken from their graves who are made to work in sugar mills and the fields at night.
—White Zombie, 1932

There's no beauty here . . . only death and decay.
—I Walked with a Zombie, 1943

IF IT IS TRUE that, as Edward Brathwaite writes, traces of African religion, fragments of ancestral rituals, echoes of African deities form "the kernel or core" of Caribbean cultures, it is also true, as Joan Dayan has argued, that the local or folk religions that germinated from them have been for the West the "mark of savagery" that has justified invasion and imperialism.[1] Pro-Western ideologues of "progress" and "civilization" have derided ritualistic practices of African origin as proof of the Caribbean folk's inability to embrace "modernity," of their incapacity for emancipation and sovereignty. Given a glimpse of Caribbean people's resolution to assert their autonomy, they are quick to invoke the titillating figure of the zombie as representative of the Afro-Caribbean folk as bogeyman.

In Haiti—Zora Neale Hurston wrote in *Tell My Horse*—"there is the quick, the dead, and then there are zombies," "the word which never fails to interest tourists."[2] Katherine Dunham, American dancer and Vodou initiate, offers two possible definitions of a zombie: a truly dead creature brought back to life by black magic "but by such a process that memory and will are gone and the resultant being is entirely subject to the will of the sorcerer who resuscitated him, in the service of good or evil"; or, "most likely," a person who, as a result of being given a potion of herbs brought from 'Nan Guinée by a bokor, "falls into a coma resembling death in every pathological sense" and is later disinterred by the bokor, who administers an antidote and takes command of the traumatized victim.[3] Zombies, Alfred Métraux argues, can be recognized "by their vague look, their dull almost glazed eyes, and above all by the nasality of their voice, a trait also characteristic of the 'Guédé,' the spirits of the dead. . . . The zombi remains in that grey area separating life and death."[4]

Wade Davis's anthropological research into the ethnobiology and pharmacopeia of zombification (recorded in his two books on the subject, *The Serpent and the Rainbow* and *Passage of Darkness*), has gone a long way to demystify a phenomenon long believed to be solely the result of sorcery and black magic.[5] Under rare circumstances, Davis argues, administration of the zombie poison (the formula for which appears in *Passage of Darkness*) provides the means by which an individual might be made to appear dead and be consequently buried. Disinterred later by a bokor who delivers an antidote, the traumatized victim remains under the control of his or her victimizer. Zombification, far from being the result of arbitrary sorcery performed by the bokor for his own personal gain, Davis contends, is a "social sanction" administered to those who have violated the codes of the secret society known as the *Bizango*, "an important arbiter of social life among the peasantry," a force "that protects community resources, particularly land, as they define the power boundaries of the village."[6]

Sorcery and poison have long been the Bizango's traditional weapons, however, and disclosure by Western researchers of the secret formula and of the local institutions in whose service it is administered has done little to dispel the belief in Haiti that anyone whose death is the result of black magic may be claimed as a zombie.[7] Zombification continues to be perceived as a magical process by which the sorcerer seizes the victim's *ti bon ange*—the component of the soul where personality, character, and volition reside—leaving behind an empty vessel subject to the commands of the bokor. Disclosure has done even less to allay the dread induced by the prospect of zombification. In the various Western horror genres the zombie may be a terrorizing, murdering creature, but Haitians do not fear any harm from zombies, although they will shun them; they may, however, live in fear of being zombified themselves. When Dunham stubbornly insisted on an expedition to visit a bokor reputed to have seven zombie wives, a frantic hotel housekeeper tearfully urged her to reconsider, earnestly cataloguing the dangers to which she was exposing herself: "Surely Mademoiselle would be made into a zombie wife or, worse still, sacrificed to one of the bloodthirsty gods and eaten by the priest and his chief *hounci*, all of whom were men. Some part of me would be left unsalted for the zombie wives, perhaps not even cooked."[8]

Death in Haiti, Maximilien Laroche has written, takes on "a menacing form in the character of the zombi . . . the legendary, mythic symbol of alienation . . . the image of a fearful destiny . . . which is at once collective and individual."[9] The accursed fate conjured by the myth of the zombie is that of the Haitian experience of slavery, of the disassociation of people from their will, their reduction to beasts of burden subject to a master. This connection is stressed by Haitian writers and scholars whenever the subject is raised, and it is at the core of many theories of Haiti's sociohistoric development. "It is not by chance that there exists in Haiti the myth of the zombi, that is, of the living-dead, the man whose mind and soul have been stolen and who has been left only the ability to work," René Depestre has argued. "The history of colonization is the process of man's general zombification. It is also the quest for a revitalising salt capable of restoring to man the use of his imagination and his culture."[10]

Visitors to Haiti are often regaled with tales of necromancy, blood sucking by *soucouyants*, and zombification—grist for the mill of sensation-seeking foreigners; the victims in the tales, more often than not, are "preferably virgins."[11] William Seabrook's *The Magic Island*, credited with serving as inspiration for *White Zombie*, the first "zombie film," tells the tale of Camille, "a fair-skinned octoroon girl" sponsored by her aunt and uncle in Port-au-Prince society, who marries a rich coffee grower from Morne Hôpital, "dark and more than twice her age, but rich, suave, and well educated."[12] Although apparently "not unhappy" during her first year of marriage, the girl nonetheless seems troubled by her husband's occasional "nocturnal excursions." On the "fatal night" of their first wedding anniversary she is told to put on her wedding dress and make herself beautiful, and is taken to an outbuilding, where a magnificent table is set. There she is forced to sit with four propped-up corpses who will, as her husband tells her, presently drink with her, clink glasses with her, arise and dance with her, and (ominously) "more." The terrified girl runs away screaming and is found the next morning lying unconscious in the valley below her home, "her filmy dress ripped and torn, her little white satin bride-slippers . . . scuffed and stained," terrorized, cowering, hysterical, and "stark, raving mad." Seabrook asks his readers to ponder "what sinister, perhaps criminal necromancy in which his bride was to be the victim or the instrument" the husband had been anticipating.

Seabrook's tale is of particular interest because it brings together a number of elements that are always present in accounts of the zombification of women: the coveting of a beautiful, light-skinned or white upper-class girl by an older, dark-skinned man who is of lower class and is adept at sorcery; the intimations of necromantic sexuality with a girl who has lost her volition; the wedding night (in this case its anniversary) as the preferred setting for the administration of the zombie poison; the girl's eventual escape from the bokor in her soiled wedding clothes (the garment of preference for white or light-skinned zombie women); her ultimate madness and confinement in a convent or mental asylum.

A review of the literature on zombification reveals, interestingly enough, that most accounts of zombified young girls draw on the same basic tale— "the most famous Zombie case of all Haiti," according to Hurston—that of the death in October 1909 of Marie M., a young upper-class woman. In one of the earliest accounts I have come across—offered by Harry Franck in *Roaming through the West Indies*—the young daughter of a prestigious family dies of loss of blood at the hands of her grandmother "and a prominent man."[13] She is buried with much pomp, the grandmother replacing with coffee the embalming fluid that was poured down her throat. Five years later, after a rumor of her existence has reached a priest through a confessional, a person believed to be the same girl is discovered in a hill town. She is wild, unkempt, demented, and has borne three children. The coffin is dug up, and in it is found the wedding dress in which she had been buried, but the autopsy proves the remains to be those of a man whose legs have been cut off and laid alongside the body.

Métraux tells the story—interesting to him "in so far as it is typical of this kind of anecdote"—of a girl from Marbial who is engaged to a young man she very much loves but who is "unwise enough to reject—rather sharply— the advances of a powerful *hungan*."[14] The spurned lover utters numerous threats, and a few days later the girl is suddenly taken ill and dies in the hospital at Jacmel. Her coffin proving to be too short, it is necessary to bend the corpse's neck to fit it in. During the wake someone inadvertently drops a lighted cigarette on its foot, causing a slight burn. Some months after her burial, unconfirmed rumors spread of her having been seen in the company of the houngan, and a few years later, during the antisuperstition campaign, the houngan is said to have repented and returned the girl, her neck bent and with the scar of a burn on her foot, to her home, "where she lived for a long time without ever recovering her sanity."

Hurston tells of how the beautiful young daughter of a prominent family dies "in the very bloom of her youth" and is buried. Five years later, a group of her schoolmates claim to have seen her in a house in Port-au-Prince. The news spreads like wildfire throughout the city, but by the time the house is searched all occupants have disappeared. Her body is exhumed, and it is discovered that the skeleton is too long for the box and the clothes found are different from those the girl had been buried in. They are neatly folded beside the skeleton "that had strangely outgrown its coffin." It is said that the houngan who had held her had died and his wife wanted to get rid of his zombies. Later, dressed in the habit of a nun, the girl is smuggled off to France. This was, Hurston concludes, "the most notorious case in all Haiti and people still talk about it whenever Zombies are mentioned."[15]

Arthur Holly, a Haitian doctor who claimed to have treated the young woman in question, offered this terse version in *Les Daïmons du culte Voudo et Dra-Po.* "The young daughter of our intimate friends was believed to be dead and was consequently buried. She was disinterred by a Vodou practitioner and recalled from her state of apparent death three days after the funeral. She is alive today and lives abroad. I was one of the physicians that attended her during her illness. The case is not a unique one in our annals."[16] C.-H. Dewisme, in an attempt to trace information on the case for his 1957 work on *Les Zombis ou le secret des morts-vivants*, found countless versions of the story: in some, as in Hurston's, she is discovered by former classmates; in others, friends of her family on a hunting trip come across her in a garden, eating with her hands "like a beast."[17] Found to have completely lost her mind, she is taken to the United States, where she is examined by the most famous neurologists and psychiatrists, who declare themselves powerless to help. In despair, her parents place her in a convent in France, where she dies many years later.

Jacques-Stephen Alexis, one of Haiti's foremost twentieth-century writers, offers a fictional version of the story in "Chronique d'un faux-amour" (Chronicle of a false love). Alexis's tale, the first-person narrative of a young zombie confined to a convent in France, couches the familiar elements of the story in an aura of unfulfilled sensuality: "Here I have been for ten years awaiting my first night of love, the night that will awaken me and bring me back to daylight, the night that will wrench me from this uncertain and colorless hinterland where I vegetate, where my head rots between two realms."[18] Back in Port-au-Prince, "the most beautiful and the richest," she had fallen in love with a young man, an "almost swarthy mulatto," "not too dark-skinned"— that would have been "an almost inexpiable crime"—but of doubtful social extraction, "although said to be very rich." (She dismisses the skin-color difference with a question—"Am I not light-skinned enough for both of us?") She is taken on a visit to his adoptive father, "an old Crésus, former satrap general, and today a great lord of the plain, a grand feudal planter who cannot measure what he owns, they say, nègre-z-'orteils [toeless negro] though he is" (135).

From the moment the old man enters the text, Alexis posits the young protagonist's awakening sensuality (her fiancé is the "salt, spirit, beauty" who has "opened the doors of life to her") against the old black sorcerer's soiling desire. "His gaze winds a forest of tangled-up lianas around me, a syrupy gaze that glides from my forehead to my nape, down my neck, my shoulders, running through my body like a cascade of ants with lecherous stings" (137). Coveting her as a madonna at whose feet he wishes to worship, he gives her the zombie poison to inhale in her wedding bouquet, and she collapses during her wedding ceremony, appearing dead to all while perfectly conscious of the grief and lamentation surrounding her. She recovers her mobility when she is disinterred and the antidote is administered; but, unable to escape despite a fierce struggle, she is condemned to live as a zombie, dressed in her white wedding dress embroidered in silver and her bride's veil until the old man dies and she is sent to her convent in France.

The various versions of the story of Marie M.'s zombification posit sexual desire—the erotic—as a fundamental component of the zombified woman's tale, hinting at, although never directly addressing, the urge to transcend or subvert race and class barriers as one of the repositories of the sorcerer's lust. The various accounts emphasize the girl's whiteness or light skin against the sorcerer's darkness (the bokor with the seven zombie wives of Dunham's *Island Possessed* is described as the darkest Haitian she had ever met); her wealth and position against his lack of social standing (a result, more often than not, of the darkness of his skin); and her buoyant, love-filled, wholesome desire against his sinister, debasing lust. The underlying truth behind this tale is that victim and victimizer are separated by insurmountable race and class obstacles that would have precluded a legitimate union even if the victim had not been physically revolted by the victimizer, as she often is; her social inaccessibility lies at the heart of her heinous zombification.

The story of Marie M. constitutes the "master narrative" of female zombification in Haiti. Its fundamental elements—found tantalizing by both Haitian and Western researchers, writers, and filmmakers—reappear throughout the century in works as disparate as Hollywood's *I Walked with a Zombie* (1943) and Depestre's *Hadriana dans tous mes rêves* (1988).

In 1932, as Haitian resistance to American occupation intensified, American film audiences were treated to *White Zombie*, the first entry in the zombie-movie genre, a minor classic distinguished by its elaboration of two seminal elements of the zombification myth: its portrayal of Murder Legendre as a Haitian "Voodoo" sorcerer (played with peculiar eeriness by Bela Lugosi), a fiend who uses zombies as workers in his sugar fields; and its focus on the ensnaring of a young white woman into Legendre's evil magic, the woman who is eventually transformed into the "white zombie" of the title.[19] The two elements intertwine in this macabre tale as they intertwine in the ideology of vilification of Haiti as the land of "Voodoo"—an ideology that has sustained American indifference to the fate of the island and its people. The terrorized Haitian peasant, transformed into a terrorizing zombie lost in the depths of his own unspeakable horrors, literally comes to embody "a fate worse than death"; all sympathy for his plight is transferred to the virginal white heroine lustfully coveted by the evil "Voodoo" sorcerer, the quintessentially innocent victim who must be rescued from her zombification before she is basely violated by racially impure hands.

Madeleine, the young protagonist of this precedent-setting tale, a fresh arrival to a phantasmagoric tropical island where walking cadavers roam the roads, is blissfully in love with a freshly scrubbed young man she met on board the ship that brought her from the United States. Enraptured by her newly found love, she is deaf to the entreaties of a rich planter who covets her, a weak man controlled by Legendre, from whom he seeks help in securing the zombie poison through which he will seek to gain possession of the girl. Given the potion to drink as she literally walks down the aisle, Madeleine falls into a death swoon at the altar and is buried in her wedding gown during what would have been her wedding night. The wedding-night motif, with its promise of carnal fulfillment, emphasizes the erotic quality of her deathlike vulnerability, as does the flimsy shroud (the wedding dress) in which she is buried and in which she will spend most of the movie. The erotic nuances of the plot intensify when Legendre (depicted as a swarthy native), filled with lust at the sight of the lovely and now will-less creature, battles the (clearly white) planter for possession of the young woman. Confronted in a later scene with the notion that Madeleine may not be dead but zombified, her hapless (and now temporarily disheveled and unshaven) husband's reaction needlessly encapsulates the sexual connotations of the developing plot. "Not alive . . . in the hands of natives . . . better dead than that!" The climactic scene of the film finds all the principals on the edge of a high cliff, death looming far below them, and its resolution reaffirms the cultural and racial hierarchies: when Legendre dies (killed by the white planter in a belated burst of decency), the zombies topple off the cliff to their deaths, while the sweet Madeleine is released from her stupor and restored undefiled to her rightful lover.

In 1943 Hollywood returned to the zombie genre in an eerily fascinating entry, *I Walked with a Zombie*,[20] loosely based on Charlotte Brontë's *Jane Eyre*. The young protagonist of the novel, Betsy, a Canadian nurse, comes to the island of San Sebastian to care for Jessica, the wife of a plantation owner. Jessica has been transformed into a zombie by a "Voodoo" curse and is now a soulless shell, weeping eerily at night and at the mercy of the "Voodoo" drums beating unnervingly after every sunset. As in *Jane Eyre*, the young nurse falls in love with the master of the estate, and the romantic triangle is eventually dissolved through the death of the zombie, who is shown to have been an unfaithful wife. (She is killed by her lover—her brother-in-law—while he is in a trance.) *I Walked with a Zombie* has been described by critics as an "enchanting film possessed of a subtlety at odds with the conventions of its genre and a beauty which might be described as otherworldly"—a not inaccurate description.[21] The movie is indeed at odds with the conventions of the zombie genre in its "imposing respect" for the supernatural, its positive presentation of Vodou, and its "evocative link to unstated themes of the island's tragic racial history and the life-death symbiosis which governs the lives of the central characters."[22] Alma, a black servant played by Teresa Harris, for example, persuasively argues for the superiority of Vodou over Christian medicine; and another black character, a singer played by famed Calypsonian Sir Lancelot, provides an authoritative narrative voice as he relates in song the history of Betsy's employers, the powerful Rand-Holland planter family.

Although thematically the movie strives to shed light on the island's history of oppression through its representation of the realities of plantation life, it is nonetheless dependent visually (and it is a strikingly visual film) on black/white oppositions that leave intact the identification of blackness with "Voodoo" and of Vodou with what is only half comprehensible and half frightening. And at the core of the movie's visual representation of blackness is a Vodou ceremony that has a white woman zombie as its centerpiece.

The scene, the longest and most haunting of the film, implicitly links slavery to the state of living death embodied by Jessica, while erotizing Jessica through its accumulation of sexually charged motifs. The sequence begins with Betsy and Jessica's journey through the rustling cane fields to a Vodou ceremony, a true voyage of penetration into a strange and foreboding world punctuated by the increasingly spellbinding beating of drums. Throughout the sequence the cinematographer alternates between shades of black and white, tracking swiftly the women's movements from light to shadow; the camera plays with the contrast between the women's light billowing costumes and the dark menacing shadows surrounding them, outlining the image of their pale faces against that of the imposing figure of Carrefour, the black guardian of the crossroads, a zombie himself, "who materializes with disquieting suddenness on their path" (see Figure 5).[23] At the ceremony itself the eroticism of the drumming and frenzied dancing of the initiates menacingly frame Jessica's passive, semiconscious fjáure. Dressed in a robe reminiscent of that of a vestal virgin being offered for sacrifice, she steps into the black vortex, the black bodies rustling past her as did the canes, their near touch eroticized as emblematic of the forbidden, her passivity alarming in that she is unable to fore-

Figure 5. The appearance of Carrefour in the cane fields in *I Walked with a Zombie.*

stall the taboo touch. Her only shield is Betsy's presence, that of a white woman possessed of her will and conscious of her whiteness as a symbol of authority.[24] Beautiful, virtuous, generous, and—as the camera constantly reminds us—white, Betsy guides Jessica through the menacing gauntlet unscathed, as she will guide Jessica's once-tormented husband into a new path of "Voodoo" free love.

Awakened by Jessica's passivity to the possibility of luring her away from Betsy and back to the *hounfort*, however, the mulatto houngan and his subservient female acolytes in subsequent evenings attempt to summon her with the drums, aided by a blond "Voodoo" doll before which he performs a highly eroticized dance characterized by jerky forward thrusts of the hips and groin. Earlier in the film the cinematographer accentuates the film's sexual imagery as he captures Betsy awakening in the middle of the night to listen to the sound of Carrefour's shuffling footsteps, framing her as she lays in bed (the movie's most frequent piece of clothing for the two female protagonists is a flimsy negligee), behind the ornate iron grille that protects her window, with Carrefour's phallic shadow standing threateningly against the wall that also holds a painting of a menacing, decaying fortress in the Gothic-romance tradition (see Figure 6).

Figure 6. The appearance of Carrefour outside Betsy's window in *I Walked with a Zombie.*

The power of the images evoked by *White Zombie* and *I Walked with a Zombie*—the association of slavery with zombification, the invocation of black/ white sexuality as the repository of the erotic, the peculiar power of white virginal women to escape from the threat of zombification unscathed—has proven lasting. They spawned countless B-movie imitations, enough to constitute a subgenre in its own right. In *King of the Zombies* a madman with a zombified wife turns the natives of a tiny island into an army of zombies to be used as mercenaries by a foreign power.[25] The wife's niece boldly struggles to wake her aunt from her lethargy but finds herself the centerpiece of a Vodou ceremony in which she is offered in sacrifice, vestallike, as the telepathic medium through whom her uncle seeks to obtain a captured American general's military secrets. In *The Plague of the Zombies* a "Voodoo"-practicing squire in Cornwall raids a local cemetery for corpses he can turn into zombies to work his tin mine, imperiling the heroine in the process.[26]

More preposterous, and more recent, examples include infamous director and screenwriter Ed Wood's *Orgy of the Dead*, in which a horror writer and his girlfriend visit a cemetery after dark and are taken captive by the Master of the Dead and the Princes of Darkness.[27] They are forced to watch various zombie women called on from the dead to dance topless to please the Master. My own choice for the winner in the ludicrous category is *Revenge of the Zombies*, a 1981 film set in Hong Kong in which a black-magic sorcerer who drinks human milk to stay eternally young preys on young people.[28] His antagonist is a young doctor who, aided by a white-magic sorcerer, fights the horde of zombies to save his fiancée from the evil magician's thirst. "I always drink human milk, and that milk keeps my body young," the poor hapless creature had been told. "Margaret, I shall drink your milk every day, understand?" The enduring power of the images these films conjure is evident in our recognition of them as tropes that encapsulate certain ways of looking at the cultural and religious syncretism of the African-Caribbean as exotic, foreign, "unknowable," and ultimately expendable. The zombies in *Zombies of Mora Tau*, which includes an oversexed white woman zombified as punishment, are summarily dismissed by the protagonist. "They're dead. They have no morality!"[29] They are images we have come to associate with the outsider's gaze bent on making an-other of the Caribbean native.

IT IS THUS surprising to find these images at the core of Depestre's *Hadriana dans tous mes rêves*, a text in which similar intertwinings of zombification and the erotic seem aimed at emptying Haitian history of its content.[30] Set in Jacmel, the story follows the apparent death, zombification, and carnivalesque wake of the beautiful (and white) Hadriana Siloé, the narrator's idealized and erotic object; it is another tale most clearly inspired by the story of Marie M. A substantial portion of the text is devoted to a detailed account of the preparations for Hadriana's wedding, planned as a "carnival without precedent," and of the elaborate Vodouesque wake that follows her death swoon at the altar. This story of a young woman's zombification and eventful restoration to a "rightful" lover is the point of departure for a somewhat peculiar meditation on Haiti's history that succeeds only in denying the significance of the devastating chronicle of its people's fate through its subordination to the narrator's single-minded quest for erotic fulfillment with Hadriana.

In Depestre's text history is depicted as a *jeu de masques*, a carnivalesque parody that reduces to a senseless game of disguises crucial aspects of Haiti's class and race divisions. From its opening pages, the beautiful Hadriana and her prominent French family are depicted by the narrator as the lynchpins of Jacmel's history, of the town's very life. In his description of the carnival figures who dance in ghostly abandon around the young woman's coffin as it rests on the town's main square, Depestre summons three centuries of Haitian history: Indian caciques, Elizabethan corsairs, barons and marquises of Louis XIV's court, black and mulatto officers of Napoleon's Grand Army, Pauline Bonaparte, Toussaint L'Ouverture, Pétion, Christophe, and, discordantly,

Stalin. But this carnivalesque celebration of death exploits the traditional classlessness of the carnival festival to deny the deeply rooted differences that divide Haitian people along class and race lines. In this indiscriminate parade all historical figures, regardless of the nature of their role or the relative value of their deeds or misdeeds, are granted equal significance. No value judgments are made, no irony accompanies the joint dance of Pauline and Toussaint or the appearance of a masque of military officers dressed as maroons. The juxtaposition of the incongruous, irreconcilable images of the Haitian military, with their record of betrayal of the people, and the Maroons who led the struggle for Haitian independence, is characteristic of the profound contradictions that abound in Depestre's representation of history in the text.

This carnivalesque dance of history, which Depestre presents as Jacmel's reverential tribute to the white, virginal Hadriana, further exacerbates the novel's failure to assign differing values to the historical figures he conjures. The people's cult of the dead Hadriana, "whom they loved and admired as a fairy" (51), seems to render null and void the struggle for independence from white control incarnated in the figures of Pétion, L'Ouverture, and Christophe, here seen dancing in homage around the white woman's coffin. Furthermore, in an odd disavowal of the hurricanes, political intrigues, and collapses in the international price of coffee that led to the downward turn in Jacmel's prosperity in the mid-twentieth century, he attributes the city's decline to Hadriana's disappearance, an event that plunges Jacmel into precipitous decay, leaving the city adrift in a sea of woes. "Together with the beauty of his daughter, time, hope, doubt, reason, compassion, tenderness, the rage to live, had also evaporated from the town of Jacmel. It seemed to have surrendered to a somber fate, tossed by waves of evil tribulations which included, in equally devastating measure, unappeasable agents of desolation and ruin, fire, hurricanes, drought, the presidency-for-life, malaria, the State, erosion, the homo papadocus, all blending into each other in a sort of unstoppable osmosis" (111).

Depestre's representation of the devastating impact of Hadriana's death on Jacmel is rendered ironic and illogical the moment it is revealed that through the decades of Jacmel's sorrowful decay Hadriana was not only alive, having managed to flee the sorcerer who had attempted to zombify her, but enjoying relative prosperity in Jamaica, where she had settled with the dowry that was still pinned to her wedding gown when she was buried. The irony intensifies when the reader realizes that the narrator's fulfillment of his erotic quest for Hadriana is in no way conducive to Jacmel's deliverance from the accursed state prompted by her disappearance. Depestre, however, circumvents the legitimate questions posed by Haiti's painful historical legacy as seen through the fate of Jacmel, declaring them to be of lesser importance than the solution of his erotic quest. And the tale ends with the assertion that the final reunion of Hadriana and the narrator signals the end of the need for a "historical" narrative because "we have chosen to hold to the belief that the joys and sorrows of love have no history" (191).

When Depestre does ponder the significance of Haitian history, to which an entire chapter is devoted, the question posed is one familiar to readers of his earlier work, that of whether the Haitian people can be seen as a collective zombie. Depestre perceives this zombification in the apparent disassociation of the people's body and their will, seen as the result of the brutality of Haitian slavery and of the Haitian racialist masquerade that assigned positive and negative essences to skin color. It is a dangerous notion in that it debases the Haitian people to "the category of human cattle, malleable, pliable to one's will" (128), denying the people's centuries-long struggle against natural calamities, dictatorship, and repression, which, however unsuccessful, has been nonetheless real. In Depestre's presentation, however, the Haitian zombie emerges as the "biological fuel par excellence, what is left of Caliban after the loss of his identity, his life having been literally cut in two: the *gros bon ange* of muscular strength condemned to eternal forced labor; the *petit bon ange* of wisdom and light, of guilessness and dreams, exiled forever into the first empty bottle found lying around" (130). The peculiarities of this view of history, which strips the Haitian people of any possibility of self-determination, are underscored by Hadriana's own escape from zombification, which implies that Hadriana, like Madeleine in *White Zombie*, being white, beautiful, and rich, can quickly recover her will, whereas the Haitian people, because they are black, gullible, and poor, are trapped in zombiedom forever. This depiction of the Haitian people as zombies negates any possibility of their transcending a history of colonialism, slavery, postcolonial poverty, and political repression because, as zombies, they are incapable of rebellion. "'Let's join our *gros bons anges* in a struggle for freedom': those are words one is not likely to hear from a zombi's mouth" (131).

Hence, in *Hadriana dans tous mes rêves*, Vodou does not fulfill its metaphorical function as the expression of the people's thirst for freedom, a connection established at the fabled meeting at Bois Caiman that started the Haitian Revolution. Depestre's exploration of the history of the Haitian people diminishes them as zombified, will-less creatures, and Vodou, usually a path to revolt and rebirth, surfaces only as the evil power threatening a beautiful white woman—a power represented by the Bela Lugosi-like sorcerer struggling to foil the narrator's efforts to "wrench Nana from death and to light the star of her flesh in our lives" (77). The narrator, like the zombie films, dismisses the historical questions as less important than his concern for Hadriana's fate, and the chapter ends with a forsaking of the meditation on history in favor of a return to the Hadriana quest. "Set aside these disquisitions so falsely imbued in mythology and in the sociology of decolonization. For the second time in your life Hadriana Siloé knocks at your door in the middle of the night. Get up and bring back the loved one to the home of her childhood!" (133).

Depestre's tale of carnival as a homage to the dead white virgin opens with a carnivalesque metamorphosis: the transformation of Balthazar Granchiré, a notorious womanizer, into a highly sexed butterfly, a sort of winged phallus that goes on a rape rampage, ravaging unsuspecting young women as they sleep. This is the most blatant, though by no means the only example of the deeply rooted sexism that pervades the text. Granchiré's metamorphosis, avowedly a punishment for his sexual transgression with a sorcerer's *femme-jardin*, ironically (and illogically) gives him license to unleash his sexual powers on unsuspecting women, allowing him, and the text, to debase women by turning them into victimized sex objects. Forced sexual "joy" is the fate of the women who fall prey to the butterfly. "The most spellbinding orgasms will wreak havoc in the beautiful lives that your satan of a phallus will have bowed to your pleasure" (26).

The figure of this grotesque *papillon* (butterfly) appears to have been inspired by a famous caco leader of that name, whose military and erotic adventures are narrated by John Houston Craige in his sensationalistic work *Cannibal Cousins*.[31] Papillon, "a terrible yegg" who earned the nickname by carving a butterfly on the back or chest of those he killed, was reputed to have skinned alive and eaten an American Marine. His tale is narrated by Craige in the context of a discussion of rampant sexuality in Haiti. Young Haitian "bucks," when not in possession of a harem, he contended, "ranged the brush waylaying desirable *tiefies*, or young women, as occasion offered. Occasion offered frequently. The *tiefies* apparently enjoyed being waylaid. Rape, I believe, implies lack of consent. I never heard of a case where consent was lacking in Haiti's black belt" (124). The objectification of women implied by Papillon's rampage and Craige's account is bolstered in *Hadriana . . .* by the portrayal of its protagonist as Sleeping Beauty, a lifeless, inanimate, passively awaiting sex object very much like the passive portraits of the zombified Madeleine and Jessica. Depestre conscientiously "saves" Hadriana from Granchiré's erotic rampage—the only young woman in the novel not "savagely deflowered"—keeping her for the narrator's ultimate pleasure at the end of the text.

The false eroticism of the text, false to the degree that it objectifies female sexuality and is built on male-centered fantasies of erotic dominance, is linked to the racially determined attitudes toward sexuality that I described above as being so intrinsic to zombie films. The text is overly concerned with sexual relations between black men and white women. Not only does Granchiré, black male-cum-butterfly, ferociously attack white and mulatto women, leaving them covered in his semen and their blood, but the text presents Hadriana's carnivalesque wake as a volcano that "reduces to ashes the legendary obstacles between Thanatos and Eros, overcoming the barriers raised between the sperm of black males and the eggs of white females" (77). The link between a woman's white skin and her role as desired erotic object is highlighted in Hadriana's meeting with the sorcerer who attempts to zombify her. His announcement that once their copulation has been accomplished, "everything that is right side out in your life as a white female will be turned wrong side out to show its blackness" (198) suggests that Hadriana's whiteness will disappear with her virginity. Hadriana succeeds in escaping that fate, but her deliverance only reinforces the correlation between her whiteness and her continued role as desired virginal (white) erotic object. This validation of whiteness, presented for the most part without irony in the text, is stressed when Hadriana enters Jamaica without a visa because "white skin, even more than a diplomatic passport, was tantamount to a visa granted by divine right" (190).

Depestre's text ultimately resists meaning, as it seems to strive to empty history of its content by placing the erotic quest above it. But the erotic quest itself is deprived of sense in the text because it negates the free erotic *jouissance* of the carnivalesque and the revolutionary aspects of Vodou in the name of the triumph of zombification and the grotesque phallic image. It is an erotic quest that relegates all Haitian people, with the exception of the narrator and his young white beloved, to everlasting zombification, devoid of the will to revolt, deprived by a brutal history of the freedom to desire.

MAYRA MONTERO's short story "Corinne, muchacha amable" ("Corinne, Amiable Girl") resonates with the tropes familiar to moviegoers, here turned inside out to expose their sexist, racist, and political underpinnings.[32] Young Appolinaire Sanglier, "wallowing in the despair of his love like a victim of a blood spell," seeks the aid of Papa Lhomond, a houngan who knows "how to work the living dead," to turn light-skinned and yellow-eyed Corinne into his zombie wife (836–837). He is spurred into action by tales of a French woman abducted and turned into a pliant zombie by a sorcerer from Hinche. Corinne, the daughter of a white priest and a prostitute, is coveted for a beauty that owes much to her being partly white; but she is engaged to marry a politically active man who is deaf and mute, aptly named Dessalines Corail; and she is disdainful of the love-sick Appolinaire. Her zombification on the eve of her wedding will be as much a punishment for her disdain as the means of guaranteeing that, after her marriage to Appolinaire, "she will not become such a whore as her mother." Appolinaire dreams of her as she will be after she returns "from the blue well of the deceased, clean and submissive like God intended, with the pale gaze of those who never think, without that scowl of disgust she gave him every time he came near" (836).

In this story, Montero is interested as much in laying bare the zombification of women as a power rather than an erotic issue as she is in linking
this issue to the larger one of the Haitian people's struggle against the Duvalier
government, here represented by the dreaded Tonton Macoutes, the regime's
feared militia. Set on the eve of an election, with Corinne's fiancé one of the
most active workers on behalf of an anti-Duvalier local candidate, the story
subtly juxtaposes Corinne's determination to choose a husband freely and the
people's struggle to elect a candidate committed to social justice. Both will
be denied this right. Montero never dwells on the pathos of Corinne's situation; no sentimentality is wasted on the fate of the brave young girl who has
dared to challenge Appolinaire's desire and the Tonton Macoute's wrath. Her
individual fate is not Montero's central concern; it is depicted as bound to
that of the Haitian people. As she lies in a deathlike stupor in her fresh grave,
with Papa Lhomond and Appolinaire racing against time to dig her up before
she suffocates, the people, her fiancé among them, are brutally attacked as
they seek to exercise their democratic right to vote.

> Smoke from old tires floated above the square, and counting on that
> being the shortest route to the cemetery, [Appolinaire] decided to
> make his way across through the bonfires. Behind the church, next to
> the garbage cans of the cabinet-maker's shop, he sighted the first
> corpses. The faces were covered with sawdust and the spilled shavings
> had stuck to their shoes. Appolinaire slowed down. He noticed the
> half-severed necks and arms and concluded they had been killed by
> machete blows. . . . When he turned the corner, without having the
> time to avoid it, he found himself facing a mob that was suddenly
> upon him, dragging him along little by little. Some men were sobbing
> loudly, their faces covered with blood and their clothes torn. . . . He
> returned to his house near dawn, avoiding the soldiers piling up
> bodies on tarpaulin-covered trucks. [844–845, 846]

The living dead remain a disquieting presence in "Corinne, Amiable Girl,"
another chapter in the narrative of the Haitian people's ongoing struggle for
freedom from political and economic oppression. Montero denies the people's
zombification through the materiality of their butchered bodies, their "half-
severed necks and arms." Appolinaire, encountering Dessalines amidst the mob
fleeing the murdering armed forces, sees his rival as "one of those who had
been brought back: very rigid arms, a fixed stare, the convulsive grin of the
mouth, the bitter grin of all creatures that like to eat vermin" (845). But this
Dessalines will not be coming back; his zombielike appearance is but the mask
of death. He is soaked in blood, with a wound, "an enormous slanting slash,"
running across his chest into his gut. The dead bodies piled up anonymously
on trucks and the still-living body of Corinne awaiting a rescue into the half-

life of zombiedom represent an unresolved historical quandary from which the zombie as metaphor can offer no deliverance.

IN *LA CATHÉDRALE DU MOIS D'AOÛT* (The Cathedral of the August Heat), Pierre Clitandre transcends the life-death symbiosis of the zombie-centered tales through the reaffirmation not of the sorcery of the bokor but of the life-giving and revolutionary qualities of Vodou.[33] Zombification has always been marginal to Vodou, and Clitandre, leaving the zombie behind, focuses instead on the relationship between history and the Haitian people's ever-changing and renewed body. Like Corinne in Montero's tale, the novel's characters are distinct individuals subsumed into the living body of the people. Although it focuses on John, a *tap-tap* (bus) driver and his son Raphael, the novel is above all a metaphorical tale of a lost people's desperate struggle to recover their history and, with it, the source of precious water that can restore them to fertility and bounty. It celebrates hope and renewal through its emphasis on the carnivalesque and its faith in the regenerating and revolutionary power of Vodou.

Central to the novel is the portrayal of the Haitian people as a body that is the opposite of Depestre's zombie, one that "fecundates and is fecundated, devours and is devoured, drinks, defecates, is sick and dying."[34] Clitandre celebrates the materiality of the Haitian people's bodies through hyperbolized, quasi-Rabelaisian, grotesque images that are overwhelmingly, although not exclusively, olfactory. The novel contains literally hundreds of references to the potent bodily smells typical of the Rabelaisian marketplace: unbathed bodies smelling like ram-goats, the abominable stench of rotting flesh, the nauseous smell of plague-ridden corpses, the stink of piss and decay, and the smell of sweat, blood, and bruises. He also presents an image of the body as mutilated, rotting corpse, as it was in Montero's tale; the text abounds in images of crushed hands, burnt bodies, cut-off penises, roasted testicles, sores, and of blood soaking and fertilizing the scorched earth. Death haunts the text, and the people are represented as subject to ever-threatening plagues, natural calamities, and repressive terror. But, as is typical of the carnivalesque, death and the dead body are depicted as stages in the renewing of the ancestral body of the people, not as the limbo of zombification. Thus, the novel treats individual deaths not as signaling an irrevocable end but as natural and necessary phases in the cycle of life. Death asserts life, thus ensuring the indestructible immortality of the people. The death of an individual, as the death of young Raphael demonstrates, is only a moment in the triumphant life of the people, "a moment indispensable for their renewal and empowerment,"[35] and is thus, as Corinne's zombification was in Montero's tale, devoid of terror and tragedy.

Images of death are counterbalanced in the text by recurrent images of the people's struggle against death through procreation. "Lost people like to have plenty of children. Fornicate all the blessed day. Say it's their only hope: pickney like the fingers of your hand, faster than death can carry them off. And so the babies come, ten, twenty, thirty at a time . . . faster than death."[36] The theme of death-renewal-fertility is underscored through repeated images of blood as a seed buried in the earth and of life springing forth not only from the human body but through fantastic profusions of roses, life-giving rain, and life-affirming eroticism.

Clitandre's interest in the erotic aspects of the grotesque image of the body is also a characteristic feature of the carnivalesque; it turns upside down the bodily hierarchy in which the head rules to make the "lower bodily stratum" prevail. Eroticism, death, and revolt set the tone for the novel from the opening, when John, impotent for a long time, prisoner of a "zombification" of sorts, lifts off the body of a white man making love to Madeleine and flings himself at her. "Three days John and Madeleine spent coiled together, moving to the tune of the serpents' hiss that whispered from their closed teeth. And like a voice from beyond the grave the song of the old madam at the bar was still humming away *Carolina Aca-o Small ear black man enragée*" (6). This image summarizes key aspects of the text: the Caribbean people's struggle against the impotence and zombification forced on them by the white colonizers, sexual activity as a metaphor for revolt, the coiled serpents as a symbol of the Vodou cult of Damballah-wèdo, and the accompanying song from the grave, which recalls the sustaining role of the ancestral loas. The earthiness of the eroticism in the novel, with the recurring images of semen and human blood, is linked to Vodou, the source of the body's (the people's) reinvigoration. "The body is joy and revival," the narrative voice asserts, and this revival of the body is achieved through the Vodou ceremony: "it is reborn every Tuesday at midnight, among the smells of burning oil and essence, in the trance, the bathing of the head, the chants, until being is transformed and the stars fall" (28).

The life-giving power of Vodou pervades the entire text. The *vèvè*, or mystical sign, for Erzulie, goddess of the erotic and divinity of dreams, presides over the first part of the novel. The power of Erzulie—"her *élan*, all the excessive pitch with which the dreams of men soar, when, momentarily, they can shake loose the flat weight, the dreary, reiterative demands of necessity"— imbues this section of the text.[37] Conceived in the spirit of expansiveness characteristic of the cult of Erzulie, where all anxieties, all urgencies vanish, the section ends with the prefiguration of the power of laughter, the volcanic laughter that erupts in the world of the lost people like a seismic shock, spreading through the Caribbean region. The supernatural laughter corresponds to the image of the netherworld in folk tradition as the place to which fear has fled after its defeat by laughter. Folk laughter, the cosmic laughter of the lost people, represents the end of the "mystic terror of the authority and truth of the past, still prevailing but dying, which has been hurled into the underworld"[38]—the defeat of the forces that have zombified the people. In Clitandre, the resulting image is that of laughter sweeping away the past, including the carnival paraphernalia, because carnival, container of the people's spirit of revolt in its temporarily sanctioned aspects, is no longer needed when true revolution is at hand. "The laugh bore away masks, decorated floats, Carnival devils, whiskers from the moustache of a former general, old dresses of women long buried, banners washed out by the rains, paper flags faded by seasons when hails of bullets re-echoed, and all the things which were passing away, grating or whining, sad and majestic puppets who had set for ever in a hollow grin" (97).

The dreams inspired by Erzulie set the stage for the second part of the tale, which is introduced by the vèvè for Petro, an invocation to the spirits of wrath and revolt. The Petro rites in Vodou were born of the rage against the evil fate suffered by Africans transported into the New World, the wrath against the brutality of displacement and enslavement.[39] The second part thus focuses on the people's open revolt against the repressive authorities, guided by the Petro loas into calling for "People power now!" (123). The Petro loas, born in the mountains, nurtured in secret, repositories of the moral strength and organization of the escaped slaves that led the Haitian revolution, help Clitandre's people retrieve their lost history of struggle and revolt, awakening them to "another shouting for armed resistance against the great epidemic of repression" (122). Even the fierce wave of repression that follows the revolt of the trade unionists, the focus of this part of the text, can no longer stem the people's thirst for freedom. Raphael, killed during the revolt, articulates the message of the Petro loas in the legacy of historical memory he leaves behind. "He had scraped it (into the old cannon) with the blade, as if he wanted to remove the rust of the Season of Neglect, as if to tell his father to keep his promise. That these brave ancestors who forged this free nation, floating like a bird on the blue Caribbean Sea, should not be forgotten" (128).

In Clitandre's novel, as in Montero's "Corinne, Amiable Girl," the grotesque/carnivalesque image of the human body functions as the repository of history, the vessel of memory through which political change will eventually be accomplished. The eroticized image of the zombified white virgin—ahistorical and insistent on relegating the Haitian people to the forever-zombified margins—has no place in these accounts of Haiti's fate. In Clitandre's account, particularly, the people-as-body is unambiguously true to itself and to its history, and, although dismembered and drained of blood at times, it is never zombified and thus is ultimately indestructible.

As an analysis of Clitandre's *The Cathedral of the August Heat* underscores, films like *White Zombie* and *I Walked with a Zombie*—early entries in Hollywood's formulation of a spectral Haiti that we have seen developed and continued in countless zombie movies and Depestre's *Hadriana dans tous mes rêves*—raise troubling questions about the subsuming of Haitian political history to an erotic quest that privileges the white woman as innocent victim. Together with images from other films of the genre (most recently *The Serpent and the Rainbow*), the images made classic by *White Zombie* and *I Walked with a Zombie* and echoed in *Hadriana* conspire to blur the reality of Haiti, that of a people for whom tragic episodes of oppression continue to be woven into the fabric of their historical present. Slavery and imperialism (and the people's brave struggle against them) color in somber hues the island's past and present history; the "zombification" of the Haitian people and the subordination of their valiant spirit to the demands of a romantic plot that demands a vindicated white heroine are a betrayal of the Haitian people's affirmation that, ideologues notwithstanding, they have the capacity for living in autonomous sovereignty and should not be made to linger on the specter of death.

Notes

1. Edward Kamau Brathwaite, *Rites of Passage. The Arrivants: A New World Trilogy* (London: Oxford University Press, 1973). Joan Dayan, "Erzulie: A Women's History of Haiti," *Research in African Literatures* 2 (summer 1994): 5; reprinted in *Postcolonial Subjects: Francophone Women Writers* (Minneapolis: University of Minnesota Press, 1996).
2. Zora Neale Hurston, *Tell My Horse: Voodoo and Life in Haiti and Jamaica* (1938; reprint, New York: Harper & Row, 1990), 179. Katherine Dunham, *Island Possessed* (Chicago: University of Chicago Press, 1969), 184.
3. Dunham, *Island Possessed*, 184–185.
4. Alfred Métraux, *Voodoo in Haiti*, trans. Hugo Charteris (New York: Schocken, 1972), 250–251.
5. Wade Davis, *The Serpent and the Rainbow* (New York: Warner Books, 1985), and Wade Davis, *Passage of Darkness: The Ethnobiology of the Haitian Zombie* (Chapel Hill: University of North Carolina Press, 1988).
6. Davis, *Passage of Darkness*, 8–10. One of the earliest of the fully documented cases of zombification concerned a young woman from Savanne Carée, Francina Illéus, known as Ti-Femme, declared dead in 1976, aged thirty, who reappeared after she escaped from her captors. Before her death she had worked as a *marchande*, or market woman. Rebellious by nature, she had left the husband chosen for her by her mother, and, breaking village taboos, she had taken a lover with whom she had a child. Her mother was suspected of asking a bokor to turn her into a zombie as punishment for her behavior. See Bernard Diederich, "On the Nature of Zombi Existence," *Caribbean Review* 12 (1983): 14–17, 43–46. Interestingly enough, many of Hollywood's zombie films employ this punishment function of zombification as a plot element, particularly in the presentation of women zombified as punishment for adultery or lustful behavior. Notable among them is *I Walked with a Zombie* (1943), where the hero's mother (who herself has for many years impersonated a *houngan*, or Vodou priest, in order to get the villagers to follow public health guide-

lines) arranges for her daughter-in-law's zombification as punishment for an adulterous affair with her brother-in-law. The "zombification" is dismissed by the family doctor and attributed to a pernicious fever. In *Voodoo Woman* (1957) the sultry title creature—amoral, lustful, and murderous—willingly becomes a subject in a science and "Voodoo" experiment that results in her transformation into a hideously scaly, murderous monster who is ultimately buried in a steamy swamp.

7. Davis's anthropological work, supported by scholarship and science, itself fell victim to Hollywood's craving for sensationalism. The film based on his book *The Serpent and the Rainbow* (1988; Universal, directed by Wes Craven, produced by David Ladd and Doug Claybourne) is replete with evil "Voodoo" sorcerers, sexual torture, and cries of "Don't let them bury me. I'm not dead!"

8. Dunham, *Island Possessed*, 187.

9. Maximilien Laroche, "The Myth of the Zombi," in *Exile and Tradition: Studies in African and Caribbean Literature*, ed. Rowland Smith (London: Longman, 1976), 47.

10. René Depestre, *Change* (Paris: Editions du Seuil, 1971), 20.

11. Harry A. Franck, *Roaming through the West Indies*, (New York: Century, 1920), 164.

12. William B. Seabrook, *The Magic Island* (New York: Harcourt, Brace, 1929), 109–115.

13. Franck, *Roaming through the West Indies*, 164.

14. Métraux, *Voodoo in Haiti*, 284.

15. Hurston, *Tell My Horse*, 194–195.

16. Arthur Holly, *Les Daïmons du culte Voudo et Dra-Po* (Port-au-Prince: n.p., 1918).

17. C.-H. Dewisme, *Les Zombis ou le secret des morts-vivants* (Paris: Edition Bernard Grasset, 1957), 146–147.

18. Jacques-Stephen Alexis, "Chronique d'un faux amour," in *Romancero aux étoiles* (Paris: Editions Gallimard, 1960), 103. All translations are mine.

19. *White Zombie* (1932), produced by Edward Halperin for Amusement Securites/United Artists, directed by Victor Halperin.

20. *I Walked with a Zombie* (1943), produced by RKO, directed by Jacques Tourneur, with James Ellison, Frances Dee, and Tom Conway in the leading roles.

21. Blake Lucas, "I Walked with a Zombie," in *Magill's Survey of Cinema: English Language Films*, 2d ser., vol. 3, ed. Frank N. Magill (Englewood Cliffs, N.J.: Salem Press, 1981), 1094.

22. Ibid., 1094.

23. Ibid., 1096.

24. Another example of white usurpation of power in the film is the revelation of the identity of the houngan as another white woman, a doctor who claims that, unable to guide the blacks to enlightened beliefs, she opted to offer them Western medicine and aids through means they could comprehend.

25. *King of the Zombies* (1941), Monogram, directed by Jean Yarbrough, produced by Lindsley Parsons, cinematography by Mack Stengler.

26. *The Plague of the Zombies* (1966), Hammer/20th Century-Fox (U.K.), directed by John Gilling, produced by Anthony Nelson Keys, screenplay by Peter Bryan, cinematography by Arthur Grant.

27. *Orgy of the Dead* (1965), F.O.G. Distributions, produced and directed by A. C. Stephen, screenplay by Ed Wood, cinematography by Robert Caramico.

28. *Revenge of the Zombies* (1981), WW Entertainment (Hong Kong), directed by Ho Meng-Hua, produced by Run Run Shaw, screenplay by I. Kuang, cinematography by Tsao Hui-Chi.

29. *Zombies of Mora Tau* (1957), Columbia, directed by Edward L. Chan, produced by Sam Katzman, screenplay by Raymond T. Marcus, cinematography by Benjamin H. Kline.

30. René Depestre, *Hadriana dans tous mes rêves* (Paris: Editions Gallimard, 1988). All translations are mine. For a longer, more detailed discussion of the novel see my essay "Authors Playin' Mas': Carnival and the Carnivalesque in the Contemporary Caribbean Novel," in *History of Caribbean Literatures*, ed. A. James Arnold, Cross Cultural Studies 3 (Amsterdam, Philadelphia: John Benjamins, forthcoming).

31. John Houston Craige, *Cannibal Cousins* (New York: Minton, Balch, 1934), 128.

32. Mayra Montero, "Corinne, muchacha amable," in *Cuentos para ahuyentar el turismo*, ed. Vitalina Alfonso and Emilio Jorge Rodríguez (Havana: Arte y Literatura, 1991), 285–306. Translated into English by Lizabeth Paravisini-Gebert as "Corinne, Amiable Girl," *Callaloo* 17, no. 3 (summer 1994). Reprinted in *Remaking a Lost Harmony: Short Stories from the Hispanic Caribbean*, ed. Margarite Fernández Olmos and Lizabeth Paravisini-Gebert (Fredonia, N.Y.: White Pine Press, 1995). References in the text are to the *Callaloo* issue.

33. Pierre Clintandre, *La Cathédrale du mois d'août* (Paris: Editions Syros, 1982). Translated into English by Bridget Jones as *The Cathedral of the August Heat* (London: Readers International, 1987). All references are to the English translation.

34. Mikhail Bakhtin, *Rabelais and His World* (Bloomington: Indiana University Press, 1984), 319.

35. Ibid., 34.

36. Clintandre, *The Cathedral*, 15.

37. Maya Deren, *Divine Horsemen: The Living Gods of Haiti* (1953; reprint, Kingston, N.Y.: McPherson, 1970), 138.

38. Bakhtin, *Rabelais and His World*, 395.

39. Deren, *Divine Horsemen*, 62.

"I Am Going to See Where My Oungan Is"

ANNA WEXLER

*The Artistry of a
Haitian Vodou Flagmaker*

*An arivan laplas deploye drapo mwen
M prale wè kot oungan mwen ye.*

*[When the laplas (ritual assistant) arrives
to unfurl my flag
I am going to see where my oungan is]*

IN THIS SONG, which marks the moment for the ritual entry of the Vodou flags from the closed altar room into the open space of the temple, the *oungan* (priest) and the flag double as points of entry for the *lwa* (spirits), directing their energies into the ceremony.[1] They almost become one, much as the oungan in another song is said to become the *poto-mitan*, or center post, through which the lwa arrive and depart from the ritual gathering.[2] My efforts to learn about the flags and how they are made initially led me away from the flags as objects and into the life of a working oungan and prominent flagmaker. As I learned more about his multiple activities as a healer/priest, the flags began to appear. As in the song, seeing the flag and seeing the oungan were intertwined events. In order to see him at all I had to look at an internal kaleidoscope of images of fraud and terror surrounding the figure of the Vodou priest—images that constantly fractured my vision of the man before me.

Haitian Vodou flags, often richly ornamented with sequins and beads, are unfurled and danced about during ceremonies to signal the spirits represented by the *vèvè* (ritual designs) or the images of corresponding Catholic saints sewn on them. Known as the *drapo Vodou*, their reflective brilliance is said to attract the spirits into the human gathering, mediating between worlds.[3] As Clotaire Bazile, the flagmaker with whom I am working, told me, sequins are used

Figure 7. Clotaire Bazile in his altar room for the Petwo lwa in Port-au-Prince. In the foreground is a small statue of a black madonna and child representing Ezili Dantò (Erzulie Dantor). *Photo: Anna Wexler.*

because "espri yo renmen limyè" (the spirits love light), because "espri a se limyè li ye" (the spirit is light).[4] (See Figure 7.)

Like the priest, who not only calls the spirits but modulates the expression of their energies throughout ritual gatherings,[5] the flags also serve to restrain the spirits[6] and to protect their *cheval*, or horse, at painful moments of transition during possession, when the spirits are said to dance in the heads of their human carriers. So, for example, the flags are sometimes used to cover the heads of those whom the lwa have entered and are now leaving to protect the horse against the pain of an abrupt departure, especially if the possession has been turbulent.[7] As active presences during important ceremonies, the flags extend the vigilance of the oungan or *manbo* (female priest), who must orchestrate the manifestations of the lwa as well as attract them with the brilliant waving banners, which signal the honor and respect of the priest and his or her association for their spiritual friends.

Aside from the *ounfò* (Vodou temple), where the flags are rolled up and usually left leaning against altars to recharge their energies,[8] they can be seen in countless galleries, "ethnic-art" stores, museums, and private collections in North America, Europe, and, to a lesser degree, Haiti and other countries in the Caribbean. The only objects to cross over in significant numbers from the ritual field of Vodou into First World art markets, they have had an aesthetic impact profound enough to dispel the phantasms that cling to Vodou, at least for the purposes of buying. The religion has long served as a magnet for the fears engendered by its history of mobilizing and sustaining resistance to colonialism and to its aftereffects in Haiti.[9] A collector described as unconcerned about the "macabre side effects" of owning Vodou flags has been quoted as saying, "People want to think objects have some power *beyond* just being great works of art, but what is more powerful than that?"[10] In the same discussion, the opportunity to purchase flags without contact with their religious milieu and those who represent it is enthusiastically reported. "Today you don't have to forge friendships with Port-au-Prince voodoo priests—their vibrant banners are purveyed in import shops, museum stores, and galleries from Columbus Avenue to Sunset Strip. 'I can buy them from wholesale suppliers at the gift show!' [claimed a dealer] who has seen her own business in ritualistic artworks increase 'five or six times' since opening in 1980."

In 1971 two French travelers who had come to Clotaire in Port-au-Prince for a card reading (divination) asked him to unroll the flags they could see resting on a cabinet in one of his altar rooms. He explained that he had not made these flags for sale but for the lwa, who had appeared in a dream to tell him he must make two flags to serve the spirits of his temple. The visitors promised to send other customers his way if he would sell them, and within two months Clotaire had set up a workshop and made several thousand dollars in sales.[11] He was the first artist to produce flags systematically for art markets; his business peaked in the mid-1980s, when he worked closely with the late Virgil Young, a collector who not only commissioned flags of Clotaire's own design but arranged for "secular vèvè flags"[12] designed by Americans, by well-known artists Betye and Alison Saar among others, to be sequined and beaded in Clotaire's workshop.[13] By 1990, following the departure of Jean-Claude Duvalier in 1986 and the resulting marked decline in tourism in Haiti because of the turbulence of ongoing political transition, the workshop was functioning only sporadically, and Clotaire's activities were again related primarily to his healing work as a oungan.[14]

The figure of the oungan in much of the anthropological literature, as well as in traveler's accounts, fiction, and film, crystallizes many of the negative images associated with the popular religion of Haiti. Often referred to as "Voodoo" in what Karen Richman has aptly termed "the quintessential hegemonic construction, representing the dominated as exotic and other,"[15] the religion has been diabolized by European and American writers since the eighteenth century, when oungan leaders of the slave revolts, like Makandal and Boukman, were said to draw their power from sorcery.[16] The identification of political resistance and bizarre practices such as ritual human sacrifice also reached a crescendo during the American occupation of Haiti (1915–1934), justifying the slaughter of the *kakos*, or guerrilla forces, who organized against the Marines.[17] As Joseph Murphy summarizes, "Each flowering of voodoo images has accompanied an effort to control real gains in black independence."[18] The vilification of the oungan in particular stemmed from the effective combination of religious and political power in the early leaders of the slave uprisings which eventually destroyed the French colonial system.

Even writers who are sensitive to the historical context of "Voodoo images" and whose personal knowledge of the religion and its practitioners transcends stereotypes often lapse in their discussions of oungan. For example, the great French ethnographer Alfred Métraux, who did his fieldwork in Haiti in the late 1940s and who demonstrates appreciation for the complex personalities and roles of the manbo he befriended, relies primarily on homophobic caricatures and allegations of sorcery when it comes to oungan. "Many houngan whom I knew seemed to me to be maladjusted and neurotic. Among them were homosexuals—impressionable, capricious, oversensitive and prone to sudden transports of emotion."[19] And, further, "have not certain houngan been accused of showing themselves to be in no hurry to cure their patients and even of aggravating an illness in order to make it more fruitful of fees? It has even been suggested that they get together with the sorcerers who have cast a spell on their client in order to learn the secret of the spell which caused the disease."[20] As the Haitian scholar Laënnec Hurbon suggests in *Le Barbare imaginaire*, the working oungan is often conflated with the sorcerer, even in the internal discourse of Vodou, because of the need to know the techniques of sorcery in order to combat them, to "ré-expédier le mal" (send back the evil).[21]

A more contemporary example is contained in *Mama Lola*, a pathbreaking life history of a Vodou priestess, in which Karen Brown constructs the first intimate and emphatic portrait of a Vodou practitioner based on her ten-year relationship with a manbo in Brooklyn, New York.[22] However, the only oungan to appear in the text are linked to sorcery or the Tonton Macoutes (members of the dreaded civilian militia created by François Duvalier) or to both. Brown also observes that in most temples the manbo handle their power gracefully, moving in and out of their authoritative role, whereas the oungan generally insist on rigid maintenance of their dominating public persona. The oungan she describes are undeniably real and numerous as types, and enact behavioral patterns of male hegemony that she rightfully challenges. However, they appear to stand in for the entire range of possibilities in the male role, which is not contextualized deeply enough in religious and political history to allow for genuine critical reflection on those who fill it.[23]

Striking exceptions to the generalized and often derogatory characterizations of oungan in much anthropological literature appear in the works of Maya

Deren, Katherine Dunham, and Zora Neale Hurston. These three women writers are known primarily as brilliant artistic innovators, Deren in film, Dunham in choreography and dance, and Hurston in fiction and folklore. Though Dunham and Hurston were academically trained in anthropology and Deren was self-taught, their appreciation and involvement in the ritual forms of Vodou were inspired at least as much by their distinct aesthetic sensibilities. A distinguishing feature of their works, especially for their periods, is their deep level of personal engagement with the spirits and rituals of Vodou, which permitted them to encounter oungan as genuine teachers rather than simply as types to be observed.[24] In Hurston's *Tell My Horse* and Dunham's *Island Possessed*, the authors describe fear as both an obstacle to and an incentive for gaining knowledge in their interactions with oungan.[25]

An extremely eloquent and candid description of such an interaction appears in *Island Possessed*. Determined to investigate rumors that a priest of the Kongo lwa, ti Couzin, practiced cannibalism and had *zonbi* (zombies) who served him as wives, Dunham and a friend set out to visit him. Her perceptions of the oungan veer constantly. At one moment she finds herself as an African American speaking comfortably about the Black Muslims and the oppression of her people to a "wise though uneducated man, with whom I could discuss sociological and anthropological subjects beyond the horizons of his own background."[26] In the next moment, the oungan is motionless and staring, and Dunham sees seven women on the verandah, also motionless and staring, who appear to be the rumored zonbi. She imagines that she is being subtly zonbified herself.

The critical juncture of the interaction results from a dramatic demonstration of the oungan's clairvoyance. Before entering one of his ounfò with his guests, the oungan turns to Dunham's friend, who had not told him of his car problems or of his plans to have it repaired at a garage in nearby Léogane, and suggests that he not leave to have his car fixed there because the owner of the garage has just died and the garage would be closed. Eager to go to the city and confirm ti Couzin's story, the two walk to the road and are stopped by a truck driver who tells them he has come from the garage in question, where the owner's death has just been announced. In her report, written after the incident, Dunham concludes that the priest's unusually keen clairvoyance and personal magnetism inspired the rumors of *zonbi* and cannibalism in his compound.

When I first started working with Clotaire in Miami in early 1992, the beautiful Vodou flags marked with his initials, CB, which I had seen in shops and galleries, were not in evidence. I had been drawn to them by their subtle color combinations and careful renderings of the vèvè which seemed to evoke the lwa more directly than the work of some other flagmakers using dramatic and whimsical narrative styles to expand the aesthetic parameters of the form. Like the collector and buyer mentioned above, however, I had separated the flags from their source. When I realized that, in Miami, Clotaire was working primarily as an oungan and not making flats, I felt that the artistry I had come in search of was missing. It was as if the flags had been rolled up again and sequestered in the ounfò, their original home. Instead of the dazzling surfaces of Vodou flags, I encountered a painful inner reservoir of malign images of oungan and their accouterments that I had assumed my critical consciousness had long since defused. I watched these images play against what I was actually experiencing in Clotaire's house and veered between states of fear, temporary relief, and profound awe like those described by Dunham in more dramatic circumstances.

The first card reading (divination) that Clotaire performed for me gave me an opportunity to look closely at objects in his altar room, where we were sitting. I was struck especially by potent-looking objects hanging from the ceiling, among them a dried fish with a black cloth doll tied to it that was crisscrossed with white string, a stuffed tubular shape in black cloth also tied with string, and a mirror hanging upside down with a cross drawn delicately in wax on its surface. Not particularly interested in providing explanations at that point, he responded to my questions about these objects with the simple phrase "pou travay . . . travay pou ou" (for work . . . work for you). Elaborating slightly, he explained that the upside down mirror was to draw back someone's lover who had strayed. Even the multiple chromolithographs of Catholic saints, each corresponding to a particular lwa, appeared to be strategically placed for action rather than passive adoration. One was hung upside down; others were placed on the floor beside plates of food and liquids.

I noted at the time that the working objects in the room made me feel distant. I interpreted the distance as a form of respect for the timing of knowledge acquisition, a gauge of how little I understood of the work these objects embodied in Clotaire's healing practice and how little I was prepared or even wanted to know about them at that point. However, I also wanted to put this distance between us, to step back from evidence of Clotaire's power as a healer; I was reluctant to find out more about the concrete purposes of the objects he had made because I was afraid to fear the man before me more.

Later that year, in Boston, when I was half asleep in a chair, I suddenly saw an image of the lwa Ezili Dantò in my mind's eye, upside down and in exquisite detail, from the chromolithograph of Our Lady of Czestochowa, the black Virgin with whom she is often identified. The suddenness and clarity of the beautiful image, its Catholic form (with which I had no great familiarity or connection), and most of all the fact that it appeared upside down shocked me. I searched through my books on Vodou for possible interpretations of this vision and came across a discussion in *Mama Lola* of the fierce nature of Ezili Dantò, which Lola's daughter illustrates by saying that if you place her image upside down and send her after someone, that person will come to you or be broken. Among the many fantasies inspired by the vision and the lines in *Mama Lola* was one in which Clotaire was responsible. The fear, which had been activated by the objects he had placed in his altar room, was all too present, painfully reminding me that I had not transcended the projections of sorcery fed by popular, racist images of diabolic oungan and their accoutrements. I was jolted into another level of confrontation with the impediments that my identity as an American white woman presented for my work.

A classic description of a ounfò and its altar—a description that moves the mind's eye from the beautiful to the bizarre—occurs in *La Reine Soleil Levée* by the Haitian novelist Gérard Etienne.[27] Noting "une pile d'objets arrangés avec un soin particulier, une certain délicatesse dans la manière d'afficher les images, de placer les articles sacrés de la religion vaudou" (a pile of objects arranged with particular care, a certain delicacy in displaying the images, in placing the sacred articles of the Vodou religion), the oungan's client observes the statues and chromolithographs of the saints and then notices a series of other items: a suitcase containing baby bottles; a pile of bras; a box the size of a coffin with a chamber pot in it containing a serpent's skin, the blood of a frog, and orange juice; a fork capped with a wad of silky hair.[28] It is as if the aesthetic presentation of the sacred images is designed to seduce the client visually into participating in the violence suggested by the more potent and seemingly bizarre objects. The stage is set for her *magnétisation* by the malevolent oungan.

The other side of the diabolization of beauty in this context is its celebration. Power is denied in both modes, in the one by making it narrowly malevolent, in the other by detaching it from suffering. In a featured article on the artist Jean-Michel Basquiat in *Art in America* entitled "Altars of Sacrifice," bell hooks remarks on the striking absence of emotional response, especially among white critics, to the dismemberment, appropriation, and prostitution of the black body so directly stated in his work.[29] Unable or choosing not to see the tragic content of his paintings, the "Eurocentric gaze" instead "commodifies, appropriates, and celebrates" in aesthetic and cultural terms images that might otherwise force the viewer to confront his or her own complicity in the death scripts written for black men in North America that Basquiat decodes and reinscribes (70). In other writing hooks links this mode of evasion to a multiculturalism that circumvents the reality of racial domination by concentrating on the more palatable concepts of ethnicity, culture, difference, and otherness.[30]

The writing on altars and other material embodiments of belief in the religious traditions of the African-Atlantic cultures sometimes share in this dissociated celebration without deep reference to the past and present sufferings that these forms inscribe, contest, and transfigure or to the social identity and ethical position of the writer. Like the deliberately surreal/grotesque cataloguing of objects on the altar in La Reine Soleil Levée described above, the celebratory aestheticizing impulse also isolates them from the network of relationships, human and spiritual, within which they are empowered to act. When I looked at the hanging objects in Clotaire's altar room, I saw only things and the projections that they stimulated, not the torments that they so intensely configure and redress.

In Island Possessed, Dunham presents ti Couzin's altar room for the lwa Kongo Moundoung in an unusually interactive and processual descriptive mode. After witnessing the dramatic precision of the priest's clairvoyance, she moves from a previously more detached survey of the sacred environment to one in which every perception of what is in the inner sanctuary—the blood on the altar, a cement pool covered with slime, a straw bundle between two poles hanging from the ceiling and resembling a body in a peasant stretcher— is keyed to her response to ti Couzin, the rhythm of challenge and disclosure that propels the encounter, her momentary connection with him beyond the distorted scenarios of spiritual fear. She almost stumbles into a pool of blood, forces herself to drink from the cement basin, and queries him about the bundle by singing a song about a zonbi being tied up with straw. She momentarily considers initiation when he traces a cross in powder on her forehead. The objects and substances are not static but signal a process of continuous transformation that cannot be morally fixed or aesthetically reified, a process that now includes her.

A passage in Mama Lola in which Brown describes the manbo activating and communing with the spirits in her altar room also stands out as quite extraordinary because we are given more than a catalogue of objects, ritual gestures, and their general referents. The description is infused with the emotional tone of that morning, each libation performed with an intensity that translates Mama Lola's anxiety about her daughter's hospitalization into poignant acts of spiritual exchange. "The dark-skinned doll representing Ezili Dantò wore a faint smile, and Alourdes smiled back at her. As the odors of the room awoke, so did its spirits, and Alourdes drew them around her. She would need their protection more on this day than on others" (261).

A notable exception also appears in broader historical context in African Vodun, where Suzanne Preston Blier discusses the bocio arts of Dahomey. She brings the psychic and material traumas inflicted by the slave trade and its aftermath to bear on her reading of these forms, arguing that the tying and binding in commoner bocio art evoke enslavement and the strength necessary to overcome its destructive legacies. The Haitian cloth-covered dolls, she suggests, may be bocio-related forms. Certainly the Haitian cloth figures employ a similar "aesthetics of shock," which evokes extremes of emotional and physical suffering and the concentrated power necessary to combat them.[31]

The people whom I met in Clotaire's waiting rooms later often reminded me of the actual violence the figures hanging from the ceiling might be remembering and redressing. A woman who appeared to be in her fifties spoke of the terror of helicopters circling the boat in which she and hundreds of others had fled Haiti, of a list of names of those who would be sent back being read over the loudspeaker at Guantánamo naval base. A younger Haitian woman cradled the side of her face with a long gash inflicted by a razor blade across it and referred to the second victimization she had experienced when she tried to testify against her assailant. The intensity of suffering related by people often fleeing desperate situations in Haiti only to encounter the systemic racism evident in the economic decline and violence afflicting many urban communities is matched by the potency of objects that affirm the possibility of survival and change in overwhelming circumstances.

I could not celebrate the aesthetic brilliance of the flags and the genius of their creator without confronting fears like those stimulated by the power of the objects in the altar room and their maker. Evidence of the active, instrumental character of Clotaire's artistry was everywhere as I saw bottles, lamps, food, and other materials prepared for his healing work. I began to see the beauty of these preparations through my fears as I came to recognize Clotaire's gifts as a healer. The same card reading that had occasioned later fantasies of sorcery also sparked this recognition by addressing my unspoken apprehensions.

He began the reading by asking me why I appeared unhappy and confused by my visit to Miami. I avoided answering his question directly, embarrassed to reveal my apprehensions and afraid that doing so would jeopardize my work with him. I referred instead to a difficult childhood that undermined my confidence in carrying out my work. He went on to respond to my unspoken fears by saying that there was no danger for me in the future connected to my work, that I would not have any "move frapman nan wout ou" (bad blows on your path),[32] and that true spiritual realities would open up to me in the process as well as recognition from the university (he predicted a fellowship). I was moved by how he used his clairvoyance to focus the reading on a sensitive area, which was the actual problem at hand, without making me feel too vulnerable. He gave my fear just enough recognition to help me go forward with my work, not only by providing reassuring information about the future but simply by acknowledging my apprehensions. He suggested that I should push more, take a more active stance toward my project.

As my fantasies about the vision of Ezili Dantò attest, I continue to re-cycle images of catastrophic spiritual manipulation. But Clotaire's reading turned these images into opportunities for more sustained attention to the bar-rier of fear I put between myself and the power of a man whose acts of beauty summon and articulate transformative spiritual energies. As ti Couzin's clair-voyance had moved Dunham beyond zonbi scenarios into a complex vision of his spiritual talents and their ritual manifestations, my direct experience of Clotaire's gift for healing made the beauty of its multiple material expressions visible by illuminating the (now) transparent obstacle of fear. I began to see the flags evoked in the exquisite attention to detail he brought to all the prepa-rations related to his work as a oungan in Miami.

The perfume bottle he prepared for me after my reading to bring me *chans*, or luck, was a miniature emblem of the artistry I was seeking.[33] Inside the small thin glass bottle with its tiny opening he had inserted a plant (called wont) with hundreds of delicate tendrils, which seemed to move and float freely there as if it were actually growing in the fragrance. The action of this plant is be-lieved to make others readily accede to the wearer's wishes, to clear the way for the realization of goals. Later in my fieldwork, Clotaire prepared a lamp to help his work with a family in Orlando whose son was in prison and whose release they were trying to obtain. The tufts of cotton rolled deftly between his fingers were transformed into seven wicks, identical in size, which were soon floating like tiny flowers of flame in the bowl of oil. With the same pre-cision he moved his hands in circles over the flames and then swept the in-visible energies into his chest—the energies of all the lwa, he explained, from all the Vodou pantheons, which he had summoned with the burning wicks. I marveled at the power of gesture in this event. Clotaire gave few words of explanation; the purpose of the lamp seemed to infuse his fingers as they skill-fully transformed the materials into an arena of floating lights for signaling the spirits. Its efficacy was already apparent in the fusion of creative act and spiritual invocation, which gave each of Clotaire's motions an almost ethe-real dexterity. The perfume bottle and the lamp were visible expressions of the precision and delicacy of gesture that he brings to the creation of trans-formative objects for his healing work. "Bagay yo mande metriz" (These things require mastery), Clotaire explained to me when preparing his table for the card reading.[34]

I observed the same flair for detail in the myriad domestic labors involved in Clotaire's healing practice. Cooking and cleaning, whether connected to a specific ritual occasion or the general well-being of the house, are carried out with the concentration brought to other ritual preparations. Whether serving coffee to clients waiting to see him, sweeping the yard, or washing the enameled tin cups and bowls with which the lwa are served, Clotaire works with a meticulous attention that is never precious or rigid; it energizes those around him and lends each task a visible aura of finesse.

As he explained later, concentration or giving full attention to whatever he does is a major expression of how he conceives his responsibilities as a oungan. Remembering and executing ritual detail correctly is critical to summoning and controlling the lwa, whose energies he must channel constructively for his healing work. The consequences of negligence are grave. To be careless about rendering a ground drawing, or vèvè, he explained, is potentially to disrupt a ceremony because the spirit being called may not recognize the pattern and other less-welcome lwa may arrive. People may die as a result of failure to concentrate or "mete tèt ou anplas" (put your head in place) to carry out a ritual service according to the requirements of tradition. Forgetting a single, apparently insignificant detail can invite serious problems: "Pou sèvi mistè, se tankou yon zè, se tankou yon zè ou manyen, ke ou bliye se zè nan men ou, ou lage latè, se konsa, men si ou pran tout bagay onè, respè, ou p ap difikilte." (To serve the spirits, it's like an egg, it's like an egg you hold, if you forget it's an egg in your hand, you let it drop to the ground, but if you do everything with honor, respect, you are not going to have difficulty.)[35] It is not the lwa themselves who create difficulties but those who serve them improperly, without the necessary vigilance and intention.

In Clotaire's work as a oungan, mastery of ritual detail translates his intense awareness of its power to heal and to destroy into tangible forms. There is an edge to acts of beauty that not only represent but activate the transforming energies of the spirits. I came to see that the principles guiding his practice as a oungan also infuse his flagmaking and the technical and formal distinction of his artistic work. The concentrated attention to detail that characterizes the preparations he makes for his healing work is also reflected in the technical excellence of his flags.

According to Virgil Young, Clotaire was the first flagmaker to achieve a consistent level of craftsmanship in his work, a "strict hand."[36] Typically Clotaire designs the pieces, drawing the vèvè for a particular spirit and the geometric borders, and designating the colors. On pieces of satin stretched on a frame usually measuring 36" x 40", each sequin is sewn on with a tiny seed bead, or *grenn*, in an extremely labor-intensive process. Sometimes the entire surface is filled in with sequins; sometimes the inner area where the vèvè appears is dotted with sequins in a style beautifully described as *simen grenn*, or scattering seeds. Clotaire insists that each sequin be sewn down tightly, evenly overlapping the one before it, that all lines in his piece are straight, and that the vèvè or image of the saint be perfectly centered within the geometric borders that usually enclose the sacred form.

When he taught me his sewing techniques in Miami, he emphasized that each time I added another sequin I must bring the needle up through the fabric right against the edge of the tiny 5mm sequin preceding it so that they overlapped evenly in straight lines and there was no space between them. He pointed out immediately any sign of carelessness in my sewing as well as in my treatment of the materials. The area outdoors where we were working was always swept clear of leaves and other debris, and if he found stray sequins on the ground, he would pick them up one by one and place them deliberately on the fabric to remind me of my negligence. He hung pieces of blue satin that had been cut away over the branch of the mango tree that shaded our work, explaining that nothing was ever wasted. These gestures both conserved materials and heightened their specificity and intrinsic power.

"Jis kenbe lin dwat" (Just keep the line straight), he later explained, is the central standard he maintains in flagmaking.[37] The same concentration required to draw a vèvè correctly or to read the cards is also essential to drawing and sewing in straight lines on the flags. This technical standard expresses another major principle that guides his activities as a oungan: direction or orientation.

> Si lin ou pa dwat ou pa gen direksyon, nan nenpòt sa ou fè, si ou pa gen direksyon, li pa bon, fòk ou kenbe dwat pou bagay la bon. Se menm jan tou si pa egzanp ou ap fè oungan, ou pa mete respè anplas, si moun pote lajan ba ou pou fè travay, ou soti kòb pou pase move pas, lwa fache tou, paske si lwa k ap travay avèk ou, fòk ou fè tout bagay, lwa kanpe depwi ou fè "whatever you do" pou moun, mistè sèvi avèk ou la, li kanpe la, li ka pale nan tèt ou, ou pa wè li, li kanpe bo kote ou pou gide ou, pou fè bagay yo dwat.
>
> [If your line isn't straight, you don't have direction; in whatever you do, if you don't have direction, it isn't good; you must keep straight for things to be good. It's the same thing if, for example, you are working as a oungan, you don't act with respect; if someone brings you money to do work, you take the money to resolve a problem; the lwa are angry also because if it is the lwa who are working with you, you must do everything; the lwa supports you whatever you do for people; the spirit collaborates with you; she or he stands there, maybe talks in your head. You don't see him or her; she or he stands near you to guide you, to make everything straight.][38]

Ritual orientation in Vodou is performed by saluting or signaling the four cardinal points with all the offerings, flags, and other objects used in the ceremony. The four points or directions demarcate the limits of space and directionality within it; they are indicated by lines that intersect in the Vodou cross, which represents the point of contact between the physical world and the domain of the lwa.[39] Clotaire insists that the basic cross of the vèvè be drawn on flat ground so that the lines provide the correct directions for ritual orientation; the lines on the flags must be drawn and sewn straight for the same reason. Directionality is not only a structural principle but one that activates contact between human and spiritual beings and also delineates the moral quality of that contact, as the above remarks of Clotaire suggest. Staying straight means honoring the directives of the lwa and the healing work for which their guidance is intended.

Like the works of the first- and second-generation oungan/painters of the Haitian Renaissance—Hector Hyppolite, Andre Pierre, and Lafortune Felix—Clotaire's flags evoke the presence of the lwa so familiar to their creator.[40] I asked two prominent curators who have seen vast numbers of the flags made for commercial markets to describe what they thought were the distinctive qualities of Clotaire's work in that context. Martha Henry noted his ability to "express the ineffable" through a "restrained subtle lyricism" in his use of color.[41] "He has the ability to communicate the nature of the lwa through his design," Candice Russell observed, pointing to his talent for expressing the intense masculine and feminine attributes of particular lwa.[42] She also compared the prominence and clarity of the vèvè in his flags to the work of certain other flagmakers whose more narrative and pictorial styles tend to reduce the impact of the central image. These observations confirmed my intuitive appraisal in more sophisticated terms. (See Figure 8.)

Clotaire's life has been continuously interwoven with the influence of the spirits since the age of twelve, when he began to receive messages in dreams and to endure physical ailments that typically announce that an individual has been designated to become a healer/priest in the service of the lwa.[43] At twenty-five, with years of diagnosing and treating others already behind him, he completed the stage of Vodou initiation known as taking the *ason*, a beaded gourd rattle, which demonstrates that one is prepared to assume the formal role of oungan or manbo. Today, more than twenty-five years later, his mastery of the role is evident in his fluid access to the lwa and his talent for translating their guiding influences into sensitive advice and powerful ritual forms. At this level of development, contact with the lwa does not necessarily require the marked change in consciousness associated with possession and dreaming but may be experienced as a more subtle, voluntary intensification of lucidity and energy that enables one to receive the guidance of the lwa in words or images.

From the beginning flagmaking has also been an expression of Clotaire's gift for communication with the spirits. He began to make flags after dreaming

Figure 8. Flag designed by Clotaire Bazile for the lwa Diobolo Bossou (a horned bull), commissioned by the collector Virgil Young in the mid-1980s. Clotaire describes this bellicose lwa as being in-between the Rada and Petwo pantheons. *Photo: Virgil Young.*

that the lwa wanted two for his temple and after receiving instructions for fabricating them, just as he had learned to draw the vèvè and make healing remedies in dreams during the early stages of becoming a oungan. Transmission of vocation in Haitian oral traditions, especially those that involve transformative activities and objects, is often experienced initially in dreams through which the lwa or other spiritual agents communicate.[44] After an intense period of instruction, he continued to receive direction from the spirits, sometimes involving stylistic changes, in heightened states of being like those described above as well as in dreams.

The distinctive formal qualities of Clotaire's work, like those identified by the curators, bring his proximity to the lwa into the realm of visual possibility so that the flags he made for commercial markets still seem to mediate between worlds like their ritual prototype. Increasingly sophisticated color patterning in the borders of his flags, for example, only enhances their spirit-evoking properties; while the geometric forms, like the split diamond and pinwheel, are uniformly repeated, the color codes appear to be consistent but are subtly fractured at points where the eye is not conditioned to repetition, like the almost imperceptible shifts in consciousness characteristic of his contact with the lwa. Breaks in the rhythmic structures of Vodou ritual drumming coordinate the timing of possession.[45] Robert Farris Thompson links flexible patterning in African-American quilts, which show strong design parallels with the flags, with break patterning in Central African textiles, which activates the "potency of the other world."[46]

In an important review of the exhibit catalogue *Black Art: Ancestral Legacy*, Freida Tesfagiorgis criticizes several essays for reducing the creative process of contemporary artists to mediumistic or "receptive" states of dream and memory through which ancestral African influences enter their work.[47] Such a focus, she contends, renders the artist passive by emphasizing the received side of inspiration rather than individual imagination and conscious intention. Although Clotaire emphasizes the contribution of the lwa to his creative development as a flagmaker, he gives equal importance to his ability to act on what he receives, to give tangible form and elaboration to his visions. His penchant for geometry in school, for example, was an important resource for designing and developing the borders for his flags after the initial impulse to use triangular shapes was given in dreams. The capacity for action is central to his definition of the effective artist and the oungan, who must act decisively and forcefully on his intuitive healing knowledge or risk the death of clients, as well as the anger and eventual loss of the lwa.[48] His sense of personal accomplishment in both areas transcends the dualism implicit in the reviewer's stance because he conceives his sensitivity to spiritual influences as inseparable from his active command and translation of these forces into ritual healing and artistic forms, a lifelong creative project.

Clotaire describes his flags as "classical," referring to his sense of their continuity with the ritual form from which they evolved. This influence can be seen in his mastery and elaboration of the techniques and design elements of the older flags, such as *simen grenn* (characteristic of ritual flags from the 1930s, 1940s, and 1950s), borders with geometric patterns, the prominence of the vèvè, and the inserting and beading of a chromolithograph, or Catholic image of a saint identified with a lwa.[49] Though developed for commercial markets, his flags exemplify aesthetic evolution within the traditions of Vodou, an ethos of creativity that Deren has described as committed to enhancing collective participation in ritual expressions directed toward the lwa rather than individualistic demonstrations of genius. Excellence in drumming and singing, she suggests, is marked by improvisation, which serves tradition, rather than by virtuoso performances; improvisation inspires the singing and dancing of other participants and hastens the arrival of the lwa (231–233). Like the master drummer Coyote, with whom Gerdes Fleurant, the Haitian ethnomusicologist, worked, Clotaire emphasizes the continuity of ritual expression as a major value. In the ceremonies at his temple, he explained, he does not permit "modernizing" of the singing and dancing, which would alienate the lwa, who are not accustomed to unnecessary innovation.[50] The aesthetic developments in his flags both recapitulate and transfigure the history of the form, moving the past into the present through improvisation, which heightens recognition of the beauty and vitality of traditional design features and techniques.

In July 1993, in Port-au-Prince, I finally saw the flag and the oungan together in a service at Clotaire's temple for Papa Zaka, the archetypal peasant lwa of the land and family roots. One flag out of several that had been recently finished in the temple and sold had been made for the ceremony. It was draped over a small chair near the ritual table that had been prepared for Zaka. Made for the chief of the Ogou, Sen Jak Majè (St. James the Elder), the warrior spirit, it also evoked Danbala, the serpent lwa and cosmic patriarch, in the blue and white patterning on the top side of the border (see Figure 9). As Clotaire explained, traditionally flags for these two lwa represent and signal all the lwa of the major Rada pantheon. From a background of deep rose satin dotted with blue sequins the saint on his white horse with his saber upright seemed perpetually ready to leap out of the border of split diamonds, where fractured patterns in rose, white, and blue appeared to both attract and contain his energy. This kinetic juncture of prolific energy and control mirrored Clotaire when Ogou was riding him. He raced through the temple brandishing a machete, striking it against the center post and the walls, and leaping into the arms of those around him. But even during this explosive possession, he could shift back instantaneously to the vigilance of the oungan, detecting a minor altercation in the crowd and defusing it, making sure that ritual protocol was maintained in the seating of a guest.

Figure 9. Central panel of a flag designed by Clotaire Bazile for Sen Jak Majè (St. James the Elder), the chief of the Ogou, and used in a ceremony for the lwa Zaka in his temple in Port-au-Prince shortly after it was fabricated in July 1993.
Photo: Anna Wexler.

Notes

Thanks to the Center for the Study of World Religions at Harvard University for a 1993–1994 dissertation fellowship, which enabled me to write this chapter. My gratitude to Gerdes Fleurant for extremely helpful discussions related to the themes of this chapter and to Lionel Hogu for expert help in transcribing and translating/interpreting interview materials. Clotaire Bazile's generosity toward me is beyond these words.

1. This song was sung for me by the flagmaker Edgar Jean-Louis. The song in its entirely goes as follows (translation by author and Lionel Hogu):

> Laplas kondi m ale
> Laplas kondi m ale
> Kondi m ale laplas o Saliyo
> An arivan laplas deploye drapo mwen
> M prale wè kot oungan mwen ye.

> [Laplas, guide me out
> Laplas, guide me out
> Guide me out laplas o Saliyo
> When the laplas arrives to unfurl my flag
> I am going to see where my oungan is.]

2. Harold Courlander, *Haiti Singing* (New York: Cooper Square Publishers, 1973).
3. Robert Farris Thompson, *Flash of the Spirit: African and Afro-American Art and Philosophy* (New York: Random House, 1983).
4. Interview with Clotaire Bazile, 3 November 1993.
5. Laënnec Hurbon, *Le Barbare imaginaire* (Paris: Les Editions du Cerf, 1988).
6. Milo Rigaud, *La Tradition voudoo et le voudoo haïtien* (Paris: Editions Niclaus, 1953).
7. Interview with Clotaire Bazile, 3 November 1993.
8. Delores Yonkers, "Invitations to the Spirits: The Vodun Flags of Haiti," in *A Report from the San Francisco Crafts and Folk Art Museum* (San Francisco: San Francisco Crafts and Folk Art Museum, 1985).
9. See, for example, Paul Farmer, *AIDS and Accusation: Haiti and the Geography of Blame* (Berkeley: University of California Press, 1992); Robert Lawless, *Haiti's Bad Press* (Rochester, Vt.: Schenkman, 1992); Hurbon, *Le Barbare imaginaire*; Joseph M. Murphy, "Black Religion and 'Black Magic': Prejudice and Projection in Images of African-Derived Religions," *Religion* 20 (1990): 323–337.
10. Virginia Lautman, "Into the Mystic: The New Folk Art," *Metropolitan Home*, June 1989, 63.
11. Interview with Clotaire Bazile, 11 July 1992.
12. Lucy Lippard, "Sapphire and Ruby in the Indigo Gardens," in *Secrets, Dialogues, Revelations: The Art of Betye and Alison Saar*, ed. Elizabeth Shepherd (Los Angeles: Wight Art Gallery, UCLA, 1990), 13.
13. Interview with Virgil Young, 12 October 1993.
14. Interview with Clotaire Bazile, 8 November 1993.
15. Karen Richman, "They Will Remember Me in the House: The Pwen of Haitian Transnational Migration" (Ph.D. diss., University of Virginia, 1992), 19.
16. Michel S. Laguerre, *Voodoo and Politics in Haiti* (New York: St. Martin's Press, 1989).
17. See Hurbon, *Le Barbare imaginaire*.
18. Murphy, "Black Religion and 'Black Magic'," 334.
19. Alfred Métraux, *Voodoo in Haiti*, trans. Hugo Charteris (New York: Schockon, 1972), 64.
20. Ibid., 65.
21. Hurbon, *Le Barbare imaginaire*, 263.
22. Karen Brown, *Mama Lola: A Vodou Priestess in Brooklyn* (Berkeley: University of California Press, 1991).

23. In contrast, see Barber's discussion of the role of self-made, or "big," men within Yoruba political structures for an example of how demonstrations of unrelenting authority and force can be seen as expressions of the protective power necessary to attract followers in reciprocal relationships, which mirror those of the òrisà (Yoruba gods) and their devotees. Karin Barber, "How Man Makes God in West Africa: Yoruba Attitudes toward the Òrisà," *Africa* 51, no. 3 (1981): 724–745.

24. In the past, participatory and self-positional, or reflexive, methods in anthropology were not generally validated. In *Voodoo in Haiti*, Métraux describes Hurston as "very superstitious" (281). And there is continued resistance within the discipline to reflexive, dialogical approaches to fieldwork and the ethnographic text. For a discussion of critical reactions to *Mama Lola*, see Karen Brown, "Writing about the Other," *Chronicle of Higher Education*, 15 April 1992, A 56.

25. Zora Neale Hurston, *Tell My Horse*, 1938, reprinted in *Zora Neale Hurston: Folklore, Memoirs, and Other Writings* (New York: Library of America, 1995). Katherine Dunham, *Island Possessed* (Chicago: University of Chicago Press, 1969).

26. Dunham, *Island Possessed*, 198.

27. Gérard Etienne, *La Reine soleil levée* (Montreal: Guérin Littérature, 1987). The unscrupulous oungan who drains the resources of the poor is a stock character in much Haitian fiction, especially the "peasant novel," now almost obsolete. See Léon-François Hoffman, "The Haitian Novel during the Last Ten Years," *Callaloo* 15, no. 3 (1992): 761–769; Jean-Baptiste Cinéas, *Le Drame de la terre* (Port-au-Prince: Les Editions Fardin, 1932); Pierre Marcelin and Philippe Thoby-Marcelin, *The Beast of the Haitian Hills*, trans. Peter Rhodes (San Francisco: City Lights Books, 1986); Edris Saint-Armand, *Bon Dieu rit* (Paris: Hatier, 1988). *La Reine Soleil Levée* is considered by Hoffman to be a "proletarian novel" that continues the tradition of naturalistic depiction of the poor, who are now displaced from the land to the urban slums.

28. Etienne, *La Reine soleil levée*, 32.

29. bell hooks, "Altars of Sacrifice: Re-Remembering Basquiat," *Art in America*, June 1993, 68–75. Reprinted in bell hooks, *Art on My Mind: Visual Politics* (New York: New Press, 1995).

30. bell hooks, *Yearning: Race, Gender, and Cultural Politics* (Boston: South End Press, 1990).

31. Suzanne Preston Blier, *African Vodun: Art, Psychology and Power* (Chicago: University of Chicago Press, 1995), 31.

32. First card reading, 5 February 1992.

33. According to Brown (*Mama Lola*), increasing and sustaining luck is a central goal of most healing work in Vodou. Good luck is not left to chance; it requires active vigilance and intervention against ever-present sources of affliction.

34. First card reading, 5 February 1992.

35. Interview with Clotaire Bazile, 3 November 1993.

36. Interview with Virgil Young, 12 October 1993.

37. Interview with Clotaire Bazile, 3 November 1993.

38. Ibid.

39. Leslie G. Desmangles, *The Faces of the Gods: Vodou and Roman Catholicism in Haiti* (Chapel Hill: University of North Carolina Press, 1992).

40. Benson suggests that "many paintings of this period…should be understood not simply as depictions but as oblations and invocations." LeGrace Benson, "Kiskeya-Lan Guinée-Eden: The Utopian Vision in Haitian Painting," *Callaloo* 15, no. 3 (1992): 730. Painting is comparable to the ritual act of drawing vèvè on the ground to call the spirits. Andre Pierre is known as the "singing painter" because he sings to the lwa as he works and receives visions of how they want to appear. Michel

Monnin, "Andre Pierre le peintre chantant," in *Haïti: Art naïf, art vaudou* (Paris: Galeries Nationales du Grand Palais, 1988).

41. Interview with Martha Henry, 18 January 1994.

42. Interview with Candice Russell, 16 January 1994.

43. See Brown's *Mama Lola* and Elizabeth McAlister's "Sacred Stories from the Haitian Diaspora: A Collective Biography of Seven Vodou Priestesses in New York City," *Journal of Caribbean Studies* 9, nos. 1/2 (1993): 10–27.

44. Alex-Louise Tessonneau, "'Le Don reçu en songe': La Transmission du savoir dans les métiers traditionnels (Haïti)," *Ethnographie* 79, no. 1 (1983): 69–82.

45. See Maya Deren, *Divine Horsemen: The Living Gods of Haiti* (1953), reprint, Kingston, N.Y.: McPherson, 1970, 1983, and Gerdes Fleurant, "The Ethnomusicology of Yanvalou: A Study of the Rada Rite of Haiti" (Ph.D. diss., Tufts University, 1987).

46. Robert Farris Thompson, "From the First to the Final Thunder: African-American Quilts, Monuments of Cultural Assertion," preface to Eli Leon, *Who'd a Thought It: Improvisation in African-American Quilting* (San Francisco: San Francisco Craft and Folk Art Museum, 1987), 21.

47. Freida Tesfagiorgis, review of *Black Art, Ancestral Legacy: The African Impulse in African-American Art*, ed. Robert V. Rozelle, Alvia J. Wardlaw, and Maureen A. McKenna. *African Arts* 25, no. 12 (1992): 41–53.

48. The Haitian term *oungan* is derived from the Fon *hungan* (chief of the hun). In her discussion of the meanings of the Fon term *hun*, Blier (*African Vodun*, 47) emphasizes those associated with action and movement, like blood, drum, bellows.

49. The collector and expert on the ritual flag Susan Tselos has indicated to me that on some of the embellished flags from the 1930s the vèvè is not framed and highlighted by distinct borders and color contrast. However, the features I noted do appear on ritual flags from the 1940s and 1950s in other collections. A documented history of the form has yet to be written.

50. Interview with Clotaire Bazile, 3 November 1993.

La Regla de Ocha

MIGUEL BARNET

The Religious System of Santería

THE MIDDLE of the sixteenth century witnessed the first arrival in Cuba of large numbers of slaves brought from Africa to work the coffee, produce, and sugar plantations around which the colony's enterprise revolved. Basely kidnapped from the coasts of the Gulf of Guinea and the jungles of the intricate Congo, they were lucrative commodities in the most cruel and inhuman exchange known to history: the slave trade. Under the whip of the Spanish master, and later of the Creole sugar autocrat, these slaves, taken from diverse places in Africa, would nonetheless impose their culture on the island. Among them, those from sub-Saharan West Africa, particularly the Yorubas, wielded the greatest influence in the process of integration into Cuba's cultural and religious systems, succeeding most quickly in holding sway over other African cultures established here long before their arrival. It is fundamental, therefore, in any attempt to characterize the divinities of the African religious systems, as well as their rituals and liturgies, to isolate cultural patterns of Yoruba origin as pivotal factors.

Elements of Yoruba culture, superstructurally much richer than the others, served as paradigms for the birth and adaptation of transcultural expressions that are still today an integral part of Cuba's cultural legacy. Yoruba mythology, comparable to the Greek in philosophical richness and poetic values, is the only solid body of ideas about the creation of the world that Cuba can boast as a legacy of traditional popular culture. This mythology—transplanted to Cuba at various historical moments, more continuously and intensely during the increase in the slave trade that marked the heyday of the sugar industry at the end of the eighteenth and beginning of the

79

nineteenth centuries—underwent crucial alterations when it clashed against other African religious forms and Catholicism. A syncretism emerged spontaneously, establishing new cosmogonic values and setting new correlations between Yoruba divinities and Catholic saints, *santos*. Its product was a complex religious system known as *Santería*, whose beliefs and ritual structures rest on the veneration of the *orichas* of the Yoruba pantheon of Nigeria as identified with their corresponding Catholic saints. This religion, perhaps as widespread in Cuba as the popular hybrid *espiritismo*, is founded on the concept of a superior triumvirate of *Olofi*, *Oloddumare*, and *Olorun*, who have authority over the rest but are not the object of direct adoration or worship, as is the case with the orichas, its subjects and messengers on earth. These orichas, directly and tangibly worshipped and not invested with abstract qualities or aristocratizing categories, intercede for people before Olofi through the supreme judge or principal messenger, *Obbatalá*, and can reward or punish them according to the conduct they exhibit in everyday life.

Pierre Fatumbi Verger, in his *Orixás*, cites Leo Frobenius as declaring in 1899 that the religion of the Yorubas became homogeneous, as it is represented nowadays, only gradually. Its uniformity is the result of progressive adaptations and amalgamation of beliefs from various sources.[1] Today, Verger contends, there is still no set, established hierarchy of the pantheon of the orichas throughout the territory known as Yoruba. Local variations attest to certain orichas occupying a dominant position in some areas while being totally absent in others. The cult of *Changó*, foremost in Oyó, is officially nonexistent in Ifé, where a local god, *Oramfé*, occupies his place, being endowed with the power of thunder. *Ochún*, whose worship is significant in the region of Ijexá, is absent from the religion of Egbá. *Yemayá*, sovereign of the region of Egbá, is not even known in Ijexá. The relative position of all these orichas is profoundly dependent on the history of the cities of which they figure as protectors. During his lifetime Changó was the third king of Oyó. Ochún made a pact with Laró, the founder of the local dynasty of kings in Exogbo, and, in consequence, water is always abundant in this region. Odudua, founder of the city of Ifé, whose sons became kings of the other Yoruba cities, retained a more historical and political than divine character. We will see below that those who evoke Odudua are not possessed or mounted by the oricha, which underscores his temporal character.

Moreover, according to Verger, an oricha's place in the social organization can vary greatly according to whether we are talking about a city where there is a royal palace (*àlafin*) occupied by a king (*aládé*) who has the right to wear a crown (*adé*) with rows of pearls hiding his face, or where there is a palace (*ilé Olójà*) that is home to the merchant potentate of the city, whose chief, a *balé*, can claim only a more modest crown called *àkòró*. In both cases the oricha contributes to reinforcing the power of the king or chief, being essentially at his disposal to guarantee and defend the stability and continuity of the dynasty and to protect its subjects. But in the independent villages, where civilian power remains weak, in the absence of the (authoritarian) state, the impact of traditional religions is very strong, and the fetishist chiefs guarantee social cohesion.

Some orichas are objects of a worship that extends throughout the entirety of the Yoruba territories—as for example, the cult of *Orìsàálá*, also called Obbatalá, divinity of creation, extends to the neighboring territory of Dahomey, where Orìsàálá becomes *Lisa* (and his wife, *Yemowo*, becomes *Mawu*, the "supreme god" of the Fon people), or even Oggún, god of the ironsmiths and of all those who work with iron, whose importance, in terms of functions, surpasses that of the original familial group. Some divinities share the same attributes in different places: Changó in Oyó, Oramfé in Ifé, Aira in Savé, are all lords of thunder. Oggún has competitors, warriors and hunters, in diverse places, such as *Ija* in the environs of Oyó, *Osóòsì* in Keto, *Ore* in Ifé, as well as *Lògunède*, *Ibaùalámo*, and *Erinlè* in the region of Ijexá. *Osayìn* among the Oyó fulfills the same role of healer as does *Elèsije* at Ifé. *Aje Saluga* in Ifé and *Osùmàrè*, more to the west, are divinities of riches. The case of *Naná Burukú*, or *Brukung*, merits separate mention. This divinity is the supreme goddess of the regions to the west of the Yoruba countries, her worship extending to more distant areas where Ifé is less influential, despite the existence of villages known as Añá or Ifé, and where the cult of Obbatalá (and Orisàálá) is totally unknown. Given the extreme diversity and countless variations among the orichas, overly structured conceptions are unconvincing.

The religion of the orichas is linked to the notion of family—an extended and numerous family, originating in one sole ancestor, encompassing the living and the dead. Out of this system of tribal or familial lineage emerges a religious brotherhood involving godfather and godchildren in a kinship that transcends blood connections to form an all-inclusive and compact horizontal lineage. This family system has been one of the most genuine characteristics of Santería in Cuba. The godmother or godfather becomes mother or father of a brood of children, forming a group popularly known as a *línea de santo*, a line or lineage of initiates. The oricha is, in principle, a divinized ancestor who during his lifetime established connections guaranteeing him control over certain forces of nature—thunder, wind, fresh or salt water—in addition to the possibility of carrying on certain activities like hunting, metallurgy, and utilizing knowledge of the properties and uses of plants. The power, *aché*, of the ancestor oricha confers on him, after his death, the faculty of temporarily incarnating into one of his descendants during the phenomenon of possession.

The path from earthly life to the condition of oricha of those exceptional beings, possessors of a powerful aché, is crystallized, as Verger has argued, in a
moment of passion preserved as legend. Changó was the object of such a mu-
tation when one day, enraged at having destroyed his palace and all those belonging to him, he climbed a hill in Igbeti, near the ancient Oyó, and
experimented with the effectiveness of a preparation intended to generate a
bolt of lightning. In another legend, Changó was transformed into an oricha,
or *ebora*, in a moment of irascibility when, feeling forsaken, he left Oyó to
return to the region of Tapá. Oyá, his first wife, accompanied him in his flight
and later, after Changó's disappearance, went underground. His other two
wives, *Ochún* and *Oba*, became rivers bearing their names when they fled, terrorized by the fulminating wrath of their common husband. Oggún became
an oricha when he understood that he had just massacred in a moment of
irreflexive ire all the inhabitants of the city of Ire, founded by him. Years later,
when he returned, he was not recognized.

These divinized ancestors did not die a natural death, understood in
Yoruba as the abandonment of the body by breath. Possessors of a very potent aché and exceptional powers, they underwent a metamorphosis in a moment of emotional crisis provoked by wrath or other violent emotion. What
was material in them disappeared, burned by that passion, and only the aché
remained—power in a state of pure energy. The oricha, as Verger has explained, is pure form, immaterial *àse*; orichas can become perceptible to humans only when incorporated in them through possession. The human being
chosen by the oricha, one of his descendants, is called *elégùn*, the one who
has the privilege of being "mounted" (*gùn*) by him. The elégùn becomes the
vehicle that allows the oricha to return to the earth to greet and receive the
marks of respect of the descendants that invoke him. The oricha, a divinized
ancestor, is a family heirloom passed on through the paternal line. The heads
of the great families, the balé, generally delegate the responsibility for worshipping the family oricha to a male or female *aláàse*, guardian of the power
of the god, who cares for it with the assistance of the elégùn, who is possessed
by the oricha under certain circumstances. The women of the family participate in the ceremonies and can become the elégùn of the paternal family's
oricha, but if they are married, their children's oricha is that of their husband's
family. Thus their position in the husband's family is somewhat marginalized.
They are considered solely as donors of children and are never totally integrated into their new home. An individual, bound by filiation to the worship
of the family oricha, can, under certain conditions indicated through divination, worship a different divinity—that of his wife after her death, for example,
or any other imposed in consequence of specific situations: ailments, difficulties in the procreation of an heir, the need to forestall a specific or indetermi-

nate threat. In such cases, the individual is involved more directly than normally in this personal veneration. One of the characteristics of the religion of the orichas is its spirit of tolerance and the absence of all proselytizing, understandable in view of the fact that each of these cults is restricted to the members of certain families.

Santería, known more rigorously as the Regla de Ocha, or religious system of the Ocha, boasts an eclectic pantheon of divinities who must be frequently gratified and appeased with festive ceremonies. In principle, a key element for practitioners of this religion is the respectful worship of the orichas through veneration, feeding, and the ritual observance of all the consecrated dates of the liturgy. This religion of the Yoruba or Lucumí—as these groups are popularly and arbitrarily known in Cuba, thanks to an allegory about a supposed port of Ulkami or Lucumí in the south of Nigeria—exerts its strongest influence on the population of Havana and Matanzas. Its rituals, music, symbolism, and vast mythological and hagiographic wealth testify to the complexity of its system. Worship of the saints, adoration of the orichas, no name is more suitable than that given by the people to this widespread Afro-Cuban cult: Santería.

The foundation or focus of Cuban Santería, as in Nigeria among the Yoruba, is the stone (*otá*) where the magic attributes of the powers (natural forces of deities) reside. These stones, generally round and polished river stones, are the containers of each of the divinities, and the practitioners must have them in their possession, at least during major rituals. The highest echelon in the hierarchy of Santería is occupied by the *olúo*, who, like the Roman emperors, must have surpassed the age of sixty, thus guaranteeing a level of maturity and experience, and the concomitant degree of intuition necessary for making predictions without the mediation of any system of divination of a material kind. But the olúo is a rare category, almost nonexistent today. In remote times, the olúos, or *olúwos,* were the foremost leaders of the community of *babalaos.* But this arrangement, a legacy from the Empire of Oyó, gradually lost its force, and the olúo's role was somewhat reduced to that of master in divination, the highest in the hierarchy. In the divination ceremonies to learn the *letra del año,* or "letter of the year," one of the main functions of the Regla de Ocha, with all of the public duty it entails, the olúo had the last word. He was the legitimate owner of secrets.

But the true ruler in Santería, because of his function as diviner, is the babalao, possessor of the attributes granted by *Orula,* god of divination, for the execution of the rituals of prophecy through the use of the *tablero of Ifá,* a series of configurations drawn on special sawdust in accordance with the casting of the *opele,* or *okuele,* chain. The babalaos introduced the Ifá system of divination once Santería took hold in Cuba, and on this basis other means of divination, such as *dilloggún*, similar in complexity and richness to the tablero of Ifá were introduced. The system of dilloggún is truly a Cuban creation, as are many other attributes of Santería, bolstering my claim that the roots of the religion may be African but its development is indeed Cuban. It remains a living and eloquent reminder of the African element so dominant in Cuban culture.

The babalao or *iyalocha*—that is, the santero or santera, equivalent in Brazil to the *pae* or *mae* of the santo—who is in charge of specific liturgies, among them that of divination through the means of shells or dilloggún, occupies a central place in the hierarchy of Santería. These "hierarchs" perform almost daily the task of introducing the *aleyos*—semi-initiates—and official practitioners to knowledge of the Yoruba mythology and its complementary rituals. Their lives are entirely dedicated to the cult of the santos and revolve around their idolatrous worship, the observance of their taboos and gratification of their whims, and the performance of religious rituals closely bound to material life. Illnesses, changes in the standard of living, threatening situations, love tribulations—everything yields to the willful designs of the orichas, who communicate their prophecies or revelations through any of the three fundamental divination systems of the Regla de Ocha: the *obi*, or coconut split in four parts—the most primitive; the dilloggún shells; and the tablero of Ifá, more prestigious but not necessarily of greater efficacy than the other two.

Anyone officiating at these complex ceremonies must be an expert. In fact, the master in the knowledge of dilloggún—known as the *oriaté*—is an individual, deemed worthy of the highest respect, to whom the hierarchs of the cult submit themselves, particularly in any matter related to the deciphering of some mystery or sortilege in the everyday life of aleyos or officiating priests. The oriaté is, moreover, the leader of the most important ceremonies of Santería, the true guide in the procedures of divination and initiation. An oriaté must be a genuine mentor, a teacher of all the steps taken by people before and after receiving the powers of an oricha or becoming official santeros.

Divination is the pivot of Santería. As in the Greek rituals of Eleusis, the Lucumí initiation ceremonies are ruled by the verdict of the gods, who determine, through the tablero de Ifá, whether a person is or is not to receive the aché, or divine grace, that will entitle him or her to proceed in the liturgical continuum that characterizes Santería. The rituals of Santería are ruled by the will of the orichas, even the right to wear sacred beads,* *guerreros*, or officially to initiate oneself by "receiving" on one's head the santo of one's

---

* Every oricha has a representative color or combination of colors that his or her devotee wears in the form of beads strung around the neck or occasionally as a bracelet. [Trans. note.]

paternal legacy. Nothing can be fulfilled in the life of the practitioner without the orichas' decree or consent; nor has the believer the right, without their sanction, to specific religious attributes.

The santos, when they are received or "settled" (*asentados*), become new members of the dwelling or house temple. They become its owners. Nothing can be done in it without first consulting them through the instruments of divination—the *registro*, or consultation, utilized by the Regla. The family and all who enter the dwelling must show consideration and respect to the santos and ancestors, whom the santero must greet every morning. Each one of the santos is sustained by a body of legend, or *pwatakis*, collected in the traditional notebooks of Santería, a sort of manual for the organization and preservation of religious traditions from generation to generation.

Foremost among the various ceremonies in Santería are those dedicated to a particular santo. They can convey a feeling of joy and gratitude toward specific santos as well as feelings of displeasure or dissent. Displeasure is occasionally expressed through the *cantos de puya*, prodding songs. There are also well-attended feasts of amusement, of absolute merriment, in which all participate equally and which the Lucumís called *bembés* or *wemíleres*. In this presumptively profane feast the sacred *batá* drums cannot be used; instead, the *güiros* or *ábwes* (carved gourds) are played, always accompanied by an iron instrument in the shape of a bell without a clanger, known as the *aggogó*, or, simply, by a *guataca* leaf. The batá, used for sacred ceremonies, initiations, or the birthday of a santo, are the *iyá*, or mother, which is the largest; the *itótele*, or medium drum; and the *okónkolo*, the smallest and most sonorous. These drums are offered food because they bear within them a spirit or semigod who possesses a magic secret, *añá*, which the drums' players and builders refuse to reveal. The enervating beat of the batá drums ceases at dusk, when the drums retire to the secret chamber, or *igbodú*, where they will rest until the next occasion, to be taken out only in the light of the sun. The ábwes follow immediately, signaling the beginning of the semiprofane or sacred feast, which will continue without set limit until past midnight. The worship of the sun is important to the Yoruba, which may be why the batá drums have been accorded the privilege of beating during the day. This practice probably hints at some ancient adoration of the god *Olorun*—the sun itself—in remote eras of Yoruba culture. The quintessential liturgical beat is known among the Lucumí as *oru*.

According to Fernando Ortiz, in the temples, or *ilé oricha*, there were three special and distinct chambers: the *igbodú*, the *eyá aranla*, and the *iban baló*.[2] The first corresponds to the sacred chamber; the second to the great *sala*, or hall, of the dwelling; the third to the patio or court, a place where nefarious forces represented by animals and ritual plants appear. The oru, or set of beats with a fixed sequence, is produced in the sacred chamber, with drums; in the salas, *moyunbando* takes place—that is, proffering invocations a cappella; in the patio invocations are proffered with drums and chorus. Almost all the oru begin with an invocation of the drums. The first divinity invoked is *Eshu Elegguá*, god of the roads and the future, the one who opens and shuts all doors and designates all crossroads. As a result of the external stimuli, a variety of interesting phenomena—gesticulation, attitudes associated with fanaticism— are exhibited in the course of the oru. Fanaticism is illustrated by the phenomenon of possession, common to all Afro-Cuban cults and of particular importance in Santería.

A possessed is a person who receives a god; the god mounts his "horse"— that is, the person's body—and forces him into contortions and gestures that characterize the deity. By the same token the possessed can dance or sing with formidable virtuosity, always, of course, in representation of that god. The god descends on the head of his *omó* (child), holding him prey to his most absolute will, forcing him to act involuntarily. This phenomenon is the result of a sort of conditioned reflex with origins in the ceremonies of initiation. The individual is conditioned to a social environment and functions in response to outside stimuli. It is rare for a stranger or someone who has never had any link to these cults to be possessed. In such cases the result has been a truly grotesque phenomenon, imitative, characterized by a completely prefabricated theatricality. Previous awareness is critical for any type of manifestation of possession to occur. Those who are entitled to be possessed by a santo and who succeed in faithfully interpreting the santo's gestures and character immediately attain a higher level of power within the social milieu where these cults are practiced. Possession thus plays as much a social and representational as a religious function because it entails the will to represent an archetype. This archetype is profoundly bound to the identity of the person who deliberately chooses to assume the traits and attributes of the deity. I believe, also, that in many cases possession attests to the determination to be something different, to assume an identify that links the possessed to the native culture. The external stimuli, like the stars, influence but do not compel. The possessed are also the bearers of a faith that makes it possible for them to become the docile "horses" of the santos who want to take possession of them.

Among the ceremonies—initiation; *itutú*, or death; *agwán*, where food is offered to Babalú Ayé; *pinaldo*, where the right to use sharp weapons to kill four-legged animals is obtained; *kofá*, where the special power of Orula is received—the *day of the drum* stands out, the day in which the person who has received a santo offers himself to the batá drum, owned by Changó, and dances before it in recognition of its significance within the cult. This ritual complex has several unique characteristics. In particular, it is one of the occasions on which a large number of people gather in the dwelling temple to witness a ceremony. The newly initiated, in ritual dress, make a ceremonial presentation before their brethren on a day marked by uncertainty and surprise. On this day all acknowledge the initiates and await their possession, the manifestation that they are truly under the protection of a santo.

Alive within the sociological body that is Santería, as its feeding cells, are the divinities that form the Lucumí pantheon. I say Lucumí and not Yoruba because I wish to clearly establish that these divinities have been transculturated and constitute a hybrid set of new forms, even if the original Yoruba elements remain dominant. In the natural and spontaneous syncretic process that began the instant the first African established parallels between African divinities and the Catholic saints, Yoruba traits were decisive in fixing the conditions of such correlations. In the face of the repressive imposition of the Catholic Church, which acknowledged no other religion, African blacks set into motion a most complex sociological phenomena when they syncretized their divinities with the Catholic saints—a give-and-take of elements and attributes that nonetheless did not alter the basic concepts transplanted from Africa.

Alluding to this syncretism, Mexican sociologist Carlos Echánove argues that if Santería lacks an explanatory theory for the aforementioned syncretisms, it does have one with respect to the almost exclusive cosmic actions of the santos. Santería has felt obliged to ask itself what happened to the sole Catholic God of the religion found in Cuba and imposed on the African immigrants, and replies thus: Olofi (also the name of a primary Mexican deity) created the world, which was initially populated solely by santos; later he distributed his powers among them (that power is the aché) so that he need not interfere at all in human fate. That is the function of the santos. Thus in santero ceremonies Olofi is seldom invoked (he is mentioned only briefly in a litany at the end), while the orichas are called on frequently.[3] The theoretical difficulties thus set aside, Santería can dedicate itself entirely to the worship of the santos. They, in fact, govern as much the extrahuman cosmos as the fate of people. Hence their extraordinary importance.

The santos number eighteen or nineteen, but the most frequently mentioned and worshipped in Santería are fewer than half that number. Much has been said about the number of divinities and of their importance or hierarchy, although nothing is categorical. Four hundred and five divinities have been identified in Nigeria, whereas in Cuba they do not exceed thirty. The passage of time has eroded the Yoruba pantheon, and many santos worshipped in the nineteenth century are almost unknown to practitioners today. However, ongoing syncretism has atomized elements of old deities and incorporated others from religions of Bantú origin or from Catholicism itself. Divinities who occupied an important place in the Yoruba pantheon of Nigeria, like

Odduá, for example, have been nearly lost in Cuba; some who had not been tutelary gods gained primacy and are today the object of preferential worship. This process of accrual and loss typifies the transfer of elements from one culture to another and gives evidence of the permeability of a religion when, forced not so much by sociological as by ecological circumstances, it has to adjust to a new environment.

In Nigeria, among the Yoruba, life is ruled by the will of the gods. "The gods are capricious and dissatisfied," Esteban Montejo said.* And these gods brought their value system, their attributes and characteristics to Cuba. In addition they adapted to or, better yet, they were adopted by humans; but in general they gained less than they lost. As Ortiz has observed, the Yoruba gods remind us frequently of the Hellenic pantheon.[4] Their hagiography is extraordinarily rich. Their avatars or *caminos* are so diverse and encompass so much history that it would be almost impossible to attempt to explain the origin of all those attributed to each divinity. These variations in the personalities of the orichas, these caminos or avatars, are almost entirely the result of a combination of factors: the dissimilar historical stages in which their lives unfolded, armed struggles that brought together different cultures and resulted in ongoing syncretism, different lands of origin, a deity's being forced by warfare to move to another place where he tried to resume his rule, different ritual observances in various groups, and other reasons still unstudied.

A significant component of Santería, as Echánove explains, is the belief that the santos manifest themselves on certain occasions—such as the initiation of a santero or the consecration of a priest—during which they descend on some of the worshipers.[5] This belief again brings to the fore how directly the Yoruba cult is linked to reality and how close people are to the orichas, who represent themselves through men and women. Assuming the garb of mortals, speaking through them, the gods of Santería exert an absolute and definitive authority over people in living and real dialogue.

LET US look now at some of the basic characteristics of the Lucumí divinities most favored in Cuba: Elegguá, Ochosi, Oggún, Orula, Changó, Yemayá, Obbatalá, Oyá, Ochún, and Babalu Ayé. Relegated to a second plane of relevance are Oba, Oricha Oke, Naná Burukú, the Ibbeyi, Inle, Aggayú Solá, Yegguá, and Osaín.

Let us begin with *Eshu Elegguá*. The importance of this divinity is indisputable. All the Lucumí ceremonies begin with an incantation, either in song

* Montejo is the protagonist of Miguel Barnet's testimonial novel *Biografía de un cimarrón* (1966), 3d ed. (Havana: Letras Cubanas, 1993), translated into English by Jocasta Innes as *The Autobiography of a Runaway Slave* (London: Macmillan Caribbean, 1993). [Trans. note.]

or by means of three knocks on some surface, to request his permission to initiate the practitioners. Elegguá has always held a privileged position. Ruler of the roads in worship, he opens or closes paths, indicates the crossroads, and is master, in some sense, of the future, the hereafter. One must consult with him about any step planned in life, especially if it involves travel or initiative. If any offering is to be made to any santo, he has to be served first, whether the offering is one of money or simply food. He is also happiness, joviality. He is fond of mischievous pranks, of playing with believers; but he can be at the same time an implacable judge who applies the most severe punishment to those who fail to fulfill his commands. He lives in a stone, in a shell, on the branch of a bush, in wooden dolls, or in an artifact resembling a pear, a mas of cement with eyes and mouth made of shells. This cement mass is an anthropomorphic artifact that is frequently present in the houses of santeros. Sometimes it is camouflaged behind a curtain or shawl or is simply replaced with a doll made of ceramic, porcelain, or bisque. Elegguá, Oggún, and Ochosi form the triumvirate of the warrior santos. The three are always together. They live in a small house, placed by believers behind the street door, and act as guardians of the house. In fact, one of Elegguá's main functions is that of guardian, although according to legend he was a diviner and gave the tablero of Ifá to Orula, who is its present master.

Argeliers Léon has written about this jesting and mischievous santo. Elebwa (as he prefers to write his name) combines the social and economic contradictions of humble people—from the slaves to those who found protection in these religious forms at later stages of Cuba's history.[6] Elebwa is sufficiently powerful to open a path—that is, to overcome the obstacles imposed on the dominated classes by the dominating class. At the same time, Elebwa protects and liberates believers from the burden of other demanding deities, like Orula and Obbatalá. Elebwa, with his elegant attire and congeniality at celebrations, represents the transcendence of the aspirations for liberation of the dominated classes. This is why Elebwa plays such an important role in Cuban Santería. He is identified with the Christ Child of Atocha, the *Anima Sola*, Saint Anthony of Padua, and lately with Saint Martin of Porres. He has countless avatars: *Echú, Aãguí, Beddún Bela, Belenke, Obi, Laroye, Sokere*. His sacred beads are red and black. Teodoro Díaz Fabelo has written of Elegguá that he rules the four corners of the world, the center, and all the paths, where he is always found in the guise of Echú.[7] He opens and closes all paths and doors, obeying solely his own most free will. Fate, the unexpected, forgetfulness, tragedy, good or bad luck, any sort of triumph, and even our own actions and hopes depend on Elegguá and Echú. He is indisputably the most influential of the Lucumí santos who have exerted their authority over Cuba.

Ochosi, a warrior, is one of those divinities of whom much is said but of whose history and attributes little is known. An old oricha, he stands guard at the entrance to the ilé. He is the representative of hunting and, like Oggún, is an expert hunter; his symbols are the bow and arrow. His colors are dark lilac, green, and black. He wears a tiger-skin cap and arrow pouch. His dance is rich in hunting pantomimes. He is the protector and saint of prisons; to have "letra de Ochosi," in popular slang, means to be on the path to jail or some impending difficulty with the law. It is said, moreover, that he was a magician and diviner in ancient Nigerian culture. Mythologically he is the son of Yemayá and brother of the herbalist and healer par excellence, Inle. His Catholic equivalent is Saint Norbert. He, Elegguá, and Oggún form the triumvirate of the warrior orichas.

Oggún is one of the oldest orichas of the Yoruba pantheon. Superior warrior, brother of Changó, he is always portrayed in the mythology as competing with him for the love of the beguiling Ochún, goddess of love and sex. Victor in the cruelest battles against Changó, he is a symbol of primitive force and terrestrial energy. He is mischievous and astute like Elegguá, but more willful. He is god of minerals, of iron, of the mountains Oggué (or Oké), and of the instruments of work. His symbols are cutlasses, shovels, hoes, chains, hammers, keys, and other objects of iron or metal. The *chirikirí*, or *alawedde*, a set of iron pieces kept in the house, also belongs to him. In Cuba he is identified with Saint Peter, who carries the keys to the kingdom of heaven. His colors are purple and green, and his dress boasts plenty of *mariwó*, vegetable fibers taken from plants from the mountains of the interior. In his pantomimic dance, he wields the cutlass, with which he clears the bush; he can be just as bellicose in war as in work. His sacred beads are purple and scarlet, or simply purple. He lives in the hills and has many avatars, but in the dwelling temple he is represented by a pot with all types of iron objects, sometimes simply by a horseshoe or a railroad spike. Himself a forger of metals, he is the protector of blacksmiths and all those who drive any type of vehicle with iron or steel parts, such as trucks and trains. According to Fabelo, through Oggún the ancient Yorubas represented the transition from the culture of nomadic hunters to that of sedentary planters.[8] Undoubtedly, he is one of the most complex divinities of Cuban Santería. Oggún, Ochosi, and Elegguá form the triumvirate of the warrior orichas.

Orula, Orunla, Orumila, or *Ifá*—these and other names could be given to this tutelary divinity in the pantheon of Cuban Santería. He is the master of the tablero of Ifá; he is the tablero itself, the master of divination, possessor of all concentrated magical powers, with mythological faculties for communicating people's future through his okuele chain and his tablero. He is respected and venerated, but there is hardly any dialogue with him because, like Olofi, he does not mount; he establishes his relationship of harmony solely with the babalao and with his *akpetebi*, or secretary, who invariably must be a daughter of Ochún. Wise, old, cantankerous, he exerts limitless power over the lives of the babalao and his clients. With a will of iron, tending to drastic decisions, this santo is one of the most beloved of Cuban Santería. About him there is a wealth of hagiography, above all because he speaks through the tablero, and his *oddú* or *letras* are always impeccably fulfilled. He is identified with Saint Francis of Assisi. His sacred beads alternate in green and yellow. To some practitioners, Orula is the true secretary of Olofi. Wisdom and intuition are recognized in this divinity, who appears as an old patriarch who sees all and knows all. Whoever wears an *irdé* (a bracelet of beads) on his wrist is supposed to possess his aché.

Changó is one of the most venerated santos of the cults of Yoruba origin in Cuba. To many he is the strongest and most important of the orichas. In Nigeria, as a brave king of the Oyó land, he occupied a primary place among the founders of the Yoruba kingdom. During his rule he won countless victories, which earned him the title of greatest Alafín of Oyó, boasted about throughout centuries by the highest hierarchs of that region. Alan Burns informs us that Changó was fourth king of Oyó, mythical king of the Yorubas, father of the nation, and its hero.[9] All legends present him as virile hero and warrior by definition. He is a womanizer and drinker, quarrelsome, courageous, and daring; made for challenges and dares, proud of his masculine virtues, boastful of his strength and manly beauty, *castigador* (a heartbreaker). When his name is pronounced, believers rise from their seats making a drinking gesture and thus salute and revere him. He is the god of music, master of the sacred batá drums, of thunder and lightning. He is a violent oricha, and his energy is manifested when he mounts his "horses," who when possessed whirl violently and thrash about. His refuge, throne, and vantage point is the royal palm. From this watchtower, his own home, he protects warriors, hunters, and fishermen. His colors are red and white, alternating in his secret beads. The double-edged ax is his principal attribute, as is the *palo mambó*, a hoe he carries in his left hand. Saint Barbara to santeros, Changó is an androgynous divinity. But nothing can undermine his manly pride and the unbeatable strength of a triumphant warrior that are his trademarks. A myth tells of how, when faced with a demoralizing defeat, he vanished right before the eyes of the astounded tribes. There was great clamoring in the land and a tempest of unequaled violence fell upon the people, with thunder and lightning. The Yoruba men felt fear and exclaimed, "Changó became an oricha!" Thus is explained, in a simple version, the deification of this god who is for his devotees an undoubtedly mortal man. His mortal condition is also attested to in a legend in which Changó had a palace made of brass with stables for ten thousand horses; after a ferocious struggle on earth he went to live in heaven, from where he governs the state, hunts, fishes, and marches forth to make war.

According to Frobenius, Changó is a mythical character, grandson of Aggayú (the desert or firmament) and descendant of *Okiskischeé*.[10] His father is *Orungan* (noon), his mother Yemayá (the mother of marine life), his favorite brothers are *Dadá* and Oggún, and his closest friend Oricha Oke. In many legends, with numerous variations, it is told how he commits incest with his mother, despite being the second son born of the womb of the goddess of maternity. Advocate of warriors, he repudiates the cowardly or pusillanimous child. Batá drums, a güiro (or *atcheré*) made of mud turtle, a Moorish horse are, among others, this god's favorite belongings. The sheep is his favorite animal, although roosters and bulls are also sacrificed to him. He throws flames from his mouth. The story is told that he swallowed fire and that lightning was born when he spewed it from his mouth as he spoke to the Yoruba people. He is feared and adored. In Nigeria worship of Changó is deeply rooted, and there are temples to this god of fire and music in many cities and small towns. His dancing pantomimes are unmistakably warlike and erotic. The erotic dances have come to acquire characteristic traits bordering on the most insolent sexuality. Present in almost all Yoruba legends, he is husband of the rivers Oyá (the warrior), Oba (the loyal one), and Ochún (the seductress), and is one of the tutelary gods.

Yemayá is the model of the universal mother and queen of the sea and of salt water. Her skirts of seven flounces announce the birth of man and of the gods. She is, to explain it in Hellenic fashion, the goddess of maternity. Her color is navy blue with some white, symbolizing the foam of the waves. On her sacred beads, seven blue beads alternate with seven white. Her dances are vivacious and undulating like sea waves; she is sometimes tempestuous and wild, sometimes calm and sensual, as when she appears in the avatar of *Asesú*. She is also the goddess of intelligence, of rationality; a harmonious personality characterizes her children. She is "jet black," the babalaos say, which is why she is compared to the Virgin of Regla, who also looks to the sea, toward the bay. Multiple legends tell of a diligent Yemayá, understanding toward her children and conciliatory. One of her most singular avatars is that of Olokún, herself a deity who lives at the bottom of the sea tied to a chain, the sight of whom can bring sudden death. Yemayá can be seen only in dreams because she covers her face with a mask of blue and white stripes. Sister of Ochún, favorite among the orichas, she is judgment and reason, but she can also be inflexible when she punishes. Majestic queen of the oceans, she is presumptuous and haughty. She protects her children in her skirt, feeds them, and raises them with absolute motherly rigor. Her emblem is the half moon, the anchor, and the silver or white-metal sun. In the tureen where she lives she also has a life preserver, seven stones (otá) gathered on the seashore, and fans with shells (cauris), also favored by her. Much has been said in the mythology about the incest she commits with her son Changó, but in some pwatakis Yemayá appears as Changó's favorite wife. She boasts a large arsenal of myths and legends and is respected by all believers, who, when she appears mounted on her horse with a *toque de santo* (the drumming that summons the gods to a ceremony), either as a haughty queen or a complacent mother, exclaim, "Oh, my Yemayá!"

Obbatalá is an androgynous god of Cuba because, like Changó, he can be syncretically represented with female attire. He is Our Lady of Mercy or the Holiest of Holy in the Catholic religion, and has special importance in the Regla de Ocha. Believers say that there are sixteen male and female Obbatalás. He is the god of purity and justice. He also represents truth, the immaculate, peace—hence his representation at times as a white dove—and wisdom. Obbatalá's first avatar is *Odúa*, in Nigeria the beginning and end, the earth and the sky. According to Verger, he is the duality earth/sea and earth/sky.[11] Odúa represents the earth, is the center itself, the axis of the earth, while Obbatalá is the sky. This duality is represented objectively in a calabash cut in two halves: the upper one, the sky, is Obbatalá; the lower one, the earth, is Odúa. Of him Ortiz has written, "Obbatalá is the celestial vault or superior gourd of the two in which the sphere was split, güiro or calabash of the world."[12] The animals emblematic of Odúa—a deity widely worshiped in Nigeria—like the deer, the elephant, and the dove, have been moved to Obbatalá's inventory, in a transcultural loan. This santo dresses all in white, his color, and he is kept on a high place, covered in cotton. He is sometimes fed meringue and coconut. In the temples of Santería stepping on cotton is prohibited, a prohibition that reminds us of the Christian interdiction against throwing away bread that has been left uneaten.* The avatars of Obbatalá are well defined in Cuba: *Odúa, Oba Moro, Ochagriñán*, and *Ayyagguna* are the principal and best known.

In the liturgy of Santería he is the head, birth, that which stands high, pure, and clean. For this reason, in the rites of initiation the color white is used as a symbol of what is born pure in life, and an *iyawó*, an initiate, spends an entire year dressed in white as a sign of being reborn to a new life within the Santería world. Obbatalá is the creator of the world, the beginning of everything. His symbolic utensil is the *iruke*, a fly whisk made of the tail of a white Arabian steed. He possesses many attributes: *aggogós* (chimes) of white metal, crowns of silver or white metal, elephant tusks, and others. Holy water belongs to him. According to certain versions he is the son of Olofi and his wife *Olodumlare*. His beads (*eleke*) are all white. He is an extremely rigorous

---

* Perhaps because both cotton and bread (the sacred host in Christian ritual) represent the deity. [Trans. note.]

santo. His devotees must behave well; they must not utter blasphemies, drink, argue, undress before anyone. Closely linked to Orula and Changó, Obbatalá, king of the world and principal head of Ocha, is a tutelary divinity within the Lucumí Olympus of Cuba.

Oyá is a severe divinity, related directly to the phenomenon of death, identified with Our Lady of the Candelaria and with Saint Theresa of the Infant Jesus. She is mistress of lightning and of the wind, and gatekeeper of the cemetery. She protects and cares for the dead and is herself the one who buries the dead. It is said that her children and protégés are less vulnerable to death than other people. Oyá is the rainbow and is represented by its seven colors, seven being her symbolic number. She "descends" seldom, but when she falls on a human head she generally arrives with strong, arrogant, and violent gestures, shaking her iruke, which is made of black horsehair. She is sister to Yemayá, Ochún, and Oba, who all fight over Changó, whom she sometimes draws away from the others and accompanies to battle, being a warrior by nature. According to mythology, Changó sometimes dresses in Oyá's clothes to fool his enemies and thus slip away or confront them cunningly. An accomplice of Changó in war, Oyá loves him but does not take care of him like Oba nor seduce him like Ochún, but rather displays her challenging personality, before which he generally surrenders in bewilderment. Her chants are grave, solemn, but of uncommon beauty; they almost always invoke justice or peace. Her sacred beads are deep scarlet red with black and white streaks. She is the mistress of copper. In Africa she is the goddess of the great river Niger and mistress of the hurricane winds and of lightning, with which she is said to conquer in battle. Together with Changó she inherited fire, and, like him, when angered, she breathes it out of her mouth. Oyá's fire, according to believers, is distinguished by being polychromous. In some Lucumí ceremonies, like that of itútu, meant to appease and refresh the dead, Oyá fulfills an important role. On the day a person dies, Oyá "descends" and shakes her iruke over the deceased's face as a signal of welcome to the cemetery. The dead must enter clean into the kingdom of Oyá (Yanza).

Ochún-Kolé is the possessor of all the virtues valued in women: coquettish, beautiful, fawning, affectionate, docile, and industrious; she is also a good dancer, sensuous, musical. She is one of those divinities whose paternity is claimed by many. She is mistress of the river, fresh water, gold, and honey. One of the largest and richest tributaries of the Niger River bears her name. Considered to be the Lucumí Aphrodite, she is goddess of sexual love and is identified with Cuba's patron Virgin, Our Lady of the Caridad del Cobre. Ochún asks in her dances "¡oñí!, ¡oñí!" ["honey!, honey!"], an aphrodisiac symbolic of sweetness, of delight, of the amorous essence of life. Her proper color is yellow, like the sandy shores of rivers. She is called with a chime (aggogó) of yellow metal, rung before the white and yellow soup tureen in which she lives. She prefers, among all animals, the haughty and beautiful peacock. An unconditional ally of the babalaos, secretary of Orula, she also possesses divining gifts which she no longer uses but which, as old blacks tell, she did in remote times.

Numerous anecdotes tell about this divinity's turbulent love affair with Changó, whom she seduces and captivates with her capricious talents. *Yeyé Cari*, as she is also called, is a symbol of the colonial mulatta, sensual and merry. She assumes the grace and elegance of the winner against Cupid; she is proud and uncivil, but on the avatar of *Iyammu* she is tranquil, profound, and grave. She lives in the sandy bottom of rivers, brushing her hair, which blends with the algae and the medusas. As Kolé, however, she lives on the roofs or cornices of houses and converses with the vulture, her favorite bird. This Ochún watches over the others and is the oldest, according to some. She works, embroiders, sews; she is always doing a domestic chore. In the avatar of *Panchágara*, however, she is irrepressible; a consummate prostitute, her mission is to wrest men away from all women, and with that in mind she does not spare any honey or gold, any erotic dance or swing of the hips.

Ochún is the protector of pregnant women; she is said to "protect the bellies" and is a goddess of powerful magnetism. She accomplishes all sorts of miracles with the calabash, which is her house and her lamp. She has, moreover, talents as a healer. It is said that she has always had a lot of money and that she keeps it together with her witch's paraphernalia within her sacred calabash. The shame she endured when her sister Yemayá caught her making love to Yemayá's husband Orula, the diviner, in a green calabash patch was so great that her daughters hate calabashes, which unsettle their stomachs and which the liturgy prohibits them from eating. In santero worship the lofty status attained by her is indisputable. Among the orichas she is one of the most venerated, perhaps the most easily and naturally adapted to Cuba, not only because of the syncretism of the patroness of Cuba, the Virgin of the Caridad del Cobre, and Ochún, but because she is thought to represent many Cuban women in her sensual grace and Creole mischievousness.

Babalú Ayé, Saint Lazarus among the Catholics, the Saint Lazarus of the crutches and dogs (*taewo* and *kiande*), is, together with Changó, one of the divinities whose worship has taken deepest root in Cuba. His mythology is somewhat confusing because although Babalú Ayé forms part of the Yoruba pantheon as a result of cultural clashes through which he came to be integrated into this culture, his true origin is Dahomean. More concretely, Babalú belongs to the *ewé-fon* (*adjá*), or *Arará*, culture, as it is known popularly in Cuba, a culture as confused and arbitrary as that of the Lucumí and Yoruba. He is the god of illness, miraculous yet severe and implacable toward those who do not obey him or forget to fulfill their promises. According to the pwatakis he was a traveler and womanizer who late in life contracted leprosy during his forays. He travels the world on his crutches preaching good habits and upstanding behavior, and receiving the veneration of all peoples. Accompanied by his loyal dogs, covered with sores and hunched over, he walks with difficulty, sounding the *tablillas de San Pedro* (three pieces of wood tied with a cord and made to sound together), which herald his arrival so that people can run away and avoid contagion. He dresses in jute cloth with strips of purple ribbon and carries the *ja*, or whisk of *corojo*-palm fronds. His characteristic herb is the ragwort-leafed centaury, with which he cleans and purifies the sick. His sacred beads are white streaked or striped with blue. He has several avatars—*Asoyí*, *Afreketé*, *Chapkuana*, and others. Chapkuana seems to have been the original and legitimate god of smallpox among the Yoruba, as recorded in their theogonic literature.

While some gods punish through madness, like Orula, or blindness, like Obbatalá, Babalú Ayé punishes and kills through gangrene, leprosy, and smallpox. All grains belong to him, as do women, whom he is supposed to counsel in love matters. He is also involved in deaths and is as wise as Orula and as just as Obbatalá. Many believers attest that not only is he the master of the chariot that takes the dead to the cemetery, like Charon in his boat, but also once the dead are in the cemetery, within its abodes, he greets them. Babalú Ayé's messengers are mosquitoes and flies, carriers of plagues and illnesses. Just as Ochún's children cannot eat calabash, Babalú Ayé's cannot eat toasted corn or corn flour unless they first offer a portion to the oricha.

The devotees of Saint Lazarus are given to flagellation. Every seventeenth of the month they dress in sackcloth, skirts for the women and pants or shirts with gold-colored buttons for the men. And on December 17, they fulfill a promise now traditional in Havana: they form a procession from a distant place, on foot, on their knees, almost crawling, pulling stones on chains, to the sanctuary of Lazareto, in the village of Rincón, where Saint Lazarus is worshipped. This sanctuary and leprosy hospital has witnessed the most spectacular acts of religious fanaticism in Cuba, lessened now with accessibility to free medical care for all under socialism.

Babalú Ayé, Saint Lazarus, he of the crutches, *Babá*, as his devotees affectionately call him, has inserted himself definitively in the religious traditions of the Cuban people. Arará or Yoruba, his origin is no longer of much concern. A transculturated divinity, he has become Cuban more by sustaining modifications in his worship than by preserving those characteristics that he brought to Cuba during slavery. Model of hybridity and fusion, Babalú Ayé maintains to this day a certain allure throughout the country.

THE SYNCRETIC PROCESS still taking place in Cuba is complex. The divinities had undergone politically and socially motivated symbiotic processes while still in Africa. Their very avatars are frequently the result of these interchanges, through which a deity loses value and becomes a demigod or a minor entity. Sometimes they keep the deity's name with additions, sometimes they assume different names; occasionally they lose attributes and remain as avatars who are worshipped unsteadily. In Cuba many divinities that belong to different tribes, of neighboring lands, have been integrated, while others have disappeared from the pantheon. Different theories proliferate about these avatars; one of them proposes that they are the incarnations of these gods in their mortal lives. But the theory that seems most historically accurate is that these entities are but local phenomena, geographically bound, who came to have a wider following, perhaps through a political and social process: a tribe imposes its god on another. This is perhaps an explanation of why some divinities gain prominence through transculturation and others lose it or grow weaker. In addition, the specific social situations that slaves faced in their new environment, in a new social and ecological reality, determined the rise of some divinities not preeminent in Africa. By the same process, others passed to a second plane, as I have already explained.

A hierarchical ordering of these divinities in relation to their powers and attributes is never definitive but is dependent on historical stages and the needs of the believers, which vary according to life-style; however, life under slavery, with the tangible presence of the bush, kept viable the divinities associated with those landscapes. Agricultural work, economic necessity, and precarious health had an impact on the preservation of Yoruba divinities like Elegguá, Babalú Ayé, Changó, Ochún, and gods of the *Monte*, healers and witches, like Inle and Osaín.

Other orichas are objects of worship and respected in Santería, but they belong to a second plane. For the believers they are bearers of magic, of spiritual powers, of hidden forces that they obey blindly. For some, these divinities occupy a preeminent space. I have put them on a second plane based on their popularity and not on their importance in specific cases: for a child of Aggayú Solá, just as for Inle's or Oricha Oke's children, these divinities occupy a fundamental space in their religious life; my ranking is purely a numerical and not a liturgical matter. Let us observe at a glance, then, some of the traits of these orichas of Santería's Olympus.

Oba is recognized as Changó's loyal and docile wife. She cut her ears in a hair-raising love sacrifice, so that he could eat *amalá* (flour) prepared with them. Domestic and diligent, she is a sad and silent oricha. She does not dance or sing because she does not mount. Her Catholic counterpart is Saint Rita, and she is sister to Ochún and Oyá. The royal poinciana tree belongs to her. *Oricha Oke* is the god of agriculture, protector of laborers and peasants. He does not dance either because he does not mount, thus he does not possess any characteristic miming gestures and is difficult to embody. He is master of the plow, lives on rooftops, and communicates with eagles and vultures. He is an old and highly respected androgynous santo, protector of the ill and "mother of the Saint Lazaruses"; he is said to protect the aged. Identified with Our Lady of Carmen, he has to be made many offerings and treated with subtlety because, as an old man, he is bothered by everything. He has been assigned an *ewé* origin, and many people from Santiago associate him with Saint Emile. His worship is limited in Cuba. The *Ibbeyi*, twins, are trans-culturated in Saint Cosmo and Saint Damien. They protect children, being children themselves. As sons of Changó, they vanquish others easily; their battles involve childish tricks and sharp wit. They are gluttons, lovers of sweets and of palm wine. They play mischievous tricks of all sorts. Obbatalá is known to spoil them. Like their father, they dress in white and red. *Inle* or Saint Raphael is the earth itself, physician of the bush, and expert healer. He can be a peasant or fisherman and is sometimes identified with Saint Ambrose. Coral and jet are his favorite stones. *Aggayú Solá* is Changó's recognized fa-ther, although since each santero has *su librito*, his notebook, some believe that he is the brother of the god of war and fire. He is the world's transporter like Saint Christopher of the Catholic faith; he is master of the gift of strength, which is why he protects longshoremen. He is also said to be master of the vast forests and their most powerful plants. *Yeggúa* is a female oricha. Virginal and chaste, she dresses in pastel colors, pinks and whites, and is close to Oyá and Babalú Ayé because she is a death-related divinity. She has been identi-fied with Our Lady of Montserrat and Our Lady of the Forsaken. Her image is that of a girl's skeleton. Few women are daughters of Yeggúa; those who are are absolutely forbidden marriage and must live a chaste and virginal life. If they do not follow that command, they are forever unhappy, according to Lucumí beliefs. *Osaín*, the mysterious herb healer, is the head herbalist, healer, and master of the secrets of the bush. He possesses the greatest knowledge of plants and their healing virtues. He is lame, one-eyed, and one-handed. He himself is a güiro, hanging on the threshold of the ilé oricha. He is identified with Saint Joseph, Saint Benito, or Saint Jerome. Lydia Cabrera's informants identified him with Saint Anthony Abad and Saint Silvester. According to some, Osaín, who has neither mother nor father, is St. Raymond the Unborn.[13] He appeared, he was not born. Like Ochosi, he is an expert hunter and has extraordinary hearing, even though he has only one ear. The güiro in which he lives is never absent in santo dwellings.

Other deities, lower in the hierarchy or less culturalized in Cuba, exist also in the complex world of Santería. Some of them are received in special ceremonies, with attributes that characterize them. They are so many that it is impossible to catalog them all in this brief space. These divinities are, among others, *Korin Koto, Boromú, Ayaó, Ogún Orí, Oggué, Ajá, Olosá, Aroni, Iroko,* and *Oroina.* Each one of these orichas underwent an adaptation to Cuban soil. Some of those who wielded the most influence among the Yoruba lost it in Cuba, and others who were only regional orichas acquired a greater importance.

WE HAVE ALREADY seen how these divinities have come to form part of Cuba's cultural legacy, some preserving original elements, others losing power and being deeply transculturized, but all of them part of the diverse pantheon of the Regla de Ocha that exists in Cuba. Today new syncretic processes contribute to form a different whole, a weaker and more complex product. These new phenomena indicate society's evolution toward new forms. A process of horizontal growth has undermined the theogonic basis of the Regla de Ocha. The old repositories of the liturgical mysteries have died, and the religion, because of large spiritual voids, has grown but without the necessary spiritual guidance or the knowledge previously treasured. New practices have generated a chaotic and unstoppable amalgam, leading practitioners into profound contradictions. But the religion of the orichas persists.

The richness of Santería's songs and dances, its mythology, and its permanent values of a purely aesthetic nature will remain. Its philosophical and cosmogonic patterns will also be validated in art and literature. Perhaps the divinities will occupy at some future time the place occupied today by those of the Greek and Roman pantheons. They will be legendary figures who will inspire writers and artists. The well of African religions in Cuba, its surface still vibrant with these divinities rising from its depth, will continue to overflow until only the faint echo of a chime will be heard, and it will be Ochún's bracelets or a nearly languid snort from Changó, exhaling the sacred fire from his mouth. Cuban Santería spreads throughout the world. Its extraterritoriality responds to the universal values that define it. *¡Moddú pue!*

Translated by Lizabeth Paravisini-Gebert

Notes

1. See Leo Frobenius, *The Origin of African Civilizations* (Washington, D.C.: Smithsonian Institution, 1899), and Pierre Fatumbi Verger, *Orixás* (Sao Paulo, Brazil: Círculo Do Livro de Sâo Paulo, 1975).
2. Fernando Ortiz, *Los tambores batá de los Yorubas* (Havana: Publicigraf, 1994).
3. See Carlos A. Echánove's *La "santería" cubana: Cultura, estilo y resistencia* (n.p., 1950). A microfilm copy of this text is available in the Caribbean collection of the University of Florida Library at Gainesville.

4. Ortiz, *Los tambores*.

5. Echánove, *La "santería" cubana*.

6. Argeliers Léon, *Música folklore: Yoruba, Banta, Abakua* (Havana: Ediciones del C.N.C., 1964).

7. Teodoro Díaz Fabelo, *Cincuenta y un pattakíes afroamericanos* (Caracas: Monte Ávila, 1983).

8. Ibid.

9. Alan Burns, *History of Nigeria* (London: Allen & Unwin, 1936).

10. Frobenius, *The Origin of African Civilizations*.

11. Verger, *Orixás*.

12. Ortiz, *Los tambores*.

13. Lydia Cabrera, *El monte* (1954; Havana: Letras Cubanas, 1993).

From *The Sacred Wild* to the City

HÉCTOR DELGADO

Santería in Cuba Today

THE FOLLOWING PHOTOGRAPHS are a living testimony to the legends and traditions that constitute a religion that has existed for more than five centuries of space and time: *Regla de Ocha*, or *Santería*. Regla de Ocha is documented in the texts of ethnographers such as Lydia Cabrera in *El monte* (*The Sacred Wild*, 1954) and Natalia Bolívar Aróstegui in *Los orishas en Cuba* (The orishas in Cuba, 1990). These images are a contemporary visual record of the worldview they describe.

Despite the fact that many elements of the rituals are normally kept secret, *santeros* and *santeras* from different sectors of Havana collaborated in this project in the hope of improving understanding between believers and the uninitiated. Here we can witness some of the ancient rites of mortals and the orishas, and the persistence of Santería in Cuban culture after thirty-five years of socialist revolution. Taken at the scene of the events in 1994, the photographs demonstrate the humble surroundings of participants from all strata of Cuban society who are united by an ancestral belief system that came to Cuba from the African continent and took root.

I am grateful for the cooperation provided by Félix (an *oriaté*) and Ana (an *iyalocha*) who opened the pathways and allowed me this rare opportunity.

Figure 10. An initiate rings Ochún's bell to greet the oricha.

Figure 11. A santero's altar.

Figure 12. Children following the tradition of their ancestors.

Figure 13. Violin playing in homage to Ochún.

Figure 14.　Offerings to the oricha.

Figure 15. Ellegguá: principal oricha, master of all the roads.

Figure 16. An oriaté (principal priest) blesses one of his godchildren.

Figure 17. An iyalocha.

Figure 18. An oriaté, using the shells, predicts the future of one of his godchildren.

Figure 19. A woman possessed by an eggún (the dead) cleanses a believer during a spiritual mass.

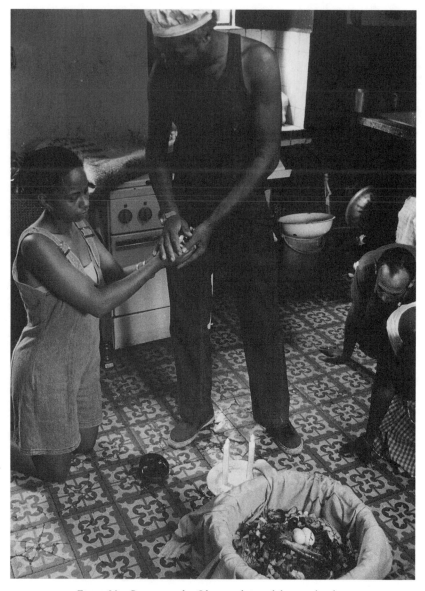

Figure 20. Ceremony for Olocun, deity of the sea depths.

Figure 21. A babalao (high priest of the Ocha) cuts the cake to be offered to the oricha.

Figure 22. Slaughter of animals to offer to Olocun.

Figure 23. Batá drums being played for the orichas.

Figure 24. An initiate in a state of possession.

Figure 25. A bembé (playing of drums for the santos).

Figure 26. Sacred ceremony where food is offered to the orichas.

Figure 27. Dancing to the beat of the batá drums.

Figure 28. Women in a convulsive state of possession.

Figure 29. Daughter of Ochún feted on her birthday.

From Monkey Tales
to Cuban Songs

JOSÉ PIEDRA   *On Signification*

SPANISH AMERICAN WRITERS represent the old inherited impositions and new self-imposed limitations of their national discourses. The resentment is not always exteriorized, for open dissent upsets the balance between overt means of cultural enslavement and hidden aims of apprentices enslaved by will or by force to seek official inscription. Originally, New World "others" bowed to a single European act: Spanish intervention. The historical implications of this intervention are negligible compared to the linguistic ones. The master code not only enslaved cultures during colonial times but also intervened in the signification of the language of independence. Imitation was a prerequisite for any form of national communication, including attempts at disavowal. The Spanish language thus perpetuated the rhetoric of a system which had become obsolete. Two options were left to Hispanic and Hispanicized dissenters: alienation, even official muteness and practical invisibility, or resentful acceptance of an uneasy compromise.

The best antidote for linguistic enslavement was to be found in fictional discourse. Mimicry of the master code, as projected in literature, could become officially tolerated, subtle mockery. Whereas the system imposed strict rules on signifiers, it was willing to enrich the ranks of signifieds with outside values. This form of linguistic gluttony reflected the typical practices of Hispanic acculturation: encouraging newcomers to contribute their own values to the presumably equitable colonial collage. Yet, if the historical imperatives behind acculturation aimed for total passive acceptance, the linguistic empire sought new subjects with a limited degree of active participation. Such a participation often was tongue-in-cheek. The history of Spanish American literature since colonial times testifies to the ironic partnership between history and literature.

Declarations of independence were accompanied by the emergence of literatures based on a mythology of compromise. White Hispanics, Hispanicized native Indians, and imported Africans united on the side of "otherness" without losing sight of the linguistic "one." Compromise consisted of a subtle balance between mimicking and mocking an oppressive code which had miscalculated the effects of reducing all the participant cultures into a Hispanic symbiosis. Refusing to compromise merely increased neglect of one's values, often rendered even more dependent on the master code as these values were turned into folklore—a trivial magnification of marginality.

The purpose of this study is to explore a variety of manifestations of the mythology of compromise. In spite of the wide range of manifestations, a central figure emerges: *el Mono*. This is an extraordinary Monkey, a literary figure hiding its essence to challenge the interpreters. Thus it appears under many guises, names, and cultural origins. Its most outstanding manifestations in Spanish America occur in Cuba, where the figure is particularly self-effacing. That quality is part of the Monkey's character: the richer and deeper the conveyed signification, the more hidden and contradictory the expression of its personality. As *Mono, Mo-Edun, Mono Sabio, Coco Macaco,* and *güije* or *jigüe*, the Monkey appears in Cuban discourse from oral tradition, as collected in anthropological works of Fernando Ortiz, Lydia Cabrera, and Samuel Feijóo, to the literary renderings by Alejo Carpentier, Nicolás Guillén, Severo Sarduy, and Miguel Barnet, among many.[1] The obvious sources for all of these Monkeys are African, but they also appear in the works of Jorge Luis Borges and Octavio Paz, who searched for theirs in Egyptian, Celtic, and Indian mythologies.

The Monkey stands for mediation and challenge because it appeases both colonialist mentalities and liberal consciences over the issue of marginal participation in the national discourse. Elitist Westerners might perceive the Monkey principle of esthetics as an incomplete mimesis of the official codes; others might view it as a New World effort to attain a syncretic equality from cultural multiplicity. Meanwhile, adamant marginals could fool them both, as the Monkey reflects the upside-down image of the system of signification. One of its most openly rebellious stances is in the black mythology and literature of the United States, where the Monkey becomes explicitly the "Signifying Monkey," mediator and challenger of all figurations of discourse.[2]

Before studying the uses of monkey-figures in Latin American literature, I propose to establish its previous historical development. Such a development not only affects the Western discipline of hermeneutics but the possibility of redefining such a discipline to accommodate the input of non-Western cultures on signification. The final emphasis will be on the Cuban application of this myth of compromise as a discourse of liberation.

Humanity's preoccupation with signification lies at the core of all mythologies. In essence, mythologies attempt to explain the knowledge gathered about natural phenomena with human languages of signs which rely on multiple, ambivalent interpretations. Presumably, the ability of mythopoeic language to communicate different interpretations in a text increases the freedom for the individual to choose among them. However, both the format of textualization and the act of signification are eminently controllable. Even if interpreters believe that the signifier and the signified are bound together by Fate and held in high esteem by Faith, they should take into account the imperial attitude of creators of myths as well as the bureaucratic biases of interpreters of mythologies. It is no wonder that all mythologies have a deified figure who mediates the revelation of knowledge (the creation of the world by *the* word) and challenges the manipulation of texts (the inscription of humanity onto *the* script).

Knowledge and Word are a persistent pair, but their partnership is not always a serene one. According to most myths, Knowledge is a divine gift to people; Word, instead, appears as humanity's approximation to divine creation. Behind the knowledge of words there is always a text of compromise which is neither God's nor humans', but it establishes a tricky relationship between the two. Western renderings of the myths of Knowledge and Word are embodied in the cult of Hermes, which leads to the system of hermeneutics. This branch of semiotics, which concentrates on the hidden links of signification, backs up Western adoration of the mystery of the written text. This type of adoration is perhaps the latest reincarnation of a deified principle which is also prevalent among non-Western mythologies, that of the "Mother of the Books."[3] The choice of Hermes as the Western "Father of the Books" is especially appropriate. He is the Greek messenger of the gods whose formal task is mediating between *Gnosis* (witnessing knowledge) and *Logos* (expressing reasons). His mediation is biased toward the latter, for his use of *Logios* (eloquence) emphasizes formal cunning. His command of *Logos* has channeled the expression of *Logios* into the shuffling of knowledge to suit his reasons.

The trends of contemporary criticism have further channeled the shuffling of knowledge into the realm of the written text. Thus, Hermes, who once ended disputes by giving ambivalent signs of compromise (such as offering the lyre to Apollo), now suggests new consoling terminology. The dueling matches between signifier and signified are settled by hermeneutics according to rules of signification, mysteriously agreed upon.

Hermes's older brother, Apollo, has been neglected in critical theory. His favorite form of mediation was the informal act of witnessing knowledge, artistically rendered with his voice. Whereas Hermes's eloquence relied on cunning to attempt social compromises, Apollo's singing struggled with personal commentaries. Hermes incurred damages against Apollo and as a consolation provided him with a formal instrument of interpretation. Such a consolation was a tricky compromise for both: Apollo disguised his voice as a musical script and instrumental execution; Hermes's gift of culture disguised but did not negate the original voice. Thus Hermes the Signer and Apollo the Singer represent parallel and mutually compromised alternatives of Signification.

In literary criticism, tradition dictated the formal triumph of Hermes over Apollo. The ensuing legacy emphasized the mythical neglect of the voice and text of "the other." One would not need to make a case history of this cultural bias to arrive at such a conclusion, but the exercise becomes valid as one finds social reasons why Hermes ceased to cooperate willingly with his brother in turning signs into texts.

The concept of the Hermes-Apollo team points toward two non-Hellenic figures, both deified monkeys from Egyptian and Indian mythologies, as well as the "Signifying Monkey"—the Afro-Anglo-American term for a widespread African principle.[4] The main link between Hermes-Apollo and these monkeys is their mediation in the creation of the World through the Word, as well as the re-creation of the Word through the Script. This type of mediation sets a liberal trend in non-Western and Western conceptions of signification. However, the Monkey principle of signification does not lead to the traumatic split between Voice and Script rampant in Western society. All Monkey-myths rely on the ambivalence of signification not to create a traumatic split but a balancing act of cultural defense. The study of the mythological alternatives to Hermes could serve to elucidate a noncolonial view of hermeneutics.

Thoth is probably the oldest of the three Signifying Monkeys. In Egyptian mythology he is both the god of wisdom and invention (under the guise of the ibis-headed man, worshipped throughout Egypt). The first aspect of this deity represents the universal Demiurge, the divine bird who hatched the world-egg by the sound of its voice. Thoth-as-ibis is not the original creator but the maker of a place for people within creation, the singer of myths. Just like Apollo, he inherits the light, an attribute from the sun-god which can be just as harmful as helpful. The two also have in common many other properties, above all, divination and prophecy. The second, much more comprehensive, aspect of Thoth represents the mediating figure between gods and people, who are the interpreters of tradition. This task is accomplished by the power of Thoth's reason and ability to convince. Just like Hermes, Thoth-as-monkey manipulates wisdom into a human language; he was first to inscribe sounds, motions, and images in hieroglyphic script.

The two sets of divinities, the Egyptian and the Grecian, may or may not have influenced each other. The question to consider is that of a common cultural campaign to mimic and mock the official relationship between the will to witness knowledge and the logic of inscription. In fact, Jorge Luis Borges, a writer not usually associated with minority points of view, has used the figure of the Monkey and specifically that of Thoth to project marginal values onto official writings. Of all the Latin American writers, he is the one who defends, at the most abstract level, the plight of any individual interpretation not prescribed by the official script.

Borges uses Thoth on at least two occasions in reference to humanity's metaphorical concerns, and calamitous consequences, in trying to find a single source of signification. On one of these occasions, "La esfera de Pascal" (The fearful sphere of Pascal), the text prepares the consideration of Thoth as a playful figure of signification with the following introduction: "It may be that universal history is the history of a handful of metaphors. The purpose of this note will be to sketch a chapter of this history."[5]

All of the metaphors which follow in Borges's text are interpretations of the core of Thoth's script: "God is an intelligible sphere, whose center is everywhere and whose circumference is nowhere."[6] However, this metaphorical projection of God as the perfect geometrical figure, according to Borges's text and the scholarship on the subject, appears as an arbitrarily deified metaphor among others. The circle of metaphors started with a Western interpretation, translation, and presumed discovery of Thoth's Script, the *Corpus Hermeticum*. This, the first Signifying Monkey text, has been conveniently shrouded in mystery, its multiple interpretations are decided upon by the social context which controls the Script. Interpretations have already "monkeyed" with the voice of Thoth and dispersed it into a virtual arbitrariness of scripts before Borges gives the reader the "last" word on the subject. "His" Pascal defines a French word in the critical vocabulary inherited from Thoth: "*effroyable*: a fearful sphere, whose center is everywhere and whose circumference is nowhere." Pascal changes "*effroyable*" into "Nature" in the finished version.[7]

The very uncertainty surrounding the Monkey Script allows the voice of Thoth to survive its multiple Western takeovers. However, survival implies in this case the Westernization of the myth. At the end, the original voice is diluted and hardly counts other than as a linguistic format inscribed in bastardized Western versions. This is in fact the reverse of the technique employed by Ishmael Reed in his *Mumbo Jumbo*, where the "Book of Thoth" is sought but no version appears. Yet, all oral interpretations of the myth contribute to re-creating the original "Text of Blackness."[8] The monkey-aspect of Thoth only applies here by inference. The ibis-aspect of the God, the scriptless voice of black creation, probably seems to Reed a less compromised solution than Borges's defense of Latin American values in a series of approximations to the "Will of Whiteness."

When Borges treats the ibis-aspect of Thoth, he does not dwell on it. One can infer that he is not seeking in Thoth an image of "pure" signification but possibly the opposite. Yet, texts like his, in spite of their calculated playfulness, turn into necessary tools to approximate the struggling liminal voice condemned to the will of script. Thus in Borges's "Ragnarök" (an old Icelandic word for *Götterdämmerung*), one of the battling gods, the twin-faced Janus, gives a mere glimpse of "distrust at the curved beak of Thoth." This signals the beginning of the end, for people begin to believe in dreams, from which emerge "heavy revolvers" with which they "joyfully killed the Gods."[9]

The superficially submissive, script-writing aspect of Thoth takes over humanity's work on signification; the revolver-carrying dreamers have killed the last illusions of unity and certainty. But Borges does not leave this concept without turning to social commentary. In his *El informe del Doctor Brodie* (*Doctor Brodie's Report*), the author uses the Ape-Men as the controllers of the illusion of an African, or perhaps South American, civilization which Doctor Brodie has just "discovered" and is faithfully recording.[10] The text, written as a report on the findings addressed to an English Queen, is so filled with obvious ambivalences that the signification of the report turns against itself. Finally, it is the threat of the Ape-Men roaming the frontiers that challenges, not the utopic civilization and codes discovered, but rather Brodie's and Borges's textual rendering of them.

The study of these parallel monkey-myths reveals the similar ways in which a given tradition protects itself from the interference of foreign codes. Thus, even if there are originators and followers in the spreading of myths, each civilization defends itself against cultured takeovers precisely by creating signifying myths about the master code or about the masters' codes. Sometimes, however, a code under siege chooses to find another to play the game of takeover. This takes us to yet another representation of the Signifying Monkey, and to how a text alien to a mythology decides to incorporate it.

The figure in question is based on the Indian myth of Hanumān, baptized by Octavio Paz as *El mono gramático* (*The Monkey Grammarian*).[11] In the original myth, as well as in the work of Paz, Hanumān accomplishes incredible leaps of textual fancy as if they were real. Moreover, the Monkey's metamorphoses claim to be as numerous as the interpretations of his complex body full of contradictory signs. The text is on him, about him, carried, and carried out, by him. In his search for the "other" he reaches out as much as within.

He begs and pays with words for his food and shelter. And he also tears his skin to reveal only temporarily serene images of duality. This holy, wandering beggar speaks in the words of Paz:

> The Great Monkey closes his eyes, scratches himself again and muses: before the sun has become completely hidden—it is now fleeing amid the tall bamboo trees like an animal pursued by shadows—I shall succeed in reducing this grove of trees to a catalogue. A page of tangled plant calligraphy. A thicket of signs: how to read it, how to clear a path through this denseness? Hanumān smiles with pleasure at the analogy that has just occurred to him: calligraphy and vegetation, a grove of trees and writing, reading and a path.[12]

And after Hanumān sees himself writing the sacred book just read, Paz comments:

> He [Hanumān] compares its rhetoric to a page of indecipherable calligraphy and thinks: the difference between human writing and divine consists in the fact that the number of signs of the former is limited, whereas that of the latter is infinite; hence the universe is a meaningless text, one which even the gods find illegible. The critique of the universe (and that of the gods) is called grammar. . . . Disturbed by this strange thought, Hanumān leaps down from the wall, remains for a moment in a squatting position, and stands erect, scrutinizes the four points of the compass and resolutely makes his way into the thicket.[13]

Hanumān is the result of a presumably neutral compromise in the witnessing of knowledge; his is the voice of rhetoric, the essential figure of speech, the critical trope par excellence. Yet his textual personality and therefore its signification transcend the set of signs by which he is represented. Finally, a transcendence of signification becomes potentially explosive. Again in the words of Paz, Hanumān is:

> a *gramma* of language, of its dynamism and its endless production of phonetic and semantic creations. An ideogram of the poet, the master/servant of universal metamorphosis: an imitative simian, an artist of repetitions, he is the Aristotelian animal that copies from nature but at the same time he is the semantic seed, the bomb-seed that is buried in the verbal subsoil and that will never turn into the plant that its sower anticipates, but into another, one forever different. The sexual fruits and the carnivorous flowers of otherness sprout from a single stem of identity.[14]

Whatever these passages tell us about the nature of signification pales in comparison with the linguistic resentment of a figure in search of a less biased discourse. Hanumān's liminal sociolinguistic figure stands against arbitrary rhetorical conventions. In fact, let us not forget that the Indian myth is evoked by a Mexican writer in Spanish according to the formal rules of Western discourse. Paz is subjecting the myth to alien configurations. But also, while the myth struggles for liberation, Hanumān plots for Paz.

The cult of the Monkey is not readily available to outsiders, unless they are willing to project on it their own struggle against parallel enslaved systems—as Borges did with the African/South American tribe and Paz did with the Indian myth. Hermes, Thoth, and Hanumān each represent defensive tactics in communication. Hermes is the source of hermeneutics as well as of the hermetic; Thoth is the presumed author of the classical hermetic treatise as well as the revealer of secrets to the initiated; Hanumān is a monkey-beggar who acts as passive recipient of the sacred script, as well as a general who is active in the exercise of the will of the marginal. All of them serve humanity as positive examples of compromise in signification.

In this view of signification, humanity emerges as an underhanded manipulator of the most secure formats. After all, quests for knowledge depend on acceptable wording; and such wording must give the illusion of security. However, when the controller of discourse is not receptive to the group's needs, then the imposed formats must be undermined with variables of signification. Both the securing of knowledge and the undermining of the formal script are part of the myth-making process. The danger arises from an abrupt tilting of the balance as not only the voice but also the meaning of human signs is battered by foreign powers.

THREE AFRICAN CULTURES enslaved in the New World developed important variants of signification to restore the cultural balance with the masters' code. Before enslavement, however, these three cultures already disguised their dependence on principles of other African civilizations. Slavery brought Africans in contact with Europeans and Euro-Americans; it also pushed together black cultures already in contact—such as the Yoruba, the BaKongo, and the Cross River Delta Efik and Ejagham. The tactics used to superficially accept and surreptitiously repel the European outsiders were practiced in a much more congenial fashion among themselves.

The Yoruba have hidden their cultural secrets in easy correspondences between their code and that of foreigners.[15] In their native land as well as in the New World, they adopted the masters' code with extraordinary defensive skills. In fact, the assimilation was mutual; syncretism did not imply submission but rather symbiosis between the colonizer and the colonized. In the resulting discourse of compromise, even if some signifiers bow to intervention, not so the signifieds. Yoruba-Western discourse consists of rhetorical deformations of the reigning model. Such deformations give the colonizer the impression that their charges are culturally flawed precisely when these "flaws" signify defensively upon the compromised discourse.

The situation of defensive compromise feeds on the ambivalent connection between signifiers and signifieds, an essential duality of all systems of signs. Yoruba and Yoruba-Cuban mythologies manifest this duality in the cult of Edun, who is the deified monkey-messenger subliminally present in the cult of the twins.[16] The cult of the twins has become much more evident than the cult of the principle behind it. That is, the objectivization of duality as a single concept accepted by the code disguises much more essential dualities of signification. The readers of such signs might assume that they know for certain the meaning of the twins, while in fact only dealing with their most superficial representation. The cult of Edun is always in precarious balance; its communication through the twins can make the difference between life and death—or, at least, life and death of the individual within tradition. A praise poem describes the twins and the particular importance of their cult under colonial siege:

> Edun orí igì
> Òyimbó ori ìtí.[17]
>
> [Monkey on the tree.
> Whiteman on the climbing ivy.]

This poem presents a mythopoeic warning against takeovers. The native speakers and written sources consulted did not reveal an original composition without the presence of white people. The uneasy duality of the twin deities, which had always existed, has incorporated the signs of colonialism. The combined effect of opposing interpretations does not translate as an admission of defeat but as a challenge to prove the interpreters' adherence to tradition. It succeeds despite native contradictions and foreign disturbances. In a sense, this is a definition of linguistic faith which is tempered but not defeated by compromise. Even Yoruba praise poems to the twins which do not contain an allusion to white people's interests warn against one-sided interpretations:

> Ibéjì ré, ọmọ ẹdun
> Ibéjì ré, ọmọ ẹdun
> Kere-kere-yàn.[18]
>
> [Behold twins, children of the monkey
> Behold twins, children of the monkey
> Become auspicious (implying "don't die").]

This composition is a clear example of language practicing what culture preaches, signifying as much by the suggestion of the format as by the multiple, liminal meanings of the words. Even for a reader who does not know Yoruba, the message is codified in (syntactic) dualities. First a perfectly symmetrical pair, then a compromising unity between the two expressed in new terms: "kere-kere-yàn." A further (semantic) interpretation yields the insistent dependence of people on an apparently lowly ancestor and the need for the reader to recognize duality in signs hidden within signs. Finally, the third line of the composition presents either a warning or an endorsement of the auspicious nature of duality in the interpretation of tradition.

The twins represent multiplicity as well as unity. On the one hand, the unity is reflected in the principle of Edun. The task of this deified monkey principle is a temporary union of signifiers and signifieds through a compromise between rhetorical disagreements. This compromise does not cancel out multiplicity, only keeps it disguised. Multiplicity, on the other hand, is openly reflected by Èṣù-Elégbéra (Eshu-Elegbara). This is a double deity embracing the strength of character to witness "pure" knowledge, Ìwà (Iwa), as well as the social power to express "applied" reason, Aṣè (Ashe). The combination of Eshu-Elegbara is well within the category of Apollo-Hermes and other two-sided myths of signification.

The Yoruba-Cuban tradition interprets the myth by turning Edun into an assistant of Eshu-Elegbara. *Mo-Edun* is the Afro-Cuban name for the transformed Edun; *Eshu-Elegguá* corresponds to Eshu-Elegbara. Whereas the latter has changed little, the former is no longer just a child of Edun but a deformation conveyed even in the etymology of the name: I [was/am to be] the Monkey.[19] To a Yoruba speaker of today this phrase is syntactically wrong; there is no explicit verb and *mo* should be used as the first person, subject pronoun with verbs in past and progressive tenses. The possibilities of the Cuban distortion of these Yoruba words all lead to a new forced acculturation of Edun, one that superficially encourages the Monkey principle to continue its task of clandestine signification for Afro-Cubans, as it has always done for Africans.

Whereas the important African concept of duality was embodied by Eshu-Elegbara, it is his Cuban companion, Mo-Edun, who now assumes the role. The duality of oral tradition has been transferred to the ambivalence of written traditions, and it still depends on a decisive social compromise. An Afro-Cuban text by Lydia Cabrera illustrates this point:

> There were once two friends of such similar tastes that, whether they were together or apart, their decisions always coincided.
>
> Now Elegba [or the Elegbara aspect of Eshu-Elegbara] was certain he could deal with his so-called perfect friendship. So he materialized one day when the friends were conversing on the street. . . .
>
> One of the comrades thought he saw a bald, black stranger, the

other was under the impression a white bearded man stood before him. (To prepare the ruse the deity had shaved off the hair on one side of his head, and kept beard and coiffure intact on the other. To compound the confusion, he changed himself into a white man on the side with hair, thus appearing fundamentally different to each friend.)[20]

At the end of the story, "as Elegba disappears, the friends are beating each other in the middle of the street."[21] Once the compromise is broken by sheer bravado, the once close partners annihilate each other. In Cabrera's text, the treacherous neutrality of Cuban culture and the struggling mulatto principles of signification could not be satisfactorily supplanted by open discord. The Yoruba-Cuban Monkey splits its power between the twins.

As ONE MOVES from the Yoruba to the Kongo cultural influences in the New World, the same Monkey principle appears to vie for a fair chance at the Euro-Cuban text. The BaKongo, or people of Kongo culture, had a traditional reaction to takeovers which makes their impact on neo-African mythologies and literatures much more difficult to study. They rejected the foreign codes by feeding the outsider with only part of their system of signification or with makeshift subsystems which would easily adjust to the will of the colonizer.

A discussion of the theoretical basis for alternative signification in BaKongo culture does not lie within the scope of this study. However, certain general characteristics should be pointed out since they passed on to Cuban discourse as linguistic techniques. BaKongo culture is based on the close partnership between the stand-still notion of a certain unity, *Nzambi*, and the self-perpetuating notion of an uncertain plurality, *Funza*.[22] There are several systems of inscription to establish the relationship of signification between these two central notions. The most relevant system for Cuban culture is one that depends on the relationship between *ndoki, nganga, nkisi,* and *simbi.* Some Western commentators have assigned to each one traditional roles relating to the realm of magic; yet they can be given a mythopoeic interpretation and applied to the realm of esthetics.

In traditional terms, ndoki is a witch, the person who materializes the relationship between the known and the unknown by the creation of fetishes— and thereby alters the natural order. The nganga is the doctor, or expert who manipulates fetishes to restore the natural order. The nkisi is the fetish itself, which serves as a positive but passive link between the individual and tradition. The simbi is an omen, the spirit of the waters whose appearance serves as a negative but active link between the individual and tradition. The spirit often materializes with monkey characteristics to warn believers that traditional relationships are being challenged.[23]

Translated into esthetic terms, ndoki is the artist's and the critic's domain, nkisi stands for the symbolic relationship between signifier and signified, and simbi becomes the challenger of signification. In such a system, the emphasis is on restoring the discourse to traditional order after adjusting it to challenging individuals and cultural variations. In Cuban discourse each of the aspects of this system of interpretative adjustments becomes both more literary, in as far as each exists mostly as a manifestation of oral or written discourse, and more detached, in that each becomes a symbolic entity with no specific personal connection. Just as Afro-Cuban religious practices went underground without losing their individuality, so did the accompanying esthetic principles lodged in a literary underworld. Thus BaKongo-Cuban concepts such as *endoqui, ñanga, (e)nkiso,* and the *Coco* or *Coco-Macaco* are protected and thrive by their subtle intrusion into Cuban literature.[24]

The margin of ambivalence in communication which permits such an intrusion undermines, without destroying, official standards. For instance, the appearance of the Coco-Macaco in oral or written versions illustrates cultural doubts or even points out fallacies in the system. In fact, from its African roots, this symbol points both to mimicry of discourse and mockery of tradition with a defensive intent. Whereas in noncolonial situations the symbol was not directed against any specific code but only against fallacies in signification, in postcolonial Cuban discourse it addressed the enslaving sociolinguistic conditions.

In essence, the main contribution of the BaKongo to the signifying skill of the Monkey is already apparent in their own poetry:

E nkewa e,
suama wusuamanga,
nkila wukusoluele,
e nkewa e.[25]

[Hey monkey hey,
hiding in the oracle,
tail telling destiny,
hey monkey hey.]

According to this poem and the system it reflects, no one can predict the message or presume to control the discourse of the monkey. The act of interpreting the message neutralizes with irony any attempt to fix the official message from the "oracle." In fact BaKongo-Cuban literary renderings by writers such as Guillén and Barnet exploit the monkey's ability to parody official claims of linguistic fixity. The words "Mono" and "Coco-Macaco" contain in themselves the possibility of parody. Thus, on the one hand, "Mono" derives from the root assigned to the first-person singular in several African and

Western languages whose legacies are present in Cuba. On the other hand, it also connotes the image of an animal which is a helpless copy of people. The word "Coco-Macaco" refers at once to a dreaded ghost and a playful monkey in both Africa and Cuba.[26] The true meaning, in both cases, is closer to a middle-ground where the expression of the "primitive" self and Western traditions of "civilized" discourse meet.

An outstanding example of this Cuban Monkey which informs on Kongo culture is Miguel Barnet's text "La lechuza y el mono" (The Owl and the Monkey), based on a legend collected by the author and others.[27] According to Barnet's text, at the time of slavery, the Owl could see by day and also by night, while the Monkey could speak fluently, as illustrated by words not commonly understood by Spanish speakers: "Diambo, malembe, diambo." The Monkey would then break into song: "Cuenda endoque cuenda / cuenda endoque diambo." The two seeing and speaking-singing animals soon became "eternal" friends according to the short text. They were engaged as a team by the proud Day to attempt to take over the attributes of the Moon—presumably the reflection of light. On the way to their mission, the Owl envisioned its role as a theft, and the Monkey felt compelled to talk about it incessantly.

By the time they arrived, the *Tojosa* (a wild Cuban pigeon) had already forewarned the Moon, who hid its desired attributes in the first total eclipse. In turn, the messenger team became recipients of the Day's anger. According to Barnet's own mythological code, the punishment was: "Lechuza, pracatatpacata? &X./ .Mono, tiquiriquitaquq?.:&X./." Barnet's version mercifully translates the mysterious code, which conveys that the Owl was deprived of day vision and the Monkey left voiceless.

Any interpretation of this text must take into consideration the coexistence of words in Spanish, KiKongo, and in Barnet's idiosyncratic language. The reconstruction of the KiKongo-Cuban script is made difficult by the fact that it is written, second or third hand, from the way Cubans would pronounce the original African words. Yet, a translation into the general phonetic script adopted for the KiKongo language for Western consumption yields a surprisingly clear and poignant message. I shall compare the KiKongo-Cuban script with a phonetic reconstruction of the KiKongo original, two contrasting English versions, and a compromise.[28]

(KiKongo-Cuban)
Diambo, malembe, diambo.
Cuenda endoqui cuenda
cuenda endoque diambo

(Phonetic KiKongo)
Dyambu, malembe, dyambu.

Kwenda ndoki kwenda
kwenda ndoke dyambu.

Two English translations illustrate the ambivalent signification already contained in the reconstructed KiKongo original:

(a)
[Word, behold, word.
Go on, fetish-maker, go on;
go on, fetish, the word.]

(b)
[Trouble, be careful, trouble
Go away, witch, (may he/she/it) go away;
go away, witch, trouble.]

A compromise can be constructed using the vocabulary of esthetics:

Discourse, the ominous, discourse.
Continue, counter-signifying, continue
continue, the counter-signifying, discourse.[29]

Although the projection of the poem unto the vocabulary of literary criticism is an educated guess, it conveys simultaneously the untranslatable dichotomy of the original. Even those who would question my interpretative rendering would have to agree that the poem is about the difficulty of communicating with words, especially with foreign ones or with native words out of context.

Moreover, the usage of a KiKongo-Cuban riddle to voice monkey-speech attains the level of grand deception. Readers familiar with KiKongo will share the advantage of understanding the "secret" code without being completely certain of its decodification. Readers not familiar with KiKongo might ignore the material as nonsense or as left pending an interpretation.

If the inclusion in Barnet's text of a nontranslated KiKongo poem as the voice of the Monkey signifies upon the arbitrariness of the sign depending on the interpreter's point of view, then the final sentence pronounced by the Day against the Owl and the Monkey would constitute the "last" words on the signification dilemma. Only Barnet and his informant might have complete access to its interpretation. Nevertheless, even the effort to conceal in apparent gibberish, or to reveal in translation, the fatal sentence leaves out significant information in the margins of signification. After addressing the sentence to *Lechuza* (the Owl) and to *Mono* (the Monkey), the text exhibits onomatopoeic words implying gestures of punishment. These onomatopoeic utterances end with a typographically rendered cross, an "X," which is a practically pan-African ideogram for control of speech and the cosmic cycle.[30] Thus the mysterious message links the punishment of the Monkey and the Owl with the end of free speech and a relative infringement on cosmic signification.

The seemingly innocuous typographical notation could also have been interpreted as the illiterate signature of the two animals. There is no favorite among all the given interpretations. As a cross of speech or of cosmos, or as the traditional signature for the illiterate, the mythology of signification continues to be polarized. It involves the Owl, a godlike bird of twilight, and the Monkey, a humanlike figure of enlightenment. The prototypical relationship between Thoth's two-sides applies here. The Egyptian God of Wisdom and Communication, Light and Shadow, Word and Script also exhibited the bird-side of "creation" and the monkey-side of "re-creation." The concept of the Indian Monkey deity, Hanumān, also applies here in a much more abstract fashion, particularly in Borges's rendering of the myth. Borges's "Ragnarök," as previously seen, transforms the Götterdämmerung into a battle between humans and gods in the twilight of their mutual signification.

In a deceivingly simple text by Barnet, this battle of signification illustrates the wide extent of its reach. Even in ridiculously disguised or deformed fashion, African traditions are preserved beyond the temporary compromise of the enslaving text.

NOT ALL manifestations of neo-African thought are this ambivalent in their methods of compromise. The Cuban interpretations of Efik-Ejagham material thrust themselves into a much more open linguistic bargaining. Contributing to this variation on the theme of compromise is that the Efik and the Ejagham cultures bargained amongst themselves for their individual traditions prior to their voyage to the New World.

In the Cross River region, Africans shared Ejagham basic principles and bargaining skills and Efik linguistic and colonial tendencies. The Ejagham, assailed by the Efik, weaved the concept of takeover into their mythology. According to Cuban renderings of Ejagham history, the Efik were permitted a cultural takeover.[31] In fact, both groups interacted symbiotically, balancing the concepts of cultural truce and colonial takeover. What the outsiders took was, at best, the most superficial level of linguistic responsibility. Even the occasional adoption of Efik terminology and traits would not deprive the Ejagham culture of control over its own ritual context. In fact, the Ejagham buttressed their culture by allowing the Efik to become the keepers of the Secret. The Secret in itself was mostly a statement on language. It was not based on letters or readily decipherable ideograms, but stood instead for a token system of signs known by its effects rather than by its causes or nature. Hence, the upkeep of such a set of signs was a symbolic concession to acculturation, and the Efik's impending cultural supremacy was turned into a cultural truce. Even linguistic concessions were under Ejagham supervision.

In any event, the colonized group masterminded the truce and the colonizers traded their de facto power for the illusory power over a borrowed secret. Moreover, not only was the takeover reduced mostly to a symbiotic relationship at the level of language, but even linguistic penetration would not guarantee in exchange a thorough knowledge of the host culture. Whole aspects of Ejagham communication, like its graphic and gestural code, prevailed and were only superficially touched by the Efik's colonial efforts. The Efik willingly accepted their ceremonial posts as keepers of the Ejagham word. Afro-Cuban mythology ensuing from this symbiotic relationship assigned to the Efik the holding of the formal "calabash," or sacred container, and to the Ejagham, its secret contents.

The two dueling cultures, in their ingenious symbiosis, arrived in Cuba by way of the *Abakuá* (Abakwa) society.[32] The Abakwa developed in the New World a strong tactic of defensive signification. The core of such a tactic was the assimilation of as many aspects as possible of the black and white codes surrounding it, to the point that the establishment considered the Abakwa as an esoteric appendage of Cuban culture. The composite cultural body emerges as a hermetic code with a subtle hold over the hermeneutic values of Cuban signs.

The Efik-Ejagham tradition upon which Abakwa social foundations are based has reserved the right to choose its own and Spanish as the main languages of expression. The mediating mythological figure between the two is a fierce rendering of the "Signifying Monkey," the *güije* or *jigüe*—from *Jiwe*, a corresponding word for monkey in Efik and Ejagham.[33]

The literature of this fierce Jiwe has been collected by Cuban experts or transposed into poems aspiring to appeal to, or already within, the mainstream. I have chosen as examples an obscure composition by a Spanish poet who lived in Cuba and a poem by a well-known Afro-Cuban poet. The similarities and contrasts between their contemporary compositions should illustrate the final jump of the Monkey from liminal mythology to mainstream literary criticism and social action.

Teófilo Radillo's "Canción del jigüe" (Song of the Jiwe) still debates the merits of the Monkey mediator between neo-African signing and Cuban singing.[34] Nicolás Guillén's "Balada del güije" (Ballad of the Jiwe) settles the dispute which has unjustly assigned written texts to Cuban whites and songs to Cuban blacks.[35] In both, the spirit of the Monkey lives above all in the text, from which the reader accompanies the Monkey in a journey of metamorphoses.

Radillo's composition exploits the ambivalences of such metamorphoses by means of: discrepancies in semantics, an erratic line of syntax, lack of cause and effect, temporal vagueness of the narrative, depersonalization of humans, and personification of Nature. As a result, in the struggle of the Monkey with the Western text, both make adjustments. Two types of voices alternate in this mutual adjustment: that of the presumably unbiased Cuban commentator who captured the Monkey principle for his or her text and that of the Afro-Cuban characters who experience the Monkey firsthand.

The commentator attempts to describe in neutral terms the origin, nature, and consequences of the Afro-Cuban myth:

> El jigüe nació en Oriente.
> El jigüe nació del agua . . .
> Al borde de la laguna,
> cuando los niños se bañan,
> vigila un jigüe moreno
> de cabellera muy larga . . .
> Tiene los dientes agudos
> y la intención afilada.[36]

> [The Jiwe was born in Oriente.
> The Jiwe came from the waters . . .
> By the edge of the lagoon,
> while the children bathe,
> a dark Jiwe is watching
> with a great length of hair . . .
> His teeth are pointed
> and his intention is sharp.]

The stanza is calculatedly ambivalent. "Oriente" may be the easternmost province of Cuba or point to the East; the "waters" could be the lagoon's or those of any other body—as the text later alludes to a river, a pond, sea waves—or it could be the Atlantic Ocean. The Jiwe, meanwhile, is both an essence and an ethereal presence, a being and a point of view. It is also a creature of the water with a will of its own or a figment of the author's imagination, a children's game, or a monster created by unhappy adults. Thus, the intruder gathers all characteristics of the mimicking-mocking Signifying Monkey.

As a creature of the text, his ambivalent origins and needs, essence and attitudes become intertwined. Even the negative aspects of his intrusion do not appear as gratuitous bursts of anger against society but rather residual resentment of needs not met by the textual rendering of his character. The voice of the Jiwe strikes the reader as a silent or muzzled voice heard through compromised acts and signs.

Presumably, in order to avert the unsatisfactory resolution of the Jiwe's signification, the poem produces two speaking voices: a Cuban Mother softly warning her child about the mystery of everyday inconsistencies, and a Cuban child complaining to the Mother that he cannot flee the obvious responsibilities for taking chances. Both of these voices contrast with the rather impersonal, or at least ambivalent, account of the figure of the intruder. The Mother speaks:

—Duermete, mi niño, pronto,
que un jigüe ronda la casa.
Ayer se asomó en el fondo
blanco de la porcelana;
ayer lo vi que corría
cerca de la guardarraya
jugando con un pedazo
de sombra de la enramada.

—El viento movía la sombra
para que el jigüe jugara.
Duermete, mi niño, pronto,
que si el jigüe se acercara
lo agarraré por las greñas,
le echaré un lazo a la pata,
y le sacaré, uno a uno,
los dientes de la bocaza
grande, como la del sapo
viejo que vive en la charca.

[Sleep, my child, soon,
a Jiwe hangs around home.
Yesterday he appeared deep
in the white porcelain shine;
yesterday I saw him running
close by the plantation path
playing with a fragment
of shadow from the undergrowth.

The wind moved the shadow
for the Jiwe to play.
Sleep, my child, soon,
if the Jiwe gets close
I'll grab a shock of his hair,
trapping his leg with a rope,
pulling out, one by one,
the teeth in his big mouth,

big as the old toad's,
the one living in the pond. (178)]

Throughout this speech the Jiwe shows its talent at metamorphoses. But even
there, the perennial compromiser has limits in attaining textual shapes: a
shadow, a running image playing with a shadow, a wind-propelled shadow. All
shadows disappear as the intruder steps in as a senseless aggressor, which the
Mother promises to entrap.

What she promises to entrap is a game of refractions, produced by the
remembrance of a menacing toad—a curious allusion to one of the favorite
ritual victims of the Yoruba and Efik gods. The aggressor becomes a refracted
shadow of the victim. When the child answers his Mother's plea, it is already
too late. He is already a victim, at least of an initiation into the deeper meanings of the Afro-Cuban code:

—Mamita, yo he visto un jigüe
ayer, cuando me bañaba
en el remanso del río:
era negro . . . y me miraba
con algo que . . . yo no sé
si eran ojos o eran brasa.
Yo tuve miedo y grité,
pero nadie me escuchaba;
quise correr y no pude,
porque el agua me agarraba . . .
Mamita, yo he visto un jigüe
bañándose en agua mansa.

[Mother, I have seen a Jiwe
yesterday, when I was bathing
in the still river waters:
He was black . . . and glared at me
with what . . . I could not tell,
may have been eyes or live coals.
Being afraid I screamed,
but nobody was listening;
I wanted to run and couldn't,
for the waters grabbed at me . . .
Mother, I have seen a Jiwe
bathing in the still waters. (178–179)]

The child has experienced both aspects of the Jiwe: the actual and the ritual.
Just as the initiated to the twin cults dedicated to Eshu-Elegbara and to Songó
(Shango), the child is exposed to a pressure on the back of the eyes, a sign of
inner vision. Thus, the Mother's admonition is not based on fear of the Jiwe

but on fear of the responsibility which awaits the child with such a vision and role.

The last part of the poem then tells the legend of the Jiwe from the point of view of the believer. There are no longer ambivalences as to its nature:

> fue el mono aquel, que se ahogó
> para que saliera el "ñanga"
> —el "ñanga" que siempre surge
> de las ondas de las aguas— . . .
> Se ahogó . . . y hoy flota en las aguas
> dormidas de las leyendas
> que arrullaron a una raza.

> [he was the monkey who drowned
> for the sake of the nganga
> —the nganga who always emerges
> from the waves of water— . . .
> He drowned . . . to float today
> in the sleepy waters of legends
> who cradled a whole race. (179–180)]

The nganga, or interpreter of Kongo tradition, becomes in Cuba a floating object of signification, bringing the "corpse" of the Monkey to the surface.[37]

This desperate dimension of the traditional African interpretation in the New World is expressed at the end of the poem. In befitting fashion, the situation is summed up in a series of parallel words:

> Jigüe-mono,
> mono-jigüe,
> ñanga-jigüe
> jigüe-ñanga . . .

> [Jiwe-monkey,
> monkey-Jiwe
> nganga-Jiwe
> Jiwe-nganga . . . (180)]

The text forces the reader to interpret each of the words—in official Spanish, unofficial Cuban, or African—or to accept on faith the multiple possibilities neutralized in a single discourse. And even though this textual tactic has been identified as defensive linguistics, on principle it does not overcome the stigma of being a deviation from the established norm. Teófilo Radillo's defensive attitude toward Afro-Cuban discourse finally delegates part of its responsibilities on the power of the nganga, i.e., on the skill of the interpreter/critic.

For full assumption of responsibilities by the Monkey-text one would have to turn to the poetry of Nicolás Guillén. The Afro-Cuban poet brought to a piercing pitch the previously cautious voice and resentful figure of the Signifying Monkey. His "Balada del güije" (Ballad of the Jiwe) fosters an aggressive use of the master code against itself. The reader who does not perceive the emergence of a black voice beneath the Eurocodified appearances of Guillén's language would at least sense a sociolinguistic note of reluctance or veiled discordance. An example from the ballad illustrates, with black and white means, a defiantly Cuban song of complaint:

> Las turbias aguas del río
> son hondas y tienen muertos;
> carapachos de tortuga,
> cabezas de niños negros.
> De noche saca sus brazos
> el río, y rasga el silencio
> con sus uñas, que son uñas
> de cocodrilo frenético.
> Bajo el grito de los astros,
> bajo una luna de incendio,
> ladra el río entre las piedras
> y con invisibles dedos,
> sacude el arco del puente
> y estrangula a los viajeros.[38]

> [The turbulent river waters
> run deep and carry the dead;
> the shell of tortoises,
> black children's heads.
> At night the arms of the river
> are raised, tearing the silence
> with its nails, the nails of
> a frantic crocodile.
> Beneath the scream of stars,
> under the incendiary moon,
> the river howls among stones,
> while its invisible fingers
> jolt the arch of the bridge,
> strangling the passengers.]

The form, language, and figures of this passage are well grounded in a traditionally Spanish mode of Western poetry. Yet, what could justifiably be interpreted as a metaphorical lament from the depth of the mainstream disguises a rich array of suppressed personal experiences in the Afro-Cuban tradition.

Along the lines of the much studied genre of the text commenting on itself, this ballad exhibits two parallel codes commenting on a textual compromise between the Western-based text and the African-inspired proto- or para-text. The ensuing discourse illustrates the issue not only of the liminal material forced by society into an official frame but also of that material forced by an author into his own frame. Moreover, not only does such a discourse deal with black materials already compromised in "mainstream" texts, but these texts are also compromised by black materials. In this regard, the prototypical text by Guillén exhibits both "defensive" and "offensive" strategies. Afro-Cuban ideas are translated not just into any official Euro-Cuban words, but into Guillén's own; alternatively, such ideas are defended by Afro-Cuban words whose meaning is not readily available to the majority of the public. In either case, material considered liminal to either the text or its interpretation creates an offensive rear guard of alternative significations.

The elements of the Monkey principle are thus manipulated by Guillén into a version of Afro-Cuban discourse which is to be sung and read with resigned despair as much as with incipient anger. Among the texts illustrating such a discourse, Guillén's "Ballad of the Jiwe" comes closest to analyzing the historical circumstances which led to the importation of the Signifying Monkey into Cuba. This "ballad" alludes to a time in which matriarchal societies predominated in precolonial Africa. It would seem that by searching into the past Guillén sought to unearth the most pure line of tradition. The search, however, required some confrontation: "shells of tortoises" alternate with "heads of black children" in the fatal flow of the river or, what is poetically equivalent, the metaphorical wombs and corpses of the offspring of tradition are dragged to the surface; the crocodile, avatar of matriarchal societies, frantically tears with its nails; the arms of the Jiwe become the arm of the river— source of life and death; the Moon, virtually a pan-African image of sacred or ritual Time, acquires an incendiary presence—burning and being burned.[39] And, finally, the "invisible fingers" of the river shake the saddest bridge in communication: the middle passage of African culture to the New World, a labor accomplished in spite of the "strangling" of the "passengers."

Considering all the deadly signs to be confronted in the Jiwe's path, beholding his figure and his message constitutes a frightening task:

> Enanos de ombligo enorme
> pueblan las aguas inquietas;
> sus cortas piernas, torcidas;
> sus largas orejas, rectas.
> ¡Ah, que se comen mi niño,
> de carnes puras y negras,
> y que le beben la sangre,

y que le chupan las venas,
y que le cierran los ojos,
los grandes ojos de perlas!
¡Huye, que el coco te mata,
huye, antes que el coco venga!
Mi chiquitín, chiquitón,
que tu collar te proteja . . .

[Pygmies with enormous navels
people the restless waters;
their short legs are twisted;
their long ears stand up.
Ah, they are eating my child,
the one of pure, black flesh,
they are drinking his blood
sucking dry his veins,
shutting his eyes tight,
his large eyes of pearls!
Flee, the nasty monkey will kill you,
flee, before the nasty monkey comes!
My little one, my big little one,
may your necklace keep you safe . . . (63)]

This stanza opens with a curious image of fear, mixing the tragicomic and the grotesque. The center figure is no longer the ominous Jiwe, but his nasty counterpart, the Coco.[40] The rebelliousness of this aspect of the Monkey appears somewhat misguided in reference to the more manageable Jiwe. And just as the Jiwe once signified upon the words of the text and vice versa, so does the Coco. Except, the textual rendering of the latter is so plagued with inconsistencies of signification that it produces an overall image of uncontrollable fear.

The Coco's image appears to be a nasty one: a being "with short legs," handicapped and clumsy, with the potential for communication just as "twisted" as his body, who goes about captivating an audience whose "long ears stand up" as much as his own. This is the traditional image of irrational fear for Cubans, which speaks to the flaws of the type of text and reader which try to "trap" the Coco as much as the difficulty of seizing it any other way. In the end, the Coco's signification is wide open. This is not just a nasty monkey but a necessary evil, or even an omen (simbi) of the break in tradition. No matter the outcome, Guillén has imposed an ambivalent, African-based signification upon the Euro-Cuban text. Thus he has reversed, by an act of sheer esthetic will, a traditional colonial imposition.

In light of the reversal of roles, the text's complaint, "Ah, they are eating my child," appears rather sarcastic. The tragicomic and grotesque touches of this phrase suggest the sacrifices implicit in a cultural compromise. The author's sacrifice consists of allowing the "devouring" of his metaphorical charge, the black child of the text; the readers' sacrifice is to accept the author's predicament. Yet, all sacrifices made in behalf of the Coco pay dividends in terms of the continuity of the discourse of blackness. Not even the interpretation of the "necklace" as a fetishistic safeguard or folkloric ornamentation will save the right wearer from the observance of Fate. Guillén poignantly underplays the importance of one of Africa's most powerful systems of signification, the textual reading of chance—of which the "necklace" is but one of the approaches.[41]

Finally, the author brings to the surface of the text a figure of worship which rejects most disguises. It is Shango, the fiery god who defends the purity of Afro-Cuban tradition.[42] Shango determines the outcome of the "Ballad of the Jiwe" and presumably that of the assailed code of blackness.

> Pero Changó no lo quiso.
> Salió del agua una mano
> para arrastrarlo . . . Era un güije.
> Le abrió en dos tapas el cráneo,
> le apagó los grandes ojos,
> le arrancó los dientes blancos,
> e hizo un nudo con las piernas
> y otro nudo con los brazos.
>
> [But Shango would not have it.
> A hand rose from the waters
> to drag him away . . . The Jiwe's.
> It opened up his skull in two,
> extinguishing his great eyes,
> tearing off his white teeth,
> making a knot of his legs
> and another of his arms. (63–64)]

Shango's intervention adds to the textual dispute between the unknown aspects of Afro-Cuban tradition and the known forms of the Euro-Cuban discourse. The deity in question is not new in its propitiatory role. According to its Yoruba-Cuban rendering, Shango has the character to defend the purity of tradition. This is the domain of Iwa, roughly equivalent to the Grecian Gnosis, which in the guise of "the gift of dancing and the mastery of the drum" Shango received from Ifa. In return for these arts, Ifa received the most direct projection of reasons, "the gift of divination," roughly equivalent to the Grecian Logos, or Word, projected unto the textual table of signification. By such an exchange, righteousness and foresight, the moral character of knowledge and the esthetic power of communication, were forever bound to each other in Yorubaland.[43] The same can be said, in Hellenic myths, of Apollo's compromise of his talents by Hermes's lyre. In Apollo's and Shango's learned codes there is still a voice claiming its own, as illustrated by Guillén's "Ballad":

> Mi chiquitín, chiquitón,
> sonrisa de gordos labios,
> con el fondo de tu río
> está mi pena soñando,
> y con tus venitas secas
> y tu corazón mojado . . .
>
> [My little one, my big little one,
> a smile through thick lips,
> of the bottom of your river
> my sorrows are dreaming,
> of your little dried up veins
> and of your soaking heart . . . (64)]

Guillén confronts the main linguistic hurdle of Afro-Cuban culture: writing as docile mirroring of a society in which both enslaved and master codes are reduced to gesturing or barely mouthing lost illusions and farfetched dreams. Guillén's text flaunts the prejudiced white words and compromised black voice, demanding in exchange the reader's gift of foresight in signification.

There is some pretended neutrality left in Guillén's attempt, but little doubt about the text being torn up by its built-in injustices. The code of blackness makes the valiant choice to accept certain historically imposed, formal compromises, without losing sight of the opportunity to exercise the power of signification. The lesson learned applies not just to blacks or to Cubans. Few people are exempt from the need to conform to a language of signs, and none is obliged to accept a partisan neutrality of signification.

Whether the critic is partial to dreams of free expression (Iwa, Gnosis, Funza) or to the controlled inscriptions of the word (Ashe, Logos, Nzambi), the rules of the game make monkeys of all. The margin of difference in signification allowed by contemporary critical theories is the domain of social as much as critical politics; and the Monkey principle signifies upon both. Even in the effort at perfect imitation there is a residue of irony, a dosage which Guillén and others have maximized without advocating a return to precolonial times, chimeric purisms, or esthetic chaos.

Yet, hidden in the lyrical truce, the Afro-American poet always keeps an extra figure of discourse and of discord. Whereas the Signifying Monkey or the Nasty Monkey partially succumbs to the peaceful kingdom of the script, the Ñeque (Nyeke), an Afro-Cuban figure of randomness, anarchy, and chaos, signifies recklessly upon the integrity of Cuban discourse.[44] Guillén ends his "Ballad of the Jiwe" battling with both the yielding Fate and the unyielding Faith of the Signifying Monkey:

¡Ñeque, que se vaya el ñeque!
¡Güije, que se vaya el güije!
¡Ah, chiquitín, chiquitón,
pasó lo que yo te dije!

[Nyeke, may the Nyeke go away!
Jiwe, may the Jiwe go away!
Ah, my little one, my big little one,
what I told you did happen! (64)]

Notes

1. Among the Cuban examples I will only discuss Barnet's and Guillén's along with a little known poem by Teófilo Radillo, a Spanish-Cuban writer. For the presence of a *güije*-like figure in Carpentier's work, see my discussion of Atilano, the hero of *Histoire de lunes*, in "A Return to Africa with a Carpentier Tale," *Modern Language Notes* 97 (1982): 401–410. Research about monkey symbolism in the work of Sarduy is still to be done; notice, for example, its appearance in connection with attempts to fit the norm as *Cobra*'s protagonist struggles with tight shoes. See Severo Sarduy, *Cobra* (Buenos Aires: Sudamericana, 1972), 12.

2. See Henry Louis Gates, "The 'Blackness of Blackness': A Critique on the Sign and the Signifying Monkey," *Critical Inquiry* 9, no. 4 (June 1983): 685–723.

3. This is the origin of the written word, according to the Koran, Chapter XIII. It was quoted by Jorge Luis Borges in a discussion on the subject of Western civilization's cult of written signification. The reference from the Koran leads Borges to suggest that all books ultimately refer to a single central illusion, of which they are but imperfect copies. "Del culto de los libros," in *Otras inquisiciones* (Buenos Aires: Emecé, 1960), 144.

4. See Gates, "The 'Blackness of Blackness,'" 688–689 and note 7.

5. Jorge Luis Borges, *Labyrinths, Selected Stories and Other Writings*, ed. Donald A. Yates and James E. Irby, trans. Anthony Kerrigan (New York: New Directions, 1964), 189–192.

6. According to Borges's text, this version of Thoth's main thought was read as a "formula" by Alain de Lille in the twelfth century. In typical Borgesian fashion, the interpretations and inscriptions of ideas fuse and overcome any semblance of the entity itself. Borges, *Labyrinths*, 190.

7. Ibid., 192.

8. Ishmael Reed, *Mumbo Jumbo* (Garden City, N.Y.: Doubleday, 1972), particularly p. 164, where the *Book of Thoth* is described as "the 1st anthology written by the 1st choreographer," and p. 188, where it is described as "the sacred Work . . . of the Black Birdman." Gates ("The 'Blackness of Blackness'") points out the importance of the ibis-aspect of Thoth, pp. 705 and 717.

9. Translated by James E. Irby. Borges, *Labyrinths*, 240–241.

10. According to the text, Dr. Brodie "preached the Christian faith first in the heart of Africa and later on in certain backlying regions of Brazil," without specifying where he met the people studied. In Jorge Luis Borges, *Doctor Brodie's Report*, trans. Norman Thomas di Giovanni (New York: Dutton, 1970), 111. Other Borges stories

corroborate the mediating position of the Monkey principle: "Hochigan" and "The Monkey of the Inkpot," in Jorge Luis Borges (with Margarita Guerrero), *The Book of Imaginary Beings*, a translation by Norman Thomas di Giovanni and Jorge Luis Borges of *El libro de los seres imaginarios* (1967) (New York: Dutton, 1978), 126 and 160.

11. Octavio Paz, *The Monkey Grammarian*, a translation by Helen R. Lane of *El mono gramático* (1974) (following a French version by Claude Esteban, included in Albert Skira and Gaëtan Picon, *Les Sentiers de la création*) (New York: Seaver, 1981).

12. Ibid., 47.

13. Ibid., 47–48.

14. Ibid., 131.

15. Of the three main cultures contributing to the Afro-American Signifying Monkey, the Yoruba influences are easiest to establish, precisely because of their skill in the superficial compromises of syncretism.

16. See chapter 13, "Twin Statuettes," of Robert Farris Thompson, *Black Gods and Kings. Yoruba Art at U.C.L.A.* (Bloomington and London: Indiana University Press, 1976).

17. I am deeply grateful to Michael Afolayan, who suggested this praise poem and whose sensitivity toward his native Yoruba language and culture has been a great help and inspiration.

18. Thompson, *Black Gods and Kings*, chapter 13, 2. Translation is Thompson's.

19. *Mo-Edun* appears in Lydia Cabrera, *El monte, Igbo-Finda-Ewe Orisha-Vititi Nfinda (Notas sobre las religiones, la magia, las supersticiones y el folklore de los negros criollos y del pueblo de Cuba)* (Havana, 1954; reprint, Miami, Fla.: Ediciones Universal, 1975), 87. Cabrera simply translates it as the Monkey. However, two etymologies are suggested by the Yoruba-Cuban word: the one given in the text and a contraction of *Ọmọ-Ẹdun*, "Child of the Monkey" (a praise usually applied to Edun's twins; see the second Yoruba praise poem quoted in the text).

20. Cabrera, *El monte*, 93–94, quoted by Thompson, *Black Gods and Kings*, chapter 4, 3–4.

21. Cabrera, *El monte*, 94.

22. For the appreciation of Kongo material I am indebted above all to John M. Janzen and Wyatt MacGaffey, eds., *An Anthology of Kongo Religion*, Publication in Anthropology 4 (Lawrence: University of Kansas, 1974), and to Tulu Kia Mpansu Buakasa, *L'Impense du discours. "Kindoki" et "nkisi" en pays kongo du Zaire* (Kinshasa: Presses Universitaires du Zaire, 1973).

23. Buakasa writes an entire book (*L'Impense du discours*) attempting, unsuccessfully, to find alternatives to the traditional translations. He decided to use the original KiKongo terminology.

24. These terms are used by the Cuban authors quoted in this paper. For example: *endoqui* or *ndoki* appears in the works of Cabrera and Barnet, *ñanga* or *nganga* appears in Ortiz's, Cabrera's and Guillén's, *(e)nkiso* or *(e)nkisi* in Cabrera's and under other names and guises in all, *Coco* or *Coco-Macaco* in Ortiz's, Barnet's and Guillén's.

25. Buakasa, *L'Impense du discours*, 297, gives the following translation: "Eh singe / tu te caches, / ta queue (ressort et) te fait reperer, / eh singe." For my alternative translation I have consulted Pierre Swartenbroeckx, *Dictionnaire KiKongo et Kituba-Français*, ser. 3, vol. 2 (Bandundu, Zaire: Ceeba, 1973), and Henry Craven and John Barfield, *English-Congo and Congo-English Dictionary* (Freeport, N.Y.: Books for Libraries Press, 1971).

26. In KiKongo, *mono* is the first person singular and *mo*, "them," or "over there"— that is, "the others"; it is in fact the root for the word for slave, *moai*. In Yoruba *mo* is the first person singular subject pronoun in past and continuous tenses, with

a special usage in Yoruba-Cuban (see the discussion of Mo-Edun in text) and *mon*, a quasi-verb indicating repetition and other "negative" implications of involvement, according to R. C. Abraham, *Dictionary of Modern Yoruba* (1946; reprint, London: Hodder & Stoughton, 1981). In Efik, *mon* is the auxiliary verb meaning "doing something" or "is about to"—that is, the essence of indirect action, a rather obtuse indication of the acting self. This is my own conclusion based on suggestions given by R. F. Adams, *Efik-English Dictionary*, 3d ed. (Liverpool: Phillip, Son and Nephew, 1953). The English word "monkey" derives from the Romance Languages, possibly from Spanish, to which it came directly from Arabic and indirectly from the Persian *maimon*. The word was first introduced to Europe by the Berber scholar Leo Africanus in the sixteenth century. Africanus, who wrote in Latin and had a classical Western education, europeanized the word into *mona*— from the Greek root for "unique," "the one," possibly contaminated by the Latin *Moneo-ere*: to call to mind, remind, advise, point out; to warn; to foretell, to teach, instruct, inform. For the most complete evolution of the word, see the historical chapter of W. C. Osman Hill, *Primates, Comparative Anatomy and Taxonomy*, vol. 6 (New York: Interscience, 1966), 3–18. For *Coco* or *Coco-Macaco*, see further discussion in text and note 40.

27. In Miguel Barnet, *Akeké y la jutía. Fábulas cubanas* (Havana: Ediciones Unión, 1978), 114–115.

28. Translation (b) was suggested to me by Wyatt MacGaffey in a letter dated 6 September 1983.

29. *Endoqui* ("signifying") and *endoque* ("signifying on") play off each other. The second is possibly a Hispanic deformation of the original, a sort of "counter-signifying."

30. The cross sign appears in precolonial Yoruba, BaKongo, and Efik-Ejagham civilizations. In Cuba, the *Abakuá* society adopted two variations on the theme of the cross: the crossed bananas and the cross with white flowers. For the sign of the crossed bananas, see Robert Farris Thompson's personal account and discussion of a similar African sign in his *African Art in Motion. Icon and Act* (1974; reprint, Los Angeles, Berkeley, London: University of California Press, 1979), 85 and note 155. For the sign of the cross with flowers, see Garófalo Mesa, *Leyendas y tradiciones villaclareñas* (Havana: n.p., 1925), quoted by Samuel Feijóo in his *El negro en la literatura folklórica cubana* (Havana: Editorial Letras Cubanas, 1980), 328.

31. See Enrique Sosa Rodríguez, *Los ñáñigos* (Havana: Casa de las Américas, 1982), 191–215.

32. Sosa Rodríguez's entire book *(Los ñáñigos)* concerns itself with this subject. See particularly pp. 115–150.

33. For a thorough definition of the term, see *"Jigüe,"* in Fernando Ortiz, *Nuevo catauro de cubanismos* (1923; revised edition, Havana: Editorial de Ciencias Sociales, 1974), 305.

34. In Ramón Guirao, *Orbita de la poesía afrocubana (1928–37)* (Havana: Ucar, García, 1983), 177–80. The poem is dated 1936.

35. In Nicolás Guillén, *West Indies Ltd.* (Havana, 1934). Edition consulted was *Sóngoro cosongo, Motivos de son, West Indies Ltd.*, *España*, 4th ed. (Buenos Aires: Losada, 1967), 62–64.

36. All of Radillo's quotes refer to his "Canción del jigüe." This passage is on pp. 177–178; from now on the page numbers are given parenthetically in the text.

37. For a dictionary definition of *nganga* in the KiKongo-Cuban dialect, see Germán de Granda, *De la matrice africaine de la "Langue Congo" de Cuba (Recherches préliminaires)* (Dakar: Centre de Hautes Etudes Afro-Ibéro-Américaines, 1973), 15.

38. All of Guillén's quotes refer to his "Balada del güije." This passage is on p. 68; from now on the page numbers are given parenthetically in the text.

39. The *Abakuá* society, which we have defined as the most important defender of

the Afro-Cuban code, is based on an Efik-Ejagham male society, which, in turn derives its ritual from a female society. See Sosa Rodríguez, *Los ñáñigos*, 81–110.

40. For the myth of the *Coco*, see Fernando Ortiz, "El cocorícamo y otros conceptos teoplásmicos del folklore afrocubano," *Archivos del Folklore Cubano* (Havana) 4, no. 4 (1929): 289–312.

41. The "necklace" most likely refers to the divination chain, which was traded by Shango to Ifa along with the most important body of African texts. Since then Shango worshippers wear, instead, red and white beads around their neck. See Fernando Ortiz, *Los bailes y el teatro de los negros en el folklore de Cuba* (Havana: Cárdenas, 1951), 124.

42. The Yoruba-Cuban interpretation of Shango is not much different from the original Yoruba interpretation, except for the syncretic association with Saint Barbara (a minor Catholic saint) and the fact that it retains its original association with divination as well as taking a firm stand on the wisdom of upholding traditional values. On the general definition of Shango's powers, see Thompson, *Black Gods and Kings,* chapter 12, 1–5.

43. See note 41.

44. For a definition of Nyeke, see "Ñeque" in Ortiz, *Nuevo catauro*, 375–378.

Ifá and Interpretation

EUGENIO MATIBAG

An Afro-Caribbean Literary Practice

The function of the babalao, *of the human, is to learn to read the language of the gods between the lines—the symbolism, the metaphor, the labyrinth of sacred writing, and the circumstantial and constant changes of each new writing.*

— JULIA CUERVO HEWITT, *Aché, presencia africana*

EDWARD KAMAU BRATHWAITE has argued that the "focus" of Afro-Caribbean culture is religious and that religion centers that culture through the transmission and use of sacred narratives that contain etiological, cosmogonic, and moral messages.[1] In religious practice, those messages are communicated in divination. Divination mediates between the earth (*aiye*) and heaven (*orun*).[2] It proffers counsel and guidance to believers at all critical junctures and transitional experiences of the life cycle. Of the three methods of divination most widely practiced in the Americas—the coconut (*obi*), cowries (*diloggún*), and Ifá—Ifá seems the most trusted and prestigious; comparing it with the other two, Miguel Barnet calls it an oracle of "higher importance but no greater efficacy."[3]

Julia Cuervo Hewitt suggests a fruitful analogy between reading and divination in *Aché, presencia africana*, where she writes that, "like the babalao, the client going for a consultation, the contemporary narrator, the testimonial narrator, and the modern reader require the same interpretative perspicacity to interlace correspondences and meaning—to interpret—to learn to read the ambiguities of the letters between the lines."[4] In Ifá, one performs a discursive, intertextual act in which myth and personal history are made to interact through the medium of language. This act recalls Giambattista Vico's writings on a "divination" practiced by the ancient "theological poets" that he called "the science of the language of the gods."[5] Edouard Glissant of Martinique bases a "vision prophetique du passé" on Viconian criteria and advances it as a means of revising and rewriting Caribbean history.[6] The corpus of Ifá in particular contains a wealth of narrative materials for the literary manifestations of poetic divination: motifs, themes, pharmacopeia, therapeutic utterances, and practical wisdom in the form of fables and proverbs. These materials have appeared in the works of such writers as José Antonio Ramos, Rómulo Lachatañeré, Lydia Cabrera, Gerardo del Valle, Alejo Carpentier, Manuel Granados, Manuel Cofiño, Miguel Barnet, Excilia Saldaña, Rogelio Martínez Furé, Nancy Morejón, and Manuel Zapata Olivella.

According to 'Wande Abimbola, the name *Ifá* refers both to a Yoruba divinity, Orúmila (also Orúmìlà), and to his system of divination.[7] As the codification and means of transmission of an entire body of knowledge, Ifá "is the Yoruba traditional thought-system *par excellence*" (vi). Through Ifá, the diviner, or *babalao*, gives counsel to the clients and makes predictions on the basis of specific alternatives. He prescribes correct behavior and appropriate sacrifice. By casting and reading the *ikin* nuts, or the more commonly used chain called *opele* (in Nigeria; *ekpuele* in Cuba), he registers the fate of a newborn, the rightness of a marriage, or the measures to be taken for carrying out a funeral. Through Ifá and the babalao, humans and *orishas* (divinities) communicate. In the mythic beginnings of the oracle, the Supreme God Olodumare (Odumare or Olorun) bestowed the palm nuts and divining tray on Orúmila, intending to use it as a means of communication between himself and the orishas. Olodumare is also said to have invented the divine language through which the oracle speaks. As Olodumare's intermediary, Orúmila is the deity of wisdom, law and order, and social harmony; as the one who bridges the distance between gods and humans, he provides guidance and reassurance in the face of life's uncertainties.[8]

For Benetta Jules-Rosette, African divination is a self-validating system of thought offering "strategies for handling problems in daily life" and therefore must be understood as mediating between the client's misfortunes and the social structure.[9] Divination may mediate between individual desire and the social context, although its "misuse" can also work against the interests of the collectivity. Among the "consensual community," the words of the oracle are considered sacred because they come directly from Ifá. They demand belief. The faith in the Ifá system and probably its efficacy are based on the related belief that each of us chooses a personal destiny, determining future success or failure, when we kneel before Olodumare prior to birth.[10] At birth we forget this destiny, but, fortunately, Orúmila was present on the day we chose it. Orúmila is therefore also called *Elérìí-ìpín*, witness of destiny, he who knows the whole of our lives and can offer advice for confronting any eventuality; he even knows the day of our deaths, and he knows how to change it, an ability that gives him the name *Oktíbìrí apajó-ikú-dà*, "the great changer, he who alters the day of death."[11]

The Ifá itself is a vast information-retrieval system that preserves, accesses, and processes the texts of mythological, naturalist, medicinal, and spiritual knowledge. At the heart of the Ifá system lie the thousands of narratives that the babalao has memorized as part of his training and that he recites to clients in consultations.[12] In the Afro-Cuban context these narratives are called *patakí*, a group of prosified verses also known as *caminos*.[13] The patakí derive from the Yoruba *ese Ifá*, the word *ese* meaning rows.[14] The diviner generally recites these verses as a part of the consultation, then goes on to interpret their meaning in relation to the situation of the client.

In divining, the babalao, whose name means "father of mysteries," uses either of two interchangeable divination instruments—the ikin palm nuts or the faster and more convenient opele chain. When cast in the correct manner, either instrument indicates a series of eight vertical markings, set in two columns of four, which constitute the configuration called an *odu* or *orgún*. With each cast, one of sixteen possible configurations results. After counting the possible configurations in two columns, we square the number of combinations (16 x 16) to get a total number of 256 odu. To each odu corresponds a set of verses, accompanying proverbs, and sacrifices, *ebbó*. The client is urged to follow the counsel provided in those verses and proverbs and to carry out the indicated ebbó in order to obtain a fortunate outcome or to avert misfortune.

The themes of the ese Ifá or patakí include some that have a universal significance and some that speak more to those acculturated in a West African or Afro-Caribbean context. William Bascom's list of themes, drawn from his collection of 186 verses, includes all of the five kinds of good; in order of their importance, each as a precondition for the succeeding one(s), they are "long life or 'not death' (aiju), money (aje, owo), marriage or wives (aya, iyawo), children (omo), and victory (isegun) over one's enemies."[15] In addition, there are five kinds of evil: "death (iku), sickness (arun, aisan), fighting (ija), the want of money (aje, owo), and loss (ofun)" (55). Death appears the most prevalent theme (thirty-six verses), followed by the desire for children (73).

Each odu corresponds to a specific set of patakí, and each patakí, to a certain orisha in one of the god's caminos or avatars. The patakí contains an ethical teaching or moral. Also, with each odu goes a corresponding *refrán*, or saying. As Cuervo Hewitt points out, the proverb contains a narrative theme illustrative of the client's past, present, and future conditions. For example, the saying "No one knows what is at the bottom of the sea" is linked with anecdotes signaling the arrival of something hidden or unexpected, the unknown. As the surprise endings of the corresponding narratives forewarn, the client for whom that odu is cast must beware of visitors and not cross the jungle (90). Olatunde Olatunji notes that most of the Ifá narratives consist of etiological stories—they tell why something in nature or in religious practice came to be.[16] Many narratives are animal fables; the orishas, or African deities, often appear as characters or supernatural agents.

Bascom emphasizes that the particular odu does not directly or simply indicate a particular prediction, ebbó, orisha, or outcome, favorable or unfavorable. Rather, the cluster of verses corresponding to the figure includes a variety of heterogeneous messages. Indeed, both positive and negative verses and predictions attach to a particular odu (42). Several deities may appear in the various verses, and different orishas may appear in the odu of some kingdoms and not in those of others; it is also true, however, that a particular orisha may dominate the verses of some odu. Bascom gives the example of the figure Iwori Meji, whose verses mention Naná Burukú and Sopona in Ifé but not in Meko, and the Meko diviners do not mention Oggún, as do those of Oyo (43).

Although Ifá is an oracle, literally an orally delivered prophecy that transmits a body of interconnected texts belonging to "oral literature," associations of Ifá with writing, language, and inscription are frequently made by native informants. In Cuba, among the most valuable resources for investigation into the field of orisha folklore and ritual are the *libretas sagradas*, notebooks and handwritten manuscripts containing personal treasuries of this sacred literature, written in part *cubano* and part *lucumí*. Migene González-Wippler recounts her *madrina's* instructions, given in the United States, to write down the Yoruba words of an invocation to Elegguá in a notebook: "I had no way of knowing that my little notebook was the beginning of my *libreta*, the traditional journal where all the santeros and their followers write down the cult's various rituals."[17] The Cuban folklorist Rogelio Martínez Furé enumerates the contents of the booklets: "In the *Libretas* we find hundreds of myths and fables, lists of proverbs, Yoruba-Spanish lexicons, sacred formulas, tales of the orishas and details of their avatars, songs, the divination systems and their secrets, the names of the herbs of the gods and their use in the rituals and popular pharmacopeia, etc. In short, all the wisdom of the ancient Yorubas and their culture, which refuses to die."[18] What is striking about this catalogue is that it lists the "genres" of "writing" included in the babalao's repertoire, and it includes the narratives and formulas that Martínez Furé refers to as "wisdom." In this written form, the santero can pass on his knowledge to his *ahijados*—godchildren, or protégés, in the practice. In Havana and other cities, libretas are mimeographed and even printed and sold, some at a considerable price.

As Martínez Furé's characterization suggests, the libretas in Cuba do the work that oral transmission would accomplish between babalao and apprentice in Nigeria. Whereas the Lucumí tradition has depended on writing for the preservation and transmission of divination narratives, the consciousness of "writing" in some form as a precondition to oracular speech can be traced back to the Yoruba culture before the colonial period. Bascom (107) links the name of Ifá to *fa*, scraping, appropriate to one who characteristically scrapes away illness and evil, or one who marks the figure of the divining tray by "scraping" the *yefa* (special sawdust) sprinkled on it. (The other name of Ifá, Orúmila, is based on the earlier name Ela, which in turn is based on *la*, to open.)

The Logic of Divination

Yoruba and Afro-Cuban believers consult Ifá in preparation for any major event. Yoruba clients tend to trust in the divination system regardless of their familiarity with the babalao or degree of trust in him.[19] When a baby is born among the Yoruba, for instance, the parents take the child to the babalao for a consultation. The babalao casts Ifá to determine which ancestral guardian soul, or *orí*, has reincarnated in the baby, thus deciding the child's fate and the taboos the child should observe as he or she grows.[20] Fate includes the subject's station in life, financial status, occupation, and the day on which the soul will return to heaven once the assigned lifespan has been completed.[21] Although the course of life is set, individuals may improve or worsen their destiny, and Orúmila may advise clients on the means of increasing blessings through prayer, sacrifice, and other ritual behaviors, on avoiding danger, and on observing the taboo.[22] A source of counsel, literature, and prophecy, Ifá has been called the Yoruba Bible. And it is apparent that the range, diversity, and lucidity of Ifá suit the purposes of all who believe and seek solutions to their problems in the oracle. In Bascom's words, "Because the verses and predictions touch on such a wide range of religious beliefs and prescribe sacrifices to so many different 'supernatural' beings and forces, Ifá divination is the focal point in Yoruba religion" (118).

Sacrifice is essential in Yoruba religion, for without it the client may not achieve the object desired or avert the danger anticipated. Part of the babalao's responsibility is to tell the client the form of sacrifice indicated by the Ifá verse. As detailed by Bascom, the form of sacrifice consists of the selection of specific plants and animals to be offered, and the manner and order in which they are to be offered (60). Among the Yoruba, all ebbó, with the exception of *adimu* (which are made to specific deities), must be offered to the shrine of Eshu, symbolized in Ifá through a rough-hewn piece of laterite placed outside the gate of the compound. The sacrifice acknowledges and placates the trickster god; it constitutes a small bribe to keep him from sabotaging the purpose of the sacrifice. Bascom records the prayer recited by the client: "Eshu, here is my sacrifice. Please tell Olorun (the Sky God) to accept my sacrifice and relieve my suffering" (65).[23] (In the Afro-Caribbean, according to Julio Sánchez, the three Eshus allied with the babalao are called Agunacue, Vivakikeño, and Kikeño Laroye [23].)

Sacrifice is thus the constant in the divination narratives, and the resolution of the problem, or the averting or mitigating of an imminent danger, depends on the exact and scrupulous execution of the prescribed offering. Barnet presents a patakí-based fable, "Why Do Birds Live in the Trees of the Bush?" (17–19), that is not only an etiological but an etymological story because it reveals the origins of the name given to sacrifice, or the ritual of purification necessary to "feed" the orishas. As the story goes, the birds take turns governing the village of Icá in the time before kings wore crowns. But then, each rule becomes a short one, because for some unknown reason the ruling bird dies after a year. The turn to rule comes to the bird called Ebbó, who, wanting to live for more than a year, departs on a journey to Orúmila's house in order to find out from the owner of Ifá how he might prolong his own life. In the course of the arduous trip Ebbó must cross an estuary, traverse a river four times atop the tortoise, and soar over walls of palm thatch. He finally reaches the house of Orúmila, only to find there a long line of animals waiting to consult the oracle. He must perch in the top of a tree and wait a year. When Ebbó finally has his turn with Orúmila, the diviner tells him that what he has been doing is what he should do in order to rule forever. This is the reason why the birds stay up in the trees, "skipping from one to the other" instead of "crawling on the ground searching for grains of corn or majá eggs." The fable concludes with a reflection on the meaning of Ebbó's name: "And when Orúmila gives counsel he always says Ebbó, which is the name of that bird that lasted so long because he climbed the trees in the bush" (19). Ebbó not only designates a ceremony of sacrifice or purification in Cuba but also signifies a spell or charm. As the fable "proves," Ebbó's forbearance and renunciation were considered sufficient "offering" to merit long dominion and longer life.

In Olatunji's view, the Ifá accords a sort of mystical legitimation to a line of action recommended by the babalao; directed along a single course, the client gains confidence and clarity from the counsel given in this manner. In narratological terms, the oracle of Ifá offers a story that may suggest the way that the clients, as protagonists of their own narratives, understand the options available at a particular juncture. For this reason they consult Ifá about certain major events or on the verge of major decisions, as with the choice of a career or a king (109).

One can suppose that the clients' faith in Ifá, their ingrained belief in the truthfulness and reliability of the system, contributes indispensably to its effectiveness and success. Failure may be rationalized, attributed to factors external to Ifá itself, including the incompetence or dishonesty of the diviner, but the system itself goes unquestioned.[24] At any rate, the client consults with one who is considered an authority or expert possessed of the means with which to transmit the word of Orúmila. With that word, divination performs the function of clarifying specific alternatives and setting a course of action for the client, thereby removing some of the doubt, indecision, and anxiety that accompany choice. As Bascom puts it, "When decisions are left to divine guidance rather than chance, the individual has far greater assurance that he is following the correct course of action. He can proceed with greater confidence; and, accordingly, in some cases he probably has a greater chance of success" (70).

In the Afro-Cuban *registro*, or consultation, prophecy and counsel are one and the same, and the forms of advice are ambiguous, flexible enough to accommodate a variety of situations: "Beware of betrayal," "Follow your own line," "Ask much of Changó," "Be careful with fire," "Do not mistreat women," "Never bathe in the water of a river," "Offer this sacrifice." Such advice often hits close to home or strikes a sympathetic chord in the client's interpreted world, giving a narrative form to otherwise inchoate experience.

Procedure

The registro, as stated earlier, relies on a "reading" of the configurations determined by a specific procedure of casting palm nuts or else the okpele necklace. The procedure is taken seriously by diviner and client, and this sacralizing attitude confers in effect a truth value on the outcome of the reading. The seriousness of the entire proceeding confers a privileged status on the babalao's pronouncements. The half-palm nuts, or *ikines*, handled by the babalao in the divination ritual come from the oil palm, *ope*, or *Elaeis guineensis idolatrica*.[25] These are the most time-honored or classic divination instruments. The results of the casting are recorded on the yefa sprinkled on the *okpón*, divining tray. A small stone, a cowry shell, a piece of bone—the client picks up one or two of these and conceals them in the fist of one hand. After a cast of the ikines or the chain, the diviner performs the *iresugbo*, or "yes/no" operation, by asking the client to reveal what she holds in either the left or right hand—

one or two pieces or nothing; the cowry means yes, and the bone, no. According to Abimbola, the client's *orí*, or divine guardian, determines which one of a number of stories will be recited and thus narrows down the selection. The babalao repeats the iresugbo, asking in this way specific questions in response to the responses given by Ifá. A dialogue with the oracle thus ensues until the babalao is satisfied that the client's problem has been addressed.[26]

Instead of the ikin nuts, the babalao may use the divining necklace, which consists of a chain of thin metal links, about fifty inches in length, interrupted by eight round or oval-shaped disks of tortoise shell or metal about an inch and a half in length. The babalao pinches the chain by the middle, letting dangle four disks on either side, then casts the chain upon a mat. Quicker, more portable, and more conveniently handled than the ikines, the opele "spells" out the figure without need for the okpón or yefa. It is used more frequently than the ikines, which tend to be used more for consultations within the family.

At the beginning of a divination, the client makes a small offering of money, a *derecho*, to Eshu, the trickster who must be propitiated so that the message meets with no obstacle or distortion. If using the nuts, the babalao proceeds by holding the sixteen ikines in one hand and then removing most or all of them with the other, trying to leave one or two in the first hand. If one nut is left, then he draws two parallel lines in the yefa sprinkled on the Ifá board, or okpón; if he leaves two nuts, he draws one line. He carries out this procedure a total of eight times, each time drawing on the okpón until the odu is completed. The actual casting of the sixteen ikin palm nuts is referred to as *dafa* or *da Ifá*, the verb that is also used to denote the act of throwing grain to chickens or pitching out water.[27]

Each of the two sides of the figure bears a name and signifies in itself. The right side, considered "male" and the stronger of the two, is the *otun*; on the left, "female" side, is *osi*. The marking of the figure proceeds from right to left, right to left, and the compound or derivative figure receives a compound name consisting of the right-side name plus the left-side name.[28] Each side permits sixteen different configurations. The sixteen major combinations, based on the occurrence of identical figures on the two sides—*meyi* or *melli*, twins—are multiplied by the sixteen minor odu (or *omo-odu*, sons of odu) contained in each major odu, making a total of 256 odu. The minor combinations of two different odu sides are called *amulu*.[29] The mythical significance of the number sixteen originates in the number of branches that extended out from the first palm tree at the center of the world, Ile-Ife, soon after its creation by Olodùmare. The first oni of Ile-Ife, Odùddua, symbolizing totality in conjunction with Obbatalá, fathered sixteen sons, each of whom ruled over a Yoruba kingdom. Further, Orúmila himself has sixteen children, to whom he taught the art of Ifá.[30]

Once the indicated verses have been recited and a particular verse has been chosen as the appropriate one by the client, the consultation may continue in the form of a series of questions posing specific and mutually exclusive alternatives. When the client presents two specific alternatives—for example, "The venture which I am considering will be good for me" versus its opposite—the diviner casts the chain two times, once for the positive statement, again for the negative statement. The casting with the higher rank indicates which of the two is the valid one.[31] A long and elaborate series of casts following this step, which Bascom outlines, continues the process initiated in the first cast and recitation of verses and further elaborates the meaning of the ese Ifá (59).

Sacred Narratives

The total number of Ifá verses seems interminable. Bascom reports that the verses vary from region to region; informants have told him that there are sixteen for each of the 256 odu, which would make a total of 4,096 (42). Because sixteen is a sacred number, however, that total is probably symbolic. Abimbola remarks that the number of ese constituting each odu is indefinite. Legendary priests of the past were said to know more than two hundred for each odu, but today a good Ifá priest will be able to recite about sixteen, and an extraordinary babalao rarely knows more than twenty. The length of the ese varies: according to Abimbola, the shortest may take as little as two to three minutes to recite, whereas some of the longest ones require more than thirty. Abimbola attributes the variety in lengths to distinct kinds of changes in the ese. First, an ese, because it is handed down orally from generation to generation, may lose sections (and entire ese from the Ifá corpus may be lost in similar manner). Second, one story or parts of one story may merge with another story. A sort of dynamic equilibrium is established by a story's ongoing growth and shrinkage within the Ifá corpus.[32]

The oracle of the Ifá offers a model for organizing narrative and for producing further narratives. Indeed, as a technology for drawing order out of chance and contingency, Ifá makes a narrative of experience and connects experience with social and cosmic patterns of meaning. Joseph Murphy confirms this notion in asserting that divination "offers the means for interpreting the meaning of random events";[33] it may help the babalao and client to plot or make a narrative of those events, especially insofar as they resemble the events narrated in the odu or pataki. As one of the pillars of the Afro-Cuban religion, Ifá divination thus constitutes a semiotic system that exhibits a complexity and unity comparable to those of highly developed philosophical systems.

The Ifá literary corpus thus serves more than just the ends of divination. It is an authentic, mobile archive of the Yoruba *epistème*. Bascom asserts that the Yoruba regard the oracle as the word of truth. Its verse narratives, proverbs, myths or "myth legends," riddles, praise names, incantations are said to contain knowledge of religion, medicine, history, science, politics. Bascom also compares the Ifá narratives to the *exempla* included by medieval priests to illustrate the message of their sermons (122). According to Abimbola, in the Ifá literary corpus of *suyere* (praise songs), the dominant poetic devices are "repetition, word play and personification."[34]

Ulli Beier refers to the ese Ifá as "the numerous inventions of the Ifá oracle, whose major function is to provide a precedent, with the help of which the babalao can advise his client on the right course of action to take. Sometimes existing religious myths can serve this purpose, but on many occasions the stories of the Ifá oracle are tales with divine protagonists, specially created for the purpose of assisting the process of divination."[35] Beier provides an example for one ese Ifá with his retelling of the story of Obbatalá and Ojiya (14–15). In that narrative, Ojiya is a blind fisherman who, having had his fish stolen by some mysterious stranger, asks the babalaos to read the Ifá for him. The oracle provides Ojiya with a song identifying the thief: he is Obbatalá, the maker of the human race, who, wearing a white gown and white metal bracelet, has used the stolen fish in a charm that would give him the power that "made his words come to pass" (15). Obbatalá begs that Ojiya not tell his secret; Ojiya begs Obbatalá to give him sight. In the end, "Obbatalá did so, and since then all Obbatalá devotees are forbidden to eat fish" (15).[36]

Aside from the Ifá verses, Yoruba also tell related prose narratives that fall into the categories of myths legends (*itan*), regarded as truth and history, and of folktales (*alo*), which are considered fiction. Many of the ese are told outside the divination context, perhaps because of Christian and Islamic acculturation.[37] Among those raised in the Yoruba religion, however, the transmission of such narratives and their repetition gradually instill an implicit belief in the system of the oracle.[38] Bascom's babalao informants tell him that all myth legends and folktales have their source in the ese Ifá; Bascom finds it more plausible that the material of those narrative forms was incorporated into the Ifá.[39]

Semantic Aspects of Ifá Narratives

As Olatunji notes, the majority of the Ifá narratives consist of etiological stories, telling why something in nature or in religious practice came to be (124). In addition, the ese Ifá, according to Bascom, perform the function of giving a realistic effect to the reading by referring to familiar natural phenomena such as plants, animals, and rituals. By anchoring the ritual in the language of common knowledge, they "substantiate the truth of the verse, with its prediction and sacrifice, and the system of divination as a whole."[40] González-Wippler offers an informal classification of the patakí in the introduction to her anthology, *Tales of the Orishas*. There she calls them explanatory "myths," and the patakí indeed exhibit repetitive features and functions according to which they may be classified. The patakís explain the creation of the world and of humanity, interactions between humans and nature, interactions between humans and the orishas, and interactions among the orishas themselves.[41] A close reading of representative patakí and a consideration of their interrelations later in this essay suggest the architectonics of the "entire edifice of the Yorubas."[42]

Speaking of the animal fables among the patakí, Julio García Cortez notes that one finds evidence of the close contact between humans and animals in them. The orishas, too, communicate and otherwise interact with animals. The animal fables fall into at least three categories: those that are "pure fantasy"; "projections of human desires, good as well as bad in which our virtues and weaknesses are reflected"; and the "explicatory" ones, which, like Kipling's just-so stories, tell us, for example, "why the cock has feathers"; in addition to explaining some custom or natural phenomenon, the explicatory ones tend to contain a moral.[43]

Although materials from the outside may be introduced and incorporated into the odu, the Yoruba diviners take care to maintain the Ifá corpus free of "adulteration" and to ensure that all additional stories or story parts are the product of true "inspiration" and come from "inside" the system. In a section both revealing and suggestive for our approach to the orisha tradition, Abimbola characterizes the content of the ese Ifá.

> Ese Ifá deals with all subjects. It deals with history, geography, religion, music and philosophy. Ese Ifá may be a simple story about a man going on a journey and asking for advice on how to make the journey successful. It may be a highly philosophical story showing the merits and demerits of monogamy. It may deal with the foundation of a particular town. There is certainly no limit to the subject matter which ese Ifá may deal with.
>
> Ese Ifá is, therefore, a story or a group of stories taken from the rich experiences of our forefathers. These stories are lists of what happened before in history. They are lists of precedents carefully laid down for us. The underlying philosophy of the whole system is that history repeats itself. It is a philosophy which points to the conclusion that we can learn from the experiences of the past.[44]

Many of the client predecessors named in the beginning part of the ese Ifá are orishas; others are deified personifications of the odu. In one ese, the clients are the four hundred orishas on the right.[45] Stories referring to the divination system itself frequently appear; they retell the system's origins, its first owners, its transferrals, its history—all certifying the system's function as purveyor of truth and counsel. Orúmila is the protagonist in many of those stories and often consults the oracle himself in the action of the ese plot.

The Syntax of Ifá Narratives

In the ese Ifá that he recorded, Bascom finds a dominant three-part pattern: a statement of the mythological case precedent, naming babalao(s), clients, and the problem; the outcome of carrying out (or not carrying out) the prescribed sacrifice, often with a section that explains what was left obscure in the first part; and an application to the present client—that is, the babalao's interpretation of the data for the client; this section is not a part of the ese Ifá proper.[46] The examples from Yoruba babalaos provided by Bascom, Abimbola, and Olatunji generally follow the pattern that names the consultation precedents and results. In the Cuban and Afro-Caribbean patakí, the pattern becomes simpler, more flexible, conversational, and improvisational, with some of the ese's plot elements, praise names, allusions, and figurative language omitted.[47]

Abimbola, in describing the African ese Ifá, outlines the four parts of its "general pattern." In the first part, the client receives the ebbó, which prescribes the sacrifice, identifying what is to be sacrificed and the orisha to whom it will be made. Warnings and advice are also given. Abimbola gives the following example: "This person is intending to marry a new wife. He is warned to make sacrifice to Osun so that the wife may be prosperous. He is warned never to flog the wife if he wants peace in his home. He should sacrifice with fifteen cowries and a big hen. Ifá says that if he observes all these warnings, success will be his."[48] In the second part of the ese, the client hears the names of the priests and clients of the divination precedents. The names may be symbolic praise names: a babalao of the savanna may be called "Giant-grass," for instance. The third part relates the previous divination. It is often told two times, in poetry and then again in prose, or is omitted if the rest of the ese suffices to send the message. Abimbola gives the example of a reference back to the precedent: "When his life was in danger of death. He was asked to make sacrifice, and he made it. He was told that he would not die." Part four of the ese reports the outcome of the previous divination and relates it, in the form of a lesson, to the present client. The past anticipates the future, so an inauspicious result before indicates an untoward result afterward, in the client's future. The babalao often has recourse to an indirect means of delivering the message—"it is veiled in philosophy and wisdom" (16). The ceremony is poetic throughout following the first part and is often chanted. A chorus sung by the priest, students, and clients sometimes concludes the ceremony.[49]

In the Cuban and Afro-Caribbean context, as would be expected, the multigeneric, syncretic, and improvised format of the notebooks, libretas, and other forms of inscription effects a change in the patakí. Cuervo Hewitt has observed that "in the manuscripts or libretas of the pataki that I have seen you can find a tendency in America to synthesize the more important elements of each odu into very short anecdotes which perhaps lose the original ese, but through which, on the other hand, the dynamic vitality of the myth-poetry in the collective, colloquial, and archetypical language of the Cuban people is gained" (77). More than a mere potpourri of texts, the combined ese linked and synthesized in the libretas thus provide a concentrated form of the odu, a form more suited than the classic Yoruba structure to the needs and concerns of the Lucumí believer.

Ifá in Afro-Cuba

To elucidate the Afro-Cuban practice, Sánchez provides a useful schema and examples, stressing that the patakís are the verses that go with corresponding odu. "Such verses begin with an introductory part in Yoruba . . . [and] contain, moreover, an illustrative story that clarifies the content of the verse. Following the verse there is an explanatory section that begins with the phrase: 'Ifá says,' which indicates the problem the client must confront and prescribes the type of sacrifice, offering, or ceremony to undertake" (50). Sánchez follows this outline with an example of a narrative containing verses, explanation, and an explicatory section (50–51).

Martínez Furé's fourteen pataki-based narratives in *Diálogos imaginarios* tell stories of original causes and of animals, gods, and humans. Orúmila and other orishas appear or are mentioned in eleven of the stories. Two of the stories are the animal fables "The Cinder-Covered Bird" and "Oturasa, Arikoshé, and Ayapá Tiroko." Of the remaining twelve, Orúmila does his work of divining and giving counsel in all but two stories. In "Iká and the Corn," it is Orúmila's friend Eshú who pushes the greedy Iká from atop his pile of corn, making him share it with the mouse and the rest of the world. In "The Son of the Babalao and the Son of Death," a *rogación*, or purification ritual, saves the babalao's son from losing a bet with the son of Death. The stories for the most part thus refer to essential components of the divination ritual, presenting and contextualizing the terminology pertinent to the ritual and listing some of the ingredients of the ebbó. The stories also legitimate the divination ritual by illustrating the consequences of carrying through—or not carrying through—the instructions of Ifá.[50]

Diálogos imaginarios classifies the entire body of patakís into the three categories of myth, fable, and legend. The myths tell the lives and exploits of the orishas, recount the creation of the world and of humans, and often explain the origins of practices or prohibitions. The fables feature animals as characters and teach moral precepts, often by castigating antisocial attitudes and behavior such as greed, envy, and lying. In legends, humans are the protagonists, with animals or orishas intervening in the action. Martínez Furé lists a number of features of this oral literature of African roots. Briefly, they are: a simple and direct style; magical realism; reiteration as a stylistic element; insertion of songs within narrations; shifts in verbal tense from past to present and vice versa; didacticism and moralizing, explicit in the end proverb; propaganda exalting the priestly caste; universal symbolism; exaltation of human and social values. In addition to these features, Martínez Furé briefly characterizes the three "levels of development and antiquity" of Afro-Cuban narrative: the oldest, of strictly Yoruba "content"; the intermediary, presenting a mixture of African and colonial cultures; and the most recent, developed in Cuba on the Yoruba model (216–217).

The most comprehensive sourcebook for Ifá proverbs, prayers, and narratives available in the United States is the one written by José María Castillo, an *obá oriaté*, or santero, with expertise in divination; the full title of his book is *Ifá en tierra de Ifá con su gran oráculo, 16 melles, 365 ordún [y] más de 1000 historia[s] y eboces*. A prefatory note informs the reader that the book is intended "exclusively for babalaos and men who have made Ifá." Throughout Castillo's book, the odu appear to be transcriptions of oral texts. They often consist of a single run-on sentence, often difficult to read because of their lack of standard punctuation. This difficulty is compounded by frequent typographical errors or idiosyncratic spellings based on pronunciation. The format is consistent for each of the 365 odu; each is announced in an upper-case heading and a graphic representation of the configuration. A proverb, a prediction, a standard injunction, the name of a plant, or a mythological motif (also at times a taboo) is printed to the right side or just below the configuration.[51]

To illustrate: Ordi Ellobe or Erdibe (IIII IOOI) corresponds to "birth of the drum"; its *egue*, or medicinal plant, is the jaguey; one must not kill mice when this sign appears. (It happens too that Erdibe is the name of the protagonist of one odu narrative.) Next comes a notice of which orishas "speak" through the odu; in the case of Erdibe it is Changó and all the rest of the *siete potencias africanas* (the seven African powers, also including Elegguá, Ochosí, Oggún, Ochún, Yemayá, and Obbatalá). The client learns that he or she, as child of the odu, can expect either luck, as did Erdibe, or money, and that he or she should "make" or receive the "mano de Ifá" (the carved figure of a hand on which the tips of the fingers represent different orishas; it is given to a babalao at the moment of initiation as a symbol of rank and power). Following on the same page are the *suyere* that are chanted in Anagó to Changó, "Orgun," and other orishas. Next comes a sample of the counsel, written in the second person and in the present tense, addressing the client's situation; and then follows the prescription of ebbó. Erdibe offers several ebbó, each one suited for a particular purpose. For the purpose of being able to return to a woman, one sacrifices a cock, five doves, and a male goat. A series of stories, some of them featuring Erdibe, follow the ebbó prescription; one story refers to the invention of the drum by Erdibe out of palm wood and goat hide—the reason he became the principal drummer to Changó (127–129).

A patakí for Ellobe Melle (IIII IIII) explains Ifá's power over death; it is retold in Lydia Cabrera's "Se hace ebbó" but received its first literary treatment in Rómulo Lachatañeré's "Orúmbila and Icú."[52] In Lachatañeré's version, Orúmila, as a favor to a desperate mother, acts to avert the arrival of Death (*Icú*) to the sickbed of a dying boy; he marks a cross with plaster on the boy's forehead and then scatters and pounds four basketfuls of *quimbombó* (okra) on the floor of the *ilé* (house). Death arrives, only to slip and slide on the mashed quimbombó and to cower at the cracking of Orúmila's whip. Death escapes into an empty bottle, which Orúmila immediately stops up. Death pleads for release from the "humiliation"; Orúmila points to the plaster cross. "Do you see this signal? It means that whoever has it is under my protection and you must therefore respect it. Do you accept my condition?" Icú does; the child recovers. From that day on, Death has the habit of hiding in open bottles, and "it is therefore very dangerous to keep them uncovered" (180). From that day on, too, Orúmila has a special dominion over Death and possesses the powerful sign that sends her away. In Castillo's version of a similar fable from the registro, Orúmila plies Icú with food and drink, then hides her scythe after she has dozed off. On her awakening, "Icú's pleas were such that she promised she would not kill him or any of his children, unless he himself offered one of them; Orúmila vanquished death and this is the reason why [his] children can save anyone on the verge of death" (8).

The story of the chameleon who killed his own mother with the power given him by Olofin is told by Castillo for the figure of Ojuani Melle (OOII OOII). Chameleon began by envying the color of the dog and later desired the power to kill with his looks (22, 23–24). Martínez Furé's "The Envious Chameleon" tells the same story. A chameleon wants to have the color of the dog. He goes for a consultation, *a registrarse*, in the house of Orúmila, who tells him neither to envy nor to desire harm for anyone, and does a rogación that grants chameleon his desire. Chameleon can change his color but now desires the power of dominating others with his look. Expressing a primary ethical principle, Orúmila cautions that "the evil one seeks for another can revert unto oneself." Insisting nonetheless, chameleon receives his *trabajo*, or spell, in the form of polvos, with the instruction that he go to his house right away. Chameleon does so, only to strike his own mother dead at the door. This matricide explains why "each time people see a chameleon they throw stones or beat it with a stick to kill it, and each time one of them climbs a tree it changes color and sticks out a thing it has on its neck" (219). The myth identifies the pouch under the chameleon's chin as a stigma of his sin and his crime.

As these examples suggest, Ifá divination supports a number of important notions in Afro-Caribbean studies. First, the texts of the Ifá literary corpus are truly Afro-Hispanic in language and reflect the transculturative process in their translation to an American context. Second, Ifá's success as communication requires a specific ritual context complete with liturgies and protocols; this context forms part of the broader context created by the religious community and its consensus of belief, and bears comparison with other discursive "communities of consensus." Third, the system of Ifá demonstrates how a social-religious discourse/practice can preserve, order, and transmit an extensive, unified body of narrative knowledge. It forms a canon of works in itself and also serves as an important source of Afro-Caribbean knowledge. Fourth, Ifá divination addresses human needs by fulfilling a therapeutic function in the community because prescriptions of medicines and of specific sacrifices are designed to solve the problems arising in the relationship between the individual and the community. Fifth, the "literature" of Ifá divination is not merely a system or set of texts but a verbal art, one requiring a performance displaying skill in memorization and recitation. Sixth, the material of pataká has been disseminated out and into the speech of the community and beyond, and manifests itself in "folktales" and other forms of literature. For the literary investigator, these aspects and functions suggest ways of seeing literature as a system with more than literary functions. Although the Ifá system maintains a certain autonomy and self-reference, it serves the human need to give form and meaning to experience. The prophetic quality of the Ifá oracle does not eliminate the literary aspect of its narrative texts because the free play of signification is built into the system as interpretation and is symbolized by the ubiquitous figure of Eshu. In Ifá, then, "literature" is medicine, therapy, counsel, soothsaying, and value clarification: it gives equipment, strategies, and instructions for living.

Northrup Frye has stated in *Anatomy of Criticism* that the "fulfillment of prophecy" in a literary work is more a structural "device" than the validation of fatalist or determinist belief: "it is a piece of pure literary design, giving the beginning some symmetrical relationship with the end."[53] Inasmuch as the Ifá system can be said to base its prophecy on "literary" foundations, it exemplifies the practices by which a community can preserve, order, and transmit narratives capable of providing coherence and structure to experience.

Notes

1. Edward Kamau Brathwaite, "The African Presence in Caribbean Literature," in *Africa in Latin America, Essays on History, Culture, and Socialization,* ed. Manuel Moreno Fraginals, trans. Leonor Blum (New York: Holmes & Meier, 1984), 103–144.
2. J. S. Eades, *The Yoruba Today* (Cambridge: Cambridge University Press, 1980), 119.
3. Miguel Barnet, *La fuente viva* (Havana: Editorial Letras Cubanas, 1983), 173. All translations into English are the editors'. Bascom says that the authority of Ifá in Nigeria is such that even when the expertise or honesty of the *babalao* is doubted or questioned, the system is not. William Bascom, *Ifá Divination: Communication between Gods and Men in West Africa* (Bloomington and London: Indiana University Press, 1969), 11.
4. Julia Cuervo Hewitt, *Aché, presencia africana. Tradiciones yoruba-lucumí en la narrativa cubana* (New York: Peter Lang, 1988), 109.
5. Giambattista Vico, *The New Science of Giambattista Vico,* 3d ed., trans. Thomas Goddard Bergin and Max Harold Fish (Ithaca, N.Y., and London: Cornell University Press, 1970), 74–75, 77–78.
6. Edouard Glissant, *Le Discours antillais* (Paris: Editions du Seuil, 1982), 132.
7. 'Wande Abimbola, *Ifá. An Exposition of Ifá Literary Corpus* (Ibadan, Nigeria: Oxford University Press, 1976), 3.
8. E. M. McClelland, *The Cult of Ifa among the Yoruba,* vol. 1, *Folk Practice and the Art* (London: Ethnographica, 1982), 13.
9. Benetta Jules-Rosette, "The Veil of Objectivity: Prophecy, Divination and Social Inquiry," *American Anthropologist* 80, no. 3 (September 1978): 551, 557.
10. Olantunde O. Olatunji, *Features of Yoruba Oral Poetry* (Ibadan, Nigeria: University Press, 1984), 110–111.
11. Ibid., 111.
12. Bascom, *Ifá Divination,* 11.
13. Julio Sánchez, *La religión de los orichas: Creencias y ceremonias de un culto afro-caribeño,* 3d ed. (Hato Rey, Puerto Rico: Colección Estudios Afrocaribeños, 1991), 50.
14. Bascom, *Ifá Divination,* 123.
15. Ibid., 54.
16. Olatunji, *Features of Yoruba Oral Poetry,* 124.
17. Migene González-Wippler, *Santería: The Religion. A Legacy of Faith, Rites, and Magic* (New York: Harmony Books, 1975), 41.
18. Rogelio Martínez Furé, *Diálogos imaginarios* (Havana: Editorial Arte y Literatura, 1979), 211–212.
19. Olatunji, *Features of Yoruba Oral Poetry,* 110.
20. Bascom, *Ifá Divination,* 115.
21. Ibid., 116.
22. Ibid., 117.
23. Sacrifice is a propitiatory act that "feeds" the orishas. The metaphor of feeding, however, tends to eclipse other functions that are reasonably attributable to sacrifice. First, sacrifice is a form of exchange. One pays something in order to get some-

thing else; one gives in order to receive, which in a dialectical manner constitutes an act of generosity toward oneself in the form of generosity toward the community. Second, sacrifice functions as a mechanism of substitution: I delay or
postpone my own death by putting an animal to death in my place. Or I may send
a sickness to a substitute. Third, sacrifice displaces aggression, directing it away
from a human or even nonhuman adversary and focusing it on another animate
but nonhuman creature. Fourth, sacrifice is more than just killing; it entails a whole
set of preparations and specific procedures; in other words, it is a ritual performance
involving setting, objects, actors, and script, and thus it is a narrative event composed of distinguishable component events—steps or stages in the process. All in
all, sacrifice exhibits the kind of reversal characteristic of magical thinking: what
is regarded as a cause is in fact an effect. Sacrifice may be perceived as a cause of a
certain outcome, but in a more abstract logic it can be seen as the outcome of a
systematic operation that relies on narrative to give it a function within the system's
signifying network.

24. Bascom, *Ifá Divination*, 70.
25. Ibid., 26.
26. Abimbola, *Ifá*, 12.
27. Bascom, *Ifá Divination*, 40.
28. Ibid., 40, 41.
29. Sánchez, *La religión de los orichas*, 49.
30. To give an approximate idea of what the major odu signify, I have abridged and
    adapted Abimbola's paraphrase in *Ifá*. The following list refers to configurations
    of the curved disks on the opele chain, with "I" meaning concave side up and "0"
    convex side up. The right-to-left order will correspond to the top-to-bottom or-
    der of the odu, and the left side will precede the right side. Keep in mind that the
    major odu are twins, doubling the figure on each side, and that some odu come
    strongly associated with an orisha name. (1) *Eji Ogbe* (IIII IIII, or four concave
    pieces up on each side): plenty of good, plenty of evil. (2) *Oyeku Meji* (0000 0000,
    or four convex pieces up on each side): death and all other evil will disappear. (3)
    Iwori Meji (0II0 0II0): enemies are around. (4) *Odi Meji* (I00I I00I): evil is close.
    (5) *Irosun Meji* (II00 II00): client should heed wife's advice; Changó. (6) *Owõrin
    Meji* (00II 00II): victory over enemies; attempts to slander client. (7) *Obara Meji*
    (I000 I000): poverty and want followed by prosperity and happiness. (8) *Okoron
    Meji* (000I 000I): good fortune; beware of enemies. (9) *Ogunda Meji*: (III0 III0):
    victory; Oggún. (10) *Osa Meji* (0III 0III): Osala and witches; many children and
    plenty of riches. (11) *Ika Meji* (0I00 0I00): long life; safety from harm. (12)
    Oturupon Meji (00I0 00I0): Egungun; twin babies and attack of witches. (13) *Otura
    Meji* (I0II I0II): Ifá and deserters; victory over enemies and many children. (14)
    Irete Meji (II0I II0I): Chankponna; death, enemies, and evil. (15) *Ose Meji* (I0I0
    I0I0): plenty of children and good fortune; victory over enemies. (16) *Ofun Meji*
    (0I0I 0I0I): greatness; safety from harm by enemies; members of client's house-
    hold should not mock strangers.
31. Bascom, *Ifá Divination*, 51.
32. Wande Abimbola, "Yoruba Oral Literature," *African Notes* 2, no. 3 (April 1963):
    13.
33. Joseph M. Murphy, *Santería: An African Religion in America* (Boston: Beacon Press,
    1988), 134.
34. Abimbola, *Ifá*, v.
35. Ulli Beier, *Yoruba Myths* (Cambridge: Cambridge University Press, 1980), xvi.
36. The total narrative situation is specular in three ways. First, this patakí, recited or
    reimprovised in the presence of the client at the Ifá divination, mirrors the ritual
    of divination itself and accordingly authenticates the veracity of the oracle. Sec-

ond, the song describing Obbatalá is sung twice, once by the babalao and again by the fisherman in Obbatalá's presence. Third, the client will be admonished to imitate the imitators of Obbatalá in not eating fish. Such abstinence will signify for the *omo-Obbatalá* (the son of Obbatalá, the client) a form of personal sacrifice and dedication to the orisha. In its performative function, the patakí thus validates itself and the divination ritual.

37. Bascom, *Ifá Divination*, 120, 130. Also Bascom, "The Relationship of Yoruba Folklore to Divining," *Journal of American Folklore* 56 (1943): 129.
38. Bascom, "Relationship," 131.
39. Bascom, *Ifá Divination*, 132.
40. Bascom, *Ifá Divination*, 128.
41. Adapted from Migene González-Wippler, *Tales of the Orishas* (New York: Original Publications, 1985), 13.
42. Ibid., 13.
43. Julio García Cortez, *Pataki. Leyendas y misterios de orishas africanos* (Miami, Fla.: Ediciones Universal, 1980), 44.
44. Abimbola, "Yoruba Oral Literature," 14–15.
45. Bascom, *Ifá Divination*, 124.
46. Ibid., 122–127.
47. Sánchez, *La religión de los orichas*, 50–51, provides a useful schema and examples of the Afro-Caribbean version.
48. Abimbola, "Yoruba Oral Literature," 16.
49. Abimbola ("Yoruba Oral Literature") records an example from Oyo of a short ese belonging to the sixth odu, Owõrin Meji. I have numbered and labeled the four consecutive parts. "[1: Sacrifices and Advice] Ifá says that this person will prosper much more than all his enemies. He should make sacrifice with one cock, two shillings and six pence. Ifá says that all his problems remain unsolved due to the damaging activities of his enemies. [2: Names of Priests and Clients of the Precedent] The-big-and-terrible-Rainbow/Cast Ifá for the Iroko tree/Of the town of Igo. [3: The Previous Divination] When it was moving too close to its enemies. [4: Result of Previous Divination and Lesson] A forest cannot be so full of trees/As to make impossible the recognition of an Iroko tree" (16). In a later, more specific exposition of the same pattern, Abimbola identifies eight parts: (1) priest names, (2) client names, (3) reason for consultation, (4) instructions, (5) client's obedience or nonobedience, (6) results, (7) client reactions, and (8) moral. In a reconsideration of Abimbola's mapping, Olatunji (*Features of Yoruba Oral Poetry*, 127–128) goes on to conflate Abimbola's "reactions" (7) with "results" (6), seeing in the reactions a continuation of the results. Appearing before those results, Olatunji's section (6) consists in the cyclical or "intrastructural" recapitulations of the introductory name citations of (1) and (2). The ese concludes with "general comments" that praise Ifá and reconfirm the importance of carrying out his instructions. The part following the introductory citation of priest names and sometimes the introduction of client names is the "narrative." In the narrative, the ese Ifá offers the case of a client, the story's protagonist, who seeks counsel from the babalao. The problem is defined; instructions prescribing sacrifice or other symbolic action are given and obeyed or disobeyed; results and reactions are described; a moralizing (or etiological) conclusion is drawn. The ese in general send the recurrent message: heed Orúmila and make sacrifice, or suffer the consequences.
50. A sample odu from José María Castillo illustrates this narrative function. The odu Eji Ogbe or (in Spanish) Ellobe Melle is formed when all the opele half-nuts turn up their concave surfaces: IIII IIII. Castillo states that "each time this letter comes up the head has to be fed. Neither passion fruit, sweet potatoes, nor eggs can be eaten." J. M. Castillo, *Ifá en tierra de Ifá. Manuel de recitaciones para santeros y*

babalaos de las reglas lucumíes (New York: n.p., 1976), 1. In one pataki corresponding to Ellobe Melle, Orúmila meets with a series of animals: monkeys, elephants, dogs. Finally he meets with the chickens, who have different names for different family roles (*gallo, gallina*). But the rudeness of the hen, *gallina*, decides her fate (9). Martínez Furé, *Diálogos imaginarios*, elaborates the pataki as a story entitled "Why Orula Eats Hens" (223–226), explaining that Orúmila eats hens (that is, receives them as offering) precisely because it was a hen—not a *gallo* (rooster), not a *pollona* (pullet), and not a *pollón* (young rooster)—that turned him away from their house. The gallo, meeting Orúmila as Orúmila walks away from the house, invites him back, only to provoke once again the rage of the gallina. After that incident, and after the gallina attempts to cast *polvo*, or magic dust, at her husband, Orúmila decides that he will gladly eat gallina but never gallo. Apart from again valorizing an attitude of reverence for the orishas, the pataki explains and justifies the specificity with which a particular sacrifice is made, in effect motivating the choice of ritual elements by referring to the details of another narrative.

51. Castillo, *Ifá en tierra de Ifá.*
52. Lydia Cabrera, *Por qué . . . (Cuentos negros de Cuba)* (Madrid: Colección del Chicherekú, 1972); Rómulo Lachatañeré, *Manual de Santería: El sistema de cultos "Lucumís"* (Havana: Editorial Caribe, 1942); and Rómulo Lachatañeré, *¡¡Oh, mío Yemayá!!* (Manzanillo, Cuba: Editorial El Arte, 1938).
53. Northrup Frye, *Anatomy of Criticism: Four Essays* (Princeton, N.J.: Princeton University Press, 1972), 139.

Romantic Voodoo

ALAN RICHARDSON

Obeah and British Culture, 1797–1807

Thomas De Quincey, searching in the *Suspiria de Profundis* (1845) for a metaphor equal to the intense depression brought on by his sister's early death, compares the power of grief over the bereaved mind to the "ignoble witchcraft of the poor African *Obeah*" in its capacity to cause even death if left to run its course. He adds an explanatory footnote on "*African Obeah*" that begins: "Thirty years ago it would not have been necessary to say one word of the Obi or Obeah magic; because at that time several distinguished writers (Miss Edgeworth, for instance, in her Belinda) had made use of this superstition in fictions, and because the remarkable history of Three-fingered Jack, a story brought upon the stage, had made the superstition notorious as a fact."[1] Although De Quincey's memory misleads him by some ten to fifteen years, Obeah or Obi, a religion practiced by black slaves in the British West Indies, had indeed become notorious toward the end of the eighteenth century when it held the British reading and play-going public under its spell for a decade. *Obi; or, Three-Fingered Jack* opened in July of 1800; the same year Charlotte Smith published "The Story of Henrietta," a Gothic novella transposed to Jamaica, in which an obscure "dread" of Obeah augments the heroine's more concrete terrors.[2] Maria Edgeworth drew on Obi both in *Belinda* (1801) and in her story "The Grateful Negro" in *Popular Tales* (1804), the latter set in a Jamaican plantation during a slave revolt. Thomas Campbell uses "Wild Obi" to characterize African barbarity in *The Pleasures of Hope* (1799); Obeah features explicitly in William Shepherd's lyric "The Negro Incantation," which appeared in the *Monthly Magazine* in 1797, and implicitly in two poems published at about the same time, "The Negro's Imprecation" and an ode on "The Insurrection of the Slaves at St. Domingo." "The Three Graves," a ballad begun by Wordsworth in 1797 and extended by Coleridge, was partly inspired (according to Coleridge's note) by Bryan Edwards's account of "the *Oby* witchcraft" in his well-known *History . . . of the British Colonies in the West Indies* (1793), and Wordsworth's "Goody Blake and Harry Gill" (1798) may owe something to Edwards as well. James Montgomery includes a passage on the "appalling" practice of Obeah among the West Indian Maroons (self-governing communities of escaped slaves and their descendants) in his antislavery epic, *The West Indies* (composed in 1807 and published two years later). The decade of British fascination with Obi closes with a burlesque set in Jamaica and England and featuring a Jamaican enchanter, A *Description of Furibond; or, Harlequin Negro*, produced at the Drury Lane during the Christmas pantomime season of 1807.

The representation of Obeah in British writing during the early Romantic period—which has gone all but entirely unnoted since De Quincey—might once have been quickly surveyed and catalogued as an overlooked variant of Romantic exoticism, analogous to literary "Orientalism" or to the depiction of the American Indian in works like Chateaubriand's *Atala*.[3] But as much recent work in the theory and history of culture has stressed, Western exoticism is rarely a matter simply of the picturesque, the novel, or the bizarre. Particularly in an era of empire building, expanding colonialist activity, and growing European domination over the rest of the globe, literary exoticism cannot easily be disentangled from political and economic developments.[4] The literary construction of the geographically or racially "other," however innocent it may initially appear (as in the cult of the "noble savage"), rarely evades some form of complicity with the making and maintaining of Western hegemony. It would be especially naive to ignore the economic, geopolitical, and ideological issues implicit in texts set in the West Indies at a time when Britain, France, and Spain were vying for dominance over the Caribbean, in a struggle profoundly affected by the French Revolution; when agitation and debate in England over the slave trade entailed a fundamental rethinking of British policy regarding its Caribbean colonies; and when the European powers were for the first time defied by a national independence movement led by blacks, the Haitian Revolution of 1791–1804. The Romantic concern with Obeah, which De Quincey calls a "dark collusion with human fears," grows out of British anxieties regarding power: the fluctuations of imperial power, the power of slaves to determine their own fate, the power of democratic movements in France, in England, and in the Caribbean. At the same time, the literary portrayal of Obeah illustrates the power of representation to generate, direct, or exorcise such anxieties. The representation of Obeah, that is to say, functions in this period rather like the practice of Obeah itself.

Like Voodoo, Obeah is a "hybrid" or "Creolized" Caribbean religion with indigenous West African roots, which includes such practices as ritual incantation and the use of fetishes or charms.[5] Although sometimes conflated, the two are distinct: Obeah has been traced to Ashanti-Fanti origins (tribes of the Gold Coast or modern Ghana region) and is more purely concerned with magic or sorcery than Voodoo, a more highly elaborated system of beliefs with origins in the Fon and Yoruba cultures (of the Dahomey or modern Benin region).[6] But for the British mind during the Romantic period, Obeah held much the same connotations as Voodoo inspires (at least popularly) now: a mysterious cult of obscure African provenance, associated with fetishes, witchcraft, and poison, with secrecy and midnight rituals, with magic potions, eroticism, and revenge. At a time when "Voodoo" had not yet entered the English language, "Obeah" tended to signify whatever forms of supernatural beliefs and religious practices the British encountered among the slaves.[7] "Certain exotic words," Alfred Métraux has written of Voodoo, "are charged with evocative power"; it is this power which "Obeah" held for Romantic period England and which my title gestures towards.[8] But it should be stressed from the outset that much of the evocative power of Obeah stemmed from associations, not only with the supernatural or with (in a double sense) "black" magic, but with political power as well, specifically with slave rebellions and the incursions and revolts of West Indian Maroons.

The role of Voodoo in slave revolts in Saint Domingue has often been stressed, from C.L.R. James's groundbreaking history of the Haitian Revolution, *The Black Jacobins*, to Michel S. Laguerre's recent study *Voodoo and Politics in Haiti*. An African from Guinea named Makandal, a Voodoo priest, or *houngan*, and guerilla leader, led a slave revolt in 1757 meant to extirpate the white colonists from the island, in part through the massive use of poison. The 1791 rebellion, which sparked the Revolution, was begun by another Voodoo priest named Boukman, who in a nighttime ceremony held before the opening battle distributed talismans and invoked the *loas*.[9] He concluded the ceremony with a prayer exalting the god of the Africans over the "god of the white man," and admonishing those slaves who wore crosses: "Throw away the symbol of the god of the whites who has so often caused us to weep, and listen to the voice of liberty, which speaks in the heart of us all."[10] Obeah functioned similarly in slave revolts in the British West Indies, with Obeahmen "essential in administering oaths of secrecy" and sometimes distributing fetishes meant to "immunize the insurgents from the arms of the whites."[11] As did Voodoo, Obeah played a role at once inspirational and practical in facilitating resistance and revolt among the slaves: it provided an "ideological rallying point" in sanctioning rebellion, afforded meeting places and leaders, and formed a repository for the "collective memory of the slaves" by preserving African traditions which could be opposed to the dominant colonial culture. Even the illusory promise of invulnerability could provide much needed morale for struggles in which the whites were almost always better armed than the black rebels.[12]

The association of Obeah and slave revolts was well known to the English writers who helped popularize Obeah (however briefly) in the Romantic period; in fact, it was this association which made "Obi" a matter of interest, rather than an obscure slave custom to be mocked and dismissed. Obeah had first been described for the English reading public in James Grainger's *The Sugar-Cane* (1764), published before the subversive connotations of Obeah had been established. Writing as a planter and physician, vaguely sympathetic to the plight of the slaves but primarily concerned with disseminating proper techniques of plantation management, Grainger includes the effects of "Obia" in a catalogue of slave diseases, real and imaginary. "Luckless he who owns / The slave, who thinks himself bewitched"; the "wretch" is sure to perish, unless "some subtle slave / (Such, Obia-men are styled)" provides an antidote or counterspell.[13] Obeah would be purely a comic matter if it did not threaten the planter's investment in human capital:

> In magic spells, in Obia, all the sons
> Of sable Afric trust: Ye sacred Nine!
> (For ye each hidden preparation know)
> Transpierce the gloom which ignorance and fraud
> Have render'd awful; tell the laughing world
> Of what these wonder-working charms are made. (4: 381–386)

Grainger's mock-heroic approach to Obeah reflects the common attitude among West Indian planters at the time, who (according to Bryan Edwards) "laughed at" the slaves' magical-religious practices as so many "harmless stratagems" for protecting their property and resolving their private quarrels. Obeah here evokes not some occult power or political threat but rather the "ignorance" of superstitious Africans and the wickedness of the "conjurers" among them; it can even be appropriated by the slaveholder, as Grainger suggests in a note: "and as the Negro-magicians can do mischief, so they can also do good on a plantation, provided they are kept by the white people in proper subordination" (14: 507). This attitude changes significantly, however, in the aftermath of the Tacky Rebellion of 1760, a "very formidable" insurrection in Jamaica led (like most slave revolts of the period) by African-born slaves.[14] As Edwards writes, an Obeah-man was the "chief instigator and oracle of the insurgents," who had "administered the Fetish or solemn oath to the conspirators, and furnished them with a magical preparation which was to render them invulnerable"; it was this incident that led the Jamaican assembly to enact a law for the "suppression and punishment" of "*Obeah* practices"—henceforth a capital offence (87–88). As a cultural signifier within British colonial discourse, Obeah shifts from denoting a harmless and appropriable "primitive" belief underscoring the cultural superiority of the British, to a "savage" custom which evinces African barbarity and must be outlawed and obliterated by the whites. The change emerges quite starkly in juxtaposing Grainger's easy mockery with Shepherd's "Negro Incantation," an ode directly inspired by Edwards's *History*:

> Haste—the magic shreds prepare—
> Thus the white man's corse we tear.
> Lo! feathers from the raven's plume,
> That croaks our proud Oppressor's doom.
> Now to aid the potent spell,
> Crush we next the brittle shell—
> Fearful omen to the foe,
> Look! the blanched bones we throw.
> From mouldering graves we stole this hallow'd earth,
> Which, mix'd with blood, winds up the mystic charm;
> Wide yawns the grave for all of northern birth,
> And soon shall smoke with blood each sable warrior's arm.[15]

The magical ingredients—bones, teeth, herbs—which are transparently ludicrous to Grainger become horrific, as potential signifiers of the "white man's doom," in Shepherd's incantation.

Edwards was not the only early writer on the West Indies to connect Obeah with revolts of slaves or Maroons. Edward Long had discussed the role of a "famous obeiah man or priest" in the Tacky Rebellion in his *History of Jamaica* (1774)—a work notorious for its virulent racism—and stated that among the "Coromantyns" (slaves shipped from the Gold Coast) the "*obeiah-men*" were the "chief oracles" behind conspiracies and would bind the conspirators with the "fetish or oath."[16] J. G. Stedman, in his *Narrative of a Five Years' Expedition against the Revolted Negroes of Surinam*, published in 1796 with illustrations by Blake, noted the "*obias* or amulets" which the rebel slaves or Maroons would wear around their necks, and which they trusted would render them "invulnerable" in battle.[17] Benjamin Moseley's *Treatise on Sugar* (1799) appends to an account of "OBI" the story of "*Three fingered JACK*, the terror of Jamaica in 1780," an escaped slave who "ascended above SPARTACUS" in his depredations and plans for revenge. As a notorious "Obiman," Jack had become "not only the dread of the negroes, but there were

many white people, who believed he was possessed of some supernatural
power." Jack was at last subdued, however, by a "christianed" slave who was
promised his freedom for producing Jack's three-fingered hand, and who believed his conversion to Christianity or "*white* OBI" rendered him immune to
Jack's sorcery.[18]

The association of Obeah with the depredations of Maroons and with
slave rebellions would not seem in itself, however, to explain the decade of
troubled fascination with Obeah in England; Long's account of Obeah and
myalism (which he considers aspects of a single cult), and the central role of
"obeiah men" in the Tacky Rebellion (aimed at the "entire extirpation of the
white inhabitants"), predates the literary vogue for Obeah by more than twenty
years (416–452). A great deal had changed, however, between 1774 and 1797.
The popular belief in the necessity of the slave system for the success of the
sugar colonies and the contemptuous attitudes toward Africa and Africans
which writers like Long developed in support of slavery had been challenged
by the rapid growth of the abolition movement, which began officially in 1787
and, following the circulation of thousands of antislavery tracts and a mass
petition campaign among a sympathetic public, almost succeeded in banning
the slave trade in 1791. But the antislavery movement had in turn become
virtually derailed, within a year of its near victory, by political developments
in France, Saint Domingue, and England itself.

The fall of the Bastille had initially found widespread sympathy in England, but Burke's *Reflections on the Revolution in France* (1790)—in which the
Paris revolutionaries are compared to a "gang of Maroon slaves, suddenly broke
loose from the house of bondage" and "ill-fitted" for liberty—anticipated by
only a few years both the pervasive English reaction against the increasingly
radical (and bloody) revolution across the Channel, and the widespread association of Jacobinism with slave rebellions in the Americas.[19] Already by the
end of 1791 a Jamaican official, terrified by the rise of Jacobin ideology among
the black revolutionaries in Saint Domingue, warned the Colonial Office that
"the ideals of liberty have sunk so deep in the minds of *all* Negroes, that wher-
ever the greatest precautions are not taken they will rise."[20] In 1792 an anony-
mous pamphlet identified the supporters of abolition as the "JACOBINS OF
ENGLAND," and the next year the Earl of Abingdon remarked in Parliament,
"What does the abolition of the slave trade mean more or less, than liberty
and equality? What more or less than the rights of man? And what are the
rights of man, but the foolish principles of this new philosophy? If proofs are
wanting, look at the colony of St Domingue and see what the rights of man
have done there."[21] Wilberforce and other leading abolitionists began to view
the popular campaign as politically dangerous, and moved to dissociate themselves from outspoken radicals like Thomas Hardy, who had declared that the

"rights of man are not confined to this small island, but are extended to the whole human race, black and white, high or low, rich or poor."[22] Burke withdrew his initial support of the antislavery movement, and by 1792 was arguing that the "continuance of the trade and servitude, regulated and reformed," was preferable to the abolition of the slave trade or of slavery itself.[23] The new mood of reaction frequently verged on paranoia, as in Clara Reeve's statement (in a 1792 treatise on education) that the West Indian slaves, in response to antislavery efforts in England, were not only "preparing to rise against their masters, and to cut their throats," but once free would come to England, "mix with the natives, and spoil the breed of the common people."[24]

In face of the anti-Jacobin reaction the abolition movement, having peaked by early 1792, rapidly declined and continued to lose momentum until 1804, when French democracy was no longer a threat and the political situation in the Caribbean had significantly changed.[25] The progress during this period of the Haitian Revolution was watched in England, for the most part, with great apprehension, particularly in the years 1793–1798, when British armies waged a protracted and disastrous struggle in Saint Domingue to conquer the colony and reinstitute slavery.[26] James writes that the British lost as many soldiers in five years of fighting against the black Jacobins—at least 40,000 dead and another 40,000 otherwise taken out of service—as they would over the entire course of the Peninsular War.[27] British fears in this period gave a fresh impetus to the growth of racist attitudes. The *Gentleman's Magazine* in 1794 declared that the "Negro race are but a set of wild beasts, when let loose without control"; Burke characterized the blacks of Saint Domingue as a "race of fierce barbarians."[28] Bryan Edwards included a harrowing "Narrative of the Calamities Which Have Desolated the Country Ever Since the Year 1789" in his *Historical Survey* of Saint Domingue (1797), ascribing the revolution to the "vile machinations" of French and English radicals (including both the French and British abolition societies) and portraying the rising black nation as "savage man, let loose from restraint."[29] He depicts massacres of white colonists in racist and blood-curdling terms: "Upwards of one hundred thousand savage people, habituated to the barbarities of Africa, avail themselves of the silence and obscurity of the night, and fall upon the peaceful and unsuspecting planters, like so many famished tygers thirsting for human blood" (63). Even Coleridge, a friend and supporter of the abolitionist Thomas Clarkson, recoiled at the "Horrors of St Domingo," describing the black revolutionaries as "degraded Savages" unprepared for freedom.[30] In this context—particularly against the background of what Genovese calls the "interlocking French and Haitian revolutions"—the literary vogue for Obeah in England seems anything but incidental exoticism.[31]

For Genovese, it is the "passage from an Afro-American religious call to holy war to the universalist claims of the Rights of Man," from Boukman's invocation of the *loas* to Toussaint's secularized, postcolonial version of Jacobinism, that marks the shift from isolated slave rebellions to a modern anticolonialist ideology posing a "new and more dangerous threat to the old regimes than anything previously encountered."[32] There were scattered recognitions of such a threat in England, such as the remark in *The Times* in 1802 that "a Black State in the Western Archipelago is utterly incompatible with the system of all European colonisation."[33] But it was largely through denying a coherent ideology or political aspirations to black insurgents, representing them instead as "savages," stirred up by African sorcerers and European demagogues and giving vent to uncontrollable, barbaric fury, that English fears of black empowerment could most readily be vented if not entirely allayed. From its dual association with slave rebellions and "African" superstition, Obeah was uniquely positioned to represent at once a tangible threat and an empty show of power which would dissipate when confronted by civilized superiority. It is not Toussaint but the Obeah-man who is made to embody British colonial anxiety in the critical decade of 1797–1807.

By 1797, British attitudes toward the West Indies had evolved into a complex and somewhat contradictory structure of feeling: sympathy for enslaved Africans in the wake of the massive abolition campaign of 1787–1792; fear of black revolt and self-determination as exemplified by the "Horrors of St Domingo"; a slowly developing consensus—which would later help facilitate the abolition of the slave trade in 1807 and of colonial slavery in 1833—that British interests would be better served by a system based on wage labor than by one based on enforced servitude. Most representations of Obeah in the early Romantic period are marked by similar complexity and ambivalence, tending to inspire pity as well as fear in relation to enslaved Africans; Obeah can evoke the slaves' legitimate grievances as well as the illegitimacy of their means for redressing them. Campbell's lines on Obeah in the *Pleasures of Hope* are unusual in appealing almost solely to terror, personifying "Obi" (according to Campbell's own note) "as the evil spirit of the African."[34] The passage occurs in a section heralding the spread of "Improvement" over the "spacious world" under the aegis of European dominion, the progress, as it were, of Progress: "Thy handmaid arts shall every wild explore, / Trace every wave, and culture every shore" (15). Although heralding an end to slavery a few lines later in the poem—"as the slave departs, the man returns"—Campbell employs Obeah to demonize the black African:

> In Libyan groves, where damned rites are done,
> That bathe the rocks in blood, and veil the sun,
> Truth shall arrest the murderous arm profane,
> Wild Obi flies—the veil is rent in twain.

While Campbell acknowledges that "Obi, or Orbiah," is known only among West Indian blacks, he does not hesitate to transfer it to "their kinsmen on the coast of Africa" (318); an instance of how Africa tended to be viewed in this period, through the lens of the slave trade, as a "dependency" or annex of the sugar colonies.[35] Campbell's fantasy of African human sacrifice arrested by the "rule" of European improvement suggests how easily antislavery sentiment could coexist with a conviction of the essential savagery of sub-Saharan Africa and its peoples, implicitly supporting the continued domination of West Indian blacks even while lamenting their enslavement; it also looks forward to the nineteenth-century British exploitation of Africa in the name of civilization and progress.

Shepherd's "Negro Incantation" (inspired by Edwards's account of the Tacky Rebellion) is more profoundly ambivalent. It begins with an open appeal to fear—"Hail! ye sacred horrors hail!"—as a "hoary wizard" named Congo invokes the "spirits of the swarthy dead" to rouse their descendants to "vengeance fell" on the white man. But Shepherd's imaginary rendition of the slaves' "words of mystic might, that seal their tyrants' fate" suggests that their intended massacre is motivated by legitimate indignation as well as by African savagery:

> Go! let the memory of the smarting thong
> Outplead the pity that would prompt to save:
> Go! let the Oppressor's contumelious wrong,
> Twice nerve the hero's arm, and make the coward brave.

"The Negro's Imprecation" (1799–1800), spoken by a slave or Maroon named Oyeo ("breathing many a curse"), similarly incites the "Spirits of the sable dead" to arise and "mark the white man's doom," while simultaneously appealing to the Christian reader's sympathy for the African's legitimate "wrongs":[36]

> Think'st thou the God thou taught me to revere,
> The God (thou said'st) who dwells enshrined above,
> Heeds not the wrongs poor Oyeo suffers here?
> But on *thy* cruel tribe looks down with *partial* love?

A comparable ambivalence marks the "Ode" on "The Insurrection of the Slaves at St. Domingo," published in *The Courier* in 1797, and spoken by a rebel slave named Orrah.[37] On the one hand the "Ode," like Campbell's *Pleasures of Hope*, plays on European fantasies of African human sacrifice, describing the victims of Orrah's "murderous band" as a "grateful sacrifice" to the "Genius" of Africa, offered up by the successful rebels "around the votive fire." But the African god—"Whidah"—is represented as having incited the slaves to a just cause:

"O, my troubled spirit sighs
When I hear my people's cries!
Now, the blood which swells their veins
Flows debas'd by servile chains:
Desart now my country lies;
Moss-grown now my altars rise:
Oh, my troubled spirit sighs
When I hear my people's cries!"

These lyrics simultaneously evince sympathy for oppressed slaves while em-bodying fears of African savagery unleashed by rebellion and heightened by just resentment. They imply that the very barbarism of the transplanted Af-ricans constitutes a reason to reform or replace the plantation system, and end the importation of fresh slaves from the dark continent, before British arro-gance and mismanagement unleash the horrors of black revenge. Their rep-resentations of African cult worship suggest at once that the slaves are more advanced than detractors like Long would suggest—possessed of cultural resources of their own, able to form not only insurrectionary plots but a forceful rhetoric of justification for them—and that they nevertheless remain danger-ously uncivilized, in need of the Christianization and "de-Africanization" which only a reformed colonial system might effect.[38]

Wordsworth and Coleridge's poem "The Three Graves"—inspired (as Coleridge writes) not only by Edwards's account of "*Oby*" but also by accounts of North American Indians—is worth noting although only tangentially re-lated to the issues I am concerned with here. For Coleridge, Obeah is princi-pally of "psychological" interest—"a striking proof of the possible effect on the imagination, from an idea violently and suddenly impressed upon it"—and the poem is set not in Jamaica but in England, its evil figure not an Obi-woman but an incestuous mother-in-law ("instances of this kind are not peculiar to savage or barbarous tribes").[39] Perhaps more closely related to most literary versions of Obeah in the period, however, is Wordsworth's "Goody Blake and Harry Gill," written the year after Wordsworth began "The Three Graves" and, like it, employing the traditional English stereotype of the witch (which both Benjamin Moseley and Charlotte Smith relate specifically to Obeah) as a vehicle for exploring the "power of the human imagination."[40] Like the West Indian slave, Goody Blake is socially marginalized, the victim of an economic system beyond her individual control; she gains her revenge from a curse which owes its effect—as does in part, in relation to its English audience, a lyric such as "The Negro's Imprecation"—to its capacity for evok-ing feelings of guilt and to the oppressor's fear of the power of *ressentiment* in the oppressed. If indeed "Goody Blake" owes something to Edwards's account of Obeah, whether directly or through Coleridge, it would constitute a particularly subtle and empathetic response, implying that there *is* power in a curse motivated by just resentment, precisely because the psychic (or moral) costs of social tyranny are as high for the master as for the slave. At the same time, the lyric's accommodation of Obeah to the English tradition of witchcraft would suggest a deflection of the social issues—slavery, colonialism—it otherwise would inevitably raise, while its psychologized treatment of social oppression could be seen as marking a certain detachment as well.[41]

Obi; or, Three-Fingered Jack and Edgeworth's "The Grateful Negro" present the two most extended literary portrayals of Obeah in the period. *Obi*, a melodrama sometimes attributed to John Fawcett, was first performed at the Theatre Royal, Covent Garden, on 2 July 1800 and was staged regularly over the next few decades.[42] The story was taken, with significant alterations and embellishments, from Moseley's *Treatise on Sugar*, published the year before. Although Moseley presents him primarily as a daring robber, in the melodrama Jack is an escaped slave, living as a Maroon, and bent on revenging himself against his former master for savagely beating him and against the white population generally for transporting him from Africa.[43] Whereas Moseley stresses that Jack, despite his "mortal hatred to white men," "was never known to hurt a child, or abuse a woman" (199), in *Obi* Jack's former master, a planter named Ormond, declares that he gave Jack the "signal punishment which . . . drove him to madness" for once daring to "attempt the honour" of his wife (5); later Jack threatens to kill Ormond's daughter, Rosa. *Obi*, like Smith's "Story of Henrietta," appeals to irrational fears of black sexuality as well as of resentment; in Smith's novella, the black rebels are depicted as "savages, always terrible in their passions, and in whom the fierce inclination for European women was now likely to be exalted by the desire of revenge" (114). But Three-Fingered Jack is given a good deal more complexity than Smith's "insurgent Maroons" (104). Jack claims that his murder of Ormond's wife was in revenge for his "beloved Olinda, whom they tore lifeless from [his] arms, as they dragged" him from his "native land"; when about to murder Ormond's daughter, he explains: "the vext spirits of my wife and child hover o'er me, like a holy curse, and claim this due revenge" (9, 23). Reading between the lines, one can even interpret Ormond's story of attempted rape as racist fantasy; Jack shows no interest in raping Rosa when she is his prisoner. When Rosa asks mercy for her captured fiancé, Jack replies with sophisticated irony, "You whites are ever ready to enforce for one another that civilized, that Christian law of mercy which our dusky children never yet partook of" (22). In allowing an openly rebellious ex-slave to point up the contradiction underlying European claims to be civilizing and Christianizing Africans by means of a barbaric and un-Christian practice, *Obi* goes beyond even works like William Cowper's "The Negro's Complaint" and John Thelwall's "The Negro's Prayer," which stand out as two of the most empathetic and least condescending examples of anti-slavery literature, but which still portray their speakers as passively supplicating rather than as actively seeking retribution; a chained and "kneeling African" was, after all, the official emblem of the abolition movement.[44]

The play's representation of Obeah is equally complex. As in Moseley's account, Jack strengthens his local reputation through giving himself out as an Obeah-man: Ormond states, "The negroes dread his incantations, and many of our colour believe him possessed of some supernatural power" (4–5). But in the play, Jack depends on the assistance of an "Obi woman" whose sorcery he himself dismisses as "mummery" (9). Scene three of *Obi*, set in the "Obi woman's" hut, presents a spectacle of African sorcery, with the black priestess working incantations over Ormond's "image made in wax" in accents reminiscent of the Witches in *Macbeth*:

> Toil him and moil him again and again,
> Sicken his heart and madden his brain;
> Till strength, and sense, and life depart,
> As I tear the last pulse from the white man's heart. (8)

But if the "Obi charm" (eighteen lines in all) seems calculated to thrill or terrify London audiences, Jack is unmoved—"Thy power is in the fear of thy votaries—and fear I know not" (9). Rather, Jack cynically manipulates the local superstitions which he himself, a materialist, scorns: "More of your charms, which, in the eye of superstition, make me invincible—and let me to my work" (10).[45] The juxtaposition in *Obi* of a staging of Jamaican witchcraft with its villain's enlightened skepticism may be taken in various ways. It is important to note, to begin with, that contemporary discussions and representations of religious practices found in or traced back to Africa were almost invariably qualified by an urge to dismiss them as "savage" superstitions, since British and other European writers on sub-Saharan Africa and black Africans nearly unanimously declared that African "culture" was too primitive to boast anything that could properly be called religion.[46] Thus Moseley introduces his account by noting that "OBI, and gambling, are the only instances . . . among the natives of the negro land in Africa, in which any effort of combining ideas has ever been demonstrated" (189); Long reduces "Negroe" religion to a matter of appetite, claiming that Africans are too attached to "their favourite superstitions, and sensual delights" to be Christianized, an index of their "barbarous stupidity" (428–429); for Edwards, Obeah illustrates the "savage and sanguinary" character of the "national manners, wars, and superstitions" of West Africa (62). (It is significant that all of these writers consider Obeah a purely African, rather than Afro-Caribbean, practice). In this way, Jack's skepticism could be read as a move to discount any truth-value that might attach to the spectacle of a belief system among African slaves by dismissing it as so much "mumbo jumbo"—to adapt a derisive term for African beliefs popularized in the same period by the explorer Mungo Park. Jack and the local blacks he terrorizes could be seen as exemplifying two different modes of savage behavior: ruthless cunning on the part of Jack, barbaric ignorance on the part of his victims.

And yet here it is an enlightened (and eloquent) former slave who sees through the mysteries of "Obi," while "many" of the local whites are taken in. Perhaps Jack is meant to evoke the specter of Jacobin "philosophy" in the hands of insurgent blacks, as in Saint Domingue; perhaps the author is himself a skeptical radical, implicitly undercutting European prejudices even in the act of playing upon them. But if an unusually sophisticated, politically radical sensibility may be intuited at work behind *Three-Fingered Jack*, any effect this might have on contemporary audiences is probably overwhelmed by the play's exploitation of melodramatic conventions and stock characterizations: the sympathetic patriarch (Ormond), the beleaguered heroine (Rosa), the heroic young man (Rosa's lover), the faithful retainers (the slaves who track down and kill Jack in exchange for freedom). It is more likely these elements to which the audience of a popular melodrama would respond than to the occasional hints of a radical critique of slavery and the subtle undermining of racial stereotypes. Jack is, in the end, presented more as a black Iago than as a Jamaican Othello. His defeat on the point of murdering a white woman, and the exposure of the power of Obeah (or the superiority of "white Obi") which that defeat implies, would undoubtedly appeal to audiences which had lived through the destruction of a British army in Saint Domingue and nervously followed accounts of the "great Maroon War of 1795–96" in Jamaica.[47] In the defeat of Jack and of "Obi" with him, the "Terror of Jamaica" and the "Horror" of Saint Domingue could be symbolically exorcised.

Maria Edgeworth treats Obeah derisively in *Belinda*, in a manner which recalls Grainger's *Sugar-Cane*, whereas in "The Grateful Negro" she portrays it much more seriously and in the explicit context of a slave rebellion. In *Belinda*, Obeah features in a comic incident involving Juba, the "faithful, affectionate," but "excessively superstitious" black servant who has followed his master, a wealthy young Creole named Mr. Vincent, from the West Indies to England.[48] Juba has offended a certain Harriot Freke, who in revenge plays on his "superstitious terror" by convincing him that "one of the obeah-women of his own country" (201) has traced him to Harrowgate in order to take his life. Although Vincent's first response is to "burst out a laughing," he worries that Juba—so much a favorite that he has named his dog after him—will indeed die from superstitious terror: "Mr Vincent knew the astonishing power which the belief in this species of sorcery has over the minds of the Jamaica

negroes; they pine and actually die away from the moment they fancy themselves under the malignant influence of these witches" (202). Fortunately,
Belinda recalls once seeing a child's experiment in drawing fiery pictures with
phosphorous, and guesses that "some imprudent or ill-natured person might
have terrified the ignorant negro by similar means"; she has a similar picture
drawn in Juba's presence, who becomes, if not altogether enlightened, "convinced that no obeah woman was exercising over him her sorceries" in the
present case. Although Edgeworth establishes her abolitionist credentials elsewhere in the novel by having Vincent recite *The Dying Negro*—a celebrated
antislavery poem—to an approving Belinda (317), the Obeah incident, a triumph of European science and rationality (even at a child's level) over African superstition, evinces the condescending and quasi-feudalistic attitude
toward West Indian slaves which she develops more explicitly in "The Grateful
Negro."

As a story in *Popular Tales*, "The Grateful Negro" is directed at a lower-
class audience at a time when many liberals like Edgeworth felt, in the wake
of the French Revolution, that popular aspirations toward a more democratic
society must be carefully contained, and the lower classes brought to see their
interests as best served not by direct political action on their part but by allowing the rising professional class to act for them. An early example of mass
propaganda literature (praised by Francis Jeffrey in the *Edinburgh Review* for
its pacifying effect on a restive populace), *Popular Tales* attempts to channel
nascent radicalism into passive support for limited reforms aimed at strength-
ening the hand of the upper middle classes.[49] Whereas Obeah had been treated
ludicrously in *Belinda* for the amusement of a middle-class readership, in "The
Grateful Negro" Obeah is evoked as the horrific analogue to a slave revolt
for the edification of English laborers—at a time when comparisons between
West Indian slaves and British wage earners were becoming frequent.[50] The
tale begins by contrasting two Jamaican planters, the dissolute and cruel
Jeffries, who tends to gamble his best slaves away, and the patriarchal Edwards,
who "treated his slaves with all possible humanity and kindness."[51] Edwards
believes in a reformed slave system with freedom phased in only gradually:
"He wished that there was no such thing as slavery in the world; but he was
convinced, by the arguments of those who have the best means of obtaining
information, that the sudden emancipation of the negroes would rather increase than diminish their miseries." His style of plantation management forms
an analogue to the program of selective reforms called for by middle-class liberals in England: "He adopted those plans for the amelioration of the state of
slaves which appeared to him the most likely to succeed without producing
any violent agitation or revolution" (400).

Jeffries's tyranny, on the other hand, has generated a conspiracy among his slaves (led, as usual, by African-born Koromantyns): "Their object was to extirpate every white man, woman, and child, in the island" (405). The head conspirator, Hector, enlists the aid of an "Obi-woman" named Esther, "an old Koromantyn negress" skilled in poison and the display of "supernatural powers"; as the tale develops, it appears that Esther in fact is "the chief instigator of this intended rebellion" (409–410). She administers the "solemn fetish oath" to Hector and his companions, and prepares a bowl of "magic poison" in which the conspirators' knives are steeped as the "sorceress" mutters incantations by the "blue flame of a cauldron" (416–418). Fortunately for the Jamaican whites, Jeffries's "best negro," Caesar (a name which evokes both the conspiracy in Shakespeare's *Julius Caesar* and the abortive slave revolt in Aphra Behn's *Oroonoko*), is indebted to the paternalistic Edwards, who has saved him from being sold to Mexico and given him a plot of his own to work in his free time. Although a fellow Koromantyn and Hector's "ship-mate" (slaves transported together frequently considered themselves mutually bound for life), Caesar chooses "honour" and gratitude to Edwards over love and friendship for Hector; he betrays the conspiracy despite the Obeah-woman's threats and the rebellion is eventually put down (411).

Exploiting well-known associations between Obeah and slave revolts, Edgeworth is able to connect revolution with savagery and superstition in a reformist, and implicitly anti-Jacobin, allegory for British laborers. It is significant that in this same period Burke not only compares the French revolutionaries to a "gang of Maroon slaves," but (in his 1796 *Letters on a Regicide Peace*) to "cannibals" as well—one of the first applications of this term beyond its originally Caribbean context.[52] Jacobin-inspired revolution and the "barbarities of Africa" had also been frequently associated, as noted above, in such accounts of Saint Domingue as Bryan Edwards's 1797 *Historical Survey*; significantly, Edwards begins by opposing the spectacle of class warfare in France to the "progressive improvement in the situation of the lower ranks" in England, which only cautious reform could effect, and ends by opposing the sudden emancipation schemes advanced by "detestable incendiaries" who would "preach up rebellion and murder to the contented and orderly negroes in our own territories" to the "slow and gradual" phasing out of the slave trade. "A perseverance in the same benevolent system, progressively leading the objects of it to civilization and mental improvement, preparatory to greater indulgence, is all that humanity can require; for it is all that prudence can indicate" (xix, 193–194). Citing Edwards's history of the West Indies as her guide to Obeah, Edgeworth tacitly draws on his connections between white and black Jacobinism, revolution and sudden emancipation, and the "improvement" of the lower ranks in England and of the slaves in the sugar colonies; it is no accident that her model planter-patriarch is named "Edwards."

Edgeworth's manipulation of the Obeah theme to preach counterrevolution and discredit sudden emancipation schemes contrasts markedly with Montgomery's lines on Obeah in *The West Indies*, which make part of a condemnation of slavery in the British possessions:

> Tremble, Britannia! while thine islands tell
> The appalling mysteries of Obi's spell;
> The wild Maroons, impregnable and free,
> Among the mountain-holds of liberty,
> Sudden as lightning darted on their foe,—
> Seen like the flash, remember'd like the blow.[53]

For Montgomery, the slave system inherently encourages revolts; the "mysteries" of "Obi" here emblematize the impossibility of subduing the escaped slaves by force, the Maroons themselves ambivalently portrayed as both "wild" savages and as heroic custodians of liberty encouraging other slaves to rebel in their turn. Montgomery's lines seem at once to acknowledge the function of Obeah in facilitating an anticolonial, Afro-centric social identity among the escaped slave communities—Laguerre calls the West Indian Maroons the "initiators of the black power movement"—while lamenting their "appalling" religious beliefs and practices, virtually forced on the more indomitable among the blacks by a shortsighted British policy, as delaying their eventual Christianization and their integration into a "civilized" postslavery colonial polity.[54]

By the time Montgomery's antislavery epic appeared in 1809, however, Obeah seems to have lost much of its horrific charge, and had begun to become once more a subject for untroubled laughter. The theater audiences that had been chilled by a melodrama on *Obi* seven years earlier were treated to a burlesque of it in *Furibond, or Harlequin Negro*, a "Grand Comic Pantomime" performed at the Drury Lane Theater on December 28, 1807—significantly, the year in which the abolition of the slave trade was finally enacted.[55] *Furibond*, as much a work of official propaganda as a popular entertainment, self-consciously heralds a new colonial order, in which slavery will be gradually phased out and West Indian blacks slowly raised to junior partnership with their British overseers—that is, allowed minimal wages for the same plantation work they previously performed without compensation. The pantomime's first scene, set in "A Plantation in Jamaica," introduces Furibond, "an enchanter who resides on the island" (presumably an Obeah-man) who attempts to "solicit the hand of Columbine," a planter's daughter, in marriage, only to be spurned with "great disgust" (5–6). Furibond summons up a familiar spirit named "Maligno," with whom he plots to win Columbine by force, eventually following her and her father, Sir Peevish Antique, back to England. Their efforts are frustrated, however, by a sympathetic though "disobedient" slave,

Harlequin, who has earned a fairy wish (in the usual accidental fashion). His first wish is to change his "sable hue" for a white skin, from which the fairy, Benigna, dissuades him: "Wilt thou the pleasures of the mind forgo[?] / I knew thy manly nature would say no" (7–9). Harlequin then wishes "for the emancipation of his fellow slaves," but Benigna responds, "Poor Afric's children sigh for liberty, / Alas!—that task was not reserved for me." Instead, she summons the "Genius of Britain" at whose signal a "figure of Britannia, with her lion, descends from the skies": "England shall stamp the blest decree, / That gives the Negro *liberty*" (9). Harlequin finally chooses a magic sword, which he employs to protect Columbine from the advances of Furibond and Maligno; their enchantments prove powerless against those of Benigna, and both "sink" in the pantomime's closing scene (26).

As *Furibond* attests, by the end of 1807 antislavery had again become a popular, even patriotic, cause. In a period of growing demand for political and social reform, abolition—as opposed to Catholic emancipation, electoral reform, or extending the franchise to the middle classes—was the only significant reform considered politically expedient.[56] Ending the slave trade could by this time be seen as more detrimental to Britain's imperial rivals than to its own colonies, which were relatively well-stocked with slave labor; it would also end the importation of Africans—widely seen as more violent, indomitable, and unpredictable than "Creole" slaves—to the West Indies.[57] Haiti, which had declared its independence from France at the beginning of 1803, was now viewed more as an unofficial ally against Napoleon (who had sent an army against it—with British collusion—in 1801) than as an enemy; Wordsworth's 1802 sonnet "To Toussaint L'Ouverture," composed when Toussaint was dying in a French prison, is an early example of British sympathy for the Haitian cause.[58] Moreover, Toussaint was by 1802 no longer a seemingly invincible revolutionary leader, but could be assimilated to the popular antislavery image of the dying, chained, or supplicating slave. As Britain began moving decisively away from slavery and toward a "universal definition of free labor" as the basis upon which to manage its colonial work forces, the abolition of the slave trade could be celebrated as both sound colonial policy and as a humanistic gesture evincing Britain's moral superiority.[59] *Furibond*, particularly in the figure of Harlequin, suggests how sympathy for oppressed slaves could again be uninhibitedly expressed for an English public no longer troubled by fears of either white or black Jacobinism, the first having been co-opted, the second significantly weakened, by Napoleon.

Nevertheless, for all its tone of self-congratulation, *Furibond* remains like *Three-Fingered Jack* a profoundly conflicted text, though for reasons of its own. Benigna's response to Harlequin's wish for a white skin may seem an uncommonly (and unexpectedly) forthright antiracist gesture, implying that

Harlequin's "mind" and "manly nature" are unaffected by his color, but much of the comedy in *Harlequin Negro* depends upon a type of crude racist humor anticipating that of the minstrel shows of the later nineteenth century. The Clown, for example, marries a "black female servant" (6) toward the end of the pantomime who almost immediately presents him with a set of cuckold's horns and a half-dozen bastard children. It is not clear from the text whether Furibond is initially portrayed as black or not (in London he changes his form into that of an English "beau"), but his implicit association with the Obeah-man, at that time quite familiar to English readers and theater audiences, together with his frantic pursuit of Columbine, suggests an appeal to the racist assumptions regarding black sexuality which surface in texts like Smith's "Story of Henrietta." And yet the "Lovers" who are joined by the benignant fairy at the pantomime's close to the delight (one assumes) of the holiday audience are Columbine and—Harlequin Negro (26). As is the case with *Three-Fingered Jack*, one must ask to what extent audience response to the play is shaped by stock roles, here the commedia dell' arte characters in particular: to what degree is Harlequin's initial presentation as a black slave counteracted by his identity *as* Harlequin, who conventionally wears a black mask?[60] Still, the apparent celebration of interracial romance which ends *Furibond* remains quite striking, particularly when contrasted with the disgust which Lamb, for one, attaches to the pairing of a "*coal-black moor*" and a "white woman" in *Othello*, and given the effective taboo on sympathetic representations of black and white erotic couplings which would characterize the theater, and later the film and television industries, for the next century and a half.[61]

After 1807, with the exception of the belated appearance of Montgomery's *West Indies*, Obeah no longer functions to represent and allay British anxieties regarding "African" power. Obeah is mentioned frequently throughout Matthew G. Lewis's *Journal of a West India Proprietor* (kept in Jamaica from 1815 to 1817), but always as superstitious "nonsense"; Lewis, like Coleridge, views its effects mainly as a measure of the "strength of imagination" among the credulous.[62] As in Grainger's *Sugar-Cane*, Obeah is once more taken seriously only when it threatens to rob the planter of one of his slaves (whose value had increased markedly as a result of abolition): "it will be truly provoking to lose him by the influence of this foolish prejudice" (134–135). Unlike Grainger, however, Lewis cannot imagine integrating the practice into a system of plantation management; he writes that Obeah has been "greatly weakened" in the island since his last visit, and hopes it might be altogether eradicated among the blacks by their baptism and conversion to "white Obeah" (95, 148).

Obeah all but drops out of sight in British writing between the publication of Lewis's *Journal* in 1834 and that of Jean Rhys's novel *Wide Sargasso*

Sea in 1966. Set principally in Jamaica during the period immediately following the end of colonial slavery, *Wide Sargasso Sea*—Rhys's antithetical rework-
ing of *Jane Eyre*—critically addresses the conventions for representing Obeah
developed by writers in the decade 1797–1807. Antoinette (Rhys's sympathetic
elaboration of Brontë's Bertha Mason), a white Creole who has grown up in
Jamaica, imagines a scene of Obeah such as those displayed in "The Negro
Incantation" or *Three-Fingered Jack*: "a dead white man's dried hand, white
chicken feathers, a cock with its throat cut."[63] The unnamed Rochester figure, who has come from England in search of a West Indian heiress, reads a
sensationalistic account of "Obeah" in a book called *The Glittering Coronet of
Isles*: "*Voodoo as it is called in Haiti—Obeah in some of the islands, another name
in South America*" (107). Rochester rationalizes Obeah as a matter of poison
but cannot help dreading it all the same; he claims to be writing a book about
Obeah in order to obtain incriminating information regarding Christophine,
the "Martinique obeah woman" who protects Antoinette until threatened with
police action and imprisonment (30, 159–160). When Antoinette prevails
against her better judgment, Christophine conjures up an aphrodisiac
(Rochester's "poison") with disastrous effect. But the narrative voice itself
never presumes to represent Obeah: rather, the practice (as Christophine in-
timates) signals what cannot be understood, or fully accepted, or assimilated
by the white characters, Creole or English: "'So you believe in all that tim-
tim story about obeah, you hear when you so high? All that foolishness and
folly. Too besides, that is not for *béké*. Bad, bad trouble come when *béké* meddle
with that'" (112). In setting the standard Eurocentric approaches to Obeah
represented by Antoinette and Rochester—demonizing it, outlawing it, eroti-
cizing it, conflating it with other Afro-Caribbean "cults"—against the narrator's
refusal to depict it at all (the scene in which Christophine produces
Antoinette's love charm is pointedly ellipsed), Rhys effectively subverts the
colonialist construction of Obeah characteristic of Romantic-era writing. In
Wide Sargasso Sea, Obeah represents what resists representation, what eludes
containment; it negatively signifies the gulf that separates even a white Creole like Antoinette (the daughter of a slaveholder) from the island's black
population and its living traditions.[64]

Peter Hulme describes two linguistic strategies available to a colonizing
culture when confronting "novelty in experience": "the novelty can be subsumed under a current signifier in an attempt to domesticate it, or it can be
marked as novel—and therefore alien—by being given a new signifier, often
one adapted from an alien discourse."[65] (The first strategy produces the "West
Indies," equating the American sugar islands with the more familiar Orient;
the second produces the "Caribbean," region of Carib, or "cannibal," natives,
who are inassimilable and therefore—implicitly—subject to eradication.) The

exotic term "Obeah" clearly denotes the practice it signifies as alien, to be banned and rooted out rather than familiarized and contained. Unlike "Caribbean" or "cannibal" or "hurricane," all words with Amerindian roots, however, "Obeah" (or "Obi," "Obia," "Orbiah") is a word of African provenance, a corruption of the Twi word *obayi* or *obeye*.[66] Obeah is marked as doubly alien: both inassimilable to European experience (despite the scattered analogies with English witchcraft), and representing a foreign, "savage" African intrusion upon the partially tamed Caribbean. As a term within the colonialist discourse in which eighteenth and early nineteenth century British writers, pro- and antislavery alike, remain enmeshed, Obeah signifies the threatening cultural difference existing between European masters and transplanted African slaves, rather than a Creolized practice suggesting the interplay of Amerindian, African, and European traditions; Edwards is representative in claiming that "the professors of *Obi* are, and always were, natives of Africa, and none other."[67]

The insistence upon the African provenance of Obeah not only contributes toward its threatening aura, however; it also enables the wishful removal of the threat—political as well as cultural—associated with it. The discursive linking of Obeah with slave revolts aligns it with what Long calls the "crafty, treacherous, bloody" character of black Africans, while its status as a superstition, and of its practicers as "pretended conjurers," suggests that both Obeah and the larger threat of black resistance it metonymically evokes can be exposed as futile, empty gestures doomed to fail when met by European superiority, whether in arms or in "civilization" (354, 416). So De Quincey, in the remark quoted at the beginning of this essay, qualifies Obeah not only as "African," but as "poor African *Obeah*," its poverty a reflex of the presumed intellectual poverty of sub-Saharan Africa. An account of "OBEAH TRIALS" included in Edwards's *History* reports that, around 1760, "various experiments were made with electrical machines and magic lanterns" upon some captured "*Obeah-men*"; one, "after receiving some very severe shocks, acknowledged that 'his master's *Obi* exceeded his own'" (92). It is this acknowledgment that every representation of Obeah in the British Romantic era presses toward, in one manner or another. By playing upon the historical associations of Obeah with slave and Maroon resistance but stripping the practice itself of any historical context, relegating it instead to the primitive, supine "Africa" or "negro land" of the colonial imagination, Romantic writers symbolically exorcise the threat of black self-determination, equating its pursuit with the empty display of a barbaric and vulnerable superstition. Like the practice it purports to represent, Obeah as constructed within colonial discourse raises fears in order to play upon and redirect them. The "master's Obi" takes as its materials, however, not blood, herbs, and grave dirt, but fantasies of "exotic" peoples and fragments of their histories and traditions.

Notes

1. Thomas De Quincey, *Confessions of an English Opium Eater and Other Writings*, ed. Grevel Lindop (Oxford: Oxford University Press, 1985), 120.
2. Charlotte Smith, *The Letters of a Solitary Wanderer: Containing Narratives of Various Description* (London: Sampson Low, 1800), vol. 2, 97. For the other works mentioned in this paragraph, see below.
3. There are scattered references to the representation of Obeah in late eighteenth and early nineteenth century British writing in both Wylie Sypher's *Guinea's Captive Kings: British Anti-slavery Literature of the XVIIIth Century* (Chapel Hill: University of North Carolina Press, 1942) and Eva Beatrice Dykes, *The Negro in Romantic Thought: A Study in Sympathy for the Oppressed* (Washington, D.C.: Associated Publishers, 1942).
4. The groundbreaking work in this regard is, of course, Edward Said's *Orientalism* (New York: Random House, Vintage Books, 1979). For a more recent study particularly relevant to European representations of the Caribbean, although it stops just short of the period I am concerned with here, see Peter Hulme, *Colonial Encounters: Europe and the Native Caribbean, 1492–1797* (London: Methuen, 1986). For a helpful overview of British attitudes toward and perceptions of the non-European world in the early colonial period, see also P. J. Marshall and Glyndwr Williams, *The Great Map of Mankind: British Perceptions of the World in the Age of Enlightenment* (London: Dent, 1982).
5. George Eaton Simpson, *Black Religions in the New World* (New York: Columbia University Press, 1978), 12; Michel S. Laguerre, *Voodoo and Politics in Haiti* (New York: St. Martin's Press, 1989), 22.
6. In addition to Simpson, *Black Religions in the New World* (esp. 51–110), and Laguerre, *Voodoo and Politics in Haiti* (esp. 22–38), see Alfred Métraux, *Voodoo in Haiti*, trans. Hugo Charteris (New York: Schocken, 1972), and Ivor Morrish, *Obeah, Christ and Rastaman: Jamaica and Its Religion* (Cambridge: James Clarke, 1982), esp. 40–48.
7. Orlando Patterson, *The Sociology of Slavery: An Analysis of the Origins, Development and Structure of Negro Slave Society in Jamaica* (Rutherford, N.J.: Fairleigh Dickinson University Press, 1967), 185.
8. Métraux, *Voodoo in Haiti*, 15.
9. Laguerre, *Voodoo and Politics in Haiti*, 52–54, 60.
10. C.L.R. James, *The Black Jacobins: Toussaint L'Ouverture and the San Domingo Revolution*, 2d ed. (New York: Random House, Vintage Books, 1963), 87.
11. Patterson, *The Sociology of Slavery*, 192.
12. Laguerre, *Voodoo and Politics in Haiti*, 70; Eugene D. Genovese, *From Rebellion to Revolution: Afro-American Slave Revolts in the Making of the New World* (1979; reprint, New York: Random House, Vintage Books, 1981), 28, 47.
13. James Grainger, *The Sugar-Cane* 4: 368–369, 378–379, in *The Works of the English Poets, from Chaucer to Cowper*, ed. Alexander Chalmers (London: J. Johnson et al., 1810), vol. 14, 507 (cited by book and line).
14. Bryan Edwards, *The History, Civil and Commercial, of the British Colonies in the West Indies* (Dublin: Luke White, 1793), vol. 2, 87–88. For the prominent role of African-born slaves in slave insurrections, see Genovese, *From Rebellion to Revolution*, 98.
15. William Shepherd, "The Negro Incantation," in *The Poetical Register, and Repository of Fugitive Poetry, for 1803*, 2d ed. (London: Rivington, 1805), 413–415; first published in the *Monthly Magazine* for July 1797 (Sypher, *Guinea's Captive Kings*, 208).
16. Edward Long, *The History of Jamaica* (London: T. Lowndes, 1774), vol. 2, 451–452, 473.

17. J. G. Stedman, *Narrative of a Five Years' Expedition against the Revolted Negroes of Surinam in Guiana on the Wild Coast of South America from the Years 1772–1777,* ed. Rudolf van Lier (Barre, Mass.: Imprint Society, 1971), vol. 2, 280, 364.

18. Benjamin Moseley, *A Treatise on Sugar,* 2d ed. (London: John Nichols, 1800), 197–198, 200.

19. Edmund Burke, *Reflections on the Revolution in France,* and Thomas Paine, *The Rights of Man* (Garden City, N.Y.: Doubleday, 1961), 48.

20. James Walvin, *England, Slaves and Freedom, 1776–1838* (Jackson: University Press of Mississippi, 1986), 115.

21. Roger Anstey, *The Atlantic Slave Trade and British Abolition 1760–1810* (London: Macmillan, 1975), 277; Walvin, *England, Slaves and Freedom,* 116.

22. Walvin, *England, Slaves and Freedom,* 113.

23. Robin Blackburn, *The Overthrow of Colonial Slavery 1776–1848* (London: Verso Press, 1988), 148.

24. Clara Reeve, *Plans of Education; with Remarks on the Systems of Other Writers,* ed. Gina Luria (New York: Garland, 1974), 91.

25. Anstey, *The Atlantic Slave Trade,* 343.

26. David Geggus, "British Opinion and the Emergence of Haiti, 1791–1805,"in *Slavery and British Society 1776–1846,* ed. James Walvin (Baton Rouge: Louisiana State University Press, 1982), 127–128.

27. James, *The Black Jacobins,* 200.

28. Geggus, "British Opinion," 128–130.

29. Bryan Edwards, *An Historical Survey of the French Colony in the Island of St. Domingo* (London: John Stockdale, 1797), xix–xx.

30. Samuel Taylor Coleridge, *Essays on His Own Times in* The Morning Post *and* The Courier, ed. David V. Erdman (Princeton, N.J.: Princeton University Press, 1978), vol. 3, 195; for Robert Southey's equally dubious reaction to the Haitian Revolution, see Geggus, "British Opinion," 145.

31. Genovese, *From Rebellion to Revolution,* 93.

32. Ibid., 93, 123.

33. Geggus, "British Opinion," 136.

34. Thomas Campbell, *The Poetical Works of Thomas Campbell,* ed. W. A. Hill (Boston: Little, Brown, 1855), 318.

35. See Marshall and Williams, *The Great Map of Mankind,* 227.

36. "The Negro's Imprecation," in *The Meteors* (London: A. and J. Black, 1799–1800), vol. 2, 53–56. The poem is signed "W. C."; I have been unable to identify these initials.

37. "Ode. The Insurrection of the Slaves at St. Domingo," reprinted (anonymously) from *The Courier* in *The Spirit of the Public Journals for 1797,* 2d ed. (London: James Ridgway, 1799), 238–240.

38. Walvin, *England, Slaves and Freedom,* 55.

39. Samuel Taylor Coleridge, *The Poems of Samuel Taylor Coleridge,* ed. Ernest Hartley Coleridge (London: Oxford University Press, 1940), 267, 269.

40. William Wordsworth, "Preface" to *Lyrical Ballads,* in *Wordsworth's Literary Criticism,* ed. W.J.B. Owen (London: Routledge & Kegan Paul, 1974), 86. For Obeah and the traditional European witch figure, see Moseley's remarks on "OBI in England" and on the Salem witch trials (*A Treatise on Sugar,* 194–195) and Smith's comparison of "Obeahs" to the witches in *Macbeth* (*The Letters of a Solitary Wanderer,* vol. 2, 97). See also Alan Bewell's discussion of "The Three Graves" and "Goody Blake and Harry Gill" in *Wordsworth and the Enlightenment: Nature, Man, and Society in the Experimental Poetry* (New Haven, Conn.: Yale University Press, 1989), 150–157.

41. The explicit source of the narrative of "Goody Blake" is an anecdote included in

Erasmus Darwin's discussion of mania: see Erasmus Darwin, *Zoonomia; or the Laws of Organic Life* (1794–1796; reprint, Philadelphia: Edward Earle, 1818), vol. 2, 307–308. Somewhat ironically, Shelley caricatures Wordsworth's later adoption of orthodox Anglicanism as his "conversion to *White Obi*" in the "Dedication" to *Peter Bell the Third*; see Frances Ferguson's interesting discussion of Shelley's remark as a critique of *The Excursion* in *Wordsworth: Language as Counter-spirit* (New Haven, Conn.: Yale University Press, 1977), 195–197.

42. See Allardyce Nicoll, *A History of English Drama 1660–1900*, vol. 4: *Early Nineteenth Century Drama*, 2d ed. (Cambridge: Cambridge University Press, 1955), 311; and New York Public Library, *Catalog of the Theatre and Drama Collections*, part III: *Non-book Collections* (Boston: G. K. Hall, 1976), vol. 20, 269–270. I have been able to locate two texts of *Obi*, neither definitive: *Obi; or, Three-Fingered Jack: A Melo-drama in Two Acts* (London: Thomas Hailes Lacy, [1800?]), a prompt-book in the Harvard Theatre Collection; and *OBI, or Three-Finger'd Jack. A Popular Melo-drame, in Two Acts*, in *Oxbery's Weekly Budget of Plays and Magazine of Romance, Whim, and Interest* 1 (1843): 93–95. The two texts agree substantially, with numerous disagreements on matters of punctuation, spelling, etc. Citations (by page) follow the prompt-book version unless otherwise noted.

43. A headnote to the *Oxbery's Weekly* version, evidently taken from some account other than Moseley's, describes "Karfa, alias Three-Finger'd Jack, the Terror of Jamaica" as a "Feelop, born in a country bordering on Gambia," who in Jamaica "headed frequent insurrections of slaves" and when these proved unsuccessful, "fled to the mountains and lived in caves" with his fellow escaped slaves (93).

44. Cowper's "The Negro's Complaint" can be found in William Cowper, *The Poetical Works of William Cowper*, ed. H. S. Milford, 4th ed. (London: Oxford University Press, 1950), 371–372; John Thelwall's "The Negro's Prayer," in *The Poetical Register, and Repository of Fugitive Poetry, for 1810–1811* (London: Rivington, 1814), 350–351. For the emblem of the abolition movement, designed by Josiah Wedgwood, see Blackburn, *The Overthrow of Colonial Slavery 1776–1848*, 139.

45. The prompt-book version reads "make me invisible"; "make me invincible," from the *Oxbery's* version (94), seems the better reading.

46. Marshall and Williams, *The Great Map of Mankind*, 242.

47. Genovese, *From Rebellion to Revolution*, 67.

48. Maria Edgeworth, *Belinda*, ed. Eva Figes (London: Pandora, 1986), 200–201.

49. Marilyn Butler, *Romantics, Rebels and Reactionaries: English Literature and Its Background, 1760–1830* (Oxford: Oxford University Press, 1981), 62. For Edgeworth's political affiliations, see Gary Kelly, *English Fiction of the Romantic Period 1789–1830* (London: Longman, 1989), 74.

50. Catherine Gallagher, *The Industrial Reformation of English Fiction: Social Discourse and Narrative Form* (Chicago: University of Chicago Press, 1985), 3–35; Blackburn, *The Overthrow of Colonial Slavery 1776-1848*, 156.

51. Maria Edgeworth, *Tales and Novels* (London: Routledge, 1893), vol. 2, 400.

52. Hulme, *Colonial Encounters*, 265.

53. James Montgomery, *The Poetical Works of James Montgomery. Collected by Himself* (London: Longman, 1850), 26.

54. Laguerre, *Voodoo and Politics in Haiti*, 68.

55. Nicoll, *A History of English Drama*, 465. Citations (by page) are from *A Description of Furibond; or, Harlequin Negro. A Grand Comic Pantomime, Performing with Applause at Drury Lane, Theatre* (London: J. Scales, [1807?]), consulted in the Harvard Theatre Collection.

56. Anstey, *The Atlantic Slave Trade*, 408; Blackburn, *The Overthrow of Colonial Slavery*, 313–315.

57. Blackburn, *The Overthrow of Colonial Slavery 1776–1848*, 310–311.

58. Geggus, "British Opinion," 140–143.

59. Frederick Cooper and Ann L. Stoler, "Tensions of Empire: Colonial Control and Visions of Rule," *American Ethnologist* 16 (1989): 617–618.

60. Henry Louis Gates notes that the figure of Harlequin has been associated with black Africans at least since the late eighteenth century, citing the speculations of Jean François Marmontel and Jean Pierre Florian in particular. He also posits a connection between the English harlequinade and the American minstrel show mediated by several harlequinades—including *Furibond*—which "contain figures of the black as Harlequin" and "combine both blackness and minstrelsy." Henry Louis Gates, *Figures in Black: Words, Signs, and the 'Racial' Self* (Oxford: Oxford University Press, 1987), 51–52.

61. Charles Lamb, "On the Tragedies of Shakespeare, Considered with Reference to Their Fitness for Stage Representation," in *The Works of Charles and Mary Lamb*, ed. E. V. Lucas, vol. 1 (London: Methuen, 1903–1905), 108. Compare Coleridge's repeated assertion that Othello is not a "barbarous Negro" but a "gallant Moor" in Samuel Taylor Coleridge, *Lectures 1808-1819 on Literature*, ed. R. A. Foakes (Princeton, N.J.: Princeton University Press, 1987), vol. 1, 55; vol. 2, 314.

62. Matthew Gregory Lewis, *Journal of a West India Proprietor, Kept during a Residence in the Island of Jamaica* (London: John Murray, 1834), 138, 353.

63. Jean Rhys, *Wide Sargasso Sea* (New York: Norton, 1982), 31.

64. Compare Gayatri Chakravorty Spivak's remarks on Christophine in "Three Women's Texts and a Critique of Imperialism,"in *"Race," Writing, and Difference*, ed. Henry Louis Gates (Chicago: University of Chicago Press, 1986), 271–272.

65. Hulme, *Colonial Encounters*, 95.

66. See Morrish, *Obeah*, 15–16, and Patterson, *The Sociology of Slavery*, 185.

67. Edwards, *The History, Civil and Commercial*, vol. 2, 84.

"An Article of Faith"

KARLA Y. E. FRYE

Obeah and Hybrid Identities in Elizabeth Nunez-Harrell's When Rocks Dance

Alma knew. Emilia had not taught her daughter obeah or even insisted that she participate in any obeah rite, yet obeah was present in their lives. Could she, Marina, have escaped it? Was it possible that she too believed in obeah without wanting to? Was it also an article of faith with her?

—ELIZABETH NUNEZ-HARRELL, *When Rocks Dance*

The history of the islands can never be satisfactorily told. . . . History is built around achievement and creation; and nothing was created in the West Indies.

—V. S. NAIPAUL, *The Middle Passage*

MARINA HEATHROW—Elizabeth Nunez-Harrell's heroine/protagonist in *When Rocks Dance* (1986)—is a character caught between two worlds, a position her creator uses to embody the fractured nature of African identity in the New World.[1] The biracial daughter of Emilia, an African woman, and Hrothgar, her English lover/keeper, Marina is "tall and arrogant, her face framed by light, almost golden hair—wild, unkempt, uncombed hair. . . . [The] bridge of her nose was long, her nostrils wide and flaring. High cheekbones set off wild, gray eyes. Her full-lipped mouth was warm and generous. Tamed. And her skin was pale, almost white, . . . breasts projecting forward . . . backside high and rigid" (67). She is thus the physical, visible embodiment of a society whose history speaks strongly of the hybridization of the Americas over the past four centuries. Her physical features—clashing, complementary, contradictory—

at once symbolize in stark relief the historical, social, and cultural processes that, as experienced by African descendants, constitute what British cultural critic Paul Gilroy has termed the "Black Atlantic."[2] On Mariana's body, and those of her mother and mother-in-law, Nunez-Harrell inscribes the shaping of African identity in Trinidad.[3]

Nunez-Harrell's rhetorical strategy establishes the dialogical opposition of dominant British culture and resistant, emergent African culture, with each pole representing specific underlying ideologies. Within or between these binaries, however, she creates a tension that reflects the ambiguity and cross-currents at the core of a fractured, hybrid, New World African identity. Through the metaphorical inscription of black/Creole bodies, coupled with a structural plot concerned with landownership, she erects a framework for the exploration of deeper, inner identity development, portrayed through the role of religion in the lives of the characters. This narrative/structural link of land/power and religion/spirituality provides the context for understanding identity within the text.

Set at the turn of the century, *When Rocks Dance* tells the story of Marina's quest for land, an extension of Emilia's desire for power and security as an African woman.[4] In late nineteenth-century Trinidad, "the whole society, including the white, the coloured and the slaves was divided on the basis of religion and language."[5] Even before the abolition of slavery, these divisions were bound to produce disparate cultures reflecting equally disparate ideologies. A strong component of the ideologies of the formerly enslaved Africans was resistance and change. Although virtually powerless, "what they certainly did was to refuse to live and work any more on the sugar plantations which to them had become symbols of their slavery and oppression."[6] Although this resistance was eventually incorporated into the Europeans' view of the Africans as lazy, Nunez-Harrell's narrative employs the enigmatic attitudes toward land and landownership demonstrated by each of the racial/class groups on the island as a primary indicator of the ideas that shape collective, but not monolithic, identity. For the Africans, for example, the attitude toward work changed when they were able to acquire and work their own land. While many of them became small businessmen and hawkers, "others, who formed a majority of the emancipated slaves, set up free villages close to existing plantations where they practiced farming on small tracts."[7] Nunez-Harrell combines this notion of self-determination with Emilia's "forefathers' love for the land—their age-old kinship with the earth"—to convey the significance of Marina's charge.

When Rocks Dance portrays people of African descent as eager to escape the bonds of slavery represented by the land but troubled nonetheless by the disconnection from landownership as the ultimate and concrete expression of the love, respect, and security that land had symbolized for their ancestors. At one point Marina attempts to articulate, through a combination of what she has learned in school and from her mother, the reason the Africans give up their land so easily: "That teacher said that the Negro hates the land because it reminds him of slavery and the whips and chains they used to make him wear on the plantation. He said that for the Negro the earth is a dirty scourge that powders his face and stops up his nostrils" (97). However, she refuses to accept this notion. Having been reared with the constant hum of her mother's regard for the land, she will set out to disprove this misconception—and the idea that lies beneath its easy acceptance, that "Negroes are slaves by nature"—through her own determined quest for landownership and the power it represents. Her quest unfolds against a backdrop that seeks to connect all the island's people of color. Nunez-Harrell sets the plights of the Amerindians, who have been forced off the island, and of the East Indians—imported to work in place of the emancipated slaves—who form an attachment to the land as settlers, against the domination of the British, who assume a "rightful legacy" to ownership of the land and domination over its inhabitants. As an actual symbol of material wealth and standing, landownership serves in the novel as a tangible text onto which is inscribed the meaning and value of power in the lives of the various groups, thus illuminating the complex relationships of the colonizers to the colonized and the colonized to each other.

In the same manner, religion, as a social and cultural practice, informs our understanding of the myriad issues related to power and identity that are raised in the narrative—issues such as language, slavery, colonialism, and ethnic/national identity formation. As Reinhard Sander notes in *The Trinidad Awakening: The West Indian Novel of the 1930s*, "Afro-Caribbean forms of dance, music, religion, philosophy, art, and oral literature appeared in response to the demands of the new environment and were used as weapons of protest against the European colonial establishment. Under cultural pressure from their rulers, the slaves and their descendants modified their customs and beliefs, syncretized European and neo-African forms, but hardly ever surrendered the core of the cultural expression."[8] Obeah is an important part of this cultural expression, a practice closely tied to and reflective of the land. As histories and cultural and anthropological studies of the various islands will attest, Obeah in various forms has been a common practice since the early days of plantation society in the Caribbean. Definitions, however, are elusive; travel writer Archie Bell best summarizes the outsider's confusion about the subject when he writes that "no one seems to be able to explain exactly what is meant by the word Obeah, or what is the belief, as it appears to have variations in the different islands, all descended, however, from African fetishism."[9] Other accounts reveal similar vagueness and variety in describing Obeah, coinciding only in defining it as being wholly associated with evil.

Prior to Nunez-Harrell's novel, other Caribbean writers portrayed Obeah to varying degrees. Kenneth Ramchand notes in *The West Indian Novel and Its Background* (emphasis mine):

> There are few indications in West Indian prose of the survival of African Cultures in West Indian secular life. But the frequent occurrence in novels of obeah and cult practices has sometimes been held as evidence of survivals in the religious field. *Few West Indian novelists see these practices as anything more, in fact, than the incoherent remains of African religions and magic; and in all cases, obeah and cult manifestations are associated with socially depressed characters.* It is possible, indeed, to be critical of the writers for having reproduced the social reality only too exactly, and without enough invention or imagination.[10]

While Ramchand's assertion and subsequent readings of Caribbean texts may hold truth for some of the novels he includes, others attempt to reflect the complexity of Obeah. Still, Nunez-Harrell revises and expands the literary treatment of Obeah through metaphoric connection to issues of power/subjectivity and its incorporation as a historically significant aspect of New World identity. Nunez-Harrell challenges the widespread negative connotation, placing Obeah in the context of resistant cultural and religious practice.

As it is applied in Nunez-Harrell's narrative, Obeah is a belief system divided into two broad categories. The first involves the casting of spells for various purposes, both good and evil: protecting oneself, property, family, or loved ones; harming real or perceived enemies; and bringing fortune in love, employment, personal or business pursuits. The second involves healing through the application of knowledge of herbal and animal medicinal properties. Obeah, thus conceived, is not a religion as such but a system of beliefs grounded in spirituality and an acknowledgment of the supernatural and involving aspects of witchcraft, sorcery, magic, spells, and healing. In Trinidad it is strongly tied to Roman Catholicism, West African–derived religions such as Shango and Rada, African-influenced Protestantism, and, to a lesser degree, Amerindian and East Indian spirituality. Hence, although it may appear strange to an outsider, particularly in the latter twentieth century, it would not be contradictory for a character to be a devout Catholic and still consult an Obeah practitioner, or for the English ruling class to uphold Protestantism and secretly seek out the Obeah-woman in dire need. Plantation records and other historical documents reveal that not only did slaves rely on the Obeah practitioners for healing, protection, and aid in personal affairs, but plantation owners often called on them, especially for medicinal purposes. As Bell reports in his narrative, "The most remarkable feature of all, perhaps, was to learn that it not only persists as a sort of underlying religion with all the negroes, but that its terrors have penetrated to the East Indians, and to a surprising extent, among the white population" (184). Similarly, Steven Vertovec notes in *Hindu Trinidad*, "The system of magic popularly known as obeah is common to Trinidadians of all religions and ethnic groups. Originally drawn from the West African obayifo systems, these magical beliefs, acts and symbols have been combined or made interchangeable with those from North India, known as ojba."[11]

Throughout its history, the natural power resulting from such widespread patronage of Obeah has given rise to strong official sanctions against the practice. For instance, the Trinidadian Slave Ordinance of 1800, seeking to curb the increasing power associated with Obeah practice, made it a crime punishable by imprisonment. In slave culture, the Obeah-man or Obeah-woman was often a leader. Often, Obeah-men and Obeah-women were responsible for leading insurrections among the enslaved. Anti-Obeah ordinances, coupled with the fear of Obeah's power among believers, contributed to much of the negativity associated with its practice. During the period following emancipation, particularly the late nineteenth and early twentieth centuries as depicted in *When Rocks Dance*, many Trinidadians attempted to dissociate themselves from any knowledge of Obeah, in part because of increased public stigma, although oral and written accounts belie this public denial.

Nunez-Harrell gives Obeah primacy as a belief system and a way of ordering the world not only among the descendants of slaves, such as Emilia, but also among white officials and landowners, middle-class blacks, Creoles, and East Indians. Her text also reflects with historical accuracy the oppositions by others to the belief in the efficacy of the "tools" (and power) of Obeah. These tools include jumbies (ghosts), gourds, grave dust and other powders, trinkets, amulets, fetishes, and poultry. Despite the intellectual and moral opposition, Nunez-Harrell suggests, the pull of Obeah remained strong enough to foster doubt in the minds of even the staunchest disbeliever and naysayer. As portrayed in *When Rocks Dance*, a syncretic mixture of African traditions, spirituality, values, and concepts of resistance, European folk beliefs, and even Americanized and East Indian ideas, Obeah reflects the complexities and contradictions of Trinidadian social, political, and religious life, and as such Nunez-Harrell employs it as a metaphor for emergent New World identity.

WHEN THE NARRATIVE opens, Martina's mother, Emilia, having forsaken the ways of her Ibo ancestors, is ostracized for living with the Englishman Hrothgar. This breach is made manifest in her life, according to a Warao Indian chief and the Ibo Obeah-man (both of whom she consults in desperation), through the repeated birth of stillborn male twins. Recognizing the error of her ways, Emilia follows the directive of the Warao (with whom the Obeah-man reluctantly concurs), who asks her to commit a terrible sacrifice of her next set of male twins in order to save her future child (12–13):

> The Warao tells the truth. The spirits of your children will haunt you. But this time, if you prove yourself, you will have a new life. This time your sons will live, but two weeks after they are born you must do as your fathers before you did. Leave your twins in the forest at the mercy of our gods. At the mercy of their divine wisdom. Do that and you will conceive again. One child. You will have one child and in that child the spirits of all your children will live. They will find a resting place. Do that and don't forget the power that has helped you.

Emilia's (re)turn to Obeah, her willingness to fulfill the sacrifice exacted, signifies her essential belief in the efficacy of her African ways. Although her alliance with Hrothgar was, in part, economically motivated, she has also "stayed in Hrothgar's bed to reclaim the land he and his people had crossed the seas and claimed . . . from her people as though God gave them the right" (6). When Marina is eight, Emilia schools her in the harsh realities that only Obeah makes it possible for the girl to experience. She gives the child "the message of her people as each African mother in the Caribbean would do: . . . a man who owned land was a sort of god. He walked with gods . . . owned a part of this earth. He belonged to no one. He could be no slave. . . . Land was his most valuable possession . . . if he had the deed to it. But if a man owned land, it did not mean that his woman owned land" (30). Emilia, in fact, loses her right to Hrothgar's land upon his death because her name is not on the deed. A symbolic, and ultimately powerless, Catholic priest attempts to right the injustice. Through Hrothgar and Emilia's relationship Nunez-Harrell constructs black female subjectivity in colonial society and intertwines the quest of African women for power and freedom from domination with the acknowledgment of "African ways," symbolized by Obeah. And by contrasting Catholicism's potential powerlessness with the strength of Obeah, Nunez-Harrell further reveals the nature of Trinidadian society. At the turn of the century, nearly "all of the black masses of Trinidad were, at least nominally, Christians, and the majority were Roman Catholic,"[12] but in the black and Creole peoples' participation in marginalized African religions the crux of the social and cultural response to colonialism is reflected.[13] In her narrative, Emilia, like most of the island's Africans, traverses the world between Catholicism and Obeah, never truly relinquishing either one. This fluidity between Roman Catholicism and Obeah is due in part to the appeal of certain aspects of Catholicism, such as the role of saints, sensuous services with incense and altars, "robes of the priest, many feasts days," which could easily be fused by the masses with non-Christian religious practices.[14] The ease with which the Creoles in *When Rocks Dance* mediate between the two belief systems suggests a perception on the part of adherents that Obeah balances or, at the least, complements the power of Christianity and the role of the dominant, hierarchical church and the society it reflects in the lives of the black masses.

Although Nunez-Harrell does not identify a specific religion, such as Shango or Rada, or portray a clearly defined, organized body of practitioners or adherents, she employs religion as a key entrée into the social and cultural world of African descendants in the island. Through religion, she illuminates the distance as well as the connections between the dominant colonial culture on the island and those who would be dominated. Not only does Nunez-Harrell explore the importance of Obeah, but she questions the dominance of Catholicism and Anglicanism in the lives of their adherents. In addition, the symbiotic relationship between Catholicism and Obeah unveils the island's complex social interrelationships. Through Obeah, Emilia gains power in her otherwise constrained world. Through the ritualistic practice of her faith, she is able to counter the effects of her materially and spiritually fruitless relationship with Hrothgar. Later, with her second white keeper, Telser, Emilia employs Obeah as a way to sustain herself in a similarly oppressive, if more materially beneficial, relationship.[15]

Through the use of oral narratives, myths, and legends from various cultures, Nunez-Harrell interweaves several underlying ideological notions within the tale of Marina's quest to own land and gain power, thereby creating a discursive hybridity. Just as she invokes Ibo ideas regarding twins,[16] Nunez-Harrell uses other legends and tales, ranging from the Amerindian legend of El Dorado to the English narratives of *The Canterbury Tales*, *Othello*, and *The Tempest*, in order to establish on a structural level the hybridity suggested within the novel.[17]

While on one level Nunez-Harrell hints at similarities and common cultural practices, beliefs, and underlying ideologies among the "people of color" on the island, her primary focus is the dichotomy and range between African and English societies. However, to the degree that other cultures reinforce her basic premise, she incorporates them. For instance, the Warao (Amerindian) chief conveys the history and "wisdom" of his nation (through the myth of El Dorado) and provides the link between the tormented, dislocated histories of Vasco de Balboa (Marina's father-in-law) and Emilia through their children. Similarly, the long-term relationship of Virginia (Marina's mother-in-law) with the "coolie" (as East Indians came to be called) Ranjit reveals the cultural isolation and solitude of the East Indians, as well as the relationship they

developed to the land. Harold Smith (Virginia's adoptive father) expresses ad-
miration for the Indians' farming ability, asserting that "Trinidad's African
people agreed with their English wardens: Give a coolie land and you make
him happy. That's all coolies live for" (168). But Hilda Smith, who "prided
herself on her knowledge of colored people," more closely expresses the dominant sentiment about East Indians when she tells her husband, "A matter of
time before the coolie does exactly what the Negro is doing now. You see,
colored people are all the same, my dear. Coolie or Negro, they all have one
desire and that is to be like us. The poor things imagine that if they could
only change their skins—at that point she would always look sympathetically
at Virginia, her black daughter—they would be white. It's more than skin,
Smithy my dear. It's culture. Civilization. Intelligence" (168). Hilda Smith's
analysis is important to the underlying ideology of the British, who are clearly
unable to see any of the island's colored as anything other than servants. In
Hilda's brief appearances, she articulates the dominant culture's racism, its often erroneous viewpoints, and underlying ideology, while realistically assess-
ing the island's social structure. In addition, her own personal narrative reveals
the deeper link between the dominant society and the masses, through Obeah.
On a structural level, Hilda's character reveals the insidious nature of these
views.

Further, Nunez-Harrell emphasizes the ways in which black society in-
ternalizes certain notions about "colored" people, reinforcing social domination and stratification. Just as Hilda Smith disparages Indians and Africans
in one breath, her loyal daughter, Virginia, harbors demeaning impressions of
Ranjit and her fellow Africans. Virginia and Ranjit are drawn to each other
because each is an outsider in his or her community. Ranjit finds in Virginia
the "very alienation and loneliness that he too suffered. And he discovered
that they shared the same desire to be more than what their conditions as
colonized people living in a British colony had forced upon them" (167). A
young woman when they met, Virginia was then "already an old maid condemned to a life of sexual frustration by a Portuguese man disenchanted with
God and religion" (167). When Ranjit discovers Virginia is a schoolteacher,
he enlists her as his tutor. She teaches Ranjit the ways of the colonizers—
music, books, manners—and looks down on him, "for in spite of all she had
taught Ranjit, in spite of his dreams, his love for music and books, he was
still and finally a peasant, a dirt farmer, a coolie. She was, or she had been
once, the daughter of Hilda Smith, the English warden's wife" (196).

Their relationship reflects the recorded historical motive of the English:
to establish a dominant society into which the Africans were to be absorbed,
"fashioned in their own image" as Raj Vasil notes in *Politics in Bi-racial Societies*; but "the balance of race relations was to be disturbed as the two existing

cultures, which were basically European and African, were joined by a completely new one from Asia. The Indians, although Caucasians, were not white; although sometimes darker-skinned than many Africans, they were not negroid. They could not fit into the traditional interplay of European and African in any predictable way."[18] Yet, underlying the friction-laden interactions in the narrative, binding the native Amerindians to the blacks and Creoles (and perhaps even the East Indians and Asians) who considered themselves "native" against the British, is Nunez-Harrell's suggestion that "the island was populated [then] and was to be populated [later] by a people who approached life's mysteries not with an intellect disengaged from their oneness with nature, but with minds open to truths whispered to them from the sea, the earth, the animals, the birds, the fish" (119).

Significantly, the ideology Nunez-Harrell describes in this passage informing the attitude toward the land and its ownership distinguishes the island's primary racial groups. The Smiths' assertions reveal the attitudes of their class and indicate that they cannot possibly know the depth of feeling for the land—and all of nature—the Africans and East Indians (and the Amerindians) possess. Nunez-Harrell articulates this affinity through the use of the history and myth surrounding Columbus's and Sir Walter Raleigh's contact with the island, and through the characters' response to elements of the land and sea. Although the island is small and may appear insignificant to outsiders, "to the people who lived there, the sea and land are varied and mysterious" (118). An important backdrop to this narrative of three women's lives is Nunez-Harrell's insistence on each group's perspective on land and landownership as a primary expression of self. When the success of this quest is articulated, this notion is the perfect demonstration of the combination of British conceptions of power with African notions of land. The attitude toward land combines with religion and religious practices as the strong overarching themes through which the reader may interpret the historical and social forces that have an impact on and shape the characters and the collective identities each represents. Nunez-Harrell employs these myths in the narrative to establish the exterior framework of Trinidadian society, which affects so gravely her characters' lives and psyches, as a reinforcement of the polarities she presents.

Through the inter- and intracultural interactions Nunez-Harrell dispels the idea of a monolithic black cultural identity, replacing it with a range of identities connecting the British to the African and vice versa. The manifestation of those identities in a collective whole rests on the shared knowledge of specific ideals, which Nunez-Harrell repeatedly conveys through the quest for land, tied to the expression of Obeah. The complexity of this "residually oral,"[19] mythohistorical narrative is further underscored in the interaction of the characters with each other, particularly the manner in which the female

characters serve as point and counterpoint for the revelation of specific cultural ideas and values reflecting identity. Within the "in-law" relationship between Virginia and Emilia, for instance, Nunez-Harrell incorporates the
tension that speaks to diverse African identities. Although both women are
of "pure" African descent, each embodies different forms of hybridity. At the
core (as Marina observes), "Virginia was much more of an African, much more
like her mother, Emilia, than she pretended to be" (202). Yet, on the surface,
Virginia scoffs at Emilia's ways, particularly her belief in Obeah, asking Marina, "And does your mother intend to cure the disease on the land with her
obeah?" (178). Likewise, Marina is embarrassed by her mother's status as a
former maid and "kept" woman, as well as her manner of dress and lack of
education and refinement. When Emilia visits, Marina, although "anxious to
see her mother," responds in embarrassment. "When the buggy stopped at the
front steps and she saw [Emilia], she regretted with all her heart that even for
one second she had allowed herself to feel the slightest need for her . . . for
there in the buggy, sitting next to her white lover, was a comic character. A
true golliwog" (219). Emilia's costume—the makeup of a white woman and
the elegant dresses of her former mistress—was meant to impress Marina, her
"schoolteacher" husband, and her mother-in-law. Instead, her daughter's "disgust and shame" was lost on Emilia, as Marina hid behind pride, while her
husband smirked at the outrageous outfit. Through scenes such as this one,
Nunez-Harrell unfolds the subtle and more obvious class distinctions that resulted from the colonial system in Trinidad, while using the larger issue of landownership and its connection to the spiritual world of the characters to convey
the island's true value system.

Trinidadian society, like that of its sister island, Jamaica, has been under
stress at differing points in its history. Nunez-Harrell exemplifies aspects of
that history as she tells the story of Marina's quest for land. Her reconstruction shifts the focus to the cultural creations that grew up in response to stress,
primarily dislocation and oppression. Prevalent in most people's lives is religion, through which the cultural ideology can be witnessed.

> We can see obeah [and myal] achieving interrelated roles in
> nineteenth-century and contemporary [Jamaican] society. Obeah is the
> art of sorcery, practiced in private, if not secret, and reflecting the
> disintegrative forces of a society under stress. . . . The obeah practitio-
> ner provided medical and jural aid for the plantation workers in a
> society devoid of these institutions in any other form. If the obeah
> specialist is fearful, he or she was also the source of comfort, healing,
> and justice.[20]

Much more than a simple religious practice, Obeah reflects a belief system as well as pain, fear, transcendence, power, and ultimate social survival. Although a great deal of the fear it inspires in the hearts of nonpractitioners derives from ignorance, a large portion of that fear can be attributed to the power it sustains in the lives of those who participate. Much like U.S. society, where cultural expressions were often viewed by the aristocracy as "quaint" and harmless, but just as often banned, nineteenth-century Trinidadian society reflected the British desire to eradicate African barbarism, but with a stronger emphasis on assimilation and the adoption of European values and forms.

As a part of Africans' cultural expression, religions that incorporated Obeah were viewed as a threat to the goals of the British. And although the British encouraged complete assimilation, they "never promised [blacks] social equality" in exchange for conformity.[21] Although few blacks who were born in Africa or had any first-hand knowledge of the continent remained in Trinidad, and "despite the influence on the [Creole] culture" of European elements "in dress, in music and in the dance," the "African element was perhaps the paramount one in [their] cultural world."[22] Similar European influence was naturally seen in the spiritual practices of African and native descendants, but here, perhaps more visibly than in any other cultural sphere, the African element remained strongest, thus placing Obeah in direct competition with the Anglican and, more importantly in this text, the Roman Catholic churches. For Alma, the village Obeah-woman, Obeah was foremost, with the Roman Catholic Church a safety net; even while she "praises the Lord" and asks Marina, "You know the Bible, chile?" (134), she "presides over ceremonies on certain nights" and places Obeah "medicine" in Marina's closet at Emilia's request. For Emilia, the pull of Obeah was strong, and even though she remained with Telser, her second lover, and professed Catholicism, "she had not deserted her African ancestors. Not even the old Ibo, if he were alive today, would accuse her of that. She was faithful to obeah" (236). For Marina's mother-in-law, Virginia, ensconced in both the Anglican Church from childhood and the Roman Catholic Church through her marriage to a Portuguese ex-priest, Obeah was frightening and induced doubts. At one point she ridicules her neighbors by saying, "They think every root and weed could cure any disease. The English people are right to stop all this nonsense. I'd burn their houses down too" (173). Yet, although she appears to dismiss Obeah's power, upon discovering a bag containing a mixture of Obeah "medicine" in Marina's closet, Virginia summons a priest to bless the house.

For Marina, a black "Creole," finding a proper context for her identity as a mixed-race woman in nineteenth-century Trinidad requires an understanding of the juxtaposition of Obeah outside and inside her life. Similarly, Virginia is characterized by the manner in which Obeah and its absence/presence manifests itself in her life. While a superficial view of Virginia's identity develops from the deconstruction of her strange relationship with her English adoptive parents and their influence on her sensibilities, a concurrent narrative plot reveals the role and impact of both Obeah and the Christian religions on her personality.

Virginia is of pure African descent but was "adopted" by the white English warden, Harold Smith, and his wife, Hilda. At the age of fifteen, when she begins to develop into womanhood, Harold initiates vague sexual advances toward his adopted daughter. Hilda arranges for Virginia's marriage to the "strange Portogee," Vasco de Balboa, with fifteen acres of land as a dowry. Given her background, Virginia is not representative of the island's African descendants and, throughout the text, reflects a construction of Creolization that is not biological but socialized. In its early portrayal, her character develops as one who is outside the realm of identity constructed by Nunez-Harrell for African descendants; instead she represents an "alternative" identity, which is just as "real" as the other. In her ironic and ambiguous insistence on the primacy of European values and ideals, Virginia embodies the subconscious struggle of African descendants with English cultural domination. Her African appearance, her "striking beauty," and "purplish black skin" are in direct opposition to her internal belief in her "whiteness." Virginia carries into adulthood the notions that Hilda embedded in her subconscious as a child; in a telling incident, as the very black Virginia holds onto a white alabaster doll at an English lawn party in Port of Spain, Hilda tells the little girl, "Never mind child. They can't see your whiteness but I can. You hold onto that wicked doll. She'll give back your whiteness to you and they'll see it too. So there" (85). This background to Virginia's socialization underscores her ironic role throughout the narrative.

Virginia's adaptation of the ideas of Hilda and her class is not easy, but it is thorough. Like them, she equates Western rationality with a superior civilization, dismissing a true belief in Obeah as a possibility for Marina, for example, because she feels the young woman is "too level-headed for that" (171). And, as with them, that exterior rationality hides an interior sense of possibility. Virginia cannot transcend race—her blackness—however, despite her proximity to the English. The class and color distinctions that Hilda ingrains in Virginia mark her as vividly constructed by a member of the dominant society—a construction that, because it lacks the grounding in "African ways" and the fluidity of that position, renders her outside both cultures. As she suppresses her Africanness, particularly her beauty, Virginia attempts to confirm her closeness to the white British. Until her epiphany at the end of the novel, Virginia inwardly identifies as "white" and feels her blackness "really belonged to the little alabaster doll that Mrs. Smith kept in her private box, the little doll that had sucked away [her] whiteness and left her black" (196).

On a micro-level the relationship between Obeah practitioners and Christianity is fraught with the same tensions revealed in the African's response to the larger oppressive colonial influence. Although on the surface such an analysis may seem reductive, Nunez-Harrell's narrative structure bears out these seemingly innocuous parallels and further supports the notion of syncretic religious practice, as portrayed through Obeah, as both resistance to and rejection of total domination. When placed in the context of social practice, these religious elements become a series of signs that reflect various forms and permutations of identity expressed in opposition to the dominant culture. Identity formation becomes not only a reflection of acquiescence to and absorption of the dominant culture but also a resistance to that which threatens to overtake. Through Virginia, Emilia, and Marina, Nunez-Harrell uses physical space and representations of the female body to connote the structure of this identity.

Nunez-Harrell's use of the term *Obeah* initially appears problematic in that unlike some other Trinidadian writers she does not indicate any religious body or group with which the practice is associated. In this narrative Obeah in and of itself is not depicted as a singular religion but as an expression of several types of spiritual beliefs and religious practice. She attributes the use of the terms *Obeah-man* and *Obeah-woman* to the practitioners and villagers, which reflects her own creative conception of the social and legal climate during this period. Nunez-Harrell's portrayal of the pervasive knowledge and assimilation of Obeah in Trinidad is evident on several levels, ranging from these narrative references and dialogue between the characters to detailed, revealing descriptions of specific ceremonies and practices. As revision of previous literary treatment, these portrayals underlie and successfully inscribe meaning related to identity and social order throughout the novel. Vasil notes that Obeah was legally defined and outlawed in an 1868 ordinance and was punishable by jail and flogging. Although the legal definition required money to be paid for the assumption of supernatural powers, "as the word was used in the late nineteenth century, it included any religious or magical practices which were considered to be African, including healing, and conjuring of all types—securing success in love and family affairs, or favourable results in litigation, or injuring enemies."[23]

Hence Obeah-man and Obeah-woman were probably not terms used publicly by Africans for fear of bringing one of their own into contact with the law, a point reflected in the novel when Marina seeks out Alma, the Obeah-woman. Marina's white skin and freckles cause the villagers of Moruga to distrust and lie to her. Even though she fears Marina's potential power because of her whiteness, the servant girl, Jane, tells her, "Ma'am, I don't know no Alma. Please, Ma'am." Nunez-Harrell incorporates this fear into her text, recognizing that, "in 1902, one did not give information about obeah to people with light skins, and Marina's pale face . . . was not above suspicion" (127). When Marina is given information by another village woman, it "was Emilia's past that gave Marina entry to the obeahwoman" (128). On this level, Nunez-Harrell reinforces the significance of West African "survivals" in the transformation of identity as well as the literary imagination through the portrayal of these permutations of belief systems in the lives of her characters.

The colonial Trinidadian society that Nunez-Harrell portrays in *Rocks* is built on an exterior/interior tension, as reflected in the expression of high/low culture on a general societal level and in the more subtle, intraracial issues. The author reflects this theme through the value-laden perspectives on land and extends it symbolically through characterization and her insistence on the significance of Obeah in her characters' lives. In interracial as well as intraracial interaction, Nunez-Harrell filters race, class, and gender issues through the lens of the specter of Obeah and further conveys this notion of exteriority/interiority through a definition of physical space. Hence, Virginia's conception of space and, by extension, land and values is shaped by the English, while Emilia's and Marina's are heavily influenced by African beliefs, a fact against which Marina struggles.

The exteriority of English society is in stark contrast to, and yet influential in determining, the interiority of the mass of African descendants—an interiority expressed through the spiritual experience. Through Obeah, Nunez-Harrell demonstrates the manner in which the English made distinctions between the races and maintained their own sense of superiority. This distinction is accomplished effectively from one perspective through Alma, the Obeah-woman, and from another through Hilda Smith, the warden's wife, who epitomized the thought, attitudes, and actions of a supposedly well-bred, superior English woman. But through Hilda Nunez-Harrell also conveys the "invisible" link between the two societies—a link that reverses the flow of influence and reveals at once the hypocrisy and human vulnerability of the English. Hilda adopted Virginia not out of pure munificence but because she and Harold had been unable to conceive a child of their own. After Virginia is married, Hilda becomes pregnant through Obeah with Virginia's "brother" Philip. When she discovers that Harold has not legally relinquished the land to de Balboa, Hilda goes back to the Obeah-woman, who tells her that Harold must release the land in order for the child to live. As Harold tells Philip long after Hilda has died, "Your mother could not resist the drums. . . . She protected Virginia from the drums, but she loved them" (252).

The historical legacy of and relationships within the de Balboa family are significant because they further illuminate the syncretic nature of Trinidadian identity and underscore the notion that hybridity is the result of this fluid social tension. Additionally, through Antonio, Nunez-Harrell presents the complex manner in which European standards of beauty underlie African conceptions of self and further the inequality experienced by women, particularly black women, on the island. In simplest terms, Antonio associated all that was good with Marina's whiteness and that which was evil with the blackness that was evident only in her "widespread nostrils" or the "rise of her buttocks." "For in his mind, only the ugly could not be trusted, and he saw infidelity, deceit, promiscuity, lasciviousness in the contours of a bony woman, her face swollen, with thick lips, bulging eyes and wide-spread nostrils mounted on a flat nose bridge. Not in the soft roundness of Marina's arms and legs, nor in the fragile paleness of her blue-veined skin, nor in the cool gray of her eyes, nor in the childlike innocence of her light-brown hair that fell naturally and artistically where it wanted" (144).

Marina's and Antonio's lives and interactions with their mothers reveal the link between religion and history. Marina married Antonio "for the land"; their personal ancestral legacies intertwine to suggest the island's enigmatic racial history and its ultimate expression over time. The narrative begins as Emilia's story, but the focus is quickly transferred to Marina's life, with her mother's involvement providing both background and timely and appropriate counterpoint throughout. Endowed with the legacy of Emilia's ties to Obeah and her deep but often misplaced love, Marina's own story can never be fully dissociated from that of her protective mother. However, much of what we learn of Marina and, through her, the island issues from her relationships with Antonio and Virginia.

For her mother-in-law, Marina represents a paradox. Virginia is drawn to Marina's partial English parentage, as represented by her light skin and eyes, "fine" features, and long, flowing hair. Marina also represents the possibility of producing "light-skinned babies," which Virginia admits she wants because her own son is so dark-complexioned. Yet, she actively resents Marina's African parentage and associates the young woman with what she considers its negative aspects, namely Obeah, a lack of formal education and refinement, and wildness/promiscuity. Marina's presence, in addition to diverting the attention of her son away from Virginia, provides a constant reminder to Virginia of the legend about the younger woman's birth and possession by the spirits of her eight dead brothers. Virginia expresses this discomfort when she says of the villagers, "'The people in this village are superstitious. It's as if they hadn't left Africa. There's a story in everything. A jumbie behind every bush. . . . ' But Virginia was uneasy. There was indeed something unusual about Marina" (76). This observation by Virginia is significant for its implied veracity. Nunez-Harrell suggests that, in fact, the island's African descendants *had not* left Africa—at least not in their resistance to total domination, socialization, and assimilation. This furthers Virginia's ironic role in the author's

subversion of the notion that the African descendant's belief system is inferior or may be easily dismissed.

Similar feelings are expressed by Virginia throughout the narrative. Although she often espouses beliefs that reflect a European sensibility, she is
racked by doubts and ultimately rejects some of those ideas. Near the end of
the novel, when Marina is fighting for her life during childbirth, she is surrounded by Virginia, Emilia, Alma, and Victoria, the midwife, and the English doctor, Glentower. At one point, Virginia, sitting by Marina's bedside,
realizes that a large shadow looms behind her. She "was not afraid. She had
an uncanny feeling that the person was a sort of protective shield between
Marina and her and the outside world. . . . The woman did not surprise her.
She was oddly familiar" (338).

Significantly, this spiritual experience, steeped in the world of Obeah, reinforces the importance of its cultural heritage and joins Virginia and Marina
with each other within its realm. Antonio too is both repulsed by and drawn
to Marina's reputed spirits. Just as Marina entered the marriage to acquire land,
Antonio, though attracted by beauty, looked to her (as his fourth wife) to
"save" him from the curse of his father, who was rumored to have killed his
first three wives—all in childbirth.

Emilia used Obeah to give Marina life and to protect her. At the same
time she attempts to shield Marina from its full effects. Similarly, Virginia has
steeped Antonio in Catholicism and attempts to use it as a tool of control.
Both mothers have succeeded in creating confusion in the minds of their children regarding religion and the spiritual world. In the end, both Marina and
Antonio resort to a belief in Obeah to save Marina and the lives of her babies. During Marina's difficult labor, Antonio visits Alma and the Roman
Catholic church. Marina's and Antonio's ambiguity throughout the text further reinforces that of Virginia, who comes full circle in the recognition of
"who she is," and of Emilia, who, when Marina falls ill, takes no chances. She
does not have much money, "but what she had, she gave to the parish priest
in Prince's Town to say a novena for Marina—nine days of Masses in Marina's
name. Now she would have both the Church and obeah on her side" (295),
reflecting a syncretism that characterizes the religious and cultural systems of
the New World black identity. Each of the characters' lives is marked by the
type of personal, yet connected, cultural journey resulting in the construction
of identities affected by the experience of a particular place in time.

By the end of the narrative, both Marina and Virginia have reluctantly
come to accept the certainty of the power of Obeah. A circularity marks the
entire narrative and is rooted in the underlying idea that no matter how arduous the journey, it eventually leads back to one's origins. In several instances,
as Hilda's visits to Alma reveal, even the English concede through word or

action that their own world-view and sense of superiority are generally built on false notions that are blind to the cultural realities of the island. Just as Hilda's visit to an Obeah-woman to help her conceive and deliver a baby reveals this hypocrisy, Philip's own uncertainty about the "absurdity" of the African's cultural practices is evident in his later attempt to force his father to sign over to him the deed to Virginia's land when he experiences "his old terror of the people who lived on this island that was not his. His fear of their power to lure white people into their mysterious, dark, underworld doings. And his fear that his mother, for all her love of daffodils and lilacs, sparkled a little when the drums pulsated on certain nights around bright fires. When women dressed in white, heads tied with white bandannas, danced themselves into a frenzy and spoke in languages few white men ever understood" (251). While Nunez-Harrell critiques the hypocrisy of the colonized society, she recognizes the validity of each of the island's cultures and explores the basic human need for myths, symbols, and ideas through which to shape and anchor their worlds.

The English views concerning the role of women and their presumed inherent inferiority relegated all women to a subordinate position in society. However, while women like Hilda Smith were granted some status based on race and economic level, women like Virginia and Emilia were forced to create their own spheres of safety, respect, and power. Both possess a sense of self and autonomy, but because each achieves limited status through her connection to a man from the dominant society, their lives are ultimately shaped by English views embedded in laws, social mores. Emilia straddles two worlds, while Virginia immerses herself wholeheartedly in English culture. These two apparent polarities are more complex however; Virginia maintains a submerged pride in her African heritage, making certain concessions to the expectations of the African villagers, and Emilia remains attached to one, then another, white lover/keeper.

Other characters also reveal the pervasive power of the English over the way Africans perceive themselves and their culture. Even Alma, the Obeah-woman, embraces the white conception of beauty, commenting that Marina is "pretty as the queen she self. White like she father" (128). In her own life, however, Alma is autonomous and seemingly free, at least from the gender constraints inherent in Victorian English rule. "Alma was as eternal as the sea washing every morning upon the lazy beaches. . . . For each generation it was the same. Alma was always there. They said it was obeah that made her food so sweet. Obeah that made her live so long. Eternal Alma, in her long white, cotton dresses and crisp white bandannas" (127). Her eternal, calming presence speaks to the effect of Obeah—"always there"—in the lives of the African villagers. In addition, her ability and relative freedom are important reminders of its power. Virginia conforms to British standards of modesty and decorum in her personal dress, and Emilia mimics what she perceives to be "the height of fashion in London." In contrast, Alma sits in the front yard of her home in a "dirty brown-striped dress, a bright red bandanna . . . staring through clouds of smoke that billowed out of her pipe" (128). Alma's "difference" is further established through her physical environment. "Indeed, surrounded by tall bushes on every side, Alma's house seemed to be in a different place altogether. A different country" (127). Her actions also reveal the link between the high church and Obeah. In one scene the Obeah-woman invokes Christianity, making the sign of the cross in the fashion of Catholics as she equates a spiritual medium's or channeler's spirit travel with Jesus's time in the tomb: "No, chile, you don't understand. Mr. Harris out dere, you tink he is in dat grave? Dat isn't Mr. Harris in de grave. Mr. Harris, but not Mr. Harris. Just like it was Jesus in the tomb, but not Jesus" (134).

When placed in the context of social practice, these religious elements become a series of signs that reflect various forms and permutations of identity, often expressed in opposition to those of the dominant culture. Nunez-Harrell uses several dichotomies to reveal the oppositions in colonial society; yet even these oppositions blur in the form of her characters, particularly Alma, Virginia, Emilia, and Hilda. In this manner, Nunez-Harrell reinforces the notion of hybridity while still subverting the oppressive nature of colonial influence and reconstructing a fictional world that acknowledges and even privileges African-centered identify.

This history has been repeated throughout the New World in countries whose official languages reflect European influence—Spanish, Portuguese, French, and English. What sustains Nunez-Harrell's narrative is the tension caused by the constant struggle against oppressive notions that is manifest in forms of resistance, such as the practice of Obeah. This same tension is evident in Alma's contradictory embrace of Marina's whiteness or Virginia's allegiance to the intricately cornrowed hairstyle she insists on wearing, then covers. Nunez-Harrell's reflection of this history through the social and cultural experiences of women reveals the diverse manifestations of social and economic oppression to which women are subjected in colonial society, as well as some of the responses to this domination.

WHEN ROCKS DANCE is a narrative about oppressive power and of tension in both the larger and the more personal worlds of its characters. Through this tension, Nunez-Harrell constructs an inner and outer tale that reveals the nature of African identity in the New World. In accepting the colonizer's designation of identity, one relinquishes the power to determine one's own relationship to the world and to others. In portraying the hybrid nature of African identity in the New World, while still defining the core of that identity through its relationship to history and the development of cultural practices, Nunez-Harrell's narrative redefines our traditional views of Caribbean culture. As with their peers in the United States, any analysis of the works of Afro-Caribbean writers must be undertaken with a sustained understanding of the impact of the social construction of race and related issues on their perceptions of and place in the world. The creative vision that inheres in Afro-Caribbean writers is predicated on the experiences of colonized subjects. Nunez-Harrell's narrative reflects, in its content and structure, the influence of Western, Anglicized education, as well as a keen awareness of its impact on the society from which she emerges. Rather than present a view that valorizes "colonized life," Nunez-Harrell constructs a syncretic narrative based on the insight of the colonized, incorporating the myths of the Western, literate history of the English, Spanish, and Portuguese with those of the oral Amerindian and African cultures to reveal the complexity of the lives of the island's people of color and original inhabitants.

Ultimately, however, the author's concern is with the specific effects of hybridity on African descendants. These ideas join her text with those of other black women in the New World—Alice Walker, Michelle Cliff, Paule Marshall, Merle Collins, among others—through a particular insistence on connections to the past, specifically the African past, as crucial to the continued survival of important ideas and values in the future. Nunez-Harrell sustains this perspective through her attention to Obeah as a grounding and rallying, albeit misunderstood, force in the lives of African Caribbeans. She further reveals the long reach of African cultures into mainstream and dominant societies. But rather than valorize African descendants or treat her characters as if they function within a vacuum, Nunez-Harrell explores the wide range of influences, innovations, and responses operative in their lives in order to render them distinctively human.

Notes

1. Elizabeth Nunez-Harrell, *When Rocks Dance* (New York: Putnam, 1986). All further references will appear in parentheses in the text.
2. Paul Gilroy, *The Black Atlantic: Modernity and Double Consciousness* (Cambridge: Harvard University Press, 1993).
3. Likewise, as the son of Vasco de Balboa, an ex-communicated Portuguese Jesuit priest, and an African mother, Virginia, Marina's husband, Antonio de Balboa, represents a commixture of conflicting histories and ideas. Although he tries to rationalize his desire to marry Marina, Antonio "knew in his heart that his resolve to meet Marina had nothing to do with this cold, rational, emotionless approach so typical of the Europeans on the island, but rather his response to the not-so-distant rhythms of his mother's buried culture" (66).
4. Early in the narrative, she tells her daughter, "You were born on the land. Beneath the cocoa. The land took you from my womb. Before I touched you, the land

embraced you. You belong to the land and you will own land one day. No, no one will force you to move from where you live. No, not like they did to me" (30).

5. Raj K. Vasil, *Politics in Bi-racial Societies. The Third World Experience* (New Delhi: Vikas, 1984), 82.

6. Ibid., 83.

7. Ibid.

8. Reinhard W. Sander, *The Trinidad Awakening: The West Indian Novel of the 1930s* (Westport, Conn.: Greenwood Press, 1988), 1.

9. Archie Bell, *The Spell of the Caribbean Islands* (Boston: L. C. Page, 1926), 186. I refer to Bell's travel narrative, a part of the Spell Series of books about places around the world, because it typifies the kind of "unscholarly" observation often tendered by travel writers, usually white males from the United States and Europe, during the 1800s and early 1900s. Bell and other travel writers usually wrote of the cultural traditions encountered with a bemused, sometimes disbelieving, and often condescending tone.

10. Ramchand gives the most detailed critical attention to the treatment of Obeah in Caribbean literature. His analyses of a range of novels provide some insight but are constrained by an apparent predisposition toward dismissing its significance as an actual (or worthy) reflection of "survival of African Cultures." Kenneth Ramchand, *The West Indian Novel and Its Background*, 2d ed. (London: Heinemann, 1983), 123–131.

11. Steven Vertovec, *Hindu Trinidad: Religion, Ethnicity and Socio-economic Change* (London: Macmillan, 1992).

12. Vasil, *Politics in Bi-racial Societies*, 157.

13. Throughout the chapter, I refer to Creole people to represent the many mixed-race groups, as well as in an attempt to recognize individuals who acknowledge(d) and/or identify(ied) this connation as a part of their heritage, even as they associate(d) themselves with the island's black masses. This encompasses a range of physical appearances. Individuals, groups, and scholars also make distinctions among French, English, and Spanish descendants who identify themselves or are identified as "white" Creoles.

   I do not attempt to subsume distinct identities through this use of the term but rather to reflect the discussions that have preceded my own as well as the construction of identity as reflected by Trinidadians and within this novel. For a more detailed historical perspective on the period, see Bridget Brereton, *Race Relations in Colonial Trinidad, 1870–1900* (Cambridge: Cambridge University Press, 1979), 193–212, who asserts that Creole society was understood by Trinidadians to include people of European and African descent and those of mixed descent but not Asian and Middle Eastern immigrants. Although certainly not the only source on the subject, Brereton provides a useful delineation of the intricate nature of late nineteenth- and early twentieth-century social stratification along the lines of "class, color, caste and race."

   For purposes of my discussion of hybridity, I subscribe to the notion that individuals often dismissed the idea of Creole (and its attendant connotations of worth) when no European blood was known and when European ideas and traditions were dominant. Hence, my use of the term at the end of the twentieth century is informed by an understanding of its complex history and etymology but proves useful in conveying certain notions of the hybridization of New World black identity over time.

14. Ibid., 158. Brereton provides further insight into Nunez-Harrell's novel and characters like Emilia and Alma through her discussion of New World "black religions." Her study describes the "fusion" of West African belief systems and Catholicism,

as well as the correlation practitioners made between the gods of West Africa and the saints of Catholicism.

15. Emilia remains with Telser, but unlike her alliance with Hrothgar, this one is characterized by a more definitive stand on the significance of Obeah. Whereas with Hrothgar she had to be secretive, Emilia and Telser have a mutual understanding. True to her "African ancestors . . . [and] faithful to obeah," Emilia knew that Telser would not interfere, for "perhaps if he did, she would see reason to leave him" (236).

16. "A woman who has twins is osu. Outcast. In my clan, her children are left in the forest to die. Or live, if their spirit is great. But the gods were kind to you. Your chi has smiled. I have prayed for you. But I can't help you now. You know in your body you carry twins again" (12).

17. Nunez-Harrell incorporates storytelling as an important device within the narrative for conveying values. At the beginning, she uses the Warao to tell Marina of her ancestors' past, including the telling of "Brer Rabbitt stories," as well as of his people's past interaction with Columbus and Sir Walter Raleigh, who chased the native Indians from El Dorado, "the city of Gold," after they had buried their treasures there. Similarly, Virginia engages Antonio, throughout his childhood, not in stories of her African ancestors but of Shakespeare because she wants him "to be like the English." Antonio tells Marina, "Before I was twelve she had read me all of Chaucer's Canterbury Tales and all Shakespeare's plays. I even memorized the soliloquies in his tragedies. 'To be or not to be, that is the question.'" (212).

18. Vasil, *Politics in Bi-racial Societies*, 85, 84.

19. I borrow this concept from Bernard Bell, *The Afro-American Novel and Its Tradition* (Amherst: University of Massachusetts Press, 1987). Bell uses the idea to describe women's texts, particularly Toni Morrison's and Margaret Walker Alexander's use of history and myth to convey an alternate, postmodern perspective of African American experience. I find this a useful concept for the discussion of writers from the Caribbean as well.

20. Joseph M. Murphy, *Working the Spirit: Ceremonies of the African Diaspora* (Boston: Beacon Press, 1994), 120.

21. Brereton, *Race Relations in Colonial Trinidad*, 153.

22. Ibid., 152.

23. Vasil, *Politics in Bi-racial Societies*, 156.

"Another Poor Devil of a Human Being . . ."

ELAINE SAVORY

Jean Rhys and the Novel as Obeah

I'm tormented by characters from heaven knows where.
—JEAN RHYS, *The Letters of Jean Rhys*

A NUMBER of studies have attempted to elucidate the concept of Obeah in Jean Rhys's texts.[1] Two major writers from the Caribbean—Edward Kamau Brathwaite and Wilson Harris—have voiced differing responses to Rhys's spiritual place in the region.[2] Brathwaite has written two important responses to Rhys. The first was in 1974, when he expressed skepticism that after the legacy of hundreds of years of slavery, racism, and colonization white Creoles could "meaningfully identify or be identified with the spiritual world on this side of the Sargasso Sea."[3] The second is a 1995 essay in which he points out that the Caribbean is a society founded on race and therefore racial identities do inform interpretations; Rhys has a white response to Obeah, albeit informed and Caribbean-centered. Harris, conceiving of the Caribbean as both the living and ancestral dead of all races, is open to the possibility that writing can discover fragments of ancient voices that speak through contemporary language; for him, Rhys's *Wide Sargasso Sea* may be read through an Arawak myth, and her ancestry can be assumed to be both white and black. Both of these positions are valid ones: Rhys herself always understood her own marginality and that of white society in the West Indies. Although her black characters speak through her voice and do not materialize in any significant way until quite late in her writing life,[4] Rhys's very isolation from community and her longing to cross racial lines eventually resulted, in the last phase of her creative work, in her discovery of voices from beyond her essential self. We can disregard neither of these two complementary visions of her place "on this side of the Sargasso Sea."

I am seeking to explore the idea of Obeah Rhys constructs in, but mainly *as* her texts, rather than Obeah's sociological or religious reality as interpreted by scholars. I propose a complex interplay in Rhys's texts between the idea of the self as isolated, imprisoned, and embattled, and the idea of the possibility of a spiritual context that could allow for release and renewal. When I suggest Rhys wrote "the novel as Obeah," I mean that she thought of writing as summoning spirits or drawing on a level of consciousness far beyond the logical or rational, which gave her the free space in which to survive her difficult life and to "earn" a proper death.[5] The numerous references to Obeah in her texts show how much the idea informed her imagination. I want to insist that Rhys's ideas on Obeah and witchcraft in Europe were just that, her ideas, and that to try to link them definitively to an insider's experiences of Obeah ritual or to link Obeah practices with the ritual opening of taletelling in the "tin-tin" folktale tradition (as Elaine Campbell attempts in her work) is to miss the way in which Rhys utilizes materials as an imaginative writer.[6]

Like both Brathwaite and Harris, Rhys understood writing to be a sacred art, requiring absolute commitment. She gave that commitment to writing, making it more important than the love of family and friends, comfort, security, or money. She also came to refer to writing itself as coming from somewhere outside herself, as a link to the world of the spiritual that had its source in her experiences as a child and adolescent in the Caribbean.[7] This connection to the spiritual links her directly to Caribbean writers such as Harris, Brathwaite, Paule Marshall, Derek Walcott, and Dennis Scott, with whom she shares the perception that resistance to oppression can be strengthened and assisted by turning to the world of the spirit.[8] Although this perception is not shared by all Caribbean writers, there is certainly an important literary extension to the role that religion and ritual have played in the history of Afro-Caribbean resistance to racism and colonialism. Rhys's texts, however, portray a conflicted, alienated awareness on the part of a white Creole of such rituals and beliefs: she knows her understanding is that of an outsider.

Rhys's texts are spare, but certain codes function as imagery does in poems, as a layered pathway of meaning. One of these codes is built from references to good and evil, God and the Devil, Obeah, ghostliness, and witchcraft. But in Rhys's fictional world moral systems do not have much coherence because those who make the rules are functionally amoral and self-interested (men, whites, the rich and socially powerful). Devising an integrated life within a context of apparent moral coherence (but actual anarchy) requires great strength and insight: Rhysian central characters are women who generally turn their anger about the situation to themselves, but with a devastating honesty about their own moral significance. They are almost all white. The exception is Selina in "Let Them Call It Jazz," whose consciousness, interestingly enough, is not spiritually aware.

The parameters of the world of the spirit in Rhys's texts derive primarily from her early experiences of religion and spirituality as two currents—Christianity and Obeah—colliding antagonistically in the black and white worlds but often flowing together within the black Dominican community. Obeah was a constantly present idea in Rhys's childhood, seeming to bring serious and threatening elements of spiritual belief into her life. In *Smile Please* (1979), she claims that the cook at her father's estate, Bona Vista, was "an obeah woman called Ann Tewitt" (15). Campbell argues that this woman (renamed Ann Twist in "Mixing Cocktails"[9]) was the ancestor of both Ann Chewitt in *Voyage in the Dark*[10] and Christophine in *Wide Sargasso Sea*.[11] Rhys goes on to describe Obeah as "a milder form of voodoo," which even in her childhood in Dominica at the turn of the twentieth century was not apparently taken seriously, yet she remembers people speaking of Ann Tewitt respectfully, in "an almost awed tone."[12]

Obeah as an underground belief system in the Caribbean was created when African religions were combined and transformed in the crucible of slavery into spiritual supports for the Afro-Caribbean community.[13] The practice was systematically outlawed by fearful colonial authorities, who attempted to destroy it in all ways possible and to construct those who practiced it as inevitably evil and destructive. The result has been a perception of Obeah as negative and fearful or, as Rhys remembers, as meaningless or trivial. No doubt there have been, as in all other religions, some corrupt and cruel practitioners who have encouraged Obeah's enemies and made their case for them, but the recuperation of African culture in recent years has led to less prejudicial views of a varied and sustaining set of beliefs that also provided medicine and therapy, both physical and psychological, and identity and spiritual guidance for the African cultural community.

Nevertheless, Obeah makes only a brief appearance in George Simpson's landmark study, *Religious Cults of the Caribbean*.[14] He cites Martha Beckwith's work on the 1920s when he defines Obeah as private, not public, involving what is called in Jamaica "conjuration." Obeah involves, according to this definition, the belief that spirits either can be summoned to hurt living people or can be prevented from doing so. The person working Obeah is in the world of magic when using the powers privately. If an Obeah practitioner works in public—for example, in a cult such as Jamaican Cumina—then Obeah usually becomes part of religious ritual.

Christianity was fostered and protected by colonial power in Dominica and was seriously implicated in racist policies, which must at times have made its messages seem illogical and perverse to a young, rebellious, intelligent, sensitive girl intended by training to stay within the white elite. Rhys preferred the less racially divisive Catholic church to the Anglican one, in which she was raised. She had gone to the Catholic convent for schooling and was once a boarder. In *Smile Please* she describes her reaction at being told she was to go to the Convent School. "I was very frightened. I cried, shrieked, clung to my mother and kicked up such a fuss that I didn't go. This wasn't altogether my fault. There was a certain prejudice against Catholicism among the white people and I'd heard many horror stories about the nuns. Also most of the girls at the convent were coloured, that is of mixed blood, another reason for general surprise at my going there" (63).

She attended classes nonetheless, and her experiences there became an important part of her imaginative education. She heard constantly about hell and purgatory; but as her parents had asked that she not be pressured into Catholicism, she was not allowed in the chapel or taken to mass. But twice she went to the service in the Roseau cathedral and enjoyed the mixing of races there. Most of the congregation were black, as few white Dominicans were Catholic at the time. The Catholic rituals, Latin, incense—all attracted the young Rhys strongly. She absorbed a strong sense of good and evil, the idea of the Devil and of God (whom she believed were equally powerful).

This profound sense of the spiritual carried over into her awareness of Carnival and its celebration three days before Lent. Rhys and her siblings were not allowed to "play mas'" so they had to watch from an open window. She was fearful of the Carnival masks and saw in the event much more than simply masking and dancing: Carnival had a spiritual undertow that alarmed her. The Corpus Christi procession, which passed the house and was watched "eagerly through the jalousies," was more appealing.[15] She describes "devout Negro women" erecting little booths along the procession route for the priest to enter, with his acolytes and the Host, leaving the young girl to wonder at their purpose and meaning. She never found out. She was entranced with the African-Dominican women who passed, dressed in glorious dresses with "sweeping trains, heavy gold earrings and necklaces and colourful turbans."[16]

Rhys's experience of Catholicism and of Carnival encompassed a tantalizing space in which the possibility of a dialogue between the African and European worlds was suggested. The figures of Caribbean folklore Rhys had learned about from her frightening nurse Meta would also inform her sense of African spirituality. The "zombies, souciants and loups-garous" of Meta's stories terrified and fascinated the young girl. Souciants, Rhys explains, are women "who came at night and sucked your blood"; zombies were "black shapeless things" who could get through a locked door and strangle a living person with "hairy hands."[17] This mythology, like that of Catholicism, was not a coherent system for Rhys, but a fragment of a world closed to her. She could never participate in the rituals of the Catholics (despite one passionate youthful period of wishing to become a nun) or in the syncretic religious practices of Dominicans of African origin. Her father was inclined to be eclectic about religion (she remembered a conversation he had with a woman about Nirvana, for he admired Buddhism).[18] And there was every encouragement to develop a general faith in the structures and rituals of spiritual modes of human experience without committing to any one system. If was as if she had no spiritual ancestry, no exact religious space in the world, unlike either Harris or Brathwaite, for whom a clear spiritual ancestry exists in the Caribbean and is a major element in their work.

When Rhys left Dominica in 1907, she traveled to a Europe less than a decade away from World War I. She lived through the war in England but experienced its powerful psychic aftershocks, which manifested themselves in increasing skepticism and nihilism, on the Continent. Her texts before *Wide Sargasso Sea*, set in Europe in the years between World Wars I and II, begin to chart a sliver of the inertia that eventually led Europe to the point where fascism was ready to overrun the entire continent. Imprisonment in the self, as opposed to the limitless innerness that many important religious traditions from the so-called Third World teach, marks Rhys's protagonists until 1939. This is their most evident sign of being trapped in a spiritually dying Europe. In her early story "Vienne" (1927) there is still a sense of connectedness with the world: "I felt a calm sense of power . . . as though I could inevitably and certainly draw to myself all I had ever wished in life."[19] But by the time Rhys publishes *Voyage in the Dark* in 1934, the self has become her protagonists' ultimate prison; it will be the self, rather than the succession of dreary rooms her heroines inhabit (though these are often described as confining) that will circumscribe the Rhysian heroine (Anna in *Voyage in the Dark*, Marya in *Quartet*, Julia in *After Leaving Mr. MacKenzie*, Sasha in *Good Morning Midnight*) and leave her the narrowest of options. Furthermore, when the Rhysian character retreats from the world into a room, her thoughts are most often directed outward, to whether she will find the money to eat and drink or for pretty new clothes and a hairdo, rather than inward.[20]

There is no sense of community for such characters, and community sustains religion, whether of African or of European origin. The recurrent motif in Rhysian texts is that the isolated self attempts to redefine moral parameters by refusing to accept what is established without coherent and effective challenge, which only has the effect of further isolating her and leading her to further self-destructiveness. In each of the five novels, the central female character could choose greater safety and community, which might eventually offer her the option of justifiable rebellion but would also place demands and restrictions on her.[21] As presented within Rhys's texts, the options open to her protagonists are neither tolerable nor logical; but the cost to each heroine of refusing them grows with each novel. The world of the spirit, then, which requires sacrifice, discipline, and community in the Caribbean context as it does in the European, is only momentarily visible to the Rhysian protagonist, and then as a pathway out of entrapment, not as a permanent opening of space and opportunity for inner change.

GOD AND THE DEVIL (and associated concepts) appear in the first four novels through the careless talk of modern European society, where they have become mere figures of speech. Such references are common and noticeable enough amidst Rhys's spare, economical prose to constitute a deliberate code. A few examples from the many in the first four novels give a sense of their connective effect: "damn tired," "evil smelling," "Oh, God," "damn covenant," "swear to God," "I'm not God Almighty," "My God," "Hell," "Good Lord," "Don't say my goodness, my badness, that's what you ought to say," "you poor little devil," "Hell to your beloved Vincent," "Damned fools," "Oh, God, God, God, God, God," "Don't go, for God's sake," "Men are devils," "Frightened as hell," "What the devil am I doing here," "Jesus, Jesus," "Poor little devil," "Shall I tell him to go to hell?," "this damned coat," "this damned terrace." But whereas they might be said, in context, carelessly, in the manner of a smart Europe drifting dangerously along, they reverberate, if we see them in the context of all of Rhys's texts, with a Caribbean sense of the moral power of words to bless or damn. This power of words becomes even more crucial to understand in *Good Morning Midnight*, which ends with a scene in which Sasha appears irrevocably to lose her soul. "He doesn't say anything. Thank God, he doesn't say anything. I look straight into his eyes and despise another poor devil of a human being for the last time."[22] The horror of what is happening here, as this woman gives herself up to a rapacious and utterly evil consumption of her inner self in a sexual act, reverberates through the apparently brave, slick statement. Such light and empty phrases referring to God or the Devil in fact reflect the spiritual defeat of a whole culture, that of white Europe in the periods leading up to and following the Second World War, periods when indeed smart and fashionable people of good education and opportunities stood by and watched fascism come close to snuffing out all hope of Europe's achieving a social order that could allow good to prevail. But the Rhysian heroine knows, underneath her facade of carelessness, exactly where normal lines are drawn, most particularly when she is determined to cross over to the side of negativity. The phrase "poor devil of a human being" is a chilling one in this sense.

That we are not intended to miss the sinister reverberation within the kind of phrase discussed above becomes evident in the text of *Wide Sargasso Sea*, for by turning back to the Caribbean of the immediate post-Emancipation era, Rhys recalls a time when phrases that referred to God or the Devil were extremely powerful and were taken to heart, especially by people of African descent, whose religious faith, while diverse and often syncretic, always revered the word and its power to achieve good or evil. Thus, Antoinettte, unlike previous Rhysian protagonists, has access to the sustaining and unconventional love as well as to the diverse kinds of religious faith of most of the people around her, and so is more morally culpable for refusing their support.

She is also at risk more quickly, for she absorbs negative statements in this culture, where words carry moral weight and where curses must be blocked and turned harmless by powerful statements or rituals. Early in *Wide Sargasso Sea*, Godfrey, Antoinette's mother's old servant, makes a number of important statements. After the horse is poisoned, he admonishes, "The Lord make no distinction between black and white. . . . Rest yourself in peace for the righteous are not forsaken" (18). It is not at all clear that he includes Antoinette's mother and herself in the company of the righteous despite appearing to be consoling. He believes, without question, "the devil prince of this world" (22). Though Christophine thinks he's "a devil" (22) and so not to be paid attention to, he clearly impresses Antoinette when one day, drunk, he tells her that her family is not righteous: "we were all damned and no use praying" (33).

However, Christophine's reputation (not proven identity) as a powerful Obeah-woman is a shield for Antoinette and her family, to whom Christophine has—in extraordinary circumstances, which include her own isolation from her people when she was sold away from home and given to Antoinette's mother—given her love and loyalty. Antoinette does not understand the moral parameters of Obeah, but she fears it and acknowledges its power. She even demands of Christophine a spell to bring back her distant and cruel husband, though Christophine is worried, with justification as it turns out, because this magic is not for *beke*, not for the whites.

Antoinette seems not to have the courage to defy her history as a slave owner's daughter or her marriage to stay to share a life with her colored cousin, Sandi, who loves her, or with her surrogate mother, Christophine. She is not ready to give up the life of a member of the white elite, a position further elevated, in colonial terms, by her status as the wife of an English gentleman. As a result she is finally imprisoned in a sort of hell in England by her husband, whose own moral limitations are the result not only of a spiritual fear but also fear of surrendering to love and attachment itself.

In a telling conversation between Antoinette and her husband, Antoinette asks him whether he has a reason for treating her badly:

"Yes," I said, "I have a reason," and added very softly, "My God."

"You are always calling on God," she said. "Do you believe in God?"

"Of course, of course I believe in the power and wisdom of my creator."

She raised her eyebrows and the corners of her mouth turned down in a questioning, mocking way. For a moment she looked very much like Amelie. Perhaps they are related, I thought. It's possible, it's even probable in this damned place.

"And you," I said. "Do you believe in God?"

"It doesn't matter," she answered calmly, "what I believe or you believe, because we can do nothing about it, we are like these." She flicked a dead moth off the table. (127)

The details of this passage are extremely important. The casual usage "My God" is more meaningful here than it might be in mid-twentieth century Europe; the man speaking is of the mid-nineteenth century, when even in Europe, matters of the spirit could be central and powerful. Although he could never deny a belief in God, his actions suggest a limited understanding of the implications of professing respect. And Antoinette, beholden to a white culture that professes the Christian God and yet enslaves, to a black culture that often defines her and her people as devils, to a loving surrogate (Christophine) who practices Obeah and saved her family from the wrath of an angry mob, then reverts the exclamation back onto her husband in the form of a real question. To him, at that moment of his answer, she looks like Amelie, a black woman and a knowing, cynical spirit whom he cannot impress for more than a moment in this "damned place." Again the casual phrase "My God," so often lightly meant in Europe, has deeper significance. Moreover, Antoinette answers his question with a fatalistic denial of the cornerstone of official decency in his English, elite culture: the profession of a God takes on another significance in a society deeply implicated in slave owning and other forms of social oppression.

What is the significance of Antoinette's death? Mary Lou Emery seems to suggest that through Antoinette's self-destructiveness her spiritual joining with black culture is achieved. She interprets the ending of *Wide Sargasso Sea* as Antoinette's discovery of her soul through identification with black experience and oppression. This approach, although recognizing the importance of the spiritual in the text, forces a positive interpretation of Antoinette's dream of self-immolation. Emery even suggests that Antoinette achieves the "traditional slave wish for wings" because at one point she feels she walks as though she is flying.[23] Emery may make this observation partly because she takes a cue from Harris's suggestion that Antoinette and Rochester are united after death; but Emery goes much further and concludes that Antoinette is united with all the people of the Caribbean in her final dream-vision.

In *The Womb of Space*, Harris points to Rhys's imaginative inheritance as being both white and black, and to the limitation of Catholic responses in interpreting the spiritual journey of Antoinette in *Wide Sargasso Sea*, offering in the process a provocative suggestion that Antoinette may be able to reach back beyond her placement in the white elite to older levels of Caribbean collective memory and that there may be an "immaterial reconciliation" between Antoinette and her husband, unnamed in *Wide Sargasso Sea* but by implication Charlotte Brontë's character Mr. Rochester in *Jane Eyre*. However, he also says that Bertha, Antoinette's other self, trapped and deadened by Rochester, is apparently damned. He separates the damned aspect of the character (Bertha) from the aspect (Antoinette) that escapes and becomes a part of the myth of the cycle of hatred turning into destruction and resolving finally into peace (125ff.).

But if Antoinette leaps, in reality, it cannot mean reunion with the black community because there is no evidence that she has faced her history in her heart and soul and come to a decision to transfer her allegiances there. Of course, she hears Tia, but what Tia is saying is ambiguous and could just as easily be an encouragement to leap into destruction as into grace. She also hears Rochester, as it were, pulling her back by calling the hated name he gave her, Bertha, but his doing so cannot be assumed to suggest any kind of reunion with him. If we read the leap, however, as a desire to free the soul from the bounds of one particular life, then we must ask what happens after that leap, after a death, in fact, that is not, in the sense of Rhys's statement in *Smile Please*, "earned." Perhaps Antoinette will leap in order to try to escape her imprisonment in self as well as her imprisonment in Rochester's house, but just as the endings of *Good Morning Midnight* and *Quartet* are chillingly indecisive, so too is this ending. We simply do not know Antoinette's spiritual fate; however, because she has not faced her history, it is unlikely that her death resolves her unhappiness.

In her unfinished autobiography, *Smile Please* (1979), Rhys sets out certain constructs of morality as echoes in her fictional texts. She describes how she thought, as a child, that God was a book, either a large one, with print, or a small one, which was probably her mother's needle-book (20ff.); later in the autobiography the Rhysian voice argues that only through writing could she earn death. The notion of earning death suggests that passing from the human to the spirit world is not automatically achieved by physically dying. The young Rhys also thought at times that Satan seemed to be all-powerful and often feared that Satan won too often in battles with God. In anger and fear, the young girl cried out against Meta, the nurse who told her stories of fearsome spirits and threatening insects, "Black Devil, Black Devil, Black Devil," reflecting her peculiarly tormented placement as a child who absorbed white values and prejudices but believed as well in the spiritual presence of black religious culture and was keenly aware of injustice in the world in which she lived.

The first "really wicked" thing Rhys's childhood self, Ella Gwendolen did (and which the adult self pronounces to have been "right") was smash the face of a fair doll given her by her "Irish Granny." This behavior clearly relates to her discovery of the significance of her name Gwendolen, meaning white in Welsh (her father's language), which she abandoned as soon as she began her independent life away from home. She was the only fair child in the family, a fact she felt as a burden because her distant and rather forbidding mother thought black babies more attractive than white. In this episode of her childhood, the young girl comes close to turning conventional white morality on its head in order to try to comprehend the puzzling and illogical fact of racism and her own self-hate as a white child tangled within it. The irony of being brought up in a racially divided society is that the prevailing moral values of that society cannot be accepted in good faith, and so the racially sensitive child becomes alienated from home and community.

Between the affirmation of faith in God (and the Devil's existence) in the early part of *Smile Please* and the denial of certain faith in God that Rhys, the adult, makes toward the end lies a lifetime of wrestling with moral entities complicated and questioned by the circumstances of this childhood and by the experiences that followed in Europe. Most important here is the late and unfinished section of *Smile Please* called "From a Diary: At the Ropemakers Arms," in which the protagonist, Rhys, is tried. She is interrogated by nameless forces and admits to not knowing whether she believes in God, but she is sure about human love. Yet she does not believe in humanity and when pressed on this point tries to say she cannot express what she means except by saying that everything, "good, evil, love, hate, life, death, beauty, ugliness," is in herself (131). The human, then, is the site of the never-resolved battle between good and evil. When pressed further, she says that she has to write, otherwise she will not have earned her death. This is an important and far-reaching statement, for by it she means that writing offers the possibility of rising above the failure of being human. The accusatory voice questioning her concludes, "But be damned careful not to leave this book about" (133), and the word *damned* seems to have a special reverberation here. It is as if, this piece having been published after Rhys's death and therefore without her final agreement, we are let into a secret contract between herself and whatever spiritual forces she perceived as informing and shaping not only her writing but the life that had to be justified by it.

The following section, called "Hell and Heaven"—"The hell of those who seek, strive, rebel. The heaven of those who cannot think or void thought, who have no imagination" (140)—ends with "*mea culpa, mea culpa, mea culpa, mea maxima culpa.*" The act of creation, then, is possibly satanic (the rebel Lucifer brought himself to inhabit the most horrific invention of all, hell). Heaven is a kind of mental inertia and not therefore available to any writer with a questioning and innovative nature. But this position brings a sense of guilt, and so the acknowledgment, Catholic in its hope of forgiveness, *mea culpa.* A list of Rhys's version of Catholic mortal and venial sins follows. The mortal sins are "pride, anger, lust, drunkenness??, despair, presumption (hubris), sloth, selfishness, vanity, there's no end to them, coolness of heart. But I'm not guilty of the last. All the others" (140). Again, the insistence that feeling, human love, is the only redeeming feature shows how mercilessly Rhys judged human inadequacy and how little she romanticized herself. A brutally severe moral judgment is being exercised here. The venial sins listed are spite, malice, envy, avarice, stupidity, caution, cruelty, and gluttony, of which the most surprising is caution, presumably included because it has been the cause of failure to explore, reconfigure life or literary form, take risks that are the only way to the remarkable achievement of new parameters. After this list the protagonist rebels against such stern admonitions and refuses to "accept all of this" any more. But when she is asked whether she is guiltless of the venial sins, the response is an exclamation, "Well. Guiltless!", which appears to be the voice of the accuser.

Noticeable throughout *Smile Please* is the lack of community to which one can turn for comfort and advice. Instead, there are sustained references to the protagonist as child or as adult being alone. Both Catholicism and Obeah function best as communal moral constructs, informing people's relations with one another even when it seems as if the individual Catholic or person who asks the Obeah practitioner for help is alone. The belief system itself is sustained and critiqued by a community.

ONE IMPORTANT form of the isolated self in Rhys's texts is the ghost. She wrote a long letter to Francis Wyndham about *Wide Sargasso Sea* and Obeah in which she mentioned that she might have developed the idea that the Antoinette who comes back from Christophine is not the one who ran away, but a zombie, a dead person raised up by the Obeah-woman.[24] But Rhys did not include this idea in the novel. Rather Antoinette is in Rhys's words "lost," in a sense a ghost of her original self but not a danger to others like the zombie of Rhys's childhood understanding.[25] Like other aspects of the spiritual discussed here, the idea of the ghost develops gradually through Rhysian texts. As early as in "Mannequin," included in her first published text, *The Left Bank*, Anna is "lost in the labyrinth" of passages behind the salons in which she works.[26] This seems an innocuous and realistic use of the idea of being lost, except that Anna later suffers a sense of claustrophobia at work after a day of being looked at and touched and thinks of running away from it, which suggests that she is in fact at some risk of losing control of her capacity to relate even to a familiar communal environment and would prefer not to be seen. At the end of the story, she is happy being alone and swallowed up in the great city. In "A Spiritualist" (1927) a bereaved husband talks complacently about his dead companion as a sweet woman but recounts how a block of marble crashes into the dead woman's closed apartment while he is visiting, an assault he interprets as her little reminder that he had failed to arrange for the marble tombstone she had wanted; a friend remarks that the dead woman must have been so disappointed to have missed him.

Being present and yet not seen is the essence of ghostly occupation of a given space. In *Quartet* Marya goes to a merry-go-round and finds it gives her a sense of greater normality, taking away a previous feeling of being "a grey ghost walking in a vague shadowy world."[27] But in *After Leaving Mr. MacKenzie*, Julia comes into a restaurant "pale as a ghost" and is seen by Mr. MacKenzie, whose response is "O God, oh Lord, she's come here to make a scene."[28] She is all too visible but somehow menacingly removed from normal discourse with others. Related to ghostliness is the sensation of being in a dream, which Anna in *Voyage in the Dark* experiences in England. At the end of this novel, recovering from an abortion, Anna lies and dreams of her Caribbean homeland: of the Morne Diablotin, which the Obeah-woman Anne Chewitt said was haunted, and of zombies and obeah and soucriants. Her self-isolation from England has become deep and significant at this point. In *Good Morning Midnight*, Sasha becomes so lost that she eventually says, "God is very cruel . . . a devil, of course" (116–117), and accepts sex with her sinister neighbor. Early on, when she meets him for the first time as he stands at her door, she thinks he looks like some kind of priest in his white dressing gown, but a priest of an "obscene, half-understood religion" (30). When she decides to act, it is to push him backward out of her doorway and shut the door. She finds this easy, "like pushing a paper man, a ghost, something that doesn't exist" (31). In *Wide Sargasso Sea* Antoinette's ghostliness becomes more and more noticeable after she is imprisoned. Her husband so describes her, assuming that his power caused the change and enjoying a sense of absolute force of will over another person. "I saw the hate go out of her eyes. I forced it out. And with the hate her beauty. She was only a ghost. A ghost in the grey daylight. Nothing left but hopelessness" (170).

Interestingly, as Antoinette takes the candle and goes out of her room in her dream, she avoids looking behind her for fear of seeing the ghost of the woman "who they say haunts this place" (187), which strongly connects to the most poignant expression of being a ghost in Rhys's work. It comes at the end of her writing career, in the story "I Used to Live Here Once" (1979).[29] The protagonist stands in a place she remembers and walks toward a house she once knew, which has changed somewhat. She meets two children and attempts to speak to them, but they do not respond to her and the boy says only, "Hasn't it gone cold all of a sudden" (176). The last line of the story is "That was the first time she knew." The degree of isolation from human community is not consciously understood until that moment. Rhys had various other ways of commenting on her own isolation. Though she sometimes saw herself as an innocuous sort of ghost, she also felt "buried alive" in Devon in 1966. She spoke of going about "in a sort of dream" but was on the whole simply amused when neighbors called her a witch and thought she worked "black magic."[30] *Smile Please* ends with a chilling reference to a frightening ghost story about a lone woman who locks her door and hears a voice behind her saying, "Now we are alone together" (148).

Rhys's Caribbean identity is sometimes questioned, but the ways in which the spiritual saturates her writing is much more reflective of Caribbean culture, especially in her lifetime, than of secular, twentieth-century European culture. She once playfully called her masterpiece, *Wide Sargasso Sea*, a devil of a book; this is the same sort of playful way she called herself a witch, as the Devonshire villagers among whom she lived in her final years believed her to be. The Caribbean aspect of this identification is the linking of defiance with spiritual forms of subversion toward an oppressive use of community. Obeah was one such form, and witchcraft, in Europe, another.

Rhys's sense of writing was that it was at best a spiritual pathway, but where it led and what parameters or vocabulary it might have she clearly could not easily define. She came, after all, from a culture where Christianity tolerated slavery, where churches could be segregated, where love was complicated by the fact of race. Her solution seems to have been to write novels that are also incantations, spells that can work only for those who understand the codes in which they are written. She has no salvation to offer: the tormented protagonists of her novels are last seen in serious danger of physical or spiritual death or both. For *beke*, the white person, the Obeah does not work the same way, as Christophine said in *Wide Sargasso Sea*. For Rhys, the novel as Obeah can only demonstrate the spiritual isolation and agony of sensitive white women from the Caribbean; it cannot take away the agony or offer an easy way out. But it does show that Rhys would have understood Brathwaite's point; in their acute consciousness of the amorality of human community, Rhys's protagonists understand also, implicitly, their own implication in oppression as well as their own flight into victimhood.

Notes

1. Louis James, *Jean Rhys* (London: Longman, 1978); Elaine Campbell, "Reflections of Obeah in Jean Rhys' Fiction," in *Critical Perspectives on Jean Rhys*, ed. Pierrette Frickey (Washington, D.C.: Three Continents Press, 1990), 59–66; Teresa O'Connor, *Jean Rhys: The West Indian Novels* (New York and London: New York University Press, 1986); Mary Lou Emery, *Jean Rhys at "World's End"* (Austin: University of Texas Press, 1990). These critics stress the identity of Dominican culture, historically, in relation to magic, religion, or Obeah, or cite mainly Caribbean sources in setting up their cases.
2. Edward Kamau Brathwaite, *Contradictory Omens* (Mona, Jamaica: Savacou, 1974). Wilson Harris, *Explorations*, ed. Hena Maes-Jelinek (Aarhus, Denmark: Dangaroo Press, 1981). Wilson Harris, *The Womb of Space* (Westport, Conn.: Greenwood Press, 1983).
3. Brathwaite, *Contradictory Omens*, 38.
4. They are Selina, in "Let Them Call It Jazz," in *The Collected Short Stories* (New York: Norton, 1987), and Christophine, in *Wide Sargasso Sea* (1966; reprint, New York: Norton, 1982).
5. See Jean Rhys, *Smile Please: An Unfinished Autobiography* (Berkeley: Donald S. Ellis/ Creative Arts, 1979), 104–105, 133.
6. These ideas are discussed by Campbell in "Reflections of Obeah."
7. See, for example, *Smile Please*, 104, where Rhys describes her fingers tingling during her first serious attempts at writing as a therapeutic exercise.
8. It is necessary only to give an example of the work of each of these writers to prove the point: Harris has already been cited; Edward Kamau Brathwaite's *Rites of Passage. The Arrivants: A New World Trilogy* (London: Oxford University Press, 1973) might be added to his essays in *Contradictory Omens*, together with Paule Marshall's *Praisesong for the Widow* (New York: Dutton, 1984); Dennis Scott's *An Echo in the Bone*, in *Plays for Today* (London: Longman, 1970), 73–137; and Derek Walcott's *Dream on Monkey Mountain* and *Tijean and His Brothers*, in *Dream on Monkey Mountain and Other Plays* (London: Cape, 1972).
9. Rhys, "Mixing Cocktails," in *The Collected Short Stories*, 36–38.
10. Jean Rhys, *Voyage in the Dark*, (1934; reprint, New York: Norton, 1982).
11. Campbell, "Reflections of Obeah."
12. Rhys, *Smile Please*, 16.
13. I do not mean to provide here any overly simplistic history of Obeah but rather to emphasize its origins in African religions and therefore its evenhandedness regarding moral issues. Obeah was an important weapon on the side of the slaves and ex-slaves in protecting their psychological strength.
14. George Eaton Simpson, *Religious Cults of the Caribbean: Trinidad, Jamaica, Haiti* (Rio Piedras: Institute of Caribbean Studies/University of Puerto Rico, 1980).
15. Rhys, *Smile Please*, 40.
16. Ibid.
17. Ibid., 23.
18. Ibid., 58.
19. Rhys, *The Collected Short Stories*, 208.
20. The sense of isolation is sometimes connected to being British or Anglo-Saxon as a minority in another culture, usually in France. In "Illusion" (1927), Miss Bruce is outwardly rather masculine, sensible, and drab, but she has a wardrobe stuffed with gorgeously colored and frivolous clothes. She is a product of British "character and training," and "after seven years in Paris she appeared utterly untouched, utterly unaffected, by anything hectic, slightly exotic or wholesome" (*The Collected Short Stories*, 140). But the clothes are like a hidden flame of spirit, kept isolated

from the world. *Wide Sargasso Sea* develops this motif most emphatically of all: Antoinette is isolated as a child, except for her connection with Tia, retreats for her honeymoon to Granbois away from the wider world that has negatively defined her in different ways, and then retreats further away from the husband who ill-treats her. The result is her confinement by her husband in the attic of his English house, but she is also in a real sense confined within herself, even as she dreams of leaping into the flames, seeing instead the pool at Coulibri and hearing Tia encouraging her.

21. In *Quartet* (New York: Carroll and Graf, 1990), the choice would be not to betray Stephan by moving in with the Heidlers (an aunt advises seeing a clergyman); in *After Leaving Mr. MacKenzie* (New York: Carroll and Graf, 1990), it is to attempt to rejoin family and stop living on handouts from men; in *Voyage in the Dark*, to go home or to find a way to become financially self-sufficient; in *Good Morning Midnight* (New York: Norton, 1986), to recognize even unlikely love (with a gigolo) and its potential to salvage the spirit; in *Wide Sargasso Sea*, to leave a cruel husband and find a way to manage life with Christophine, as a part of Caribbean society, or to love Sandi and challenge racist conventions about love and sexuality.

22. Rhys, *Good Morning Midnight*, 189.

23. Emery, *Jean Rhys at "World's End,"* 57, 187.

24. Jean Rhys, *The Letters of Jean Rhys*, ed. Francis Wyndham and Diana Melly (New York: Viking Press, 1984), 261ff.

25. Ibid., 263.

26. Jean Rhys, *The Left Bank* (London: Cape, 1927).

27. Rhys, *Quartet*, 46.

28. Rhys, *After Leaving Mr. MacKenzie*, 22.

29. Rhys, "I Used to Live Here Once," in *The Collected Short Stories*, 387–388.

30. Rhys, *The Letters of Jean Rhys*, 300, 89.

The Shaman Woman, Resistance, and the Powers of Transformation

BRINDA MEHTA

A *Tribute to Ma Cia in Simone Schwarz-Bart's* The Bridge of Beyond

Shamans occupy a central position in Caribbean and other traditional non-Western cultures, serving as valuable storehouses of myth, folklore, sociocultural values and practices, and the healing arts. Constituting the fabric of cohesion and self-consciousness, especially in rural communities, shamans have been posited as persons of distinction with exemplary powers of (self-)mastery. Mircea Eliade is careful to separate the shaman from traditional faith healers, "witch-doctors," and "sorcerers" by stating that the shaman is a dominating figure who distinguishes himself (or herself) by the nature and intensity of an "ecstatic" experience that gives access to higher levels of transcendence than other members of the community can reach.[1] This level of mastery is highlighted by the fact that the shaman remains the subject of the mystical experiences; in other words, the shaman is able to communicate with the spirits of the other world and their different permutations (nature and animal spirits, ancestral spirits) as a human being without necessarily being "possessed" or manipulated by them. The shaman orchestrates and controls the lines of communication without serving as a passive receptacle for the voices from beyond. But communication with the spirits is not a unilateral process for the sole benefit of the shaman, who alone can manipulate and interpret spiritual manifestations effectively. In several cultures where shamanism coexists with other systems of belief, priests, magicians, or fakirs act as assistants who may help initiate the process of communication. However, their complicity stops at the level of initiation, as their powers are not as wide-ranging as those of the shaman, which inhibits them from actual participation in the ecstatic flight. Moreover, Eliade's definition does not suggest that the shaman's voice is univocal; communication with the spirits is based on a pattern of reciprocity in which the shaman can hold his or her own.

Eliade qualifies the specificity of the ecstatic flight by explaining that "any ecstatic cannot be considered a shaman; the shaman specializes in a trance during which his soul is believed to leave his body and ascend to the sky or descend to the underworld" (5). This definition brings to light three prerequisites essential to the shamanic experience: a position of distinction, an altered state of perception, and the powers of transformation. These exceptional qualities have been vital to the shaman's role as preserver of the cohesiveness and structure of communities that have been faced with several historical and socioeconomic crises that have threatened the general well-being of the group. These crises can be broadly characterized as colonialism, capitalism (with its preponderance of bourgeois ideologies and blind importation of Western value systems), racism, and sexism. Traditional cultures, which have been splintered at the core of their being, are still reeling under the adverse impact of these crises.

The Caribbean is situated within the parameters of this tragic reality, with a history characterized by slavery, indentured labor, genocide, and violent socioeconomic upheaval. Systematically dispossessed, devitalized, and marginalized by the constraining politics of the imperialistic powers, the peoples of the Caribbean have been the victims of a veritable raping of their lands and identities—of their very being—thereby conforming to the deflective norm of specular representation practiced by the colonizers.[2] However, the history of the Caribbean peoples is one of courage and resistance based on a refusal to remain passive and acquiescent. This resilience, which has characterized national liberation movements and individual attempts at self-affirmation alike, has found its roots in the cultural and spiritual values of the community preserved by the shaman and has served as a counterforce to colonial authorities. In this context, the shaman has mobilized the collective energies of the group through a "call to action" based on strategies of interconnection.

The purpose of this study is not to essentialize the colonial experience in the Caribbean by using the shaman as a universal presence or provider of survival and resuscitation techniques; shamanic beliefs and practices have their own regional specificity in the Caribbean even though they share the common legacy of the importation of African religious practices during the period of slavery. My analysis is limited to the role of the female shaman in a specific French Antillean context, that of the island of Guadeloupe, based on a reading of Simone Schwarz-Bart's *Pluie et vent sur Télumée Miracle* (1972) (English title: *The Bridge of Beyond*). I discuss several topics in an attempt to postulate a (w)holistic representation of the shaman woman in Guadeloupan culture: (1) general attitudes toward female shamans, (2) the importance of female shamans in the elaboration of female subjectivity, (3) female shamans as paradigms of resistance for women to counter the forces of sexism within the community, and (4) female shamans as spiritual mentors to ensure the preservation of women-centered belief systems.

Although shamans work for the general well-being of the entire community, male and female, I would like to emphasize that the strong presence of female spiritual models, sensitive to the particular concerns of women in traditional male-centered societies, is a vital key in the process of female actualization. This point is substantiated by the fact that although ample academic research valorizes the special powers of the male shaman, parallel efforts to qualify women's access to ecstasy and transcendence have confined them to the realm of witches, hysterics, and conjurer women. However, it is also true that men of color have been subjected to the same unidimensional representations as women through an imposition of Western belief in the "higher" orders of Cartesian rationality.

Edouard Glissant, Dany Bébel-Gisler, Gérard Etienne, and other Caribbean and Third World scholars stress the importance of recognizing and valorizing underlying cultural motifs in Caribbean and other non-Western texts as an example of responsible scholarship in order to avoid the pitfalls of cultural/textual imperialism within the realm of literary analysis. Too often, non-Western texts are subjected to the imposition of Western value systems that lead to their marginalization and objectification. The imposition of the Western cultural lens, the myopic Western "eye"/"I", results in misconceptions and distortions that have the ultimate effect of making these texts "objects of Western hegemonic discourse leading to a particular cultural colonization," as Chandra Mohanty affirms.[3] She further states that "colonization almost invariably implies a relation of structural domination, and a suppression—often violent—of the heterogeneity of the subjects in question" (52). In other words, Western readings of Third World texts position them as the "exotic Other," which falls short of the Western norm.

Glissant and Bébel-Gisler define the cultural specificities of the Caribbean in terms of a cultural repossession that "reinstates us in the true essence of our beings; it cannot be assumed for us by others."[4] The two scholars privilege cultural modes of resistance and self-affirmation as effective tools for (self-)empowerment within a specific geographical location. This strategy involves the legitimization of certain "mystical," "irrational," "non-representable" modes of affirmation scorned by Western materialists seeking reductive, tangible, and easily identifiable responses and explanations. While denouncing this "positivist yearning for transparency," Trinh Minh-ha exposes the

Western agenda. "This is the way the West carries the burden of the Other. Naming is part of the human rituals of incorporation, and the unnamed remains less human than inhuman or sub-human. The threatening Otherness must, therefore, be transformed into figures that belong to a definite image-repertoire."[5] A phenomenon that is immediately visible is easily conquerable. The "cultural conquering" of texts is a ploy to intercept and divert any discourse that runs counter to Western hegemonic discourse. The literary subordination of non-Western texts is aimed at inscribing them within the parameters of a unified, essentialized discourse. Homi Bhaba's analysis of the unilateral specificities of colonial cultural critiques of Third World texts leads him to conclude:

> Colonial discourse is an apparatus of power . . . an apparatus that
> turns on the recognition and disavowal of racial/cultural/historical
> difference. Its predominant strategic function is the creation of a
> space for a subject people through the production of knowledge in
> terms of which surveillance is exercised and a complex form of
> pleasure/unpleasure is incited. It (i.e. colonial discourse) seeks
> authorization for its strategies by the production of knowledge by
> colonizer and colonized which [is] stereotypical but authentically
> evaluated.[6]

Stereotypical representations have led to what I term "homogeneous reproductions of thwarted Caribbean literary figures," who are almost always analyzed in terms of their victimization, mythification, and orientalization, irrespective of their individual socioeconomic and geographical locations.

The relevance of this digression is that it attempts to show how and why Caribbean authors are making concerted efforts to reclaim their cultural heritage through the reinscription of the cultural in literary production and thus to restabilize the cultural imbalance of power. This strategy of transformation serves as a direct response to Western scholarship that sees cultural motifs and transfigurations as mythical, ironic, and often humorous "insertions" in an otherwise static and petrified representation of Caribbean realities. For Caribbean authors moving beyond purely ornamental Western prescriptions, cultural motifs symbolize a return to the sources, a reconnection with an otherwise "threatened utterance."[7] Within the parameters of this redefinition, literary characters in Caribbean literature take on a new and valorized significance. Cultural figures like the shaman, the griot, cease to participate solely in the enhancement of the "local" or "exotic" flavor of the text and become involved instead in a more (self-)conscious examination or reevaluation of the literature's sociocultural and historical specificities. In this way, the character of the female shaman Ma Cia in *The Bridge of Beyond* functions as a meta-

phor, as a transformative reflection of Guadeloupean history and all the var-
iegated permutations of cultural resistance, as will be developed later.

Gay Wilentz's interesting and informative study *Binding Cultures: Black
Women Writers in Africa and the Diaspora* links the idea of transformation to
the fabric of women's lives, highlighting women's "natural" propensity to cir-
cumvent permanence and immobilization through a heavy investment in the
oral heritage. Wilentz explains the importance of oral re-creations in black
women's writing:

> Through the cultural retentions that have survived since slavery,
> these women are attempting to reflect, (re)discover and (re)articulate
> their African roots; their aim is to help build communities more in
> line with African cultural values. As women they take on their
> traditional role as educators of past and future generations to voice
> their heritage, which has been distorted and effaced for many in the
> Black community through imposed dominant cultural values and
> attempts at assimilation. Pertinent to their aim is a use of the orature
> in their writings as a method of uncovering and recovering their
> collective past.[8]

Women's access to oral history serves as a rite/write of passage for female
individuation and self-affirmation, calling for a reinsertion of the feminine in
literary expression to rectify the traditional exclusion of black women from
literary production. The repressed mother tongue finds a new articulation in
the works of Simone Schwarz-Bart, Maryse Condé, Myriam Warner-Vieyra,
to name only a few Francophone-Caribbean women writers, precisely through
the process of "matrifocal generational continuity,"[9] initiated by the "Original Mother" and passed down to future generations of daughters. Women writers engage in a process of narrative mothering, which Bernice Johnson Reagon
defines. "One can use the concept of a mothering generation to mean the way
the entire community organizes itself to nurture itself and its future generations."[10] The act of mothering is based on a pact to cement intergenerational
bonds through a primeval linkage with the Mother, the original creator and
maker of stories. However, this recovery of the past is not based on an idealized mystification of the African cultural roots in Schwarz-Bart's text. Ma Cia's
spiritual reconnection with her past serves as a mobilizing force for the women
of her community, while, at the same time, exposing the inequities inherent
in the male-dominated societal configurations and the infringement of
women's rights and privileges. This ambivalence is re-created in *The Bridge of
Beyond*, where the situation of the women is more complex than that of their
male counterparts, as they are the victims of a double alterity evidenced in
their marginalization by Western imperialistic structures as well as by

patriarchal systems within their own communities. Caught in an unsatisfactory double bind, women in the Caribbean have had to rely, for the most part, on their inner resources and creativity to deal with the vicissitudes of day-to-day reality.[11]

The *vécu féminin* depicted in *The Bridge of Beyond* inscribes its female characters in a hostile environment where they are obliged to single-handedly fulfill many social roles—mother, worker, lover, role model to future generations of women. This multifaceted stance has necessitated the acquisition of "two hearts" (41), a strong back capable of enduring hardships, and a strong chest, evidenced in the proverb, "However heavy a woman's breasts, her chest is always strong enough to carry them" (12)—in other words, a strong body capable of withstanding the pressures faced by women in a vulnerable male-dominated milieu still traumatized by the ambivalent impact of the colonial experience. Schwarz-Bart describes one of her major female characters, the legendary Queen Without a Name, as "talented, a real Negress with two hearts and she had made up her mind that life was not going to lead her up the garden path. In her view a human back was the strongest, toughest, most flexible thing in the world, an unchanging reality, stretching far beyond the eye's reach. On it descended all the ravages, all the furies, all the eddies of human misery" (41). Underlying the specification of physical endurance is a strong sense of spiritual transcendence—"stretching far beyond the eye's reach"—emphasizing an elevated plane of consciousness necessary to surmount "unchanging reality." It implies that spiritual consciousness helps one to rise above static, petrified reality. The spiritual component is an integral part of the physical and vice-versa. Resistance is ensured by the active co-working of both components. The principle of complementarity that characterizes several African and Asian traditions is crucial to an understanding of the realm of influence of the shaman, who serves as a mediator to link two seemingly unrelated entities. The function of Ma Cia in the text is precisely to furnish that particular space, construct that particular bridge in the psyche of the female characters, especially Toussine and Télumée (Toussine's granddaughter), who experience the full import of her shamanic capacities, enabling them to achieve epic levels of self-representation.

Strongly influenced by West African religious practices, spirituality in Antillean society is based on a holistic culture in which all forces of nature are united by a primeval Mother spirit. Plants, animals, humans, inanimate objects constitute a harmonious ensemble gravitating toward a centrifugal feminine force responsible for maintaining levels of connection between various species. The principle of interconnection is not based on the either/or paradigm of exclusion or distinction, but more on an intimate understanding of natural and human forces and, as Maryse Condé states in *La Parole des femmes*, on an inherent complicity between the two.[12] A natural, preinstitutionalized religion is evoked in Condé's novel *Moi, Tituba, sorcière noire de Salem* (1986), where another female shaman figure, Mama Yaya, imparts valuable knowledge to her protégée. "Mama Yaya," Tituba affirms, "taught me the sea, the mountains, and the hills. She taught me that everything lives, has a soul, and breathes. That everything must be respected. That man is not the master riding through his kingdom on horseback."[13]

Natural religions based on strong, animistic beliefs have always favored the equal participation of women because they are located in an atemporal, mythical time before the imposition of hierarchy and categorizations. Mythical time does not refer to an archaic, regressive, prehistorical period, but to a particular *hors-temps*, which undermines the unilateral vision of "institutionalized" time; institutionalized time is based in the fundamental structure of "masculine" and "feminine," "male" and "female," where the "feminine" and "female" is always posited as the negative, inferior instance. Hélène Cixous has written that the "organization by hierarchy makes all conceptual organization a subject to man. Male privilege is shown in the opposition between activity and passivity, which he uses to sustain himself."[14] Conceptual or institutionalized time works to the advantage of the male, legitimizing the marginalization of women within the confines of mythical time.

The primacy of the male has led to the traditional muting of the female, an eclipsing of the mother culture, which is based on equal citizenship. The function of the female shaman, who, indeed, situates herself within the parameters of preinstitutionalized time, is to use her superior powers of transcendence to reclaim the heritage by decentering conceptual organization. This reclaiming does not seek to replicate a pattern of imposition by destabilizing the accepted/acceptable order of things. Rather, it stresses the reassertion of female space within the community, a space that is not confined or reduced solely to the task of acting as a satellite to the male partner's hopes, fears, dreams, and ambitions. The opening of female space, initiated by the shaman, is vital to women's ontological experience because, according to Vicki Noble, it leads to "a gradual mastery of oneself, and a healing or recovery from the chronic dis-ease of our time. Once a woman has done the work of remembering herself, she is much more able to change the world effectively."[15]

Ma Cia personifies the primordial mother spirit who has survived her original displacement or dislocation by the male order to arrive at an altered or higher perception of reality, a (w)holistic vision capable of surmounting ordinary, petty reality. This exceptional vision is highlighted in several textual passages and is placed within a physical and spiritual context. Télumée's first impression of Ma Cia is that of "a subtle face that spoke of ecstasy" (35); on the next page, she comments, "There was something about her, this friend of

Queen Without a Name. And what was it? It was those eyes—huge, transparent, the sort of eyes people say can see everything, hear everything, because they never shut, even in sleep" (36). The mysterious, trancelike physical
appearance of Ma Cia serves as a lens to project the inner workings of a highly
sophisticated level of consciousness capable of a multivisioned, global perspective. Ma Cia's superior understanding of the human condition is evidenced
in a conversation with Toussine and Télumée. Commenting on the injustices
suffered by black people at the hands of their white masters, Toussine remarks,
"And after that sadness here is another: to see the fires go out and the pup-
pies playing in the embers" (38). While basically agreeing with Toussine, Ma
Cia takes the conversation a step further by stating, "With your permission,
my friend, I'd say it is a piece of sadness, not a whole one. The whole sadness
was the fire. But the fire is out, and it's a long time now since the White of
Whites was in the ground, rotten meat that will not grow again. And even
the embers will not last forever." Ma Cia's higher vision enables her to con-
textualize situations by going beyond the narrow confines of unpleasant reality. She is able to extricate herself from the pain and suffering that characterize
the daily situation of black peoples worldwide by projecting her vision onto a
more favorable space that "will not last forever" (38). In this way, her perspective, which takes into account "the big picture," offers a glimmer of hope
to future generations. Ma Cia is presented as a paradigm of resistance for
Toussine and Télumée, urging them to fight and overturn the inequities of
their particular situations by subscribing to strategies of survival capable of
transcending tragic, human reality. This resistance is even more pertinent to
the women described in *The Bridge of Beyond*, providing them with the necessary "oppositional space" in their search for selfhood, independent of impe-
rialist and patriarchal definitions and expectations of the feminine.

If, as stated before, Ma Cia embodies the archetypal mother principle,
the very nexus of creation and civilization, why would her obliteration from
the annals of his-story be deemed necessary? What are the particular dynamics of the mother principle, and how can the "return to the mother" reinitiate
women to what Noble calls "a reawakening . . . [of] the instinctual senses and
the empowerment needed to act on what our bodies know to be true" (12).
In evoking the primacy of the mother principle, J. J. Bachofen writes, "The
maternal principle, like the life of nature, knows no barriers. The idea of moth-
erhood produces a sense of universal fraternity among all men, which dies with
the development of paternity. The family based on father right is a closed individual organism, whereas the matriarchal family bears the typically universal character that stands at the beginning of all development and distinguishes
material life from higher spiritual life."[16] The mother principle is characterized by its global qualities of universality and all-expansiveness. The mother

and her archaic powers are located at the point of origin, at the source of creation and development. The progressive aspect of the mother principle is evidenced in its transgression of boundaries and limitations; it creates utopia based on three basic principles that should constitute the foundation of all civilization—liberty, equality, sorority/fraternity. The mother principle finds its sustenance in its close ties with the earth, in its communion with the forces of nature and in its establishment of a harmonious rhythm with the surrounding environment.

This harmony was disrupted by the intrusion of the male principle concretized by the colonial experience; it created a disequilibrium in the otherwise synchronized rhythms between humans and nature. Women were particularly vulnerable to this rupture; they had to deal not only with the inequities of the white master but also with the destabilized psyche of their menfolk, anxious to re-member their threatened manhood by replicating their own humiliations (suffered at the hands of the oppressor) and projecting them onto their women. As a result, the maternal principle suffered a double burial, necessitating the presence of the shaman to revive the lost heritage and create a healing space for women. This space, re-created in the text by the recurrent use of water imagery, encountered for the first time in the French title, *Pluie et vent sur Télumée Miracle* (Rain and wind on Télumée Miracle), symbolizes the resurgence of the archetypal female principle, which provides the necessary framework for the narrative development of the story.

Healing space is vital to any process of female selfhood because it provides the essential locus of reintegration for women who have been as alienated from themselves as from others as a result of what Noble describes as a "male dispersion" of the female. The aftereffect of male dispersion has been a general anesthetizing of women-centered feelings and instincts, which have been "replaced by false, externally imposed rules and ideas about ourselves and the world."[17] Woman has thus been the victim of a double reality—an inner, psychological reality in which she is the subject of her experiences, and an external, social reality that has been imposed on her and has objectified her, to the detriment of the full realization of her inner being. Schwarz-Bart's heroines in *The Bridge of Beyond* are all victims of the subject-object dialectic; with the exception of Mama Victory they are unable ultimately to break the bonds of dialectic logic and position themselves as independent agents. This is particularly a problem for Toussine and Télumée, but their distinction is assured by the strong presence of a spiritual alter-ego, Ma Cia; Ma Cia is able to solder together their fragmented and fractured sense of self into a unified whole, although her doing so does not in any way minimize their individual attempts at self-affirmation, which earn them the venerable titles of Queen Without a Name and Télumée Miracle. Their transcendence is limited in the sense that it is relegated to a mastery of terrestrial circumstances. This sense of limitation is evidenced in Télumée's admission that "whenever [Ma Cia] was at the point of telling me the secret of metamorphosis, something held me back, something prevented me from exchanging my woman's shape and two breasts for that of a beast or flying succubus, and so there the matter rested" (130).

Ma Cia, who is "closer to the dead than to the living" (33), procures her higher vision from her ability to synchronize the forces of the sacred and the profane, the visible and the invisible, which enables her to reach a point of consciousness where "her ordinary human form . . . [is] insufficient for her" (33). Ma Cia is only a "secondary" character whose personal story is a *méta-récit* in the general functioning of the text. However, the influence that she wields is enormous in its capacity to affect every member of the community who comes into contact with her. I assert that each individual story presented in the text gravitates around Ma Cia's story, which serves as a *fils conducteur*, or unifying force, in the narration. Her minimal textual presence does not detract from the pervasiveness of her spiritual presence, which, like the process of osmosis, permeates the structural fabric of the text.

Ma Cia occupies a position of distinction within the community, which maintains a certain attitude of deference toward her as is demonstrated by the varying reactions of the members of the community to her presence. While shamans in general are treated with much respect and veneration, there is a definite ambivalence toward the female shaman in the text by the male members of the group. This ambivalence is manifested in Old Abel's encounter with Ma Cia, where she is presented as a negative, malefic spirit, capable of doing harm.

> One day, Old Abel told the story of how Ma Cia had given him the scar he had on his arm, a scratch from the claws of the flying Negress. He was coming back from a night fishing when the two huge birds started hovering over his head. One of them had breasts instead of wings, and Old Abel recognized Ma Cia by her transparent eyes and the breasts he'd seen one day as she was washing in the river. As soon as he recognized her, Ma Cia circled down and alighted on the branches of a nearby flame tree, which began to move around Old Abel, followed by all the other trees, their eyes rustling. (33)

Old Abel's description associates Ma Cia with a bird of prey anxious to swoop down and mutilate its victim. Anger and aggression are evoked in his portrayal of Ma Cia, which contrasts sharply with Télumée's first impression of her. "At that moment, an ordinary-looking little old woman came out of the cabin. She was barefooted and wore a full Creole dress. . . . As she glided swiftly toward us over the clay soil, I saw a subtle face that spoke of ecstasy and involuntarily closed my eyes" (35). Although both descriptions underline an ethereal quality in the character of Ma Cia, capable of inspiring awe in the beholder, Télumée's awe, unlike Old Abel's, is not tempered by a defensive attitude or by attempts to control her fear through displacement. While recognizing Ma Cia's uniqueness, Télumée is not intimidated by it. She sees the humaneness of Ma Cia's personality characterized by "the snaky tiny body almost like a child's, and the weathered face, peeling in places. And the more I looked at her, the more she seemed just like everyone else, an ordinary little old woman from Fond-Zombi" (36). These human qualities are accentuated by Ma Cia's sly sense of humor and her hearty appetite. "I don't know whether it's a fancy of the dead or the living, but the smell of the stew I've got on the stove is going to my head—I can feel the meat melting in my mouth. So come along" (35). Télumée perceives Ma Cia to be an ordinary woman who nevertheless has a special vocation in life, as opposed to Abel, who categorizes her as a woman transformed or possessed by evil spirits. This perception of woman in her Medusa-like form, capable of castrating her male victims, is, in fact, a backhanded compliment paid to Ma Cia and her exceptional powers of transformation.

Woman's body, as a source of life and creation, has been fetishized by the male psyche in male-dominated societies. Considered to be an object of repulsion and intense attraction simultaneously, the female body has been subjected to a long tradition of physical aphasia destined to minimize its "destructive" effects. The female body is considered dangerous when it is capable of autonomous action, as is evidenced by Ma Cia's extraordinary ability to transcend human form. Her powers of transformation are based on a complete mastery of her body, displaying a sense of inner authority and creative energy. Anne and Barry Ullanov associate the creative impulse with hagocracy, qualifying it as "the hag's drive to be her own self, independent of others, with her own purposes to effect, her own resources to pull from."[18] Traditionally, the term *hag* has had the same pejorative connotation as the term *witch* in its application to the feminine. Mary Daly, in her study *Gyn/Ecology*, associates hags and crones with the notion of mature women who have acquired a sophisticated level of wisdom, enabling them to travel into a particular feminist time and space in which they govern.[19] In this way, hagology is the creation of political space, ensuring female (self-)representation and affirmation unmediated by masculine perceptions. This space is private, self-reflective, beyond the comprehension of the masculine, a space women can call their own.

Old Abel's attempts to infiltrate and trespass on private female space, his transgression of its rules of access, lead to a reprimand symbolized by "a scratch from the claws of the flying Negress" (33). By encroaching on female space,

Abel tries to demystify the feminine by reducing it to a unidimensional corporeal representation, evidenced by his references to Ma Cia's exposed body
parts. Reductive logic, based on binary oppositional forces, characterizes male
modes of thought, which seek to confine women to a subcaste, redefining them
in terms of their reproductive capacities. Women who have passed the reproductive stage, as in the case of the menopausal Ma Cia, or who are incapable
of producing children, like infertile Télumée, have been dispossessed of their
bodies by the male order. Télumée's empty belly is rejected by her companion Elie, who believes that the attainment of complete womanhood is contingent on the ability to reproduce.

Feelings of alienation or despair that might result from social rejection
are transformed into positive, creative energy within the realm of supportive
female space through the mediation of Ma Cia, who initiates Télumée to the
process of repossession, a particular psychic conditioning. After repossession,
"the female body is more than a sensual receptor, more than a physical vehicle; it is an instrument of superconscious awareness."[20] It is now the subject
of multilayered levels of representation—the spiritual, the physical, and the
emotional, combined harmoniously to reach a level of consciousness where it
"will rise over the earth like a cathedral" (35)—in other words, over limited
masculine projections of the feminine.

Ma Cia's power is thus pure woman power, symbolizing the force of women
in the Caribbean as textualized in *The Bridge of Beyond*. Her influence extends
over a pre-Oedipal space of intense symbiotic bonding between women, the
original Eden.[21]

> Next morning Grandmother gave me a peculiar look . . . and said:
> "We're going to see Ma Cia." Turning toward the mountain, we took a
> little path overgrown with weeds. At first there were only ferns, then
> on either side of the path there appeared clumps of malaccas, tama-
> rinds and Chinese plum trees with their tempting fruit. . . . The path
> came out into a clearing, a huge disc of red, sun-baked earth, in the
> middle of which stood a rickety little cabin. It seemed to belong
> entirely to the spirits of the forest that rose up not far off against the
> hesitant light of dawn. (34–35)

Pre-Oedipal space is natural, intrauterine space, which facilitates the creation and endurance of primeval bonds between mother and daughter; this
relationship—characterized by psychoanalysis as the most intense of all
relationships—is rudely disrupted, in later stages, by the Oedipal configuration. This one-to-one rapport with the mother is replicated in the text by the
instinctual understanding and caring that exists among Ma Cia, Toussine, and
Télumée. Ma Cia, who is presented as Toussine's spiritual (pre-Oedipal) sis-

ter, assumes the function of Télumée's spiritual mother upon the death of Toussine. In fact, the Ma Cia-Toussine-Télumée trio constitutes a three-dimensional representation of the complete Woman, with the union mother-sister-daughter, a formidable force, symbolizing a Holy Trinity of female orientation. The impact of this force is evident in the hesitation demonstrated by the community to pronounce Ma Cia's name, echoing one of the tenets of the holy commandments. Toussine explains this sentiment to Télumée. "It's true people are afraid to talk about her, and that it's dangerous to pronounce her name" (35).

Pre-Oedipal space is threatening to men because within it women's stories are told, her-story is created. Valuable knowledge and teaching skills are learned from the mother and then passed on to future generations. This education comprises an acquisition and appreciation of cultural and social values, basic survival techniques, and communion with nature (whose cycles correspond with the female cycles) in an effort to achieve mastery. The acquisition and transmission of a particular female legacy ensure its (self-)preservation despite its obliteration from the annals of his-story. Thus, Ma Cia gives Télumée several important lessons in history, stressing the fact that any understanding of self is based on an intimate knowledge of one's own historicity. Evoking Guadeloupe's tragic colonial history, Ma Cia comments, "Have they succeeded in breaking us, crushing us, cutting off our arms and legs forever? We have been goods for auction, and now we are left with fractured hearts" (130). Despite her anger and resentment, Ma Cia's words bring to light the valuable truth that continued oppression can only strengthen the powers of resistance among the people. External forces will intensify internal forces of endurance, enabling her people to reach an elevated place of (self-)consciousness. "But though we are almost nothing on the earth, I *can* tell you one thing: however beautiful other sounds may be, only Negroes are musicians" (124). Suffering embellishes to the point of creating sweet music and poetry within the soul.

Ma Cia's mission in life is to provide a changing, rejuvenating force within her community, a transformative energy capable of breaking down outmoded patterns of thinking and living. Her philosophy is a progressive one, encouraging her people to move "beyond survival," to break the mold of stereotypical perceptions of black people as complacent and apathetic ("I could hear in the wind, over the scorched earth, the voice of Ma Cia: 'A Negro? A headless, homeless crab, that walks backwards,'" 58) by taking charge and assuming collective responsibility for their own destinies. This call for change, this movement to raise group consciousness is Ma Cia's vocation, her special calling, misunderstood by the very people she would like to mobilize and free from mental and physical lassitude: "The people still couldn't make her out: for them she was a 'freak,' a 'loonie,' a 'temporelle,' but all this only made her shake her head and smile, and she went on doing what God had created her for—living" (41).

The change recommended by Ma Cia is internal and calls for an introspective journey based on a reevaluation of one's own principles and ideals. External change is possible only when the individual is willing to undergo a rigorous process of soul searching to come to terms with his or her own insecurities, prejudices, negativity, and strengths. Her philosophy is radical in that she challenges the general mind set of her community, content to objectify itself in its abjection without taking action. Her message is particularly severe to men in her community, for whom her position as a female "caller to arms" is doubly suspect. The collective psyche remains intractable, no matter how dire the need for change, leaving the task to a committed few, like Ma Cia, who comments, "And there are some who fly at night while others sleep" (124).

Ma Cia's message has a more receptive audience in the women of the group who act as the mainstay of change, eager to transform their double alterity, based on sexist and racist models, to a more favorable level of representation. Ma Cia's strategies for female empowerment are based on a sharing of her powers and a distribution of her knowledge, as mentioned before, as is evidenced in her emotional and spiritual tutelage of Télumée. Once again, female empowerment is based on the ability to transform the status quo to one's own advantage through the acquisition of certain skills. As Télumée describes her apprenticeship with Ma Cia, "And we'd get up and go for a walk in the forest, where Ma Cia initiated me into the secrets of plants. She also taught me to get rid of faintness and tics and sprains. I learned how to set people and animals free, how to break spells and turn sorcery back on the sorcerers" (130).

Ma Cia's powers are socialistic in their orientation, working toward the general good of the community, both past and present. Her services to relieve her people of their dis-ease are extended to the dead as well, embodying the African belief that life and death are not two mutually exclusive spaces but a continuum based on a cyclical rhythm of self-perpetuation. Today's ancestors become tomorrow's children and vice-versa, symbolizing an ongoing process of maturation.[22] Cyclical thinking is thus an integral part of Ma Cia's message, reminding her people that they will rise to the same heights of glory as their African ancestors. Their current abjection is only a phase in the larger cycle of total rejuvenation, a getting rid of the bad blood to purge the body of all impurities, as is demonstrated in Ma Cia's interpretation of Toussine's dream:

Then Grandmother was leaning close to her friend and telling her a dream. She was bathing in a river, and dozens of leeches were around her head. One of them attached itself to her forehead, and she thought, "it's drawing off the bad blood. But mightn't it be a sign of approaching death?" . . . "What do you mean, death?" cried Ma Cia briskly. "The leech was just drawing off the bad blood, and that's the long and short of it. When your hour comes . . . you'll find yourself in a strange country with trees and flowers you've never seen before. Don't pay attention to any dream but that." (36–37)

The idea of shedding one's skin to reach a new level of consciousness is illustrated by the different metamorphic transmutations of Ma Cia's body, demonstrating, once more, the notion of continuum as a means of transcendence. Shamanic traditions make ample use of animal symbolism to delineate the specific capacity of the shaman to assume various "natural" forms during the ecstatic flight. According to Eliade, the assuming of animal or ornithomorphic forms by the shaman forges a new identity—the shaman becomes an animal spirit capable of flying like a bird or barking like a dog. Animal language, states Eliade, is a variant of spirit language itself, the secret shamanic language, constituting a direct line of communion with the "other" world. This "special" language establishes a communion between human and animal that enables the shaman to become familiar with the secrets of nature, a superior, transcendental knowledge. Eliade equates animal spirits with the ancestral spirits who function as the shaman's guide in his or her supraterrestrial experiences (104).

Ma Cia's shamanic transformations initially take the form of a bird and a horse, two symbols of ascent in shamanic imagery. Her ecstatic journey marks a progression epitomized by her ability to fly to the sky to establish contact with the celestial spirits. Noel King in *African Cosmos: An Introduction to Religion in Africa*, affirms that in Africa the majority of the spirits are celestial, hence the shamanic flight is manifested by an ascension trance.[23] The "flight," according to ethnologists, is a metaphor for superior intelligence, a secret understanding of certain metaphysical phenomena and truths. This understanding of the inexplicable or of the nonrepresentable enables shamans to manipulate their human form and transcend their mortal state without necessarily waiting for death in order to be able to do so. In this way, the shamanic act manifests a certain victory over death or, in other words, a coming to terms with death that is not finite. Télumée describes (in)finite space as "a solemn place where time had ceased and death was unknown" (132). This process of coming to terms with death perhaps accounts for Ma Cia's "happy" transformation into a dog at the end of the text. Télumée describes the transformation: "Ma Cia was waiting for me, her forepaws crossed one over the other, and as I came near I recognized her curious mauve, fluted nails. . . . Ma Cia began to run around me, licking my feet and hands with relish. . . . I suddenly felt like going for one of our usual walks, and Ma Cia came with me, frisking about and yelping happily" (131–132). The dog, a funerary symbol marking the passage to the underworld, symbolizes the downward part of Ma Cia's flight, bringing her full circle in her total ecstatic experience. In this way, Ma Cia embraces total reality by bridging the gap between the different cosmic zones of earth, sky, and the underworld. Her rite of passage has been marked by a perilous, but successful, crossing of several bridges, inaccessible to the un-initiated, to return to the Origin, the lost Eden. This forgotten paradise has been described by the Indian philosopher A. K. Coomaraswamy as a solipsis-tic space that transcends opposites and abolishes the polarity that typifies the human condition to reach an ultimate vision, an ultimate reality.[24]

This ultimate vision makes Ma Cia the "Ultimate Womanist," "commit-ted to the survival and wholeness of entire peoples."[25] Her universal messages of interconnectedness, unified resistance to oppression, sisterhood, and respect for the environment are important guidelines for all liberation movements aimed at autonomy. Ma Cia's narrative presence and functions furnish the nec-essary frame of reference for the successful raising of group consciousness and self-consciousness by serving as a manifesto for all peoples, even though her particular powers are evidenced most effectively by the women of the com-munity. Through the immortal, transcendent figure of Ma Cia, Schwarz-Bart pays tribute to the pervasive presence of her spiritual foremothers, the pur-veyors and preservers of a proud Antillean heritage.

Notes

1. Mircea Eliade, *Shamanism: Archaic Techniques of Ecstasy* (Princeton, N.J.: Princeton University Press, 1964).
2. A specular image is an inverted mirror image that is negative in its representa-tion. It is a deflective rather than reflective image.
3. Chandra Talpade Mohanty. "Under Western Eyes. Feminist Scholarship and Co-lonial Discourses." *Boundary 2* 12, no. 3; 13, no. 1 (spring/fall 1984): 333–358. Reprinted in *Third World Women and the Politics of Feminism*, ed. Chandra Talpade Mohanty, Ann Russo, and Lourdes Torres (Bloomington: Indiana University Press, 1991)
4. Edouard Glissant, *Le Discours antillais* (Paris: Editions du Seuil, 1982), 18. See also Dany Bébel-Gisler, *Léonora: L'Histoire enfouie de la Guadeloupe* (Paris: Edition Seghers, 1985).
5. Trinh T. Minh-ha, *Woman, Native, Other* (Bloomington: Indiana University Press, 1989), 54.
6. Homi Bhaba, "The Other Question—The Stereotype and Colonial Discourse," *Screen* 24, no. 6 (1983): 23.
7. Marie Denise Shelton, "Women Writers of the French-Speaking Caribbean: An

Overview," in *Caribbean Women Writers*, ed. Selwyn Cudjoe (Wellesley, Mass.: Calaloux, 1990), 346.

8. Gay Wilentz, *Binding Cultures: Black Women Writers in Africa and the Diaspora* (Bloomington: Indiana University Press, 1992), xvi.

9. This term was coined by Beverly Stoeltje of the University of Texas and is quoted by Wilentz, *Binding Cultures*, Introduction.

10. Bernice Johnson Reagon, "African Diaspora Women: The Making of Cultural Workers." In *Women in Africa and the Diaspora*, ed. R. Terborg-Penn, S. Harley, and A. Benton-Rushing (Washington, D.C.: Howard University Press, 1987), 177.

11. Simone Schwarz-Bart, *The Bridge of Beyond*, trans. Barbara Bray (Portsmouth, N.H., and Oxford: Heinemann, 1982). French original: *Pluie et vent sur Télumée Miracle* (Paris: Editions du Seuil, 1972). Page numbers are from the translation.

12. Maryse Condé, *La Parole des femmes: Essai sur des romancières des Antilles de langue française* (Paris: L'Harmattan, 1979).

13. Maryse Condé, *Moi, Tituba, sorcière noire de Salem* (Paris: Mercure de France, 1986). See also the English translation: *I, Tituba, Black Witch of Salem*, trans. Richard Philcox. (Charlottesville: University Press of Virginia, 1992), 6.

14. Hélène Cixous, *The Newly-Born Woman* (Minneapolis: University of Minnesota Press, 1986), 64.

15. Vicki Noble, *Shakti Woman: Feeling Our Fire, Healing Our World: The New Shamanism* (San Francisco: Harper, 1991), 5.

16. J. J. Bachofen, *Myth, Religion, and Mother Right*, trans. R. Manheim (Princeton, N.J.: Princeton University Press, 1970), 80.

17. Noble, *Shakti Woman*, 4.

18. Anne Ullanov and Barry Ullanov, *The Witch and the Clown: Two Archetypes of Human Sexuality* (Wilmette, Ill.: Chriron, 1987), 12.

19. Mary Daly, *Gyn/Ecology: The Metaethics of Radical Feminism* (Boston: Beacon Press, 1978). Also consult Karen Smylely-Walace, "The Female Self in Schwarz-Bart's *Pluie et vent sur Télumée Miracle*," *French Review* 59, no. 3 (1986): 236–248.

20. Noble, *Shakti Woman*, 45.

21. See Ronnie Scharfmann, "Mirroring and Mothering in Simone Schwarz-Bart's *Pluie et vent sur Télumée Miracle* and Jean Rhys's *Wide Sargasso Sea*," *Yale French Studies* 62 (1981): 88–106.

22. Noel King, *African Cosmos: An Introduction to Religion in Africa* (Belmont, Calif.: Wadsworth, 1986).

23. Ibid.

24. A. K. Coomaraswamy, *Figures of Speech or Figures of Thought* (London: n.p., 1946), 486.

25. Alice Walker, *In Search of Our Mothers' Gardens: Womanist Prose* (London: Woman's Press, 1984), xi–xii.

Sorcerers, She-Devils, and Shipwrecked Women

IVETTE ROMERO-CESAREO

Writing Religion in French-Caribbean Literature

The Caribbean is a land of taking root and wandering.
—EDOUARD GLISSANT, *Poétique de la relation*

RELIGION HAS ALWAYS played an important part in crafting a gendered and racial identity, whether it is wielded as a weapon for repression or as a force for liberation. French-Caribbean literature written by women often focuses on religion—as well as family, education, and the workplace—and its function within the colonial framework. Myriam Warner-Vieyra's *Le Quimboiseur l'avait dit* (*As the Sorcerer Said . . .*),[1] Simone Schwarz-Bart's *Pluie et vent sur Télumée Miracle* (*The Bridge of Beyond*),[2] Jacqueline Manicom's *La Graine: Journal d'une sage-femme* (The seed: Journal of a midwife),[3] and Dany Bébel-Gisler's testimonial narrative *Léonora: L'Histoire enfouie de la Guadeloupe* (Leonora: The hidden history of Guadeloupe)[4] all explore the importance of role models for women within religious and family structures in the quest for a Caribbean identity.[5] These texts center on women's appropriation of religious beliefs and practices in positing a gendered/racial self.

Suzette Destinville (Zetou) in Warner-Vieyra's *Le Quimboiseur l'avait dit*, a young Guadeloupan girl in an insane asylum in France, creates an alternative world into which she retreats not only to survive the traumas of being uprooted from her homeland but also to explore the sequence of events leading to her internment. With the dream of pursuing her studies, Zetou leaves behind her father and siblings in Guadeloupe to live with her wayward mother and her mother's white lover in Paris, only to find herself betrayed at every turn. Tricked into servitude in her mother's house, she is raped by her unofficial stepfather, Roger, and lured into an ongoing "relationship" with him. Almost sold off to a despised man many years her senior, she discovers her mother's cold-blooded collusion with every abuse she has suffered. Her experience parallels that of the African slave—ocean crossing, servitude, destruction of the family, abuse by the white "master," and "sale" to another white man. When she overhears her mother and Roger laughing about their plans to marry her off to obtain financial favors from her future husband, Zetou flies into a rage, attacking them both. They call the police, accuse her of madness, and smugly watch her being dragged away and confined to a mental hospital.

Her triple alienation—migration to a foreign country, maternal entrapment and betrayal, and banishment to a mental hospital—places Zetou in a state from which the only escape is her spiritual lifeline to her island and her memories of home. Zetou's story hinges on the hometown sorcerer's warnings of the tragedies that would befall her once she left her land. Stemming from that central idea, the character's momentary well-being and relief are tied to retrospection about elements of Afro-Caribbean beliefs. Religious beliefs and practices in *Le Quimboiseur l'avait dit*, as well as in other French-Caribbean works written by women, provide the possibility of an imaginary return to or affirmation of a homeland, which simultaneously links Caribbean life to Africa (Guinea).

In the French Antilles, the idea of leaving one's birthplace, by choice or involuntarily, is a highly complex matter as it is tied to particular family structures, traditions, and religious beliefs regarding life and death. A person is literally "tied" to the homeland by virtue of the fact that the umbilical cord, along with the placenta, is usually buried close to his or her birthplace under a young tree on the family's plot of land. The person should be buried in the same place; if this is not possible, the water used to bathe the corpse should be thrown on the ground where the umbilical cord is planted. This practice, which originated in West Africa, provides a sense of attachment to place and community.

The narrator of *La Graine*, a midwife in a Parisian hospital, laments the loss of this attachment and lack of ceremony regarding birth as she reminisces about customs in her native land, Guadeloupe; the placenta, called *maman-ventre*, is entrusted to the father, who buries it under a young mango or breadfruit tree. She calls this the "landmark [*point de repère*] for every Christian." Throughout the text she expresses pity for newborn infants who are not bound to any place in particular. "Children who are born at Sainte-Cécile and in other hospitals in Paris have nowhere on earth a tree under which their *maman-ventre* is buried" (68). They have no sense of "connection" with the earth, no landmarks, and, consequently, no place [*nulle part*]. Léonora, the narrator of *Léonora: L'Histoire enfouie de la Guadeloupe*, likewise comments, "When you come into this world, you are unbound from your mother to be reattached to the earth by planting your umbilical cord at the same time a coconut tree is planted." Because the tree marks the land where one is born and dies, a person will remain alive in memory as long as the tree is standing. "From the time of our birth to death, we are attached to her [the land]. It is she who makes us live. All of us, living beings, are tied to the dead, to the earth" (87). The narrator illustrates two aspects of the same practice. First, she underlines the historically signifying function of the tree under which the umbilical cord is buried. The cord not only attaches one to the earth but also nourishes the tree that will serve as a landmark for one's existence: it is a living monument to one's life. Second, she affirms our relationship not only to the earth but also to the dead.

While Manicom refers to the umbilical cord as "the landmark" of all people, Léonora makes a clearer connection between this tradition and the worship of dead ancestors characteristic of Afro-Caribbean beliefs. In the chapter entitled "The Motherland, Land of the Ancestors, a Piece of Oneself That One Cannot Sell," Léonora explains the importance of the plot of land, which she considers sacred and essential for the survival and unity of the family and the preservation of memory. "Like the fingers of your hand, the members of the family are attached to the land. The thumb was already there, the others arrived, all the way to the little finger. All together, they form a large body. To sell the land of the ancestors is to unbind the family because what kept it together no longer exists. Selling the land that your father or mother left you, is like selling your father or mother; it is not to recognize that they gave birth to you" (80). Although this practice stresses family unity, it also points to the importance of landownership in the name of the survival of memory (ancestry). In *Fonds des nègres*[6] Marie Chauvet explores the problems that arise from subdividing and selling off the family plot, and she explores the problem of losing it to outside forces in *Colère*;[7] in *Colère* the family burial ground has been appropriated by the Tonton Macoutes. In *Le Quimboiseur l'avait dit*, ties to the land (the family plot) are problematical; Zetou's thirst for knowledge and decision to seek it elsewhere are punished by the unleashing of tragic events in her life.

The disintegration of the family, however, is actually precipitated by Zetou's mother, Rosamonde, whose decision to abandon her home, husband, and children is based on ambition and racism. Rosamonde is a traitor who despises her community and considers herself superior to her own people. "The local people preferred my grandmother, *who was one of them*, to my mother, who had always put on grand airs as she had been to the big school in town, the one where you could get your School Certificate. There were also rumours that she had never forgiven my grandmother for having married her off to a fisherman who could hardly read and, *what was worse, one of the darkest-skinned men in the village*" (15; emphasis added).

For Rosamonde, education provides an escape from the community she has always rejected—first to the "big school in town" and finally to France. Zetou's desire to learn, however, centers on her thirst for the "truth" about her African heritage, as she rejects the story of her Gallic ancestry taught to her in the local school. For Zetou, education would provide access to a black history rather than assimilation to a white world. Although Zetou describes Rosamonde as light-skinned and very beautiful, her cold, bristling contemptuousness impresses Zetou the most. She exposes Rosamonde's hypocrisy, thirst for power, and desire to emulate whites while taking advantage of her own people, in particular her own daughter. Rosamonde sides with the oppressor as she destroys her family—condemning her daughter to servitude and then having her locked away—and is compared to Roger, the French authorities whom Zetou fights to escape, and, finally, to the white traders who brought the first slaves to the Caribbean. "A feeling of hatred that I had never felt before blurred my vision—hatred for these two people against whom I now hurled myself, but also hatred for all the white people who had always deceived us, humiliated and mocked us, since my first ancestor was wrenched from the African coast" (68). After this epiphany Zetou refuses to think of the present. Her life in France acquires surreal qualities—"like something out of a strange dream, peopled with fantastic faces and forms"—as she favors her imaginary excursions back home, which seem more real to her. "I directed my thoughts to my village which I ought never to have left" (5). Because "as far as she was concerned, nothing form Cocotier had any value," Zetou's mother had bought her the "smallest possible suitcase" in order to make her leave home without taking any of her "little souvenirs": bags, shell necklaces, fruits, and other items that could remind her of island life (45). The passageway to the past (or what the narrator calls a "passport to dreams") and an "idyllic" life in her village of Cocotier can by accessed only through the recollection of traditional, magicoreligious practices, which enable her to find "the way home," both to her Caribbean village and to an identification with African roots.

Zetou's first flight from her surroundings at the hospital is introduced by the recollection of a popular dictum: "days of disaster send no warning before them" (4). Thoughts of the disastrous turn of events in her life combine with memories of death and rituals of mourning in Guadeloupe. The syncretic nature of Caribbean beliefs is apparent in her detailed description of the activities surrounding wakes: the coexistence of Christian practices, exemplified by the repetition of rosaries, and African-based oral tradition, storytelling about fantastic animals (Compère Lapin) or she-devils (*la diablesse, la djablesse*, or *la guiablesse*). The uncomfortable marriage between Christian and African-based beliefs is exemplified in the description of the sorcerer's consultation room: along with the cabalistic figures on the ground, the coconut-shell lamp, and the geometric figures in chalk (*vèvès*), there is a statue of Christ and two crosses, one wooden and the other drawn in chalk (46). Christian practice, however, is considered repressive. Zétou recalls that the village priest, Father John, would exhort the people "to chastity, goodness, charity and many other virtues" making the mass much longer than necessary; he would not permit women into church without head coverings, and he "could see sin everywhere." Although the church as an institution is seen as somewhat superfluous and most certainly intrusive in Zetou's eyes, the actual building, Saint Sophie's Church, serves practical purposes. Being the only brick structure in the village, it provides shelter from cyclones or tidal waves.

Dany Bébel-Gisler's *Léonora* conveys a similar perception of Christianity—the church provides protection for Father Celeste during his hunger strike and subsequent persecution by the authorities—but the narrator goes much further in her criticism of traditional Catholicism and in her support of liberation theology. *Léonora* carefully describes the innovative, community-oriented changes that empower the townspeople. The author adds another dimension to the amalgam of rituals by including Indian religious practices, in particular the feast held in the name of the goddess Maliémen (Mariammam).[8] Mariammam, the goddess of chicken pox, is a fierce mother figure who must be appeased if one is to request her protection.[9] *Léonora* focuses on the inclusiveness of the feast, which is open to everyone ("without distinction of skin-color," "all black folk who wanted to come were invited, too"). The description of the arrival of Maldévilen (or Madoura Viran, the war god who guards the temple and Mariammam) in these ceremonies resembles descriptions of African-based rituals: "People whispered 'Maldévilen is coming.' He arrived, illuminated by torch bearers. His costume seemed made of light. He entered the circle and danced, spinning and spinning. Then a white rooster was given to him. He brought the animal's neck to his mouth and in one clean bite, severed it and drank its blood" (42). The resemblance to other rituals (Guadeloupan Quimbois, Cuban Santería, and Haitian Vodoun, to name a few) may explain the acceptance of Indian ritual on some islands: the war god is similar to Shango (Santería) or Ogún/Ogoun (Santería, Vodoun); offerings (rice, coconut, milk, jewelry, embroidered cloths, flowers) for Mariammam are important; and animal sacrifice (roosters or male goats) is central to the ceremony. Through religion, Indian culture has had a definite impact on Guadeloupan life. Indian gods and goddesses, in particular Mariammam, are considered to be extremely powerful, and many black Guadeloupans believe them to be effective in solving their problems.[10]

At variance with Bébel-Gisler, Schwarz-Bart, Opal Palmer Adisa,[11] and many other Caribbean women writers whose works portray images of both destructive and constructive women/goddesses, positive female figures are not to be found in Myriam Warner-Vieyra's treatment of the supernatural. Their absence is unusual given Afro-Caribbean mythology's numerous manifestations of female divinities, who are generally related to the power over life and death, seduction, femininity, aspiration to a higher nature in humankind, protection, love, fertility; they are commonly divided into either "good" or "evil," or more complex attributes. In Vodoun, for example, there are many manifestations of Erzulie, some known to protect and others to harm: Erzulie Frieda Dahomey, Erzulie Mansour, Erzulie Ge-Rouge, Erzulie Mapionne, Gran Erzulie, Erzulie Lemba, La Sirène, La Balianne, Brigitte, Mai-Louise, Ti-Quitta, Marinette-Congo, Marinette Bras-Chêche, and Marinette Pied-Chêche. However, the most clear-cut contrast can be seen in the Erzulie Frieda and the Erzulie Mansour divinities, who represent two different poles: light-skinned Erzulie Frieda, the goddess of love, is the epitome of femininity, beauty, coquetry, and seduction, which Erzulie Mansour is the generous, caring and giving, dark Madonna who represents motherly love, sacrifice, and protection. Santería, in the Spanish-speaking Caribbean, also has many female divinities representing different principles. The major female *orisha* (divinity) in Santería and related religions is Yemayá, who is known for her role in the creation of the world and the human race: it is she who caused the universal deluge, and it is from her bones that both man and woman were created.[12] Yemayá, as goddess of the sea and maternity, and river goddesses like Oshún and Oyá, who represent death and love respectively, are in many ways like the variform manifestations of Erzulie, as they rule similar principles. These female figures play an important role in the Caribbean imaginary and have been appropriated or reinterpreted by Caribbean women writers.

Positive, powerful female figures are lacking in *Le Quimboiseur l'avait dit*, however, thus contributing to the bleakness, alienation, and despair of Zetou's narration. While Bébel-Gisler's Léonora speaks of Maliémen, heroic family members, and the survivors of popular stories (like Persillette, who outsmarts the evil *soucounyan*[13]) and while Schwarz-Bart offers a chain of strong women headed by sorceress Ma Cia (a positive force for women and a monster in men's eyes), Warner-Vieyra prefers a male figure to represent Afro-Caribbean magic. The *quimboiseur* (sorcerer) is the voice of doom in Zetou's life—"I was only sixteen and the future was filled with bad omens. . . . As the sorcerer had said: 'The gods of Africa were not favourable'"(65)—and is incapable of saving her from her destiny[14]—"The river does not wash away what is meant for you" (47). Most of the female characters in the novel are depicted as either helpless (her grandmother) or evil (her schoolteacher, her mother), and the only female figure representing supernatural powers is *la diablesse*, the terrifying she-devil.

In Caribbean oral tradition, as documented in *Pluie et vent*, *Léonora*, and *Le Quimboiseur l'avait dit*, the diablesse is a beautiful woman with long silky hair, frequently found at a party, on a bridge, in the woods, or close to a river, elegantly dressed. She is recognizable by her feet: "On a moonlit night, la Diablesse would come to dance. La Diablesse! A beautiful woman with light skin, a scarf on her pretty head, gold earrings, a long dress fastened up on one side, revealing an embroidered slip underneath, but also, if one looked closely, with the hoof of a donkey replacing one of her feet."[15] The man who perceives her is charmed by her grace and beauty and led into the woods never to be seen again. Occasionally he is discovered the next day at the foot of a cliff, his neck broken, or if he is lucky, he may find himself in a ravine or ditch from which he will have difficulty finding his way home.[16] In *Léonora*, the diablesse seduces and tricks men. She sings, dances, and entices them to leave the party with her. After sleeping with her, "the unlucky one would awaken with only a bunch of bones in his arms" (156). Furthermore, says Léonora, the diablesse seeks revenge if she is turned away from a party with whips or cigarette smoke (said to repel she-devils) by leading people to "phantom" *léwoz* (parties) with the sounds of distant drums that seem to change directions as people attempt to find them. (In Puerto Rican popular culture a similar belief centers on a beautiful woman dressed in white who entices men to her "home," only to have them discover that her dwelling place is actually a cemetery.) In *Pluie et vent*, this she-devil, called *la Guiablesse*, is described as the most wicked of spirits, "the woman with the cloven hoof who feeds exclusively on your desire to live, and whose charms drive you sooner or later to suicide" (5). A similarly monstrous figure is the *bête a man Ibé*, a sorceress who wanders at night with one human foot and one horse or donkey hoof, shrieking and dragging a long iron chain around her waist.[17] Unlike the diablesse, the bête a man Ibé is reputed to be frightful and is sometimes described as having the form of an animal.

In *Le Quimboiseur l'avait dit*, the she-devil appears in relation to a mysterious mountaintop reputed to have huge pools of boiling water and burning craters. After a party a young man from Zetou's village meets a beautiful girl who asks him to return home with her: "After they had walked for more than an hour and he could no longer recognise the area, he grew suspicious and refused to go any further, deciding to stay where he was till daybreak. The girl grew angry, slapped her companion's face and went away. When the sun rose, the young man saw that he had stopped a few feet from one of these pools of boiling water and he realised that the beautiful girl was one of the mountain she-devils" (8). This she-devil anecdote leads into the story of the

Bastille Day dance on 14 July 1946 where Zetou's mother met "the white man," Roger. This story is embedded in a discussion of the perceptions of color in Zetou's family ("My father was one of the darkest people in the village and my mother among the lightest," 9). In many cases the she-devil, described as light-skinned with silky hair, entraps men by dancing with them through most of the night, suggesting that men who are tricked by the diablesse are punished for choosing the light-skinned over the black woman. Rosamonde, in turn, is described as a light-skinned, seductive beauty who dances through the night with "the white man" who has "picked her out" and, shortly after, she sets sail for Le Havre, opting for a "white" world and its enticements.

A second example of memory of the homeland being bound to religious practices is a discussion of bathing. Zetou speaks of her need to steep in past life "just as we used to soak ourselves in a bath of certain leaves back home, to wash away the effects of the evil eye and regain our high spirits with the return of good luck" (14). She is referring to what is called a *bain démarré* in the French Caribbean, a special bath taken to rid oneself of problems. There are also *bains de la chance*, or good-luck baths, which can be taken in the ocean or at home with sea, river, or rain water and various herbs. Léonora speaks of going to the seaside with other young girls carrying "selected herbs with which to rub our bodies in the water, to unbind our extremities, to take our *bain démarré*. It was necessary to chase away all the bad things that had entered our bodies."[18] However, she acknowledges the limitations of the baths. "This bath of leaves was supposed to eliminate everything it could. Whatever it could not eliminate, would not be eliminated." This is echoed in *Le Quimboiseur l'avait dit* when the sorcerer suggests his impotence in the face of fate. "The river does not wash away what is meant for you" (47). In *Pluie et vent*, the narrator, Télumée, likens the bain démarré to a rebirth; she emerges from the water as a new woman with renewed strength. "Still singing, I ran to the river and jumped in, immersing myself again and again. . . . At this very moment I have left my grief at the bottom of the river. It is going downstream, and will enshroud another heart than mine" (114). She also stresses the healing properties—for both body and soul—of the special baths prepared by Ma Cia, which help her recuperate from the string of tragic events in her life. Télumée would always arrive at Ma Cia's yard to find "a big earthen pan waiting for [her] outside her cabin, in the sun, full of water dark with all kinds of magic leaves—paoca, calaba balsam, bride's rose, and the power of Satan" in which she would steep, ritualistically ladling the contents nine times over her head, to "leave behind all the fatigues of the week."[19]

Since *démarré* means to untie the knots that obstruct one's life, it is not surprising that in *Le Quimboiseur l'avait dit* bathing provides access to long-lost feelings of well-being. At the hospital Zetou is obsessed with taking a bath.

When denied a bath she retreats to her remembrances of Cocotier. Several bathing scenes echo throughout the novel; two memories that immediately follow the prohibition of a bath at the mental ward are the joys of bathing in the Corossol River on Saturday afternoons, and the bain démarré at the sorcerer's, both of which provide the relief inaccessible to her in the ward. In the first one she recalls swimming, playing, and splashing with other children, and washing her hair with a prickly-pear infusion. The river is central to her recollections of the community because people also went there to fill their bottles with drinking water and to do the washing. Mention of an infusion to wash her hair foreshadows the infusion of herbs with which the sorcerer attempts to dispel Zetou's bad luck: "After ten to fifteen minutes he came back carrying a large tub filled with a mixture of greenish water and leaves. He told me to undress and get into the tub. The water was warm and gave off an undefinable but pleasant smell. The sorcerer took the leaves and rubbed my body, while repeating incantations in a strange language—that of the Gods of Africa, no doubt" (47).

The scene of the bain demarré, which combines several sensory images, is important as it exemplifies the function of memory in the narrator, especially the use of water as a unifying topos. Zetou strings together images of water—the bathtub at the hospital, the ocean and her father's fishing boat, the Corossol River, the bain demarré and the sorcerer's mention of the river's limitations, the ocean crossing with Rosamonde and Roger, and back to the river in her village, and so on until the final scene. The sorcerer's incantations in another language in the bath scene are essential for they further the mnemonic linkage with another ocean crossing—the Middle Passage—from Africa in the days of the slave trade, and back to Africa in the imaginary return to Guinea.

Although the sorcerer, Papa Logbo is called a quimboiseur in the text, his description fits the definitions of several different types of magicoreligious figures: *sorciers, quimboiseurs,* and *gadé zaffés.*[20] According to Ary Ebroïn, sorcerers and quimboiseurs have persisted in Guadeloupan life in spite of attempts to eradicate them throughout the years by criminalizing their activities. These sorcerers can be distinguished as: those who read the past, present, and future in the flames or the designs made by melting wax of candles; healers, who practice white magic and utilize "good" herbs; gadé zaffés, who work with secrets such as conjuring; and good or evil quimboiseurs.[21] Sociologist Dany Bébel-Gisler includes the quimboiseurs (*kenbwazé,* according to her spelling of Creole vocabulary) under descriptions of gadé zaffés (*gadédzafé*). She defines the *gadédzafé* literally as one who looks into someone's business, "celui qui regarde dans les affaires" (310). The gadédzafé, many of whom are women, use magic and invoke the gods to solve problems of the heart, business, and health, or to help people find the causes of their miseries. She further distinguishes the gadédzafé, from the kenbwazé: the gadédzafé provides aid on a psychological level and gives advice, while the kenbwazé uses *kenbwa*, material artifacts designed to ensure certain positive or negative results.

Representing ties with Africa, Papa Logbo appears as a stereotypical tribal man of the past. "His sole garment was a piece of red material tied at his waist and he wore a necklace made of shells and the teeth of animals that I had never seen before." The narrator's emphasis on the unknown—"animals that I had never seen before" and "incantations in a strange language"—points to her lack of familiarity and contact with her African heritage. She is unable to read or understand the signs she sees: a wooden cross above the door, another cross "drawn in white chalk in the middle of which was fixed a pair of scissors," wooden statuettes "projecting their shadows up to the roof of corrugated iron, from which hung a tangle of strings," and inscriptions and geometric drawings on the walls. Everything she sees in Papa Logbo's hut is a tangle of signs that she is incapable of deciphering; his "writing" is as mysterious as the incantations he pronounces. "He traced a cabalistic figure on the ground, composed of a double triangle that looked like a star. He wrote some letters and figures in it" (46).

As incomprehensible as his language may seem, Zetou is nonetheless fascinated by it because, for her, it represents a history she has only just begun to learn about, in spite of the misleading lessons she receives at school. "Contrary to what I had been taught up till then, I discovered that our ancestors were not only the Gauls, but Negroes, snatched from their own country in the Gulf of Guinea, in Angola, in Cape Verde, Senegal, etc." (23). Having been expelled from school for sharing her newly discovered knowledge—"our ancestors were black men, slaves that came from Africa"—with her teacher, Mrs. Paule, Zetou remains bewildered by her misreading of physical signs. While Mrs. Paule screams furiously ("Your ancestors, perhaps, not mine!"), Zetou "couldn't believe that her [Mrs. Paule's] ancestors had simply been Gauls" as she observes that she "was a big stout Mulatto with a nose so flat it looked as though her mother had sat on it when she was born, and with thick lips and very crinkly hair" (24). Papa Logbo, on the contrary, holds the key to a world Zetou yearns to know. "I was so full of wonder that, forgetting my shyness, I asked him, 'Have you ever been to Africa, Papa Logbo?'" The sorcerer's answer—"Yes, my child. I go back there every day, several times a day, to consult our gods" (47)—includes Zetou in that world. This inclusion will stand in sharp contrast to the exclusion and utter isolation she will suffer as she moves further and further away from the ties to her African heritage. Zetou's last night in Cocotier, the bright, moonlit night when she set out with her grandmother to visit Papa Logbo with their offerings—"a chicken, a large

yam, a candle, and some money to pay for the consultation"—is the last pleasant moment she remembers.

As the sole representative of a religion that is meaningful, albeit mysterious, to Zetou, the sorcerer becomes the most important figure in the text.
He is the guardian of the crossroads to different worlds, and he alone has access to them all. His role is reminiscent of the Fon figure of Legba. "While
Legba's six siblings preside over the six domains of heaven and earth, Legba
rules over all."[22] Papa Logbo is Papa Legba, the divine trickster who traveled
across the Middle Passage with slavery and is still alive in African, South
American, North American, and Caribbean cultures. One of the most important figures of Fon and Yoruba mythology, he is known as Legba in Benin
(Fon), Papa Legba in Haitian Vodoun, Papa La Bas in North American
hoodoo, Esu-Elegbara in Nigeria (Yoruba), Echu-Elegua in Cuba, and Exú in
Brazil.[23] He is considered to be a prankster or implacable judge, guardian of
houses, and ruler of the roads; "one must consult with him about any step
planned in life, especially if it involves travel or initiative."[24] As master of
the crossroads, Papa Legba also plays an important role in connecting the past
and the present, granting access to memory. "Never metamorphosed out of
history or embellished into dream, Legba opens the way to memory, not fantasy."[25]

Known as a "the divine linguist" who speaks all languages, Eshu/Legba
mediates between gods and men. Like Hermes, he is a messenger and interpreter of the gods, ruling hermeneutics and translation. According to West
African mythology, Eshu/Legba created the system of divination known as Ifá
(the god to which he taught this art) and its interpretation. Thus he is known
as the "path to Ifá."[26] This system of divination consists of the reading and
exegesis of patterns formed by throwing sixteen palm nuts or cowry shells. To
each cryptogram corresponds a fixed verse, which must be interpreted. "These
verse texts, whose meanings are lushly metaphorical, ambiguous, and enigmatic, function as riddles, which the propitiate must decipher and apply as is
appropriate to his or her own quandary."[27] Furthermore, Eshu/Legba is the care-
taker of *ase*, the "word" or "power" that created the universe. According to
Henry Louis Gates, ase can be translated as *logos*, the word as audible and visible sign of reason.[28] It may be too tempting to see in Papa Logbo's name a
combination of Legba/Logos; what is undeniable here, however, is his role as
mediator between different worlds through the use of the word—pronounc-
ing incantations in "strange" languages, writing, reading signs, deciphering,
and translating.

Papa Logbo's central role as mediator in the narrator's life is problematic
in this novel. Religion, in the Latin sense (*re-ligare*) means to "tie again," to
develop connections. Although religion, represented by Papa Logbo/Legba,

allows Zetou to find the frail threads connecting her to her homelands—the Caribbean (Cocotier) and, ultimately, Africa—these connections are not physical but symbolic; they remain in Zetou's imagination as disjointed memories. She has developed a simulacrum of a community deployed to replace a "re-linking" with a historical community. Zetou, as opposed to the narrators of *Léonora* and *Pluie et vent*, breaks with a tradition of women's embodied religious practice grounded in empirical materiality and substitutes for it a symbolic conception of religion.[29]

In both *Léonora* and *Pluie et vent* women go beyond images and words, metaphors and symbols. In *Pluie et vent* Télumée's grandmother, Reine Sans Nom (Queen Without a Name), claims there is an "invisible thread" going from home to home keeping the community together; this symbol is rooted, however, in practices that nourish this sense of community and make the connection a reality (95). When Télumée (like Zetou) denies her bodily existence, wishing she could dissolve into thin air, the women of the community present themselves:[30]

> And then, when they went by my yard, it was as if they deliberately *laughed louder* than before, some of them even *singing cheerful songs and hymns of deliverance*. . . . So they went to and fro in front of my cabin, and from time to time a woman would break away from the group, lift imploring arms heavenwards, and *cry in a high-pitched voice, "Be born, come down to change our fates."* And hearing her I'd have the strange feeling that she was throwing me a thread in the air, throwing a light, light thread toward my cabin, and then I'd be visited by a smile.[31]

Here, women are the mediators between gods and mortals, between Télumée's imaginary world and their own. They have no need for Legba, for they are the ones who stand at the crossroads, controlling the word and its utterance. They laugh, sing (hymns of deliverance!), invoke, provoke, and will Télumée back to life among them. One of the women, Adriana, even seems to transform into a formidable goddess; she "heaved herself up and I saw her enormous bulk silhouetted against the grass, the setting sun making that towering flesh look like a block of granite" and utters pronouncements, echoed by the chorus of women surrounding her:

> "It's true, you're right, Ismène, something keeps this little Negress from touching land, and she may go on a long while, a long while, voyaging like that. And yet, I Adriana, I beat my breast and tell you she *will* come to shore." "She will," Ismène declared at once, ingenuously, "she will come to shore, she will, she will." Then addressing me directly from the other side of the road, the good Adriana said in a vibrant voice that was almost a cry: "Télumée, my dear little

countrywoman, you stay in your grass, there's no need to answer us today. But one thing I wanted to tell you this Christmas day: you will come to shore." . . . Night was near, and somewhere in the distance singing arose, shrill voices still imploring, Be born and change our fates.[32]

In this and similar scenes, men are noticeably absent. In the quotes above, there is no telling whom they are invoking when the women implore, "Be born, come down to change our fates." It could be a male or female deity, or it could be Télumée herself, for when she changes her own fate to become a sorceress/healer, she will be helping her community as mediator between the spirit world, the natural elements, and humans. *Léonora* presents similar figurative and literal connections in the community within the framework of both traditional, African-based practices and Christian liberation theology.

In *Léonora* and *Pluie et vent* women are responsible for exegesis and utterance. Reading and speaking become two aspects of a single social practice. Léonora focuses on the sense of empowerment she acquires when Father Celeste changes the traditional church structure by decentering or dethroning the male figure (from his position in front of the congregation and perched above the pulpit), substituting Creole for the language of those in power (Latin, French) and instituting community-run Bible readings. In the new church, people sit in a circle and take turns selecting passages and interpreting them. Léonora revels in the way she and the community are able to make connections between biblical interpretations and day-to-day experience, learning how to find solutions for their immediate problems and ultimately deciding to take direct action to change their reality. She also stresses the importance of taking the skills she develops through religious practice—reading, writing, interpreting, public speaking—to the realm of political activism.

In *Pluie et vent* the most powerful figure is Ma Cia, the sorceress, who can read and interpret the signs of the spirit world as well as those of nature and the human body. Unlike Papa Logbo, who keeps his knowledge a secret from Zetou, Ma Cia initiates Télumée into the "secrets of plants" and teaches her "the human body, its centres, its weaknesses." She learns "how to set people and animals free, how to break spells and turn sorcery back on the sorcerers" (130)—in other words, she learns how to read and interpret (sorcery, spells) and write (to send the spells back): "rumour spread that I knew how to do and undo, that I knew secrets . . . and I was raised to the rank of seer and first-class witch" (156). Télumée stresses the wholistic coexistence of body and soul, the help she can provide to heal both physically and emotionally. "People climbed up to my cabin and put in my hands the grief, confusion, and absurdity of their bruised bodies and bruised souls" and "[they] pressed and begged me, forced me to take their troubles on my shoulders, all the woes of body

and soul" (157). She assists her community as they suffer the onslaught of miseries caused by drought, disease, and the "Strike of Death," in which strikers
die at the hands of white factory owners. "Then I'd light a special candle and
make signs, some that I learned from Ma Cia and others I'd heard about,
and yet others again that came to me out of nowhere, because of the foam
and the cries."[33] Not only does Télumée "write" ("make signs") the way she
has been taught, but she also creates new "vocabulary" (signs) according to
the changing needs of the community.

Although language is central to her role as mediator, her religion is completely anchored in the body. She avoids learning the last skill Ma Cia offers
to teach her, the secret of metamorphosis—"something held me back, something prevented me from exchanging my woman's shape and two breasts into
that of a beast or flying succubus" (130)—thus refusing to deny her identity
as a woman. What marks both *Léonora* and *Pluie et vent* is the inseparability
of national, racial, and gender identity and of interpretation and practice. Their
conscious roles as women in their respective religious practices determine how
the female characters read, write, interpret, and shape the world around them.
The narrators in these texts "write" religion as a link between women, the
thread or umbilical cord that binds women to each other and to their lands.

In contrast, Zetou displays little sense of gender identity with any of the
women in her life. Despite fond memories of her grandmother, sister, and Mrs.
Felix (her boyfriend's mother), they are unimportant in Zetou's life; her mother
and her teacher, Mrs. Paule, betray her, not only as women, but, more important, as black women, both denying blackness and sabotaging her attempts to
find her roots. They seem as alien to Zetou as the other—mostly French—
girls in the mental ward. The only important figures in her life are male: her
father, her boyfriend (Charles), Roger, Papa Logbo, and at the hospital, Dr.
Edward, a "young coloured man" chosen to tend to her because she would be
"more at ease" with him (4). Mystification and difficulty in reading characterize Zetou's relationship with men: her father is the strong, silent type, of
whom she mostly remembers his back; her communication with Charles is
broken when both his and her letters are intercepted by her mother (she literally cannot read him); she misreads Roger's interest in her. What she notices about Dr. Edward is his illegible writing. "The doctor was writing
something that I couldn't make out in a hieroglyphic handwriting on a blank
sheet of paper" (12). Although he tries to help Zetou, he is unable to anchor
her in reality. He does the contrary; by keeping her sedated, he contributes to
the imaginary wanderings that lead her nowhere. Papa Logbo's role as a junc-
tion where religion, remembrance, and different worlds meet has already been
mentioned. Although Zetou is able to conjure up thoughts of home through
religious images, she is never able to return. By choosing a male as the exegete

(as guide, director, and interpreter), she relinquishes the possibility of an active role in reading/writing/interpreting or proposing an alternative social order.

While in other texts the umbilical cord—related to women, childbirth, and mothering—provides metaphorical and physical grounding, in *Le Quimboiseur l'avait dit* the link to other worlds is symbolized by a phallus. Legba, frequently represented with an eternally erect penis, is characteristically oversexed and not to be trusted with women.[34] He is often "selected to be 'intermediary between this world and the next' at the end of myths that recount his sexual prowess. The pun here is on copula(te) and intercourse. Legba's sexuality is a sign of liminality, but also of the penetration of thresholds, the exchange between discursive universes."[35] Zetou is unable to identify with this figure, who offers a link, or copula(tion), that can be only metaphorical and mystifying, remaining in the realm of the imaginary. Religion, written by a male in *Le Quimboiseur l'avait dit*, exists as ideology rather than practice.

The same chasm between ideology and practice can be observed in Zetou's search for Africa. Although she draws a parallel between her unpleasant experiences and those of the African slave and seeks to access Africa through Papa Logbo, she is unable to bridge the chasm between the symbolic and the real. Through Papa Logbo she glimpses an exoticized, unreadable Africa, made all the more attractive by its remoteness and mystery.[36] In both *Léonora* and *Pluie et vent* links with Africa are kept alive through generations of oral history. *Pluie et vent* offers a genealogy tracing the Lougandor family's roots to Africa and the "living" proof of a survivor, Ma Cia, born into slavery.[37] *Léonora* also provides a witness, Anmann, whose parents-in-law were among the last slaves taken clandestinely to Guadeloupe after the abolition of slavery. Anmann tells a story of a sorcerer who takes runaway slaves back to Africa— "he did his sorcery, broke the two eggs [stolen from the master]; a great ship appeared before them and they returned to Africa"—thus showing how resistance was reflected through the imaginary, aided by "the beat of the drum and the story-teller's voice" (301). This story, however, is preceded by an account of "real" abuses of slavery as told to Anmann by the survivors themselves. In *Léonora*, *Pluie et vent*, and *La Graine* Africa does not appear as the mythical, idealized "nonplace" that it is for Zetou. In the first two, African legacy provides an important reference, and both texts develop a sense of Caribbean identify and community. *La Graine* focuses on migrants in Paris groping with a Caribbean identity: it stresses solidarity with African migrants (as well as Spaniards, Portuguese, and Latin Americans) not as idealized "others" or a missing link necessary for the understanding of Caribbean-ness, but as "real" people sharing similar problems of racism, sexism, and classism. And *Le Quimboiseur l'avait dit* is a good example of the contradictions of *négritude* and the idea of a return to Africa as an alternative to a colonized Caribbean mentality, an idea criticized by Maryse Condé.[38] Helmtrud Rumpf's "Rhizome verus racine: Deux concepts d'identité dans les Caraïbes francophones" beautifully describes the differences between the search for a mythical African past as opposed to the creation of a sense of Caribbean and/or African-diaspora unity.[39] She compares the first to a vertical *marronage* (the quest for roots) and the second to a horizontal *marronage* (the lateral growth of rhizomes—ties to a community). By neither taking into account the political and class realities of the "desired" continent nor proposing political solutions, nationalist ideologies based on travel/departure/escape replace the possibilities of revolutionary action in situ or development of a nonontological, historical sense of Caribbean collectivity.

Zetou's fictionalization of Africa mirrors the exoticism of her memories of home—an exoticism she relies on to avoid the pain of reality. "I had to put off as long as possible 'the moment of truth,' in order to keep the present at bay" (5).[40] The tension between Zetou's exoticization of Cocotier and the "true" story is announced in the "introduction" to her narration:

> This is a story which might have begun: "Once upon a time, there was a little girl who lived in a tiny little village on an island that was as big as two coconuts. Her mother was the most beautiful person in the village and her father was a fisherman who sometimes took the little girl out to sea with him. She had a friend who was the smartest little boy on the island, the one who always knew everything. They ran barefoot and bareheaded all over the island. They swam in the river, gorged themselves on fruit, saturated themselves with sunshine." . . . And then the story would end: "the little girl grew up to be as beautiful as her mother, married the clever, little boy and they lived happily ever after and had lots of children." In fact it didn't turn out like this at all. (1).

Although "it didn't turn out like this at all," her spontaneous recollection is close to this fictionalized rendering. Finally, she is able to face neither the "drama" that Dr. Edward has made her relive nor the "calamity" described in her sister Zelia's letter—a flood; a bus accident and the tragic death of her boyfriend, Charles, and his father, Mr. Felix; her brother Jose's loss of an arm; and many others dead or injured. Instead of joy at the sight of her packed suitcase, ready for her return to Cocotier, she loses "all notion of time and place," is "plunged into an alien world, behind a wall of darkness," and is no longer able to communicate with others. "I opened my mouth but no sound came" (72). In the closing lines, she finds herself at the bottom of a boat: "The only thing I could see from the bottom of the boat was a man's broad naked back—his glistening muscles, wet from perspiration, were reassuring in their strength—and a tiny white cloud hanging in a blue sky" (73).

Like Zetou, we, as readers, no longer know whether she is still in the mental ward or back on her island. Does this strong, reassuring back belong to her father, Papa Logbo, or to a fictional Maroon escaping in a boat? If this male figure represents a Maroon, then her break with the reality of the hospital—the white world—is *marronage* of sorts: madness is her only escape.[41] Whether she is imagining Papa Logbo's naked back or actually seeing her father rowing her "home" (Cocotier? Africa?), she cannot survive the trip. Her lifeline severed, she is helpless and voiceless, trapped within a world of symbols. Zetou remains drifting somewhere in the "middle passage" with only a tiny white cloud in sight and no landmarks to guide her to shore.

Notes

1. Myriam Warner-Vieyra, *Le Quimboiseur l'avait dit* (Paris: Présence Africaine, 1980); Myriam Warner-Vieyra, *As the Sorcerer Said . . .* , trans. Dorothy S. Blair (Essex: Longman, 1982). All references are to the translation.
2. Simone Schwarz-Bart, *Pluie et vent sur Télumée Miracle* (Paris: Editions du Seuil, 1972); Simone Schwarz-Bart, *The Bridge of Beyond*, trans. Barbara Bray (Portsmouth, N.H., and Oxford: Heinemann, 1982). All references are to the translation.
3. Jacqueline Manicom, *La Graine: Journal d'une sage-femme* (Paris: Presses de la Cité, 1974).
4. Dany Bébel-Gisler, *Léonora: L'Histoire enfouie de la Guadeloupe* (Paris: Edition Seghers, 1985). All translations are mine.
5. Although there are references to works from Haiti (Marie Chauvet) and Martinique (Edouard Glissant), I have chosen to focus on literature from Guadeloupe, in particular Warner-Vieyra's *Le Quimboiseur l'avait dit*. Other texts that would have provided interesting points of comparison are Françoise Ega's *Le Temps des madras: Récit de la Martinique* (Paris: Editions Maritimes et d'Outre Mer, 1966), and her *Lettres à une noire: Récit antillais* (Paris: L'Harmattan, 1978).
6. Marie Chauvet, *Fonds des nègres* (Port-au-Prince: Editions Henri Deschamps, 1961).
7. Marie Chauvet, *Amour, Colére, et Folie* (Paris: Editions Gallimard, 1968), a trilogy printed in a single volume.
8. More than forty thousand East Indians were transported to Guadeloupe between 1854 and 1889, after the French turned to India in order to preserve the plantation economy after the abolition of slavery (1848). The East Indians, who took the place of the slaves on the sugarcane plantations, were from the lowest caste, the "untouchables."
9. I would like to thank Uma Narayan (Vassar College) for explaining this deity's characteristics and function in Indian society. Mariamma is most commonly worshipped in rural communities in India, which explains her popularity among the agrarian population, mainly Indian and black, of Guadeloupe.
10. Bébel-Gisler, *Léonora*, 306.
11. See Opal Palmer Adisa, *Bake-Face and other Guava Stories* (Berkeley, Calif.: Kelsey Street Press, 1986).
12. Of the fourteen gods born of Yemayá, five are female deities. See Migene González-Wippler's *Santería: African Magic in Latin America* (New York: Original Publications, 1989), 27–29.

13. The *soucounyan* (or *soucougnan*; also called *volant*) is a word of African origin meaning human beings transformed into balls of fire. According to oral tradition, they suck people's blood (much like the vampires of European origin). This power, usually attributed to old women, is either inherited or acquired through a pact with the devil. (For the story of Persillette and the soucounyan, see Bébel-Gisler, *Léonora*, 22–33.)

14. Ironically, her last name is Destinville (*destin*—destiny; *ville*—city).

15. Bébel-Gisler, *Léonora*, 156.

16. Ary Ebroïn, *Quimbois, magie noire, et sorcellerie aux Antilles* (Paris: Jacques Grancher, 1977), 93.

17. Ibid., 95.

18. Bébel-Gisler, *Léonora*, 101.

19. Schwarz-Bart, *Pluie et vent*, 129.

20. A similar figure is that of Papa Longoué, in Edouard Glissant's *La Lézarde* (Paris: Editions du Seuil, 1958), who serves as a mediator between different worlds: the Caribbean (present) and Africa (past).

21. Ebroïn, *Quimbois, magie noire*, 157.

22. Henry Louis Gates, *The Signifying Monkey: A Theory of African-American Literary Criticism* (Oxford: Oxford University Press, 1988), 23.

23. See Melville J. Herskovits, *Dahomey: An Ancient West African Kingdom*, vol. 2 (New York: J. J. Augustin, 1938), for a history of Legba in Dahomey (People's Republic of Benin). For an extensive analysis of Esu-Elegbara/Legba in different traditions, see Gates, *The Signifying Monkey*.

24. See Miguel Barnet, "La Regla de Ocha: The Religious System of Santería," in this book.

25. See Joan Dayan, "Vodoun, or the Voice of the Gods," in this book.

26. Gates, *The Signifying Monkey*, 15.

27. Ibid., 10.

28. *Ase* is also the name given to iron altars in the Fon tradition. According to Edna G. Bay's *Asen: Iron Altars of the Fon People of Benin* (Atlanta, Ga.: The Museum, 1985), "The slender metal sculptures called asen are tangible reminders of the interdependence of the living and the dead. The centerpiece of a variety of ceremonies, asen establish a sacred space, a place for the communion of family members in the world of the living with those of the parallel world of the dead" (5). Although their professions provide obvious reasons for their choices, it is interesting to compare Bay's and Gates's choices of definitions. While Gates focuses on the abstract meanings of *ase* (word, energy, power), Bay stresses both the symbolic and material values of the *ase* as objects with simultaneously sacred and utilitarian functions—monuments, sacred places/spaces for communion, and means of recording family histories. See my discussion (below) of women writing religion as materially grounded/embodied practice versus the male logocentric/phallocentric adherence to the symbolic realm.

29. Manicom's *La Graine* explores the problem of linking community, religion, and national, racial, class, and gender identity, in both metaphorical and material terms, by presenting tensions between the traditional woman (from Cocotier) and the nameless narrator, a midwife/nurse who spurns traditional religious beliefs. Manicom's characters oscillate somewhere between the powerless women of *Le Quimboiseur l'avait dit* and the empowered women of *Léonora* and *Pluie et vent*:

30. The village women's perceptions of Télumée seem equally to fit Zetou's state:
    "But my dear," said another voice, "don't you see this person can't hear or understand? I even wonder whether we'll ever see her again as she used to be, in the flesh."

"Yes, you're right, something stops her from touching land and she could go on sailing through the air a long time without ever setting foot on any continent." (110)

31. Schwarz-Bart, *Pluie et vent*, 109–110; emphasis added.

32. Ibid., 111.

33. Ibid., 157.

34. The figure of the oversexed sorcerer appears repeatedly in Caribbean literature. One example is the houngan in Chauvet's *Fonds des nègres*.

35. Gates, *The Signifying Monkey*, 27.

36. The denial of coevality has been well analyzed by Johannes Fabian in *Time and the Other: How Anthropology Makes Its Object* (New York: Columbia University Press, 1983).

37. As Schwarz-Bart points out about her work, lougan is a Wolof word meaning a plot of land. By using this Wolof term, she roots the family tree in the African continent—"Un nom donc ancré dans le continent d'origine"—while maintaining the importance of the family plot of land in the Caribbean. Simone Schwarz-Bart, "Sur les pas de Fanotte," *Textes et Documents* 2 (1979): 13–23. The family tree included at the beginning of *Pluie et vent* also points to both African and classical mythology: Télumée inherits the syncretism of the different worlds braided into the Caribbean imaginary, as exemplified by the mythological names of her great-grandparents, Minerve and Xango.

38. See Maryse Condé, "Pourquoi la négritude? Négritude ou révolution," in *Les Litteratures d'expression française: Négritude africaine, négritude caraïbe* (Paris: Editions de la Francité, 1973), 150–154.

39. Helmtrud Rumpf, "Rhizome versus racine: Deux concepts d'identité dans les Caraïbes francophones," in *Born Out of Resistance: On Caribbean Cultural Collectivity*, ed. Wim Hoogbergen (Utrecht: Centrum voor Caraibische Studien, 1995).

40. Although Manicom's *La Graine* does not center on a mythical past, there is only one instance where the homeland is presented as an exotic, idealized, and surreal place. The narrator, worn out by the everyday reality of the maternity ward where she works, dreams of going "home" to an Edenic island full of tropical flowers, where she sees herself as an infant returning to the mother's womb.

41. Rumpf, "Rhizome versus racine." I would like to acknowledge Ana Echevarría for sharing her views on madness as *marronage*.

Trans-Caribbean Identity and the Fictional World of Mayra Montero

MARGARITE FERNÁNDEZ OLMOS

The spaces that the nomad's imagination encompass exist
within a circumference of seasons, and national borders
have no meaning for him.

> —JAN CAREW, *Fulcrums of Change*

When the anthropologist arrives, the gods depart.

> —Haitian dictum

IN THE CARIBBEAN, a region characterized by migration and displacement, one's country of origin—and the place in which one chooses to resettle—can assume tremendous importance. The colonial condition, as well as constant political turmoil, have made Caribbean peoples more aware of differences than of similarities. Even among those who share a common language, as in the Hispanic Caribbean, the question of one's national loyalties may arise in any attempt by writers to reflect a larger transnational creative landscape.

One author whose works endeavor to expand trans-Caribbean consciousness is novelist Mayra Montero, who was born and raised in Havana but has lived in Puerto Rico for most of her adult life. Montero's works express a fascination with Afro-Caribbean spirituality and its potential as a unifying dimension of Caribbean cultural identity. Critical acclaim for her work, including her novel based on Haitian sugarcane workers in the Dominican Republic, has not precluded interviewers, however, from asking her "what a Cuban author who lives in Puerto Rico is doing writing about Haitians who emigrate to the Dominican Republic." According to Montero, the reply is contained within the question, "like a snake biting its own tail. In the center of the circle traced by the serpent there is an entire universe of symbols, certainties, and dearly cherished relics. . . . What I really wish to do is . . . demonstrate that despite the isolation and the lack of communication that clearly exist among the Caribbean peoples, there are certain defining characteristics, commonalities, and, above all, a sincere eagerness on the part of all artists to break through that isolation."[1]

The vacuum created by this polarization is being addressed by Montero and other artists whose search for common points of reference is, in part, an attempt to end the Caribbean writer's historical legacy as nomad and exile in his or her own land. These artists' Afro-Caribbean vision is an amplification of earlier movements at the beginning of the century; contemporary authors are going beyond a limited national vision, however, to explore a trans-Caribbean ethos.

THE COMPLEX and elusive nature of "Caribbeanness" defied essentialist definitions long before postmodernists declared such exercises futile and meaningless; respected writers and intellectuals nonetheless continue the attempt. Roberto González Echevarría, for example, in his search for particular features that might lead to a definition of a literature of the Hispanic Caribbean and give coherence to Hispanic Caribbean society, considers that a "most important characteristic is the conception of a syncretic social myth giving a sense of national and regional identity, a myth whose outward manifestation is popular music."[2] And Antonio Benítez-Rojo's postmodernist search for Caribbean cultural specificities becomes a rhythmic rereading of the region that is ultimately lured into singularizing Caribbean cultural features based fundamentally, albeit not exclusively, on African-based traditions:

> What [E. Duvergierd] Hauranne tried to represent with his pen, his compatriot [Frederic] Mialhe and the Spaniard [Victor Patricio de] Landaluze tried to communicate through painting and lithography, also in the past century. Their respective compositions *Dia de Reyes (La Habana)* and *Día de Reyes en La Habana* work to capture the rhythms of the drums, of the dances, of the songs, of the fantastic dress and colors that this annual holiday, where the slaves were freed for one day, set out upon Havana's streets in an enormous carnivalesque spectacle. It is precisely this rhythmic complexity, rooted in the forms of the ritual sacrifice and directed toward all of the senses, that gives pan-Caribbean cultures a way of being, a style that is repeated through time and space in all its differences and variants. This polyrhythm of planes and meters can be seen not just in music, dance, song, and the plastic arts, but also in the cuisine—the *ajiaco*—in architecture, in poetry, in the novel, in the theater, in bodily expression, in religious beliefs, in idiosyncracies, that is, in all

the texts that circulate high and low throughout the Caribbean region.[3]

Intellectuals at the beginning of the twentieth century grappled with this issue as well, with limited success. The intense search for a national identity in the Hispanic Caribbean can be traced to the period of the emergence of the *negrista*, or *afrocriollo*, movement in the 1930s and 1940s, described by Richard Jackson as the "Harlem Renaissance of Latin America" and one of the "first genuinely 'American' literary movements in this century in Latin America."[4] According to Jackson, *Afrocriollismo* was part of the general search for authenticity and return to "roots" that permeated Latin American culture at the time; the Afrocriollo movement was unique, however, in its lasting effect.

> There was fascination with the sights, movements, sounds, and rhythms of the black world, which white authors in Latin America tried to capture in song, ballet, prose, and poetry, but the *Afrocriollo* movement did not owe its existence to Cubism and other European *isms* of the time; nor was it an entirely artistic or literary movement. The *Afrocriollo* movement was a crisis-oriented phenomenon in which racial, social, and ethnic forces merged to produce a heightened awareness in Latin America of blacks and blackness. The result of this focus was a movement that had a lasting impact on Latin American literature. European primitivism was rampant, as was the fashion for African and Afro-American art, but the living reality of the black and the necesssity of coping with this pervading influence were the motivating forces behind the black's emergence as a literary theme and as a producer of literature. (21–22)

The scrutiny and reevaluation of local values in the Hispanic Caribbean was not focused exclusively on African-based local culture, however; studies such as Antonio Pedreira's *Insularismo* in Puerto Rico, among others, examined the issue of individual and national identity from a variety of perspectives, in many cases Eurocentric, fostering a tradition that has continued in subsequent generations of Cuban, Puerto Rican, and Dominican intellectuals.[5]

To the extent that their scrutiny has led to an inclusive vision, the results after six decades have been uneven. In Cuba the information regarding Cuban culture furnished by such intellectuals as Fernando Ortiz, Juan Marinello, and Jorge Mañach paved the way for what would become an expanded and inclusive vision of *cubanía*, or Cubanness. The 1959 Cuban Revolution made enormous strides in this regard with its impetus to delve into the historical origins of Cuban society; Miguel Barnet's *The Autobiography of a Runaway Slave* and Roberto Fernández Retamar's *Calibán and Other Essays* are but two examples of an alternative vision of official history that questions the limited, Hispanicized interpretations of cubanía and of Caribbean culture in general.[6] Not only have the contributions of Afro-Cuban culture been recognized, but the revolution has also enthusiastically promoted black culture and literature in general, a policy that received official sanction in statements such as Fidel Castro's famous declaration during the fifteenth anniversary celebration of the Bay of Pigs invasion, in which he described Cubans as an "Afro-Latino peoples." The vitality and persistence of Santería worship in Cuba today after more than three decades of socialist revolution is but one example of the durability and pervasive influence of African-based culture in Cuban society.

In Puerto Rico and the Dominican Republic a similar systematic effort has not been forthcoming. Despite sporadic individual efforts, a Hispanicist identity still predominates, as exemplified by such incidents as the 1988 outcry in Puerto Rico against an attempt by a local politician to name the Centro de Bellas Artes after the black Puerto Rican promoter of *plena* and *bomba* music, Rafael Cortijo. Juan Flores, whose earlier award-winning essay exposed the racialist and Eurocentric bias in Pedreira's *Insularismo*,[7] notes that in 1992 the issue of race and culture was still unresolved in discussions of the island's national identity.

> But the hubbub over the appropriate legacy of Rafael Cortijo signals the continuing relevance of *Insularismo* in especially sharp relief, and at a time when the very interrogation of culture and identity, the "master narrative" of any collective cultural history, has come under grave suspicion. . . . For the long introspective quest leads not so much to some hidden "essence" of our identity, some primordial "¿qué somos?", but to a sharper understanding of the dynamic within Puerto Rican culture and its place among the cultures with which it most directly interacts. If it is to be more than a "mere rhetorical adscription," the recognition of blackness necessarily points beyond the shores of the island to the rest of the Caribbean and Latin America and to the cultural dynamic in the United States. In this respect, the Eurocentric, elitist view, in the manner of Pedreira, constituted the very intellectual insularity that his book called upon his compatriots to overcome. Discovering and valorizing African "roots" has comprised a second stage, after the first one marked off by *Insularismo*, in the theoretical definition of Puerto Rican culture, and that stage has only come to full articulation in the past decade. Yes, there is a national culture, as Pedreira did affirm, after all, with all his gloomy reluctance, but it is grounded on the popular, African-based traditions of that culture.[8]

Cultural fusions and fissions are also crucial issues in the Dominican Republic, where cultural distinction has been a key element in the country's political and cultural separation from its neighbor to the west in Hispaniola. The roots of the problematical relationship between the Dominican Republic and Haiti date at least from the period of Haitian domination of Santo Domingo, from 1822 to 1844, when Dominican national identity crystalized as an antithesis to all that could be identified as Haitian. But the racialist campaign against African-based culture continues to be waged a century and a half after the Dominican Republic's successful struggle for independence from its island counterpart.

In *Race and Colour in Caribbean Literature* G. R. Coulthard attributes the rejection of the Afro-Antillean literary movement in the Dominican Republic in the 1930s and 1940s to the expressed attitudes of the Rafael Trujillo regime, which held in 1954 that "the Negro in the Dominican Republic . . . has been absorbed completely, has given up any African atavism and has adjusted to the system of Dominican Culture which has deep Spanish roots."[9] This official position, which had the force of law under the dictatorship, was upheld by the regime's ideologues, including the long-time president of the country, Joaquín Balaguer. The elevated position given to Hispanicism in the Dominican cultural hierarchy is apparent in such works as Balaguer's 1947 study, *La realidad dominicana*, in which he expounds on Dominican attachment to Hispanic culture and what he perceives as a Haitian threat to Dominican economic, racial, and national integrity, a threat that still haunts the political landscape, as witnessed by the revived anti-Haitian sentiments expressed by Balaguer supporters during the 1994 presidential campaign.[10] The alleged Haitian origins of one of Balaguer's main opponents, José Francisco Peña Gómez, was emphasized in negative and openly racist attacks in the months preceding the elections, with particular stress placed on claims of Peña Gómez's adherence to Vodou religious practices. Any discussion of these border cultures as spaces in which to contest cultural identities must take into account not only the long history of stormy relations between the two countries but also the actual massacre of twelve to twenty-five thousand Haitian nationals ordered by Trujillo in 1937, precisely on the northern frontier that separates the two countries.

The continued denial of the role of African-based traditions and popular experience in the definition of national culture, as well as the exclusion of the significance of ethnic and gender minorities, confers an added importance and urgency to the role of artists such as Montero, the language and substance of whose works correspond to Edward Kamau Brathwaite's description of a "literature of African experience" in the Caribbean.[11] Among Brathwaite's categories are "Rhetorical Africa," a static, romantic writing that reflects

African-based culture in marks or signals but is generally based on ignorance or naivete; a "Literature of African Survival," a more conscious approach that incorporates African cultural survivals in Caribbean society, particularly the folk tradition, but offers little insight or interpretation; and the "Literature of African Expression," defined by a shift from rhetoric to involvement that "has its roots in the folk . . . [attempting] to adapt or transform folk material into literary experiment" (81). For Brathwaite, an author must possess a true understanding of the folk tradition in order to be able to "move fearlessly into this enigmatic alternative world" (90).

Montero is among the new generation of Caribbean authors who no longer simply reclaim an African heritage from the past but recognize "the heterogeneity that is the distinguishing feature of Caribbean life and consciousness, a disposition that, far from being disabling, may well constitute a special source of strength, implying as it does the potential for new beginnings."[12] The notion that reclaiming an African heritage might encompass a special source of strength coincides with Montero's comments on her childhood experience of Afro-Caribbean religion in Cuba, which determined her fascination with Vodou and affected the direction of her literary creativity.

> I was born in Havana and raised in that City of Columns, as Alejo Carpentier so rightly named it. But as far back as I can remember, since my childhood, since forever, I yearned for the balconies of an old mansion in Port-au-Prince; the hubbub of shouts, cries and barking in the markets of Cap Haïtien; the interminable ceremonies in Damballah's honor that were celebrated on the plantations of Artibonite, and the Vodou drum beats which greeted Baron Samedi, undisputed lord of the cemeteries.
>
> Madame Loulou, the old woman who impacted my childhood, came into the world in France but was taken to Haiti when she was only several months old. There she grew, there she knew freedom and sorrows; she discovered the secrets of the sacred wild—she would lower her voice when referring to the Mont des Enfant Perdus—and slept beneath the tree of death. . . .
>
> It was this unforgettable old woman who placed the first ceremonial necklaces on me, and it was she, in the final analysis, who taught me that Haiti was the land of adventure, an adventure unseen by tourist eyes nor by those of hurried anthropologists—an adventure prepared in secret, for the use and abuse of a chosen few, for their glory and sometimes as well for their ruin. . . .
>
> What I have wished to emphasize is the fact of having been born in Cuba, the fact of growing up there, gave me a broad and I suppose unbiased vision of my own Caribbean identity. . . . All of that, combined with the reality of emigration, which took me to live in a

country as complex as Puerto Rico, created in me an unorthodox concept of Antillean reality, something which is present in all three of my published novels.[13]

In the same lecture Montero remarks on the pervasiveness of Cuban Santería in her upbringing in Havana, where, despite a Catholic education in parochial schools run by Spanish nuns, she and her classmates would search for and easily encounter examples of African religious culture, which she describes as "las más variadas, enriquecedoras y alucinantes muestras de religiosidad popular" (the most varied, enriching, and hallucinating examples of popular religiosity).

Montero's first novel, *La trenza de la hermosa luna* (The braid of the beautiful moon), reflects her fascination with Haitian culture as it interacts with the waning regime of Jean Claude Duvalier, with an emphasis on the importance of Vodou as a political force.[14] Montero's 1991 novel, *La última noche que pasé contigo* (The last night I spent with you), also takes place in the Antilles, following the sexual romps of a middle-aged couple on a Caribbean cruise;[15] it has led some critics to describe Montero as a "transnational figure defining a larger postmodern Caribbean."[16] Following this trend are her novels *Del rojo de su sombra* (The red glare of his shadow)[17] and *Tú, la oscuridad* (You, darkness),[18] both of which also revolve around Haitian themes: *Del rojo de su sombra* explores the harsh, mysterious world of Haitian emigrants in the Dominican Republic, and *Tú, la oscuridad* follows the adventures of a North American herpetologist in his quest for a rare frog species in the Haitian wilderness.

Of all her novels *Del rojo de su sombra* most clearly affirms Montero's transnational and trans-Caribbean reputation. Its subject is *Gagá*, a socioreligious practice followed by Haitians and their descendants in the sugarcane regions of the Dominican Republic. Related to what Dominican anthropologists such as Carlos Deive[19] generally refer to as "Dominican Vodou"—a parallel religious tradition dating from the eighteenth century and resulting from the flight of Haitian slaves to the eastern portion of the island under Spanish control— Gagá is a specific religious society with roots in *rará*, the Haitian traveling groups who dance, play music, and display their rituals and traditions in neighboring villages during the Christian Holy Week before Easter Sunday. Brought to the Dominican Republic by emigrating Haitian sugarcane workers, these *rará* rites were later transformed and reinterpreted by Dominican folk practice and beliefs. Gagá is therefore an interesting example of nontraditional Caribbean syncretism: instead of a hybridity between the European and the colonized, Gagá exemplifies a secondary type of syncretism, one between (ex)colonized peoples.

Given the historical relationship between the Dominican Republic and Haiti, it is not surprising that little interest has been shown by Dominican researchers and intellectuals in the subject; caught within its attachment to Hispanic tradition and its rejection of Haitian culture, Dominican society has been unable to appreciate this significant sector of its own culture. Montero's novel is dedicated to three individuals who have made Gagá the focus of their research: Puerto Rican archeologist José Francisco Alegría-Pons and Dominican folklorist, Soraya Aracena, who have lived with Gagá practitioners, among the poorest and most exploited of Dominican laborers, and documented their rites;[20] and North American June Rosenberg, whose 1979 book on the subject was the first study of its kind.[21]

According to Alegría, Gagá is a cult dedicated predominantly to the powerful deities or *loas* of the Vodou pantheon known as the *Petró*. With ceremonies similar to those of Vodou, Gagá initiation and devotional rituals are jealously guarded by the family of members who form an intimate society; in Gagá one also discovers the magic stones, seeds, sacred shells, and other objects required to honor and call forth the "bitter and violent" deities of the Petró cult, referred to by Dominican believers as *seres*, or beings (33). Considering Gagá a Dominican variant of Vodou, Alegría notes the particular devotion of Gagá to the loas referred to as the *guedé*, the spirits of the underworld and death as well as of eroticism, sensuality, and fertility. Rosenberg, however, has argued that "this syncretic complex of Gagá is, in our estimation, specifically Dominican, perhaps even based on Dominican carnival elements from the past century. It is, moreover, a structural reorganization of the Vodou religion in its Dominican and Haitian manifestations" (17).

Among Alegría's observations of a Gagá community in the area of San Pedro de Macorís during the late 1980s are the following: (1) Gagá is not a product by and for Haitians exclusively. (2) Gagá is an ongoing "evolutionary process," a Dominican-Haitian syncretism that has created and re-created a new formula (or cultural pattern) that includes Dominicans and Haitians equally in a unique syncretic variant. (3) The dynamic, transformative pattern created by this Dominican-Haitian syncretism extends to a wide range of sociocultural factors: religious (beliefs, ideas, and practices); social (family and group organization); linguistic (the combination of Creole and Dominican Spanish); culinary (the preparation of sacred foods); economic (the elaboration of the paraphernalia associated with rituals) (61-62).

The main Gagá festivity occurs during the Christian Holy Week. On the evening of Holy Thursday the ritual known as the *levantamiento de la silla,* or the lifting of the chair, where members vow fidelity for a period of either five or seven years, is celebrated. Then the gathered are baptized, as are the musical instruments that will be used during the journey. At dawn on Good Friday the members leave their living quarters, or *bateyes*, to visit other towns, taking their music and their dances.

The organizational structure of the Gagá follows that of the support *sociétés*[22] surrounding the *humfo*, or religious community in Haiti, modeled in turn on the Haitian governing hierarchy. The Gagá is likewise modeled closely on the Dominican governing hierarchy, with a *dueño*, or maximum leader, followed by a president, head of the armed forces, ministers, colonel and lieutenant colonel, majors, queens, secretary, treasurer, a police force, musicians, and a female chorus. Rosenberg has observed that the structure of the group reflects that of the general society in which they live, with the diverse categories an indication of prestige and authority. "They offer an identity which is far removed from the possibilities of these individuals in society in general. . . . The social structure of the group reflects the values of the larger society" (203). During their wanderings, the Gagá collect money to be distributed among the group on the evening of Easter Sunday, when they return to their homes. Despite the carnival-like atmosphere of the festivities, the basis of the Gagá ritual is profoundly religious; isolated from Hispanicized Dominican society, the Gagás have created their own social structures and their own means of dealing with their world.

This hybrid religious society, with its peculiar social structures, forms the core of Montero's *Del rojo de su sombre*. The genesis of the novel is revealed in the "Author's Preface," translated here in its entirety:

> Each year, on the island of Hispaniola, Haitians by the tens of thousands cross the frontier from Haiti to cut sugarcane in the Dominican Republic. These Haitians or "Congos" as they are called on the other side of the frontier, drag along their wives and children, and all await, without exception, a life of privation and untold misery, in working conditions that duplicate those of the cruelest slave regimes.
>
> In these circumstances, which are usually prolonged until their final days, they have no recourse but to bind themselves to their religious beliefs, to the images of their gods, also called "mysteries" or "loas," which they bring with them from Haiti. It is then that they group themselves into "Societés" or societies, and little by little organize the so-called Gagá: a cult, a fiesta, a hermetic and laborious brotherhood that few manage to penetrate. A Vodou priest of much prestige becomes the "dueño" of the Gagá and spiritual director of the flock of which his "majors," the men of higher rank, and the "queens," the women with most mettle, are the more prominent. Their main festivity, during Holy Week, is based on a dazzling journey or pilgrimage throughout the countryside surrounding the cane fields. This journey, full of ritualized stopping points, is prolonged for three days,

until Resurrection Sunday. Sometimes the Gagá wanders, covering great distances of the country, and frequently on its way it will meet up with another Gagá. The encounter can be quite cordial, or on the contrary extremely bloody, depending on the unpredictable mood of the "gods."

This novel narrates true events which took place several years ago in an area of La Romana. It is the story of love, of hate and of death between a "hungan" or Vodou priest and a well-known and respected "mambo" or priestess in the region. The names and some of the places have been altered to protect informants. Behind a case which the Dominican police dismissed as a simple "crime of passion," beats the spell of a war that has yet to be settled. (9–10)

The novel that follows (complete with a glossary of Vodou and Gagá terms) is about the exceptional Zulé, a Gagá *dueña*, or priestess/leader, identified in the tale with the multiple variations or manifestations of the deity Erzulie-Fréda, and her passionate, fateful struggle with her adversary-lover, the infamous and terrible Similá Bolosse, an ex-Tonton Macoute and *bokor*—that is, a *houngan*, or priest, who works "con las dos manos" (with the forces both of good and of evil)—who is compared in the novel to the loa Toro Belecou.

Zulé is the captivating daughter of a houngan born in Haiti; she flees with her father, Papá Luc, after a terrible curse destroys her mother and young brothers. As a young girl her spiritual talents emerge during a Gagá ceremony, after which her father is forced to hand her over to a powerful *dueño* who becomes her mentor, protector, and lover, and whose religious community she will eventually inherit. Zulé develops into a young woman among the Haitian and Dominican laborers in the cane fields, their harsh and often violent existence abated only by their religious beliefs and strong sense of community.

The novel traces Zule's spiritual evolution, the intuitive powers that lead her to forbidden areas of the psyche and eventually to the leadership of her own Gagá, a responsibility that can include conducting religious ceremonies, counseling members of the community, and performing such delicate and dangerous tasks as rescuing the zombie wife of a Gagá member from the "Lake of Danger," a human "herd" in which she is obliged to work for others. Montero's richly textured novel does not ignore the physical hardships of life in the bateyes nor the abuse and "benign neglect" of the Dominican authorities, but those difficulties are counterbalanced by the passion and strength derived from the characters' spiritual beliefs.

Written in the mysterious language of the mystical world of its characters, the novel flows back and forth between the physical world and the spiritual sphere of the loas or seres, and at times these worlds are indistinguishable. The action builds gradually to the irrevocable confrontation between Zulé and

Similá Bolosse, who, working with his Tonton Macoute allies in Haiti, has orders to infiltrate the Dominican labor camps and assure a safe route throughout the countryside and the coastline for the export of contraband. Zulé, as dueña, must lead the fight to defend her Gagá's autonomy; she must also struggle against her sexual attraction to her powerful rival.

> "Do you want an alliance or do you still want to make war?"
>
> The daughter of Papá Luc, with a razor switch held high and wooly hair flying loose, looks more than ever like Maîtresse Erzulie Fréda, the hot whore with a deep-seated heart, lover of perfumes and white-colored foods, of all that is made of wheat and smells of milk. It is told by the saints that Maîtresse Fréda was bent on savoring Toro Belecou's cum. But Toro Belecou began to humiliate her, abusing her at night, obliging her to drink of the white urine that flowed from black serpents back in those days.
>
> "I don't need pistols," Similá insists. "If you want war, you'll get a machete."
>
> Erzulie Fréda decided to avenge herself. She walked in the night and searched in the wilderness for the most savage of all the loas, one they call Belie Balcan; she offered him a goat, which is what he likes best, and begged him to trample down Toro Belecou. Belie Balcan accepted the offering, assuring her that in exchange he would bring back the bull's blood. But the truth is he never fulfilled his promise.
>
> "You, cheating *dueña*, oh yes, you like to fire bullets, don't you. You went over to Galeana Troncoso, you asked for her men and left the brute Honoré in their place. . . . Does Honoré Babiole know that I plucked out his brother Truman's eyes?"
>
> Zulé begins to walk towards the bokor, as meekly as if she had just been offered a golden drink, a menthol cigarette, an enormous jet-black prick, all the things that are most pleasing to Maîtresse Fréda.
>
> "You are better off with an alliance, *dueña* Zulé. We'll live together in the Colonia Engracia or in the camps of the Colonia Tumba. And in the off-season we'll go to the Lake of Danger to watch over the herd. What's your answer, *dueña*?" (171)

The choice of a female spiritual leader, a *mambo*, is a significant one. The ethnologists Maya Deren and Alfred Métraux both consider the mambo to be equal in rank to her male counterpart, thereby conferring on women a rank in the religious hierarchy that is denied them in the larger society; the fact that women and men are peers in the practice of Vodou has led Joan Dayan to describe the religion as a "locus of feminine strength."[23] As a mambo Zulé commands an authority in spiritual and earthly matters that includes not only the role of spiritual and physical healer but also negotiator with the spiritual world, with other Gagá leaders, and with the Dominican authorities. Like the Vodou houngan, a mambo must perform rituals that are crucial in preserving the collective's cultural traditions.

Montero's preface mentions "a war that has yet to be settled." But which war is she referring to? The novel offers several possibilities. There is, of course, the struggle of an oppressed people to keep their traditions alive, to invent and reinvent themselves, the heroic search for a mythical oasis that will counteract the spirit-crushing forces of poverty and racial discrimination. Miguel Barnet's observations on the African contribution to Cuban culture apply equally here. "The culture that the African constructed in Cuba was an entirely defensive one. . . . The culture of the African is revolutionary by nature; it is a method of inward liberation and a way of seeking security. Prayer, revelation, spells, dance rituals, all are directed toward finding salvation."[24]

There is also the spiritual struggle between good and evil, life and death; this struggle is an element of most religious rituals, and the Gagá is no exception. Gagá ceremonies culminate on Easter Sunday, with resurrection being the mainstay of their beliefs. The author has remarked that the novel is, above all, "a reflection on passion, a passion on two levels and surrounded by a special mysticism (observe the scene in which Zulé withdraws, like Jesus Christ, to meditate, and returns to find all her 'majors' asleep as in the biblical passage).[25] The erotic and passionate nature of the mystical Zulé, therefore, should not mislead us; George Bataille's work exposes the relationship between sacrifice, death, and eroticism, and it is well to recall that the theme of resurrection is not only one of the dominant components in syncretized Gagá but also of *Ghedé*, the Vodoú Petró loa strongly identified with the Gagá belief system and a figure repeatedly invoked throughout the novel. Zora Neale Hurston has remarked that Ghedé is a loa identified in Haiti with the common people; he belongs to the peasants and has the distinction of being the one loa who is entirely Haitian, with no European or African antecedents.[26] Deren reminds us that Ghedé is lord of that eroticism beyond good and evil as well as the keeper of the cemetery, uniting death and the erotic in one paradoxical figure.

> Ghedé is the dark figure which attends the meeting of the quick and the dead. This is the loa who, repository of all the knowledges of the dead, is wise beyond all the others. And if the souls of the dead enter the depths by the passage of which Ghedé is guardian, the loa and the life forces emerge from that same depth by the same road. Hence he is Lord of Life as well as of Death. His dance is the dance of copulation; in the chamber dedicated to his worship, the sculptured phallus may lie side by side with the three grave-diggers' tools. He is the protector of children and the greatest of the divine healers. He is the final appeal against death. He is the cosmic corpse which informs man of

life. The cross is his symbol, for he is the axis both of the physical cycle of generation and the metaphysical cycle of resurrection. He is the beginning and the end.[27]

By invoking such figures the novel lends itself to a more literal interpretation of passion and redemption outside of the Christian tradition. Throughout the novel the main characters are referred to interchangeably by their earthly names and as their loa spiritual counterparts. The narrator identifies Zulé's adversary and lover Similá with the deity or loa Toro Belecou, also known in Vodou as Taureau-trois-graines, or Bull with Three Testicles, a bizarre characteristic that the virile Similá character and the taurine loa share. And Zulé is combined in the novel with the earthly representation of the Vodou loa Erzulie-Fréda, both virgin and goddess of love, a spirit created on Haitian soil whose varying and often paradoxical emanations correspond in the novel to the actions and contradictions of its protagonist. At once promiscuous, passionate in love, and attracted to both sexes like Erzulie-Fréda, militant and vengeful like Ezulie-gé-rouge, and victimized like the long-suffering Erzulie-Danton, Zulé confounds and reinvents herself throughout the novel, as does her romanticized and textualized loa counterpart who, according to Dayan, "whether the pale and elegant Erzulie-Fréda or the cold-hearted, savage Erzulie-gé-rouge, dramatizes a specific historiography of women's experience in Haiti and throughout the Caribbean" (6). Zulé is a fitting counterpart to her virile lover and enemy Similá; another of the loa Maîtresse Erzulie's many manifestations is Erzulie-Toro (Erzulie the Bull).

Following Zulé and Similá's passionate encounter, Similá's identification with Toro Belecou is accentuated by a physical mask created by a snowy downfall of crushed tree pods. On the eve of Similá's departure the fuzzy pods had begun to fall, "dispersing a multitude of white buds" and causing havoc in the cane fields.

> Similá Bolosse, still breathless from the romps of their farewell, wanted to go out and delight in the landscape of whirling cotton in which most everyone was spinning. When he returned he heard Zulé burst into laughter, the first and the last he would hear in those ten days. She searched for a piece of mirror for him to glance at himself: the wandering fuzz had stuck to his face which was now the exact face of the most feared and rancorous loa of the Pantheon: it was the face of Toro Belecou. He observed himself solemnly and enraptured, made more vain by the invincible mask it had made of him. Then he half-closed his eyes, began to sway, and hum a tune as powerful and ethereal as the deluge falling on the fields.
>
> M'tòro m'beglé,
> nâ savân mwê . . .

Tòro mwê tòro, sa ki mâdé pu mwê,
ou a di o
mwê mem kriminel.

[I am a bull,
I bellow in my savannah . . .
A bull, I am a bull,
he who asks for me
tell him I am a criminal.]

Zulé offered him denim pants and Dominican sandals, and he had woven for himself a shoulder sack of braided palm leaves. He began to walk without uttering a word and without removing the snowy substance from his face, and the *dueña* followed to the exit of the compound. There they both stopped and she fell to the ground to lick his feet; to humbly embrace his knees; to thrust her hungry mouth against his wily cock where, from their triplet origins, the three legendary milky streams converged. . . . Then she watched him depart, herself covered by the wind-swept fur, unable even to pronounce his name, voiceless to reclaim him, a tearful whore like Maîtresse Fréda, submissive and grand like the Virgin Erzulie. (95–96)

The loa Erzulie has been described by Deren as "the dream impaled eternally upon the cosmic cross-roads where the world of men and the world of divinity meet, and it is through her pierced heart that 'man ascends and the gods descend'" (145). Appropriately, Montero's novel ends with the dream— Zulé-Erzulie—literally impaled by Carrefour (Dominicanized as Carfú in the novel), the Lord of the Crossroads, in the body of his *serviteur* and earthly counterpart Jérémie Candé, Zulé's ex-lover, whose surprising aggression against Zulé can be described as either jealous fit or uncontrolled spiritual possession. As a result, in this novel— in a dramatic mythical turnabout and reversal of the ultimate "master narrative" of redemption—the sacrificial victim whose death consolidates the warring factions and leads to collective salvation is a black woman of Haitian origin through whose love and passion "man ascends and the gods descend."

In *Del rojo de su sombra* Montero organically interconnects such postmodern tools as feminism, ethnography, mysticism, and an analysis of otherness with localized circumstances to enhance our understanding of Afro-Caribbean spirituality and culture. Her work reflects what Julio Ortega has observed of other Latin American novels that also have "their roots in the common scene of International Modernism, while, at the same time, confronting it with its own needs, problematizing it, and parodying it. They likewise go beyond existing definitions and frameworks by giving their postmodernity an even more critical accentuation, voicing yet new aesthetic needs and social revindications."[28] The works of authors such as Montero, with their recourse to myth, are an important contribution to a Caribbean ethos based on the creation of new myths, the rearticulation of old ones, and a renewed sense of self–re-creation.

Notes

1. Mayra Montero, lecture given in Italy on 16 February 1994. All translations, unless otherwise indicated, are my own.
2. Roberto González Echevarría, "Literature of the Hispanic Caribbean," *Latin American Literary Review* 16 (1980), 17.
3. Antonio Benítez-Rojo, *The Repeating Island: The Caribbean and the Postmodern Perspective*, trans. James Maraniss (Durham, N.C.: Duke University Press, 1992), 79–80.
4. Richard L. Jackson, *Black Literature and Humanism in Latin America* (Athens: University of Georgia Press, 1988), 20, 31.
5. Antonio S. Pedreira, *Insularismo* (1934; San Juan: Edil, 1968).
6. Miguel Barnet, *The Autobiography of a Runaway Slave*, 1966, trans. Jocasta Innes (London: Macmillan Caribbean, 1993); Roberto Fernández Retamar, *Calibán and Other Essays*, 1972, trans. Edward Baker (Minneapolis: University of Minnesota Press, 1989).
7. Juan Flores, *Insularismo e ideología burguesa en Antonio Pedreira* (Havana: Ediciones Casa de las Américas, 1979).
8. Juan Flores, "Cortijo's Revenge," in *On the Edge: The Crisis of Contemporary Latin American Culture*, ed. George Yúdice, Jean Franco, and Juan Flores (Minneapolis: University of Minnesota Press, 1992), 188, 193.
9. Quoted in G. R. Coulthard, *Race and Colour in Caribbean Literature* London: Oxford University Press, 1962), 38.
10. Joaquín Balaguer, *La realidad dominicana* (Buenos Aires: Imprenta Ferrari Hermanos, 1947).
11. Edward Kamau Brathwaite, "The African Presence in Caribbean Literature," *Daedalus* 103, no. 2:2 (spring 1974), 81.
12. Abiola Irele, "Editorial," *Research in African Literatures* 25, no. 2 (summer 1994), 2.
13. Mayra Montero, lecture on 16 February 1994.
14. Mayra Montero, *La trenza de la hermosa luna* (Barcelona: Editorial Anagrama, 1987).
15. Mayra Montero, *La última noche que pasé contigo* (Barcelona: Tusquets Editores, 1991).
16. María Acosta-Cruz, "Remaking Culture: Postmodernism in Hispanic Caribbean Fiction," unpublished manuscript.
17. Mayra Montero, *Del rojo de su sombra* (Barcelona: Tusquets Editores, 1992).
18. Mayra Montero, *Tú, la oscuridad* (Barcelona: Tusquets Editores, 1995).
19. Carlos Esteban Deive, *Vodú y magia en Santo Domingo* (Santo Domingo: Museo del Hombre Dominicano, 1975).
20. José Francisco Alegría-Pons, "Aspectos de la religiosidad popular en Puerto Rico," in *Gagá y vudú en la República Dominicana* (Puerto Rico and Santo Domingo: Ediciones el Chango Prieto, 1993).
21. June Rosenberg, *El gagá: Religión y sociedad de un culto dominicano* (Santo Domingo: Editora de la UASD, 1979).
22. "This term refers to all people connected with a specific hounfor and defines them as a communal entity. While the hounfor itself is referred to in the name of the

houngan, it is understood as being under the sponsorship of the *société*, which has a separate name. The *société* may even include members who live in town and attend only the most important ceremonies, but upon whose assistance the priest can rely should he need to raise money for an expensive ceremony, to arrange transportation, to be advised on building, etc. As the collective unit at the basis of the religious structure, the *société* is represented by two heavily embroidered ceremonial flags. Carried by two flag bearers, these banners are used to salute the loa and as a mark of respect to any distinguished guest at ceremonies. When one arrives at a ceremony, the accepted greeting is '*Bonjour, la société.*'" Maya Deren, *Divine Horsemen: The Living Gods of Haiti* (1953; reprint, Kingston, N.Y.: McPherson, 1970), 154.

In *The Serpent and the Rainbow* (New York: Warner Books, 1985), Wade Davis describes his experiences with the *Bizango*, secret *sociétés* described as a type of underground government, "the very conscience of the peasantry, a quasi-political arm of the vodoun society charged above all with the protection of the community. Like the secret societies of West Africa, those of Haiti seemed to [Michel] Laguerre to be the single most important arbiter of culture" (212). And Benítez-Rojo mentions the Holy Week processions, a "type of inverted carnival," of the *bande rara* made up of emigrant Haitian sugarcane workers in the eastern provinces of Cuba who were members of the local Bizango sects, "issuing warnings and threats of punishment to anyone who flouts the life pattern expected of him by the community," Benítez-Rojo, *The Repeating Island*, 166.

23. Joan Dayan, "Erzulie: A Women's History of Haiti," *Research in African Literatures* 2 (summer 1994), 6.

24. Miguel Barnet, "The Culture That Sugar Created," *Latin American Literary Review* 16 (spring-summer 1980), 42.

25. Mayra Montero via personal correspondence.

26. Zora Neale Hurston, *Tell My Horse: Voodoo and Life in Haiti and Jamaica* (1938; reprint, New York: Harper & Row, 1990), 219.

27. Deren, *Divine Horsemen*, 37–38.

28. Julio Ortega, "Postmodernism in Latin America," in *Postmodern Fiction in Europe and the Americas*, ed. Theo D'haen and Hans Bertens (Amsterdam: Rodopi, 1988), 206.

Glossary

aché or *ashe* or *asé, àse, asè, ase*—The "word" or "power" that created the universe in Santería, originating from the supreme god, Olodumare.

Aggayú Solá—In Santería, Changó's father, master of the gift of strength, of the vast forests and their most powerful plants.

agwán—In Santería, a ceremony in which food is offered to Babalú Ayé.

ahijados—"Godchildren," or protégés, in the practice of Santería.

aleyos—semi-initiates in the practice of Santería.

ange—See *loa*.

ason—A sacred beaded gourd rattle belonging to Voudou priests and priestesses and used in Rada ceremonies.

babalao or *babalocha* (male) and *iyalocha* (female)—A priest (priestess) who occupies a central place in the hierarchy of Santería, guides the initiate's development, and is in charge of specific liturgies, among them divination.

Babalú Ayé—One of the divinities whose worship has taken deepest root in Cuba; the god of illness; miraculous yet severe and implacable toward those who do not obey him or forget to fulfill their promises.

bagi—In Vodou, the sanctuary room containing the altar to the loa, an elaborately furnished habitation, where the loa can find on display its special things; not only are these pieces of property tokens of devotion, preserved by the houngan, but they make up the lineaments and capture the idiosyncrasies of the loa.

bain démarré—In the French Caribbean, a special bath given to wash away the effects of the evil eye and bad luck. There are also *bains de la chance*, or good-luck baths, which can be taken in the ocean or at home with sea, river, or rain water and various herbs.

balé—Heads of the great families in Santería; they generally delegate the responsibility for worshipping the family oricha to a male or female *aláàse*, guardian of the power of the god, who cares for it with the assistance of the *elégùn*, who is possessed by the oricha under certain circumstances.

batá drums—Used for sacred ceremonies, initiations, or the birthday of a loa. In Santería there are three: the *iyá*, or mother, which is the largest; the *itótele*, or medium drum; and the *okónkolo*, the smallest and most sonorous. These drums are offered food because they bear within them a spirit or semigod who possesses a magic secret, *añá*, which the drums' players and builders refuse to reveal.

bête a man ibé—In Guadeloupe, a sorceress who wanders at night with one human foot and one horse or donkey hoof, shrieking and dragging a long iron chain around her waist.

Bizango—One of the most important of the secret societies of Vodou, an important arbiter of social life among the peasantry; protects community resources, particularly land, by setting power boundaries within the village and inflicting punishment on those who violate its codes.

bocor or *bokor* or *boco*—A houngan who can use his supernatural powers for evil.

brûler zin—Initiation ceremony of the "boiling pots," during which the initiate who knows how to "tie fire" is elevated to the status of *kanzo*.

camino de Orula—In Santería, the way of knowledge and enlightenment.

camino de santo—In Santería, the way of the spirit or orichas.

caminos—See *patakí*.

cave-mystère—House of the loa, containing one or more altars to the gods. Each god has his or her own altar, which contains a mélange of objects, flowers, plates of food and drink, *cruches* or *govis*, the earthenware jars or bottles belonging to the spirits of the dead, and *pots-de-tête*, which contain the hairs or nail parings of the initiates to keep them safe.

Changó or *Shango*—A virile hero and warrior, one of the most venerated of the tutelary gods of Cuban Santería; a womanizer and drinker, quarrelsome, courageous, and daring; the god of music, master of the sacred batá drums, of thunder and lightning.

cheval or *horse*—Person "mounted" or possessed by an oricha or loa.

coco macaco—See *mono*.

crise de loa—That moment when a god inhabits the head of his or her servitor, articulating the reciprocal abiding of human and god.

day of the drum—Central ceremony in Santería, the day in which the person who has received a santo offers himself to the batá drum, owned by Changó, and dances before it in recognition of its significance within the cult.

derecho—A small offering of money made by an initiate of Santería to Eshu, the trickster, who must be propitiated so that the message of divination meets with no obstacle or distortion.

Déssounin (*dégradation* in the north of Haiti)—The major death ceremony in Haitian Vodou.

dilloggún—One of the three systems of divination in Santería; utilizes cowry shells.

djab (*djablesse* if a woman)—Devil spirit who seduces and tricks men.

drapo Vodou—Richly sequined and beaded banners unfurled and danced about during ceremonies to signal the spirits represented by the vèvè (ritual designs) or by the images of corresponding Catholic saints sewn on them; their reflective brilliance is said to attract the spirits into the human gathering.

dueña—A Gagá priestess/leader.

ebbó—Ceremony of offering or sacrifice; in Ifá divination, one such offering is presented to the shrine of Eshu to acknowledge and placate the trickster god and to bribe him not to sabotage the sacrifice.

elégùn—The human being chosen by the oricha, the one who has the privilege of being "mounted" (gùn) by him; the elégùn becomes the vehicle that allows the oricha to return to the earth to greet and receive the marks of respect from the descendants who invoked him.

Eshu Elegguá or *Elebwa, Esu-Elegbara, Legba, Eshu-Elegbara*—In Santería, a double deity who has the strength of character to witness "pure" knowledge, ìwà (iwa), as well as the social power to express "applied" reason, asè (ashe); ruler of the roads in worship, he opens or closes paths, indicates the crossroads, and is master, in some sense, of the future, the hereafter.

Gagá—A socioreligious practice followed by Haitians and their descendants in the sugarcane regions of the Dominican Republic; it has roots in *rará*, Haitian traveling groups who dance, play music, and display their rituals and traditions in neighboring villages during the Christian Holy Week before Easter Sunday.

gros bon ange or *ombre-cadavre*—One of the three parts of individual identity in Haitian Vodou, the double of the material body—something like *spiritus* but understood as the shadow cast by the body on the mind.

Guédé—The spirits of the underworld and death as well as of eroticism, sensuality, and fertility.

güije—See *mono*.

hounfort or *ounfò*—The temple, surroundings, and ceremonial altar of Haitian Vodou; includes a central dwelling of one or more rooms, circumscribed by the *peristyle* (or *tonnelle*), in the middle of which is the *poteau-mitan* (*poto-mitan*), or center post, that images the traffic between heaven and earth.

houngan or *gangan* or *oungan*—In Vodou, a religious leader who initiates new hounsi and facilitates the community's contact with the deities and ancestral spirits.

hounsi or *spirit wives*—The Vodou servitors, most often women, who have been initiated into the mysteries and have passed the trial by fire (the brûler zin); they are born anew as *hounsi kanzo*, as opposed to *hounsi bossale* (from the Spanish *bozal*, wild or untamed).

Ibbeyi—The mischievous twins, protectors of children in Santería.

Ifá—See *Orula*.

ikin nuts—Half-palm nuts handled by the babalao during the divination ritual.

Ilé oricha—Abode of the orichas in Santería, with three special and distinct chambers: the *igbodú*, the sacred chamber; the *eyá aranla*, the great *sala*, or hall, of the dwelling; and the *iban baló*, the patio or court, where forces represented by animals and ritual plants appear.

Inle—In Santería, the earth itself, physician of the bush, and expert healer.

l'invisible—See *loa*.

itútu—Funeral ceremony in Santería.

iyalocha—See *babalao*.

jigüe—See *mono*.

kofá—In Santería, a ceremony in which the special power of Orula is received.

konesans (connaissance)—A basic stage of participation in Vodou; knowledge of special lore, which gives power to the houngan or mambo.

laplas (laplace)—Ritual assistant in Vodou.

Legba—See *Eshu Elegguá*.

letra del año or *letter of the year*—A New Year's divination ceremony in Santería.

libretas sagradas—In Santería, notebooks and handwritten manuscripts containing personal treasuries of sacred literature, written in part *cubano* and part *lucumí*.

loa or *lwa* or *mystère, ange, saint, invisible*—Supernatural being in Vodou; usually translated as god or divinity, but more a genie or spirit. The *loa héritage* or *loa racine* is either connected to the family land or inherited directly from parents or ancestors. Whether inherited loa that come with the land, those loa "in your blood," or the loa *maît-tête* (master of the head) received in initiation, they are always distinguished from the bad gods who cannot be trusted, the *loa volé* or *loa acheté*; these bad gods are paid or enticed into service by a bocor or ritual specialist who might have more money or other tempting "goods" than the houngan.

madrina—See *padrino*.

maman-ventre—Placenta; in Guadeloupan tradition it is entrusted to the father, who buries it under a young mango or breadfruit tree, which becomes the child's "landmark," or *point de repère*.

mambo or *manbo*—Vodou priestess (see *houngan*).

manger-loa—One of the most important ceremonies in Vodou, at which a loa is fed his or her preferred food; any variation in the expected offering can result in the loa's desertion or revenge.

Mono, or *Mo-Edun, Mono Sabio, Coco Macaco*, or *güije* or *jigüe* or *Jiwe*—The monkey, a significant figure in Cuban religious and folkloric discourse.

mystère—See *loa*.

mystic marriage—Marriage with a loa in Vodou.

Naná Burukú—An old and highly respected androgynous deity, protector of the ill and the aged in Santería.

Oba—A sad and silent oricha; Changó's loyal and docile wife; domestic and diligent.

Obbatalá or *Orìsàálá*—An androgynous god in Santería, the god of purity and justice; he also represents truth, the immaculate, peace—hence his representation at times as a white dove—and wisdom.

Obeah or *Obi* or *Obea*—A belief system divided into two broad categories. The first involves the casting of spells for various purposes, both good and evil: protecting oneself, property, family, or loved ones; harming real or perceived enemies; bringing fortune in love, employment, personal or business pursuits. The second involves healing through the application of knowledge of herbal and animal medicinal properties. Obeah, thus conceived, is not a religion as such but a system of beliefs grounded in spirituality and an acknowledgment of the supernatural and involving aspects of witchcraft, sorcery, magic, spells, and healing.

Ochosi—An old oricha in Santería, a warrior and hunter, the protector and saint of prisons; Ochosi, Elegguá, and Oggún form the triumvirate of the warrior orichas.

Ochún-Kolé or *Ochún*—A Santería goddess, possessor of all the attributes valued in women: coquettish, beautiful, fawning, affectionate, docile, and industrious; defined as a mulatta oricha, mistress of the river, fresh water, gold, and honey.

Oggún or *Ogoun* or *Ogou*—One of the oldest orichas of the Yoruba pantheon; superior warrior, rival of Changó, a symbol of primitive force and terrestrial energy; himself a forger of metals, he is the protector of blacksmiths. Oggún, Ochosi, and Elegguá form the triumvirate of the warrior orichas.

Olofi—In Santería, the creator of the world, which was initially populated solely by santos; later he distributed his powers among them so that he need not interfere at all in human fate.

olúo—Occupier of the highest echelon in the hierarchy of Santería; must have surpassed the age of sixty, which guarantees a level of maturity, experience, and the concomitant degree of intuition necessary for making predictions without the mediation of any system of divination of a material kind.

ombre-cadavre—See *gros bon ange.*

opele, okpuele, or okuele chain—Commonly cast by the babalao during a divination ritual, its pattern is read to determine the fate of a newborn, the rightness of a marriage, or the measures to be taken for carrying out a funeral. When cast in the correct manners, it indicates a series of eight vertical markings, set in two columns of four, which constitute the configuration called an *odù* or *orgún.*

oriaté—Master of diloggún, deemed worthy of the highest respect, an individual to whom the hierarchs of Santaría submit themselves, particularly in any matter related to the deciphering of some mystery or sortilege. An *obá oriaté* is a santero with expertise in divination.

Oricha Oko—God of agriculture, protector of laborers and peasants in Santería.

orichas (orishas) or santos—Deities of Santería, spirits of Yoruban ancestors or divinities often identified in new correlations with Catholic saints. An oricha is pure form, immaterial àse, and can become perceptible to humans only when he is incorporated in them through possession.

Orula or *Orúnla, Orúmila,* or *Ifá*—Tutelary divinity in the pantheon of Cuban Santería, master of the tablero of Ifá and of divination, with mythological faculties for communicating people's future through his opele chain and his tablero.

Osaín—Santería's mysterious herb healer, master of the secrets of the bush.

ounfò—See *hounfort.*

oungan—See *houngan.*

Oyá—A severe divinity in Santería, related directly to the phenomenon of death, mistress of lightning and of the wind, and gatekeeper of the cemetery.

padrino or *madrina*—The godfather or godmother, head of the ilé, or religious community; becomes mother or father to a family of children, forming a group popularly known as a *línea de santo,* a line or lineage of initiates.

pataki or *caminos*—A group of prosified verses used in Santería divination.

peristyle or *tonnelle*—A structure, part of the hounfort, in the middle of which is the *poteau-mitan,* or center post, which images the traffic between heaven and earth.

petit bon ange—In Haitian Vodou, one of the three parts of individual identity, the source of consciousness and affect; depends on the loa for protection, for keeping it steady and bound to the person.

Petro (Petwo)—Family of Creole loas originating in Haiti but owing greatly to traditional Kongo religion; born in the mountains of Haiti, nurtured in secret; repositories of the moral strength of the escaped slaves who led the Haitian Revolution.

pinaldo—In Santería, a ceremony in which the right to use sharp weapons to kill four-legged animals is conferred.

quimboiseurs or *kenbwazé*—Sorcerers in Guadeloupe's Quimbois; they can be good or evil and fall in several categories: those who read the past, present, and future in the flames of candles or the designs made by melting wax on candles; healers, who practice white magic and utilize "good" herbs; *gadé zaffés* (*gadédzafé*) who work with secrets such as conjuring.

Rada—Pantheon of loas in Haitian Vodou, of Dahomean or Yoruban origin.

registro—In Santería, consultation that relies on a reading of the configurations determined by a specific procedure of casting palm nuts or the opele, or okuele, chain.

rogación—Purification ritual in Santería.

Santería—A complex religious system whose beliefs and rituals rest on the veneration of the orichas of the Yoruba pantheon of Nigeria as identified with their corresponding Catholic saints. Santería is founded on the concept of a superior triumvirate of Olofi, Olodumare, and Olorun, who have authority over the rest but are not the object of direct adoration or worship, as are the orichas, who are their subjects and messengers on earth.

santero and *santera*—An initiate in Santería; unconditionally dedicated, rigorously disciplined, and committed to a particular oricha for life.

santos—See *orichas*.

shaman—A figure who distinguishes himself or herself by the nature and intensity of an ecstatic experience that gives access to levels of transcendence higher than other members of the community can reach.

Shango—See *Changó*.

siete potencias africanas—The seven African powers of Cuban Santería: Elegguá, Changó, Ochosí, Oggún, Ochún, Yemayá, and Obbatalá.

tablero of Ifá—A series of configurations drawn on special dust in accordance with the casting of the opele, or okuele, chain; used in Santería for divination purposes.

Vèvè—A mystical design representing the attributes of a loa traced on the ground with maize flour, ash, coffee grounds, or brick dust.

Vodou, or *Voodoo*, *Vodoun*, *Vaudon*—From the word used by the Fon tribe of southern Dahomey to mean spirit, god, or image; a religious system whose beliefs and rituals center on the worship of the loas, which can have multiple emanations depending on locale, on a particular ritual, on the composition of the hounfort, or on their association with particular individuals or family groups. The reciprocal abiding of human and god, which is the cornerstone of Vodou practice, is articulated through the phenomenon of possession, or the *crise de loa*.

wanga—In Vodou, charms or spells.

Yegguá or Yewá, an aspect of Oyá—A death-related oricha in Santería whose daughters are forbidden marriage.

Yemayá—In Santería, the universal mother, queen of the sea and of salt water, the goddess of intelligence, of rationality; sometimes tempestuous and wild, sometimes calm and sensual, as when she appears in the avatar of Asesú. A harmonious personality characterizes her children.

zombi or *zombie* or *zonbi*—A living corpse, a person whose soul is believed to have been extracted by a sorcerer and who has been thus reduced to slavery.

Works Cited

Abimbola, 'Wande. *Ifá. An Exposition of Ifá Literary Corpus*. Ibadan, Nigeria: Oxford University Press, 1976.

———. "Yoruba Oral Literature." *African Notes* 2, no. 3 (April 1963): 12–16.

Abraham, R. C. *Dictionary of Modern Yoruba*. 1946. Reprint, London: Hodder & Stoughton, 1981.

Adams, R. F. *Efik-English Dictionary*. 3d ed. Liverpool: Philip, Son and Nephew, 1953.

Adisa, Opal Palmer. *Bake-Face and Other Guava Stories*. Berkeley, Calif.: Kelsey Street Press, 1986.

Alegría-Pons, José Francisco. "Aspectos de la religiosidad popular en Puerto Rico." In *Gagá y vudú en la República Dominicana*. Puerto Rico and Santo Domingo: Ediciones el Chango Prieto, 1993.

Alexis, Jacques Stephen. *Les Arbres musiciens*. Paris: Editions Gallimard, 1957.

———. "Chronique d'un faux-amour." In *Romancero aux étoiles*, 101–149. Paris: Editions Gallimard, 1960.

Anstey, Roger. *The Atlantic Slave Trade and British Abolition 1760–1810*. London: Macmillan, 1975.

Bachofen, J. J. *Myth, Religion, and Mother Right*. Trans. R. Manheim. Princeton, N.J.: Princeton University Press, 1970.

Bakhtin, Mikhail. *Rabelais and His World*. Bloomington: Indiana University Press, 1984.

Balaguer, Joaquín. *La realidad dominica*. Buenos Aires: Imprenta Ferrari Hermanos, 1947.

Barber, Karin. "How Man Makes God in West Africa: Yoruba Attitudes toward the Òrìsà." *Africa* 51, no. 3 (1981): 724–745.

Barnet, Miguel. *Akeké y la jutía. Fábulas cubanas*. Havana: Ediciones Unión, 1978.

———. *Biografía de un cimarrón*. 1966. 3d ed. Havana: Letras Cubanas, 1993. Translated into English by Jocasta Innes as *The Autobiography of a Runaway Slave*. London: Macmillan Caribbean, 1993.

———. "The Culture That Sugar Created." *Latin American Literary Review* 16 (spring-summer 1980): 38–46.

———. *La fuente viva*. Havana: Editorial Letras Cubanas, 1983.

Bascom, William. *Ifá Divination: Communication between Gods and Men in West Africa*. Bloomington and London: Indiana University Press, 1969.

———. "The Relationship of Yoruba Folklore to Divining." *Journal of American Folklore* 56 (1943): 127–131.

Bastide, Roger. *African Civilizations in the New World*. London: C. Hurst, 1971.

———. *The African Religions of Brazil: Toward a Sociology of the Interpenetration of Civilization*. Baltimore, Md.: Johns Hopkins University Press, 1978.

Bay, Edna G. *Asen: Iron Altars of the Fon People of Benin*. Atlanta, Ga.: The Museum, 1985.

Bébel-Gisler, Dany. *Léonora: L'Histoire enfouie de la Guadeloupe*. Paris: Seghers, 1985.

Beier, Ulli. *Yoruba Myths*. Cambridge: Cambridge University Press, 1980.

Bell, Archie. *The Spell of the Caribbean Islands*. Boston: L. C. Page, 1926.

Bell, Bernard. *The Afro-American Novel and Its Tradition*. Amherst: University of Massachusetts Press, 1987.

Benítez-Rojo, Antonio. *The Repeating Island: The Caribbean and the Postmodern Perspective*. Trans. James Maraniss. Durham, N.C.: Duke University Press, 1992.

Benson, LeGrace. "Kiskeya-Lan Guinée-Eden: The Utopian Vision in Haitian Painting." *Callaloo* 15, no. 3 (1992): 726–734.

Bewell, Alan. *Wordsworth and the Enlightenment: Nature, Man, and Society in the Experimental Poetry*. New Haven, Conn.: Yale University Press, 1989.

Bhaba, Homi. "The Other Question—The Stereotype and Colonial Discourse." *Screen* 24, no. 6 (1983): 18–36.

Blackburn, Robin. *The Overthrow of Colonial Slavery 1776–1848*. London: Verso Press, 1988.

Blier, Suzanne Preston. *African Vodun: Art, Psychology and Power*. Chicago: University of Chicago Press, 1995.

Bolívar Aróstegui, Natalia. *Los orishas en Cuba*. Havana: Ediciones Unión, 1990.

Borges, Jorge Luis (with Margarita Guerrero). *The Book of Imaginary Beings*. Trans. Norman Thomas di Giovanni and Jorge Luis Borges. New York: Dutton, 1978.

———. *Doctor Brodie's Report*. Trans. Norman Thomas di Giovanni. New York: Dutton, 1970.

———. *Labyrinths, Selected Stories and Other Writings*. Ed. Donald A. Yates and James E. Irby. Trans. Anthony Kerrigan. New York: New Directions, 1964.

———. *Otras inquisiciones*. Buenos Aires: Emecé, 1960.

Brathwaite, Edward Kamau. "The African Presence in Caribbean Literature." *Daedalus* 103, no. 2 (spring 1974): 73–109. Reprinted in *Africa in Latin America. Essays on History, Culture, and Socialization*, ed. Manuel Moreno Fraginals, trans. Leonor Blum, 103–144. New York: Holmes & Meier, 1984.

———. *Contradictory Omens*. Mona, Jamaica: Savacou, 1974.

———. "A Post-Cautionary Tale of the Helen of Our Wars." *Wasafiri* 22 (autumn 1995): 67–78.

———. *Rites of Passage. The Arrivants: A New World Trilogy*. London: Oxford University Press, 1973.

Brereton, Bridget. *Race Relations in Colonial Trinidad, 1870–1900*. Cambridge: Cambridge University Press, 1979.

Brown, Karen. *Mama Lola: A Vodou Priestess in Brooklyn*. Berkeley: University of California Press, 1991.

———. "Writing about the Other." *Chronicle of Higher Education*, 15 April 1992, A56.

Buakasa, Tulu Kia Mpansu. *L'Impense du discours. "Kindoki" et "nkisi" en pays kongo du Zaire*. Kinshasa: Presses Universitaires du Zaire, 1973.

Burke, Edmund. *Reflections on the Revolution in France*, and Thomas Paine, *The Rights of Man*. Garden City, N.Y.: Doubleday, 1961.

Burns, Alan. *History of Nigeria*. London: Allen & Unwin, 1936.

Butler, Marilyn. *Romantics, Rebels and Reactionaries: English Literature and Its Background, 1760–1830*. Oxford: Oxford University Press, 1981.

Cabrera, Lydia. *Anagó: Vocabulario lucumí*. Miami, Fla.: Ediciones Universal, 1986.

———. *El monte, Igbo-Finda-Ewe Orisha-Vititi Nfinda (Notas sobre las religiones, la magia, las supersticiones y el folklore de los negros criollos y del pueblo de Cuba)*. Havana, 1954. Reprint, Miami, Fla.: Ediciones Universal, 1975, and Havana: Letras Cubanas, 1993.

———. *Porqué . . . (Cuentos negros de Cuba)*. Madrid: Collección del Chicherekú, 1972.

Campbell, Elaine. "Reflections of Obeah in Jean Rhys' Fiction." In *Critical Perspectives on Jean Rhys*. ed. Pierrette Frickey, 59–66. Washington, D.C.: Three Continents Press, 1990.

Campbell, Thomas. *The Poetical Works of Thomas Campbell*. Ed. W. A. Hill. Boston: Little, Brown, 1855.

Carew, Jan. *Fulcrums of Change*. Trenton, N.J.: Africa World Press, 1988.

Castillo, J. M. *Ifá en tierra de Ifá. Manual de recitaciones para santeros y babalaos de las reglas lucumíes*. New York: n.p., 1976.

Césaire, Aimé. *Discours sur le colonialisme* (Discourse on colonialism). Trans. Joan Pinkham. New York and London: Monthly Review Press, 1972.

Chauvet, Marie. *Amour, Colère, et Folie*. Paris: Editions Gallimard, 1968.

———. *Fonds des nègres*. Port-au-Prince: Editions Henri Deschamps, 1961.

Cinéas, Jean-Baptiste. *Le Drame de la terre*. Port-au-Prince: Les Editions Fardin, 1932.

———. *L'Héritage sacré*. Port-au-Prince: Editions Henri Deschamps, 1945.

Cixous, Hélène. *The Newly-Born Woman*. Minneapolis: University of Minnesota Press, 1986.

Clifford, James. *The Predicament of Culture: Twentieth-Century Ethnography, Literature, and Art*. Cambridge: Harvard University Press, 1988.

Clitandre, Pierre. *La Cathédrale du mois d'août*. Paris: Editions Syros, 1982. Translated into English by Bridget Jones as *The Cathedral of the August Heat*. London: Readers International, 1987.

Coleridge, Samuel Taylor. *Essays on His Own Times in* The Morning Post *and* The Courier. Ed. David V. Erdman. 3 vols. Princeton, N.J.: Princeton University Press, 1978.

———. *Lectures 1808–1819 on Literature*. Ed. R. A. Foakes. 2 vols. Princeton, N.J.: Princeton University Press, 1987.

———. *The Poems of Samuel Taylor Coleridge*. Ed. Ernest Hartley Coleridge. London: Oxford University Press, 1940.

Condé, Maryse. *Moi, Tituba, sorcière noire de Salem*. Paris: Mercure de France, 1986. Translated by Richard Philcox as *I, Tituba, Black Witch of Salem*. Charlottesville: University Press of Virginia, 1992.

———. *La Parole des femmes. Essai sur des romancieres des Antilles de langue française*. Paris: L'Harmattan, 1979.

———. "Pourquoi la négritude? Négritude ou révolution." In *Les Litteratures d'expression française: Négritude africaine, négritude caraïbe*, 150–154. Paris: Editions de la Francité, 1973.

Coomaraswamy, A. K. *Figures of Speech or Figures of Thought*. London: n.p., 1946.

Cooper, Frederick, and Ann L. Stoler. "Tensions of Empire: Colonial Control and Visions of Rule." *American Ethnologist* 16 (1989): 617–618.

Coulthard, G. R. *Race and Colour in Caribbean Literature*. London: Oxford University Press, 1962.

Courlander, Harold. *Haiti Singing*. New York: Cooper Square Publishers, 1973.

Cowper, William. "The Negro's Complaint." In *The Poetical Works of William Cowper*, ed. H. S. Milford, 4th ed., 371–372. London: Oxford University Press, 1950.

Craige, John Houston. *Cannibal Cousins*. New York: Minton, Balch, 1934.

Craven, Henry, and John Barfield. *English-Congo and Congo-English Dictionary*. Freeport, N.Y.: Books for Libraries Press, 1971.

Cuervo Hewitt, Julia. *Aché, presencia africana. Tradiciones yoruba-lucumí en la narrativa cubana*. New York: Peter Lang, 1988.

Daly, M. *Gyn/Ecology: The Metaethics of Radical Feminism*. Boston: Beacon Press, 1978.

Darwin, Erasmus. *Zoonomia: or the Laws of Organic Life*. 2 vols. 1794–1796. Reprint, Philadelphia: Edward Earle, 1818.

Davis, Wade. *Passage of Darkness: The Ethnobiology of the Haitian Zombie.* Chapel Hill: University of North Carolina Press, 1988.

———. *The Serpent and the Rainbow.* New York: Warner Books, 1985.

Dayan, Joan. "Erzulie: A Women's History of Haiti." *Research in African Literatures* 2 (summer 1994): 5–31. Reprinted in *Postcolonial Subjects: Francophone Women Writers.* Minneapolis: University of Minnesota Press, 1996.

de Granda, Germán. *De la matrice africaine de la "Langue Congo" de Cuba (Recherches préliminaires).* Dakar: Centre de Hautes Etudes Afro-Ibéro-Américaines, 1973.

Deive, Carlos Esteban. *Vodú y magia en Santo Domingo.* Santo Domingo: Museo del Hombre Dominicano, 1975.

Denis, Lorimer. "Le Cimetière." *Bulletin du Bureau d'Ethnologie* (Port-au-Prince) 13 (1956): 1–16.

Depestre, René. *Bonjour et adieu à la négritude.* Paris: Editions Robert Laffont, 1980.

———. *Change.* Paris: Editions du Seuil, 1971.

———. *Hadriana dans tous mes rêves.* Paris: Editions Gallimard, 1988.

———. *Pour la révolution, pour la poésie.* Montreal: Editions Leméac, 1974.

———. *A Rainbow for the Christian West.* Translated with an introduction by Joan Dayan. Amherst: University of Massachusetts Press, 1977.

De Quincey, Thomas. *Confessions of an English Opium Eater and Other Writings.* Ed. Grevel Lindop. Oxford: Oxford University Press, 1985.

Deren, Maya. *Divine Horsemen: The Living Gods of Haiti.* Kingston, N.Y.: McPherson, 1970.

A Description of Furibond; or, Harlequin Negro. A Grand Comic Pantomine, Performing with Applause at Drury Lane, Theatre. London: J. Scales, [1807?].

Desmangles, Leslie G. *The Faces of the Gods: Vodou and Roman Catholicism in Haiti.* Chapel Hill: University of North Carolina Press, 1992.

Dewisme, C.-H. *Les Zombis ou le secret des morts-vivants.* Paris: Edition Bernard Grasset, 1957.

Díaz Fabelo, Teodoro. *Cinquenta y un pattakíes afroamericanos.* Caracas: Monte Ávila, 1983.

Diederich, Bernard. "On the Nature of Zombi Existence." *Caribbean Review* 12 (1983): 14–17, 43–46.

Dobbin, Jay D. *The Jombee Dance of Montserrat: A Study of Trance Ritual in the West Indies.* Columbus: Ohio State University Press, 1986.

Dunham, Katherine. *Island Possessed.* Chicago: University of Chicago Press, 1969.

Dykes, Eva Beatrice. *The Negro in Romantic Thought: A Study in Sympathy for the Oppressed.* Washington, D.C.: Associated Publishers, 1942.

Eades, J. S. *The Yoruba Today.* Cambridge: Cambridge University Press, 1980.

Ebroïn, Ary. *Quimbois, magie noire, et sorcellerie aux Antilles.* Paris: Jacques Grancher, 1977.

Echánove, Carlos A. *La "santería" cubana: Cultura, estilo y resistencia.* N.p., 1950.

Edgeworth, Maria. *Belinda.* Ed. Eva Figes. London: Pandora, 1986.

———. *Tales and Novels.* 10 vols. London: Routledge, 1893.

Edwards, Bryan. *An Historical Survey of the French Colony in the Island of St. Domingo.* London: John Stockdale, 1797.

———. *The History, Civil and Commercial, of the British Colonies in the West Indies,* 2 vols. Dublin: Luke White, 1793.

Ega, Françoise. *Le Temps des madras: Récit de la Martinique.* Paris: Editions Maritimes et d'Outre Mer, 1966.

———. *Lettres à une noire: Récit antillais.* Paris: L'Harmattan, 1978.

Eliade, Mircea. *Shamanism: Archaic Techniques of Ecstasy.* Princeton, N.J.: Princeton University Press, 1964.

Emery, Mary Lou. *Jean Rhys at "World's End."* Austin: University of Texas Press, 1990.

Etienne, Gérard. *La Reine soleil levée.* Montreal: Guérin Littérature, 1987.

Fabian, Johannes. *Time and the Other: How Anthropology Makes Its Object.* New York: Columbia University Press, 1983.

Farmer, Paul. *AIDS and Accusation: Haiti and the Geography of Blame.* Berkeley: University of California Press, 1992.

Feijóo, Samuel. *El negro en la literatura folklórica cubana.* Havana: Editorial Letras Cubanas, 1980.

Ferguson, Frances. *Wordsworth: Language as Counter-spirit.* New Haven, Conn.: Yale University Press, 1977.

Fernández Retamar, Roberto. *Calibán and Other Essays.* 1972. Trans. Edward Baker. Minneapolis: University of Minnesota Press, 1989.

Fleurant, Gerdes. "The Ethnomusicology of Yanvalou: A Study of the Rada Rite of Haiti." Ph.D. diss., Tufts University, 1987.

Flores, Juan. "Cortijo's Revenge." In *On Edge: The Crisis of Contemporary Latin American Culture,* Ed. George Yúdice, Jean Franco, and Juan Flores. Minneapolis: University of Minnesota Press, 1992.

————. *Insularismo e ideologia burguesa en Antonio Pedreira.* Havana: Ediciones Casa de las Américas, 1979.

Franck, Harry A. *Roaming through the West Indies.* New York: Century, 1920.

Frobenius, Leo. *The Origin of African Civilizations.* Washington, D.C.: Smithsonian Institution, 1899.

Froude, James Anthony. *The English in the West Indies or The Bow of Ulysses.* New York: Scribner's, 1888.

Frye, Northrup. *Anatomy of Criticism: Four Essays.* Princeton, N.J.: Princeton University Press, 1972.

Gallagher, Catherine. *The Industrial Reformation of English Fiction: Social Discourse and Narrative Form.* Chicago: University of Chicago Press, 1985.

García Cortez, Julio. *Patakí, leyendas y misterios de orichas africanos.* Miami, Fla.: Ediciones Universal, 1980.

Gates, Henry Louis. "The 'Blackness of Blackness': A Critique on the Sign and the Signifying Monkey." *Critical Inquiry* 9, no. 4 (June 1983): 685–723.

————. *Figures in Black: Words, Signs, and the 'Racial' Self.* Oxford: Oxford University Press, 1987.

————. *The Signifying Monkey: A Theory of African-American Literary Criticism.* Oxford: Oxford University Press, 1988.

Geggus, David. "British Opinion and the Emergence of Haiti, 1791–1805." In *Slavery and British Society 1776–1846,* ed. James Walvin. Baton Rouge: Louisiana State University Press, 1982.

Genovese, Eugene D. *From Rebellion to Revolution: Afro-American Slave Revolts in the Making of the New World.* 1979. New York: Random House, Vintage Books, 1981.

Gilroy, Paul. *The Black Atlantic: Modernity and Double Consciousness.* Cambridge: Harvard University Press, 1993.

Glissant, Edouard. *Le Discours antillais.* Paris: Editions du Seuil, 1982.

————. *La Lézarde.* Paris: Editions du Seuil, 1958.

————. *Poétique de la relation.* Paris: Editions Gallimard, 1990.

González Echevarría, Roberto. "Literature of the Hispanic Caribbean." *Latin American Literary Review* 16 (1980): 1–20.

González-Wippler, Migene. *Santería: African Magic in Latin America.* New York: Original Publications, 1989.

————. *Santería: The Religion. A Legacy of Faith, Rites, and Magic.* New York: Harmony Books, 1975.

————. *Tales of the Orishas.* New York: Original Publications, 1985.

Guillén, Nicolás. *Sóngoro cosongo, Motivos de son, West Indies Ltd., España*, 4th ed. Buenos Aires: Losada, 1967.

Guirao, Ramón. *Orbita de la poesía afrocubana (1928–37)*. Havana: Ucar, García, 1983.

Harris, Wilson. *Explorations*. Ed. Hena Maes-Jelinek. Aarhus, Denmark: Dangaroo Press, 1981.

———. *The Womb of Space*. Westport, Conn.: Greenwood Press, 1983.

Herskovits, Melville J. *Dahomey: An Ancient West African Kingdom*. Vol. 2. New York: J. J. Augustin, 1938.

———. *Life in a Haitian Valley*. With an introduction by Edward Brathwaite. Garden City, N.Y.: Doubleday, 1971.

———. *The New World Negro*. Bloomington: Indiana University Press, 1966.

Hill, W. C. Osman. *Primates, Comparative Anatomy and Taxonomy*. Vol. 6. New York: Interscience, 1966.

Hoffman, Léon-François. "The Haitian Novel during the Last Ten Years." *Callaloo* 15, no. 3 (1992): 761–769.

Holly, Arthur. *Les Daïmons du culte Voudo et Dra-Po*. Port-au-Prince: n.p., 1918.

hooks, bell. "Altars of Sacrifice: Re-Remembering Basquiat." *Art in America*. June 1993, 68–75. Reprinted in bell hooks, *Art on My Mind*. New York: New Press, 1995.

———. *Yearning: Race, Gender, and Cultural Politics*. Boston: South End Press, 1990.

Hulme, Peter. *Colonial Encounters: Europe and the Native Caribbean, 1492–1797*. London: Methuen, 1986.

Hurbon, Laënnec. *Le Barbare imaginaire*. Paris: Les Editions du Cerf, 1988.

Hurston, Zora Neale. *Tell My Horse: Voodoo and Life in Haiti and Jamaica*. 1938. Reprint, New York: Harper & Row, 1990. Also reprinted in *Zora Neale Hurston: Folklore, Memoirs, and Other Writings*. New York: Library of America, 1995.

Irele, Abiola. "Editorial." *Research in African Literatures* 25, no. 2 (summer 1994): 1–3.

Jackson, Richard L. *Black Literature and Humanism in Latin America*. Athens: University of Georgia Press, 1988.

James, C.L.R. *The Black Jacobins: Toussaint L'Ouverture and the San Domingo Revolution*. 2d ed. New York: Random House, Vintage Books, 1963.

James, Louis. *Jean Rhys*. London: Longman, 1978.

Janzen, John M., and Wyatt MacGaffey, Ed. *An Anthology of Kongo Religion*. Publication in Anthropology 4. Lawrence: University of Kansas, 1974.

Johnson Reagon, Bernice. "African Diaspora Women: The Making of Cultural Workers." In *Women in Africa and the Diaspora*, Ed. R. Terborg-Penn, S. Harley, and A. Benton-Rushing. Washington, D.C.: Howard University Press, 1987.

Jules-Rosette, Benetta. "The Veil of Objectivity: Prophecy, Divination and Social Inquiry," *American Anthropologist* 80, no. 3 (September 1978): 549–570.

Kelly, Gary. *English Fiction of the Romantic Period 1789–1830*. London: Longman, 1989.

Kincaid, Jamaica. "In the Night." In *At the Bottom of the River*. New York: Random House, Vintage Books, 1985.

King, Noel. *African Cosmos: An Introduction to Religion in Africa*. Belmont, Calif.: Wadsworth, 1986.

Lachatañeré, Rómulo. *Manual de Santería: El sistema de cultos "Lucumís."* Havana: Editorial Caribe, 1942.

———. *¡¡Oh, mío Yemayá!!* Manzanillo, Cuba: Editorial El Arte, 1938.

Laguerre, Michel S. *Voodoo and Politics in Haiti*. New York: St. Martin's Press, 1989.

Lamb, Charles. "On the Tragedies of Shakespeare, Considered with Reference to Their Fitness for Stage Representation." In *The Works of Charles and Mary Lamb*, ed. E. V. Lucas, Vol. 1. London: Methuen, 1903–1905.

Laroche, Maximilien. "The Myth of the Zombi." In *Exile and Tradition: Studies in African and Caribbean Literature*, ed. Rowland Smith, 44–61. London: Longman, 1976.

Lautman, Virginia. "Into the Mystic: The New Folk Art." *Metropolitan Home*, June 1989, 63.

Lawless, Robert. *Haiti's Bad Press*. Rochester, Vt.: Schenkman, 1992.

Léon, Argeliers. *Música folklore: Yoruba, Bantú, Abakua*. Havana: Ediciones del C.N.C., 1964.

Lewis, Matthew Gregory. *Journal of a West India Proprietor, Kept during a Residence in the Island of Jamaica*. London: John Murray, 1834.

Lippard, Lucy. "Sapphire and Ruby in the Indigo Gardens." In *Secrets, Dialogues, Revelations: The Art of Betye and Alison Saar*, ed. Elizabeth Shepherd. Los Angeles: Wight Art Gallery, UCLA, 1990.

Long, Edward. *The History of Jamaica*. 3 vols. London: T. Lowndes, 1774.

Lucas, Blake, "I Walked with a Zombie." In *Magill's Survey of Cinema: English Language Films*, 2d ser., vol. 3, ed. Frank N. Magill. Englewood Cliffs, N.J.: Salem Press, 1981.

McAlister, Elizabeth. "Sacred Stories from the Haitian Diaspora: A Collective Biography of Seven Vodou Priestesses in New York City." *Journal of Caribbean Studies* 9, nos. 1/2 (1993): 10–27.

McClelland, E. M. *The Cult of Ifa among the Yoruba*. Vol. 1, *Folk Practice and the Art*. London: Ethnographica, 1982.

Manicom, Jacqueline. *La Graine: Journal d'une sage-femme*. Paris: Presses de la Cité, 1974.

Marcelin, Pierre, and Philippe Thoby-Marcelin. *The Beast of the Haitian Hills*. Trans. Peter Rhodes. San Francisco: City Lights Books, 1986.

Marshall, P. J., and Glyndwr Williams. *The Great Map of Mankind: British Perceptions of the World in the Age of Enlightenment*. London: Dent, 1982.

Marshall, Paule. *Praisesong for the Widow*. New York: Dutton, 1984.

Martínez Furé, Rogelio. *Diálogos imaginarios*. Havana: Editorial Arte y Literatura, 1979.

Mesa, Garófalo. *Leyendas y tradiciones villaclareñas*. Havana: n.p., 1925.

Métraux, Alfred. *Voodoo in Haiti*. Trans. Hugo Charteris. New York: Schocken, 1972.

Minh-ha, Trinh T. *Woman, Native, Other*. Bloomington: Indiana University Press, 1989.

Mohanty, Chandra Talpade. "Under Western Eyes: Feminist Scholarship and Colonial Discourses." *Boundary 2* 12, no. 3; 13, no. 1 (spring/fall 1984): 333–358. Reprinted in *Third World Women and the Politics of Feminism*, Ed. Chandra Talpade Mohanty, Ann Russo, and Lourdes Torres. Bloomington: Indiana University Press, 1991.

Monnin, Michel. "Andre Pierre le peintre chantant." In *Haïti: Art naïf, art vaudou*. Paris: Galeries Nationales du Grand Palais, 1988.

Montero, Mayra. "Corinne, muchacha amable." In *Cuentos para ahuyentar el turismo*, Ed. Vitalina Alfonso and Emilio Jorge Rodriguez, 285–306. Havana: Arte y Literatura, 1991. Translated into English by Lizabeth Paravisini-Gebert as "Corinne, Amiable Girl." *Callaloo* 17, no. 3 (summer 1994). Reprinted in *Remaking a Lost Harmony: Short Stories from the Hispanic Caribbean*, ed. Margarite Fernández Olmos and Lizabeth Paravisini-Gebert. Fredonia, N.Y.: White Pine Press, 1995.

———. *Del rojo de su sombra*. Barcelona: Tusquets Editores, 1995.

———. *La trenza de la hermosa luna*. Barcelona: Editorial Anagrama, 1987.

———. *Tú, la oscuridad*. Barcelona: Tusquets Editores, 1995.

———. *La última noche que pasé contigo*. Barcelona: Tusquets Editores, 1991.

Montgomery, James. *The Poetical Works of James Montgomery. Collected by Himself*. London: Longman, 1850.

Moral, Paul. *Le Paysan Haïtien: Etude sur la vie rurale en Haiti*. Port-au-Prince: Editions Fardin, 1978.

Morrish, Ivor. *Obeah, Christ and Rastaman: Jamaica and Its Religion*. Cambridge: James Clarke, 1982.

Moseley, Benjamin. *A Treatise on Sugar*. 2d ed. London: John Nichols, 1800.

Murphy, Joseph M. "Black Religion and 'Black Magic': Prejudice and Projection in Images of African-Derived Religions." *Religion* 20 (1990): 323–337.

———. *Santería: An African Religion in America*. Boston: Beacon Press, 1988.

———. *Working the Spirit: Ceremonies of the African Diaspora*. Boston: Beacon Press, 1994.

Naipaul, V. S. *The Middle Passage*. London: André Deutsch, 1962.

"The Negro's Imprecation." In *The Meteors*, vol. 2, 53–56. London: A. and J. Black, 1799–1800.

New York Public Library. *Catalog of the Theatre and Drama Collections*. Part III, *Nonbook Collections*. 30 vols. Boston: G. K. Hall, 1976.

Nicoll, Allardyce. *A History of English Drama 1660–1900*. Vol. 4, *Early Nineteenth Century Drama*, 2d ed. Cambridge: Cambridge University Press, 1955.

Noble, Vicki. *Shakti Woman: Feeling Our Fire, Healing Our World: The New Shamanism*. San Francisco: Harper, 1991.

Nunez-Harrell, Elizabeth. *When Rocks Dance*. New York: Putnam, 1986.

Obi; or, Three-Fingered Jack: A Melo-drama in Two Acts. London: Thomas Hailes Lacy, [1800?].

OBI, or Three-Finger'd Jack. A Popular Melo-drame in Two Acts. Oxbery's Weekly Budget of Plays and Magazine of Romance, Whim, and Interest 1 (1843): 93–95.

O'Connor, Teresa. *Jean Rhys: The West Indian Novels*. New York and London: New York University Press, 1986.

"Ode. The Insurrection of the Slaves at St. Domingo." Reprinted (anonymously) from *The Courier* in *The Spirit of the Public Journals for 1797*, 2d ed., 238–240. London: James Ridgway, 1799.

Olatunji, Olatunde O. *Features of Yoruba Oral Poetry*. Ibadan, Nigeria: University Press, 1984.

Ortega, Julio. "Postmodernism in Latin America." In *Postmodern Fiction in Europe and the Americas*, Ed. Theo D'haen and Hans Bertens, 193–208. Amsterdam: Rodopi, 1988.

Ortiz, Fernando. *Los bailes y el teatro de los negros en el folklore de Cuba*. Havana: Cárdenas, 1951.

———. "El cocorícamo y otros conceptos teoplásmicos del folklore afrocubano." *Archivos del Folklore Cubano* (Havana) 4, no. 4 (1929): 289–312.

———. *Nuevo catauro de cubanismos*. 1923. Revised edition, Havana: Editorial de Ciencias Sociales, 1974.

———. *Los tambores batá de los Yorubas*. Havana: Publicgraf, 1994.

Paravisini-Gebert, Lizabeth. "Authors Playin' Mas': Carnival and the Carnivalesque in the Contemporary Caribbean Novel." In *History of Caribbean Literatures*, ed. A. James Arnold, Cross Cultural Studies 3. Amsterdam, Philadelphia: John Benjamins, forthcoming.

Patterson, Orlando. *The Sociology of Slavery: An Analysis of the Origins, Development and Structure of Negro Slave Society in Jamaica*. Rutherford, N.J.: Fairleigh Dickinson University Press, 1967.

Paz, Octavo. *The Monkey Grammarian*. A translation by Helen R. Lane of *El mono gramático* (1974). New York: Seaver, 1981.

Pedreira, Antonio S. *Insularismo*. 1934. Reprint, San Juan: Edil, 1968.

Piedra, José. "A Return to Africa with a Carpentier Tale." *Modern Language Notes* 97 (1982): 401–410.

Ramchand, Kenneth. *The West Indian Novel and Its Background*. 2d ed. London: Heinemann, 1983.

Reed, Ishmael. *Mumbo Jumbo*. Garden City, N.Y.: Doubleday, 1972.

Reeve, Clara. *Plans of Education; with Remarks on the Systems of Other Writers*. Ed. Gina Luria. New York: Garland, 1974.

Rhys, Jean. *After Leaving Mr. MacKenzie*. New York: Carroll and Graf, 1990.

———. *The Collected Short Stories*. New York: Norton, 1987.

———. *Good Morning Midnight*. New York: Norton, 1986.

———. *The Left Bank*. London: Cape, 1927.

———. *The Letters of Jean Rhys*. Ed. Francis Wyndham and Diana Melly. New York: Viking Press, 1984.

———. *Quartet*. New York: Carroll and Graf, 1990.

———. *Smile Please: An Unfinished Autobiography*. Berkeley: Donald S. Ellis/Creative Arts, 1979.

———. *Voyage in the Dark*. 1934. Reprint, New York: Norton, 1982.

———. *Wide Sargasso Sea*. 1966. Reprint, New York: Norton, 1982.

Richman, Karen. "They Will Remember Me in the House: The Pwen of Haitian Transnational Migration." Ph.D. diss., University of Virginia, 1992.

Rigaud, Milo. *Secrets of Voodoo*. New York: Arco, 1969.

———. *La Tradition voudoo et le voodoo haïtien*. Paris: Editions Niclaus, 1953.

Rosenberg, June. *El gagá: Religión y sociedad de un culto dominicano*. Santo Domingo: Editora de la UASD, 1979.

Rumpf, Helmtrud. "Rhizome versus racine: Deux concepts d'identité dans les Caraïbes francophones." In *Born Out of Resistance: On Caribbean Cultural Collectivity*, ed. Wim Hoogbergen. Utrecht: Centrum voor Caraibische Studien, 1995.

Said, Edward. *Orientalism*. New York: Random House, Vintage Books, 1979.

Saint-Amand, Edris. *Bon Dieu rit*. Paris: Hatier, 1988.

Sánchez, Julio. *La religión de los orichas: Creencias y ceremonias de un culto afro-caribeño*. 3d ed. Hato Rey, Puerto Rico: Colección Estudios Afrocaribeños, 1991.

Sander, Reinhard W. *The Trinidad Awakening: The West Indian Novel of the 1930s*. Westport, Conn.: Greenwood Press, 1988.

Sarduy, Severo. *Cobra*. Buenos Aires: Sudamericana, 1972.

Scharfman, Ronnie. "Mirroring and Mothering in Simone Schwarz-Bart's *Pluie et vent sur Telumée Miracle* and Jean Rhys's *Wide Sargasso Sea*." *Yale French Studies* 62 (1981): 88–106.

Schwarz-Bart, Simone. *The Bridge of Beyond*. Trans. Barbara Bray. Portsmouth, N.H., and Oxford: Heinemann, 1982.

———. *Pluie et vent sur Télumée Miracle*. Paris: Editions du Seuil, 1972.

———. "Sur les pas de Fanotte." *Textes et Documents* 2 (1979): 13–23.

Scott, Dennis. *An Echo in the Bone*. In *Plays for Today*, 73–137. London: Longman, 1970.

Seabrook, William B. *The Magic Island*. New York: Harcourt, Brace, 1929.

Shelton, Marie Denise. "Women Writers of the French-Speaking Caribbean: An Overview." In *Caribbean Women Writers*, ed. Selwyn Cudjoe. Wellesley, Mass.: Calaloux, 1990.

Shepherd, William. "The Negro Incantation." In *The Poetical Register, and Repository of Fugitive Poetry, for 1803*, 2d ed., 413–415. London: Rivington, 1805.

Simpson, George Eaton. *Black Religions in the New World*. New York: Columbia University Press, 1978.

———. *Religious Cults of the Caribbean: Trinidad, Jamaica, Haiti*. Río Piedras: Institute of Caribbean Studies/University of Puerto Rico, 1980.

Smith, Charlotte. *The Letters of a Solitary Wanderer: Containing Narratives of Various Description*. 2 vols. London: Sampson Low, 1800.

Smylely-Walace, Karen. "The Female Self in Schwarz-Bart's *Pluie et vent sur Télumée Miracle*." *French Review* 59, no. 3 (1986): 236–248.

Sosa Rodríguez, Enrique. *Los ñáñigos*. Havana: Casa de las Américas, 1982.

Spivak, Gayatri Chakravorty. "Three Women's Texts and a Critique of Imperialism." In *"Race," Writing, and Difference*, ed. Henry Louis Gates. Chicago: University of Chicago Press, 1986.

Stedman, J. G. *Narrative of a Five Years' Expedition against the Revolted Negroes of Surinam in Guiana on the Wild Coast of South America from the Years 1772–1777*. Ed. Rudolf van Lier. 2 vols. Barre, Mass.: Imprint Society, 1971.

Swartenbroeckx, Pierre. *Dictionnaire KiKongo et Kituba-Français*. Ser. 3, vol. 2. Bandundu, Zaire: Ceeba, 1973.

Sypher, Wylie. *Guinea's Captive Kings: British Anti-slavery Literature of the XVIIIth Century*. Chapel Hill: University of North Carolina Press, 1942.

Tesfagiorgis, Freida. Review of *Black Art, Ancestral Legacy: The African Impulse in African-American Art*, ed. Robert V. Rozelle, Alvia J. Wardlaw, and Maureen A. McKenna. *African Arts* 25, no. 12 (1992): 41–53.

Tessonneau, Alex-Louise. "'Le Don reçu en songe': La Transmission du savoir dans les métiers traditionnels (Haïti)." *Ethnographie* 79, no. 1 (1983): 69–82.

Thelwall, John. "The Negro's Prayer." In *The Poetical Register, and Repository of Fugitive Poetry, for 1810–1811*, 350–351. London: Rivington, 1814.

Thompson, Robert Farris. *African Art in Motion, Icon and Act*. 1974. Reprint, Los Angeles, Berkeley, London: University of California Press, 1979.

———. *Black Gods and Kings. Yoruba Art at U.C.L.A.* Bloomington and London: Indiana University Press, 1976.

———. *Flash of the Spirit: African and Afro-American Art and Philosophy*. New York: Random House, 1983.

———. "From the First to the Final Thunder: African-American Quilts, Monuments of Cultural Assertion." Preface to E. Leon, *Who'd a Thought It: Improvisation in African-American Quilting*. San Francisco: San Francisco Crafts and Folk Art Museum, 1987.

Ullanov, Anne, and Barry Ullanov. *The Witch and the Clown: Two Archetypes of Human Sexuality*. Wilmette, Ill.: Chriron, 1987.

Vasil, Raj K. *Politics in Bi-racial Societies. The Third World Experience*. New Delhi: Vikas, 1984.

Verger, Pierre Fatumbi. *Orixás*. Sâo Paulo, Brazil: Circulo Do Livro de Sâo Paulo, 1975.

Vertovec, Steven. *Hindu Trinidad: Religion, Ethnicity and Socio-economic Change*. London: Macmillan, 1992.

Vico, Giambattista. *The New Science of Giambattista Vico*. 3d ed. Trans. Thomas Goddard Bergin and Max Arnold Fish. Ithaca, N.Y., and London: Cornell University Press, 1970.

Walcott, Derek. *Dream on Monkey Mountain and Other Plays*. London: Cape, 1972.

———. "Laventville." In *Collected Poems, 1948–1984*. New York: Farrar, Straus & Giroux, 1986.

Walker, Alice. *In Search of Our Mother's Gardens: Womanist Prose*. London: Woman's Press, 1984.

Walvin, James. *England, Slaves and Freedom, 1776–1838*. Jackson: University Press of Mississippi, 1986.

Warner-Vieyra, Myriam. *As the Sorcerer Said. . . .* Trans. Dorothy S. Blair. Essex: Longman, 1982.

———. *Le Quimboiseur l'avait dit*. Paris: Présence Africaine, 1980.

Wilentz, Gay. *Binding Cultures: Black Women Writers in Africa and the Diaspora*. Bloomington: Indiana University Press, 1992.

Wilson, Edmund. *Red, Black, Blond and Olive: Studies in Four Civilizations (Zuni, Haiti, Soviet Russia, Israel)*. London: W. H. Allen, 1956.

Wordsworth, William. "Preface" to *Lyrical Ballads*. In *Wordsworth's Literary Criticism*, ed. W.J.B. Owen. London: Routledge & Kegan Paul, 1974.

The Works of the English Poets, from Chaucer to Cowper. Ed. Alexander Chalmers. 21 vols. London: J. Johnson et al., 1810.

Yonkers, Delores. "Invitations to the Spirits: The Vodun Flags of Haiti." In *A Report from the San Francisco Crafts and Folk Art Museum*. San Francisco.: San Francisco Crafts and Folk Art Museum, 1985.

Zapata Olivella, Manuel. *Changó, el gran putas*. Bogota: Rei Andes, 1992.

Zimmerman, Marc. "The Unity of the Caribbean and Its Literatures." In *Process of Unity in Caribbean Society: Ideologies and Literatures*. Minneapolis: Institute for the Study of Ideologies and Literature, 1983.

Notes on Contributors

MIGUEL BARNET is an internationally acclaimed Cuban ethnographer, poet, novelist, and short-story writer. His *Biografía de un cimarrón* (1966) has been widely translated and is a forerunner of the testimonial genre in Latin American literature. Among his many works are *La Canción de Rachel* (1970), *La vida real* (1986), *Con pies de gato* (1993), and *La Regla de Ocha* (1995).

JOAN DAYAN is a professor of English at the University of Arizona. She has published extensively on American Romanticism and Caribbean literature. Her books include *Fables of the Mind: An Inquiry into Poe's Fiction* (1987) and *Haiti, History, and the Gods* (1996). Dayan is currently at work on a study of chain, classification, and deterrence at the Arizona State Prison Complex in Florence.

HÉCTOR DELGADO is the photographer of the Cuban Union of Artists and Writers (UNEAC). His works—which focus on the African roots of the Cuban carnival as well as the religion of Santería—have been exhibited in Canada, Mexico, and the United States, and have appeared in several books, including Miguel Barnet's *La Regla de Ocha* (1995).

KARLA Y. E. FRYE is an assistant professor of English and African-American literature at the University of Alabama. Her research interests include women's writings in the African diaspora and feminist theory.

EUGENIO MATIBAG is an associate professor of Spanish at Iowa State University in Ames. He has published articles on Caribbean culture and literature in *Postmodern Culture, Dispositio, Journal of Interdisciplinary Literary Studies*, and *L'Heritage de Caliban* (ed. Maryse Condé), and is the author of *Afro-Cuban Religious Experience: Cultural Reflections in Narrative* (1996).

BRINDA MEHTA is an associate professor of French at Mills College in Oakland, California, where she teaches courses in the nineteenth-century French novel,

Francophone African and Caribbean literatures, feminist critical theories, and postcolonialism. She is the author of *Corps infirme, corps infâme: La femme dans le roman balzacien* as well as of articles on Francophone African and Caribbean literatures in *The French Review, Revue Francophone,* and *Journal of Caribbean Studies* among others.

MARGARITE FERNÁNDEZ OLMOS is a professor of Spanish at Brooklyn College. She has lectured extensively on contemporary Latin American literature and has published essays in numerous journals and anthologies. She is the author of *La cuentística de Juan Bosch: Un análisis crítico-cultural* (1982) and *Sobre la literatura puertorriqueña de aquí y allá: Aproximaciones feministas* (1989). She coedited *Contemporary Women Authors of Latin America: New Translations and Introductory Essays* (1983) with Doris Meyer. Her most recent books are *El placer de la palabra: Literatura erótica femenina de América Latina* (1991), *Pleasure in the Word: Erotic Writings by Latin American Women* (1993), and *Remaking a Lost Harmony: Short Stories from the Hispanic Caribbean* (1995), all coedited with Lizabeth Paravisini-Gebert, and *The Latino Reader* (1997), with Harold Augenbraum.

LIZABETH PARAVISINI-GEBERT is an associate professor of Caribbean and Latin American literature at Vassar College. She coauthored *Caribbean Women Novelists: An Annotated Critical Bibliography* (1993) with Olga Torres Seda and is the author of *Phyllis Shand Allfrey: A Caribbean Life* (1996). Her other books include *Ana Roqué's Luz y sombra* (1991), *Green Cane and Juicy Flotsam: Short Stories by Caribbean Women* (with Carmen Esteves, 1991), and three collections coedited with Margarite Fernández Olmos: *El placer de la palabra: Literatura erótica femenina de América Latina* (1991), *Pleasure in the Word: Erotic Writings by Latin American Women* (1993), and *Remaking a Lost Harmony: Short Stories from the Hispanic Caribbean* (1995). She is at work on a book-length study on "Race, Gender, and the Plantation in Caribbean Women's Fiction" and has recently completed a monograph on the works of Jamaica Kincaid.

JOSÉ PIEDRA is an associate professor of Romance Languages and Literature at Cornell University. His numerous essays have appeared in *Callaloo, Dispositio, New Literary History, Transition, Diacritics,* and *Modern Language Notes,* among other journals and collections.

ALAN RICHARDSON is a professor of English at Boston College. He is the author of *A Mental Theater: Poetic Drama and Consciousness in the Romantic Age* (1988) and *Literature, Education and Romanticism: Reading as Social Practice 1780–1832* (1994). He is also coeditor of a collection entitled *Romanticism, Race and Imperial Culture 1780–1834* (1996).

IVETTE ROMERO-CESAREO is an assistant professor of Modern Languages at Marist College. She has published on a variety of topics in the fields of Caribbean literatures and art, cultural studies, and women's studies. In addition to completing a book on testimonial narrative in the French Caribbean, she is presently coediting two collections of critical essays: *Aesthetics and Social Movements* with Mario Cesareo and *Writing in the Wake: Women Travelers and the Caribbean* with Lizabeth Paravisini-Gebert.

ELAINE SAVORY (formerly Elaine Fido or Elaine Savory Fido), a poet and scholar, has written extensively on Third World women's literature. She is the coeditor of *Out of the Kumbla: Caribbean Women's Literature* (1990) and is currently working on a book on Jean Rhys. She teaches Caribbean and African literature at the New School for Social Research in New York.

ANNA WEXLER has worked as a counselor and art teacher in educational and clinical programs for Haitians living in the Boston area. Her doctoral thesis in progress at the Harvard Graduate School of Education is a study of the artistry of Clotaire Bazile, a Haitian Vodou priest and flagmaker. Her poetry has been published in several journals, including most recently the Boston-based review *Tanbou*.

Index